WORLD PEACE

VOLUME FOUR

DEBT AND PEACE

Suresh Chandra Mallick
Pritam Mallick

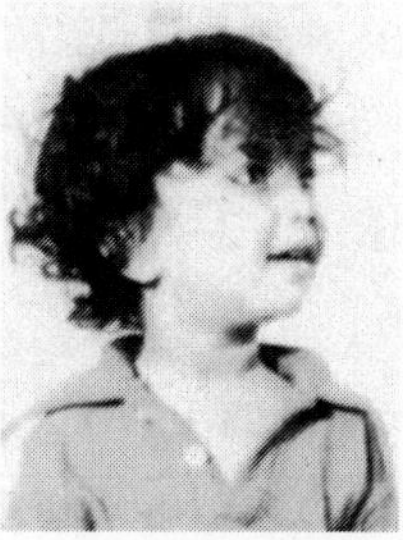

DEBT AND PEACE

Published by: Institute of Development Studies and Policy research, Pritam Bhawan, 93 Dharma Vihar, Khandagiri, Bhubaneswar 751030 (Orissa), INDIA

ISBN: 978-81-924851-3-3

First Edition

Price: US $

Dedicated to

Mr. Barack Hussein Obama
The 44th President of the USA and
Nobel Laureate in Peace

PROLOGUE

The world's leaders agreed to take actions on a range of global challenges at the United Nations Headquarters, New York in 2005. These challenges are: development, terrorism, peace building, peace keeping and peacemaking, responsibility to protect the common man, human rights, democracy and rule of law, management reform, environment, international health, humanitarian assistance, and updating United Nations charter[1]. But we feel that two more important challenges must be included and solved at the earliest. These are: **debt** and **starvation.** As long as these two economic and humanitarian crises are not solved, world peace would be delayed and vis-à-vis the global challenges would be multiplied rather than solved. Today 1.3 billion people live on less than US $1 per day and 2.8 billion people live on less than US $ 2 per day. At least 72 countries spend less on education or health care than debt servicing.

The WORLD PEACE Volume four covers 'Debt and Peace', which is an attempt to assist more than 50 percent of human population, who are indebted. Till date, 54 least and less developed countries and 58 low-middle-income countries are burdened with debt overhang, debt servicing and starvation deaths of poor people. The world's most impoverished countries are forced to pay over $100 million every day to the

---

[1] 2005 World Summit, High Level Plenary Meeting, UN Headquarters, New York, 14-16 September, 2005

rich world in debt repayments, while poverty kills millions of their people for want of food, drinking water and medicines. This manuscript emphasizes on **debt relief** as the most effective instrument to solace the poor countries of the world.

In this monograph, we have suggested how world peace could be established through debt relief by the creditors. We have illustrated the problems encountered by the least and less developed countries and other indebted countries to meet the Millennium Developed Goals (MDGs). The irony is that resource-rich countries encounter poverty worldwide and these countries are unable for debt servicing. There occurs illiteracy, unemployment, and absence of healthcare facilities, starvation, pre-mature deaths, corruption, terrorism, road blockades, political instability, lawlessness and natural disasters. The media highlights the necessity of debt relief for these poor countries. The un-serviceable debts hinder economic growth of the poor countries of the world. Hence, the rich countries can be the saviors of these low-income and low-middle-income countries by granting debt relief. (Ch-I)

Research studies by world organizations, countries, economists, and planners on debt relief have been described in Chapter- II. In the Chapter- III, country classification, groups, poor pockets of the world have been explained. Moreover, the mendicancy of the people of six countries has been highlighted to focus the relevance of debt relief of all low-income countries. In Chapter- IV, the procedure of availing debt relief has been analyzed and the benefit/loss of the poor countries has been explained through assessment reports of the countries. We have also included the recommendations of international forums on debt relief. (Chapter- V)

In Chapter VI, the activities of forerunners of debt relief campaign organizations have been included and their self-less struggles for the poor people of sub-Saharan Africa, South Asia, Caribbean and Pacific countries have been reported. They are struggling hard to see that poor people of LDCs lead a better life through debt relief and live in peace. They are the torchbearers of the greatest peace movement to encourage and globalize world peace in this twenty-first century before 2015.

The activities of the developed countries particularly the G-8 countries have been placed in Chapter VII. We emphasize the role of G8 countries as these countries have the capacity and capability to make poverty history. Similarly the activities of multilateral organizations like the United Nations Organization, the World Bank, the International Monetary Fund, and Paris Club have been analyzed in Chapter VIII. In Chapter IX, we have explained how world peace is achievable through debt relief. We have also cited how Greek philosophers suffered and even sacrificed their lives for the cause of human welfare.

The reports of committees, conferences or news items of international or national newspapers have been utilized to enumerate poverty of people and the need of debt relief. We are deeply indebted to all committees and authors, who have contributed their thoughts and suggestions for completion of this manuscript. We are really obliged to Google search engine, and Www world atlas Com, which contributed enormously for writing this monograph. We shall appreciate constructive criticism aiming at improvement of the subsequent editions of the book. Our hearts will be filled with joy even if a small step towards debt relief and world peace is contemplated through this endeavour. We thank Dr. Bikram Mallick, Dr. Gopinath Parida, Mrs. Bina Mallick, Priyam Mallick and Mrs. Priyambada Mallick, for their cooperation in completing of the manuscript.

October 15, 2012 Suresh Chandra Mallick

ACRONYMS

AAP : Africa Action Plan
ACFID : Australian Council for international Development
ADB : Asian Development Bank
AFDF : Africa Development Fund
AFRODAD: Africa Forum and Network on Debt and Development
AGOA : African Growth and Opportunity Act
AIDS : Acquired Immuno-Deficiency Syndrome
ALDE : Alliance of Liberals and Democrats for Europe/Association of Lutheran Development Executives
APEC : Asia-Pacific Economic Cooperation
APR : African Peer Review
ASEAN : Association of South- East Asian Nations
Aus AID : Australian Aid
BC : Before Christ
BCEAO : West African Regional Central Bank
BOT : Built Operate and Transfer (Projects)
BPoA : Brussels Program of Action
CAFOD : Catholic Agency for Overseas Development
CCA : Common Country Assessment
CEM : Country Economic Memorandum
CPO : Country Program Online

CSO : Civil Society Organization
DAC : Development Assistance Committee

DART : Disaster Assistance Response Team
DC : Development Committee
DFID : Department for International Development
EBRD : European Bank for Reconstruction and Development
ECOSOC: Economic and Social Council (UN)
ESAF : Enhance Structural Adjustment Facility
FAO : Food and Agriculture Organization (UN)
FAQ : Fair Average Quality
FDI : Foreign Direct Investment
FfD : Financing for Development
FSF : Financial Stability Forum
FTAP : Fair and Transparent Arbitration Act
FY : Financial Year
G-24 : Group of Twenty Four
GATS : Trade in Service
GAVI : Global Alliance for Vaccines and Immunization
GCAP : Global Call to Action against Poverty
GDP : Gross Domestic Product
GNE : Global and National Economics
GNI : Gross National Income
GNP : Gross National Product
GSP : Generalized System of Preference
HCB : Cahora Bassa Hydro-Electricity Company (Mozambique)
HDI : Human Development Index
HHI : Harvard Humanitarian Initiative
HIPC : Heavily Indebted Poor Countries
HIV : Human Immuno- Deficiency Virus
IBRD : International Bank for Reconstruction and Development
ICP : International Comparison Program
ICSID : International Center for Settlement of Investment Disputes
ICT: Information and Communication Technology
IDA : International Development Association
IDP : Internally Displaced Persons
IEO : Independent Evaluation Office
IFAD : International Fund for Agricultural Development
IFC : International Finance Commission

IFF : International Finance Facility For Immunization
IFI : International Finance Institution
ILO : International Labour Organization
IMF : International Monetary Fund
IMFC : International Monetary and Finance Committee
INR : Indian Rupees (currency)
JSA : Joint Staff assessment (IMF / WB)
Lao PDR: Lao People's Democratic Republic
LDC : Least Developed Country
LDC : Low Developed Country
LDYS : Liberal Democrat Youths and Students
LLDC : Least and Less Developed Country / Least among less developed Countries
LRA : Lord's Resistance Army
MDB : Multilateral Development Bank
MDG : Millennium Development Goals
MDRI : Multilateral Debt Relief Institutions
MEFMI: Macro Economic and Financial Management Institute of Eastern and South Africa
MIGA : Multilateral Investment Guarantee Agency
MNC : Multi National Corporation
MTEF : Medium Term Expenditure Frame Work
NBER : National Bureau of Economic Research
NEPAD: New Partnership for Africa's Development
NGO : Non Government Organization
NHDR : National Human Development Report
NLTPS : National Long-Term Planning Strategies
NPV : Net Present Value
NREP : National Rural Employment Program
OA : OXFAM America
ODA : Official Development assistance
OECD : Organization for Economic Cooperation And Development
OED : Operation Evaluation Department
OPEC : Oil Producing and Exporting Countries
OXFAM: Oxford Committee for Famine Relief
PAF : Performance Assessment Framework
PARPA: Action Plan for Reduction of Absolute Poverty (Mozambique)
PEP: Private Enterprise Partnership (Africa)
PPP : Purchasing Power Parity

PRGF : Poverty Reduction and Growth Facility
PRS : Poverty Reduction Strategy
PRSP : Poverty Reduction Strategy Papers
PSIA : Poverty / Social Impact Assessment
RCCHE: Research Center for Civic and Human Rights Education
RER : Real Exchange Rate
RLEGP : Rural Landless Employment Guarantee Program
RPHA : Rapid Public Health Assessment
SAARC: South Asian Association for Regional Cooperation
SADC : South African Development Community
SAFTA : South Asian Free Trade Area
SAP : Structural Adjustment Program
SAPTA : South Asian Association for Cooperation
SIP : Small Investor Program
SWAPs: Sector Wise Approaches
TA : Technical Assistance
TB : Tuberculosis
TFC : Twelfth Finance Commission
UNCTAD: UN Conference on Trade and Development
UNDAF UN: Development Assistance Framework
UNDP : Unite Nations Development Program
UNESCO: United Nations Educational, Scientific and Cultural Organisation
UNFPA : United Nations Population Fund
UNICEF: United Nations Children's Emergency Fund
UNO: United Nations Organisation
WAIFEM: West Africa Institute for Financial and Economic Management
WB : World Bank
WBI : World Bank Institute
WFP : World Food Program
W.H.O.: World Health Organisation
WTO : World Trade Organisation

+++++

CONTENTS

Prologue
Acronyms
Contents
Introduction

Chapter I: Debt – A Global Challenge: 19 - 35
Problems in Poor Countries, Natural Wealth and Poverty, Causes of Debt Crises, Debt Relief and Media, and Conclusion

Ch II: Research Studies on Debt Relief: 36 -95

Chapter III: Indebted Countries Appeal for Debt Relief 96 -156
Country Classification, Country Reports - Burkina Faso, Ethiopia, Mozambique, Uganda, Bangladesh, India, Problems Can be Solved and Conclusion

Chapter IV: Necessity of Debt Relief: 157 - 216
Debt Relief, Necessity of Debt Relief, Debt relief under HIPC Initiative, Poverty Reduction Strategy Papers, Engagement of UNDP in PRSP Process, Review of Poverty Reduction Strategy Process, World Bank Operation Evaluation Department, Evaluation by

the IMF and the World Bank, Envisaged Methodological Approach, Joint World Bank and IMF Report, The World Bank: Full Debt Cancellation, HIPC Initiative Progress Report, Sunset Clause, Debt Forgiveness as Imperialism and Conclusion

Chapter V: International Forums in favour of Debt Relief: 217 - 253
Peoples Millennium Forum, South Asian Association for Regional Cooperation, Commonwealth Civil Society, Commonwealth HIPC Ministerial Forum (2005), Bangkok Recommendations, Commonwealth Ministerial Debt Sustainability Forum (2009) and Conclusion

Chapter VI: International Advocacy for Debt Relief: 254 - 300
African Forum and Net Work on Debt and Development, Jubilee Debt Campaign (UK), Liberal Democrat Youth and Students (LDYS), CAFOD (Catholic Agency for Overseas Development), Churches and Religious Organizations, OXFAM, Women's Environment and Development Organization, Make Poverty History and Conclusion

Chapter VII: G-8 Countries and Debt Relief
Dilemma in Granting Debt Relief: 301 - 376

G-7 Toronto Summit (1998), G-7 London Summit (1991), G-7 Lyon Summit (1996), G-8 Koln Summit (1999), G-8 Okinawa Summit (2000), G-8 Genoa (Italy) Summit, 2001, G-8 Gleneagles Summit (2005), G-8 L'aquila Summit (2009), Four Ministers on a Common Cause, Joint Progress Report, Joint Report on Progress on Cologne Debt Initiative, Canada Announces Debt Relief for Asian Countries, G-8 Proposals for HIPC Debt Cancellation, G-8 Africa Action Plan, Motion for Resolution in the European Parliament, G-8 Agrees Cancellation of World Bank and IMF Debt, Contribution of German Government, The Multilateral Debt Relief Initiative (MDRI) The G-

20 Leaders' Statement: The Pittsburgh Summit (2009), Summary and Conclusion

Chapter VIII: World Organizations and Debt Relief: 377-455
United Nations Organizations, Third UN conference on LDCs, 2001, The Development Agenda, The World Bank, Debt Relief at a glance, MDRI, Avoiding the need for another Debt Relief Initiative, The International Monetary Fund, Factsheet IMF, Fact Sheet 2011, Paris Club, Two Important Committee Reports on the World Bank and the IMF, US House Banking and International Relations Committee, Meltzer Commission, The World Bank: Hype Versus Substance and Conclusion

Chapter IX: World Peace Is Possible: 456 – 488
The IMF Crimes against Humanity, Dis-investment Campaign, Debt Cancellation Should Be Implemented, Learning from History, Opinion of Mr. Gordon Brown, WB and IMF reject 100 percent Debt Relief, Where We Stand Now, and Problems can be Solved, The IMF desperately needs a non-European, Measurement of Peace and Conclusion.

Annexure: 489
Authors Index: 490 - 495
Subject Index: 495 - 498

INTRODUCTION

World peace is achievable through reduction of debt or waiving out debt at the shortest possible time. Debt relief is not a slogan; it is a request, a prayer, a demand and a challenge to all the developed countries for award of amnesty to the low-income countries and developing countries as these countries are financially unsound for debt servicing. Debt relief is the moral duty and responsibility of the rich countries as they have received more money as compared to the grants and loans they have given to the poor countries. Today, 1.3 billion people manage their livelihood with less than US $1 per day, 2.8 billion people earn less than US $2 per day and one billion people are food-insecure. Hence, the rich, industrialized and developed countries, foreign funding institutions, International Monetary Fund, and international banks should accept humanitarian and moral responsibility to award debt relief to the debtor countries for creating an environment for world peace.

Debt burden causes migraine to the debtor countries and it blocks economic progress; hampers social security; shrinks public sector institutions and chokes the prospects of hundreds of millions of world's poorest people. Now, the question is why the poor people remained poor and why the poor countries are unable for debt servicing. The reasons may be: the rich countries award abundant debt in hard currencies for social welfare projects, which are not economically viable. Simply they invest their surplus funds for money lending, which pushes the poor countries to enter into debt trap. The debtor countries borrow foreign funds for development projects; but the political leaders, government officials and contractors misappropriate a major share of the borrowed funds; and these funds are converted into private properties. The governments of the poor countries spend the amount through false receipts without considering that debt must be repaid.

It is observed that neither the creditors grant credit for productive purposes nor the debtors utilize the borrowed capital in profitable projects. As a result, the borrowed capital emerges as punitive and cursing measure for the poor people of developing countries.

This alarming situation prevails in all the HIPCs and low-income countries. The debt burden continues to grow; poor countries pay more than what they receive; and they are now placed in debt bondage. The budgetary allocation on education and health care is earmarked less than debt servicing. The pay and pension of government officials has crossed the state gross domestic product. Expenditure on populist measures, corruption in project work, occurrence of frequent natural calamities, general elections, inaction of planning and monitoring machinery in government departments, entry of tainted politicians in administration and lethargic jurisprudential procedure have contributed, if not stagnant economies, but slow moving economies in about 78 countries.

Why as many as 54 low-income countries and 58 low-middle-income countries are insolvent of debt servicing even today? Why the donor organizations grant huge amount of credits to poor countries for uneconomic projects? These debts to governments have created massive corruption at all levels. Perhaps, the funding institutions, public sector banks and rich countries are granting funds to the poor countries for investment of their (creditors') idle money for their (creditors') own benefits, but they speak differently. It is alleged that these investments do not contribute to the welfare of majority of the poor people.

It is therefore necessary that the United Nations, the World Bank, the International Monetary Fund, the G8 and the OECD should formulate a peace process for the benefits of billions of people living in this beautiful world for a better and secure future.

Can we make this world an abode of permanent peace? The world has avoided world war for more than six decades and why we cannot avoid the world war for the next six centuries? If the problem of poverty and debt over dues are not solved; if the world organizations delay in adopting suitable and effective measures for debt relief, the World War III may be caused for poverty related issues.

The world community has the capacity to solve the problems of 'debt and starvation' in all the LDCs and LLDCs as an economic approach to ensure world peace. Debt relief is the confirmed route to encourage WORLD PEACE.

The world community needs a safer and peaceful world. Man, by nature, is an architect of development not destruction; he searches for peace not pain; creates friendship not enmity and prefers divinity not devil nature. Each individual should opt for peace, progress and prosperity for achieving WORLD PEACE. And it is possible.

+++++

Chapter-I

DEBT:
A GLOBAL CHALLENGE

In a well-ordered society, the securing of one's livelihood should be and is found to be the easiest thing in the world.

Mahatma M.K. Gandhi, December 22, 1921

Debt is both an advantage and a problem. Debt is necessary for development but it should be properly utilized. Mis-utilization, under-utilization, no-utilization of debt or investment of debts in long-term un-productive projects becomes a burden on the state exchequer. The habit of borrowing funds from the multilateral and bilateral organizations by the politicians of the poor countries has landed these countries to a point of no return. Each year these countries borrow to service the old debt. External debt increases as it is to be paid in hard currency. The problem occurs when a country is unable to service the dues by sacrificing the present development efforts.

Debt relief is somewhat an ambiguous term used variously to refer to rescheduling and refinancing; debt reduction and debt-service reduction; or both. Debt restructuring is a general term for debt rescheduling and debt refinancing. But we understand that debt relief is a political and economic slogan for assisting the poor countries and controlling these countries economically and politically for a number of decades.

The oil producing and exporting countries (OPEC) such as Iraq, Iran and Kuwait could amass huge fortunes through sale of crude oil and these countries deposited the amount in Western banks. At the end of Seventies the world suffered from recession, low commodity prices and a high interest rate. Hence, the unutilized hard money was loaned out to the underdeveloped newly independent third world countries, which needed funds for developmental projects. These countries spent the amount recklessly without considering the benefit-cost analysis and incurred further loans. Ultimately the debt burgeoned to such an extent that the countries could not undertake debt servicing and these countries availed fresh loans for debt servicing. The refinancing and rescheduling of foreign debt and devaluation of home currency could not assist the poor countries, rather invited more fiscal troubles. The debt burden increased to a sky limit. Therefore, the poor countries increasingly resorted to new borrowings. Funds for new investment became scarce, economic growth slowed and debt dynamics were set off that became unsustainable in many cases. Developing (including middle-income) country debt rose from $500 billion in 1980 to $1 trillion in 1985, around $2 trillion in 2000 and $ 2.554 trillion as on December 31, 2003 and $2.8 trillion by the end of 2005. The low-income countries owe a total of US$ 523 billion debt to all creditors. Of this, the African continent alone has a debt stock of US$ 330 billion and still spends US$ 15 billion every year in debt service to rich countries and the international financial institutions. In short, all the heavily indebted poor countries (HIPCs) and most of the developing countries are today unable for debt servicing as these countries have already entered into the debt trap.

Initially, creditors believed the debt service problems of the poor countries are of temporary period. Accordingly, debt relief took the form of payment rescheduling, sometimes coupled with new packages of loans. Indeed, an elaborate mechanism was developed to ensure that all of a country's bilateral creditors contributed equally. Creditor governments formed a committee to agree on the needed debt relief, in consultation with the IMF, and to take up possible steps that all creditors offered terms at least as favorable as those agreed by the Committee. Hosted by the French Treasury, this committee became known as the "Paris Club". Repeated Paris Club rescheduling for many debtors led official lenders to recognize that a new approach was needed for these countries that went beyond rescheduling debt service. At summits of the G-7 industrialized countries in Toronto (1988), Trinidad (1990), London (1991), and Naples (1994), new and increasingly concessional mechanisms were devised to bring more lasting relief. Thus, increasing amounts of debt reduction were written into terms of Paris Club rescheduling, so that by 1994 when the Paris Club began to offer "Naples terms" at the rescheduling, about two-thirds of the stock of official debt was cancelled. Around $60 billion in debt and debt service has been cancelled through the Paris Club process.

Yet, the debt of the poor countries remained high. By the mid-1990s, it was evident that the combination of existing debt relief mechanisms, new official assistance, and policy packages aimed at reducing borrowing needs were still not enough to reduce debt to sustainable levels. In October 1996, the IMF and the World Bank jointly announced the HIPC Initiative to provide a comprehensive solution to the problems of poor country indebtedness.[2]

The HIPC Initiative aims at ensuring that no poor country faces a debt burden it cannot manage. The Initiative entails coordinated action by international financial community, including multilateral organizations and governments, to reduce to sustainable levels the external debt burdens of the most heavily indebted poor countries. In September 1999, the HIPC Initiative adopted a number of modifications to provide faster, deeper and broader debt relief and to strengthen the links between debt relief, poverty reduction and social policies. The enhanced HIPC Initiative calls for macroeconomic adjustment and structural and social policy reforms - including higher spending on social sector programs like basic health and education - in the debtor countries.

Problems in Poor Countries

Debt has been choking the world's weakest economies and blocking economic progress for billions of the world's poorest people. Most of the poor families of these countries are illiterate, unemployed, lack of shelter, food insecure and they suffer from jaundice, typhoid, and malaria. The agriculture sector suffers from low productivity, inaccessibility of markets, fewer prices for saleable surplus, high interest rate, no insurance coverage, and inequality in land distribution. The government machinery is corrupt, inefficient and lacks transparency. The government opts for higher wages, undeclared wars, frequent amendments of Acts and policies, and invests funds in populist projects without consideration of benefit-cost analysis. In some cases the project, which could be completed within 2-3

---

[2] The Logic of Debt Relief for the Poorest Countries, International Monetary Fund

years, takes 20-30 years and the amount of investment increases 20 to 25 times. The poor countries treat external debt as grants even before the government functionaries receive the amount. Both grants and loans are mis-utilised by the government. So rescheduling of debt relief cannot solve the problem of poverty permanently.

As Denise Froning observes, the poor countries face too many problems in addition to overwhelming debt, many of, which are precisely what caused the debt accumulation in the first place. Many factors - disease, poverty, lack of education, lack of institutions, lack of transportation infrastructure, lack of food, lack of business, lack of security, lack of foreign investment, and lack of prospects - continue to stifle the economic growth of these countries, and they will continue to do so after debt relief. Without a change in these circumstances, debt relief will be only a short-term palliative, and these countries will find themselves back in the same predicament that they now face. The researcher further explains that poor countries must improve domestically in a number of areas; their poverty cannot be attributed entirely due to external factors. Although these countries face some valid domestic woes, many of the excuses for poverty are invalid. A lack of natural resources, for instance, does not fully account for the poverty the HIPCs face. The author concludes that bad leaders, corruption, bad institutions and lack of rule of law are responsible for poverty of nations and suggests that breaking the cycle of indebtedness will require several actions: (a) forgive debt, (b) encourage trade through regional customs arrangements, (c) eliminate all tariffs and quotas on HIPCs; and (d) finally, the author believes that economic freedom is vital and, in the end, the only truly humane solution.[3]

---

[3] Denise Froning, "Will Debt Relief Really Help?", *The Washington Quarterly*, The Centre for Strategic and

Natural Wealth and Poverty

A number of poor countries have abundant natural resources like mines and minerals, oil deposits, forests, rivers, and cultivated land. Now, these countries have plenty of cheap and abundant labour force, technical know-how, and easy credit facility. Yet these countries are unable to utilize the funds for productive purposes. Unless the natural resources are utilized in productive ventures, the output is properly marketed; the low-income countries cannot achieve economic growth. The governments can hire expertise, can make viable projects for progress; and can generate surplus funds to repay back the debt.

Ayittey[4] opines that Africa, where most of the world's 41 HIPCs are located, is awash in natural wealth, from diamonds, gold, and oil to arable agricultural land. The continent has abundant natural potential. This potential, however, remains largely unrealized. Citing examples such as Russia, some argued that such resources are more a curse than a blessing, but that arguments do not explain the lack of development capacity. Different countries have become developed through utilization of resources. He makes the important distinction between African people and the leaders of African nations. It is not the African people who squander development opportunities. Too often, it is African leaders, who seize both native wealth and foreign aid, are successful in plunging their countries into war and they plunder their money, through the exploitation of resources like diamonds and stealing massive amounts of foreign aid. Ayittey delineates four

---

International Studies and the Massachusetts Institute of Technology, Summer 2001, 24:3, pp.199 -211

[4] George Ayittey, *Africa in Chaos* (New York: St. Martin's Press, 1998) and Ayittey, "How the West Compounds Africa's Crises," *Intellectual Capital*, June 29, 2000, located at http://207.87.15.232/issues/Issue 387/item9858.asp, quoted from Denise Froning, ibid.

institutional pillars that are essential for lasting development in Africa: independent judiciaries, an independent central bank, free media, and neutral armed forces.

Ruchir Sharma (2004)[5] explains that historical evidence on the role of natural resources in economic development is terribly mixed. While some of the leading industrialized economies, starting with United States in the nineteenth century and later Australia, Canada, Sweden and Norway, all relied heavily on the export of natural resources to develop their economies, more recent experience suggest that oil riches can wreck havoc on a country's economic and political systems. Oil can be poison for a variety of reasons, ranging from oil-induced sloth to waste and corruption. Countries largely dependent on oil revenue often end up being run by authoritarian regimes that gain their power by controlling oil assets. Money flowing through weak structures leads to perverse outcomes. Only those countries that have strong institutions in place have been able to avoid the resource curse, such as Norway and Botswana of late. The US was able to exploit its natural resources to be held privately and yet reserve the right to intervene and prevent monopolies. Russia's economic fate will really dictate in which the debate over oil tilts.

Joseph E. Stiglitz (2004)[6] says abundant natural resources can and should be a blessing not a curse. We know what must be done, but what is missing is the political will to make it so. There is a curious phenomenon that economists call the *resource curse* – so named because, on average, countries with large endowments of natural resources perform worse than

---

[5] Sharma, Ruchir "When the bountiful is not beautiful", *The Economic Times*, Kolkata, dated August 10, 2004, P4

[6] Stiglitz, Joseph E., "The Resource Curse Revisited", The Economic Times, Kolkata, dated 12.08.2004, P4

countries that are less well endowed. Yet some countries with abundant natural resources do perform better than others, and some had done well. Why is the spell of the resource curse cast so unequally? Thirty years ago, Indonesia and Nigeria - both dependents on oil - had comparable per capita income. Today, Indonesia's per capita income is four times that of Nigeria. A similar pattern holds true in Sierra Leone and Botswana. Both are rich in diamonds. Yet Botswana averaged 8.7 per cent annual economic growth over the past thirty years, while Sierra Leone plunged into civil strife. The failures in the oil-rich Middle East are legion. Economists put forward three reasons for the dismal performance of some richly endowed countries:

First, the prospect of the riches orients official efforts to seizing a larger share of the pie, rather than creating a larger pie. The result of this wealth grab is often war. At other times simple rent-seeking behaviour by officials, aided and abetted by outsiders, is the outcome. It is cheaper to bribe a government to provide resources at below-market prices than to invest and develop an industry. Therefore, it is no surprise that some firms succumb to this temptation.

Second, natural resource prices are volatile, and managing this volatility is hard. Lenders provide money when times are good but want their money back when, say, energy prices plummet. (At the old adage has it, banks only like to lend to those who do not need money). Economic activity is thus even more volatile than commodity prices and much of the gains made in a boom unravel in the bust that follows.

Third, oil and other natural resources, while perhaps a source of wealth do not create jobs by themselves, and unfortunately, they often crowd out other economic sectors. For example, an inflow of oil money often leads to currency appreciation – a phenomenon called the *Dutch Disease.* He further explains that secret bank account not only supports terrorism, but also facilitates corruption that undermines development. Moreover, oil money helps someone else's economy.

Causes of Debt Crises

Dijkstra and Hermes (2003) have explained that debt payment problems may arise because of two reasons: Expectations and assumptions on the future do not hold, or there are market failures and distortions in international financial capital markets.[7]

During debt finalization, actors make assumptions on the future, in particular, on the expected rate of returns to investment. In the case of sovereign borrowing, expectations on the future exports and government revenues are important. These two will tend to be related to GDP. If the loans carry variable interest rates, assumptions must also be made on the future behaviour of the interest rate. In 1980s, there were unexpected rises of interest rates and unexpected falls in export volumes in developing countries. Moreover, the international financial markets do not always work according to neo-classical assumptions. In general, three types of distortions can be distinguished: interest rates are not fully determined by supply and demand factors, lender's decisions are not always based on expected returns, nor, thirdly, are borrowers' decisions.

---

[7] Dijkstra, G. and Hermes, N, "The Debt Crisis, International; Responses, and Results of Debt Relief", Report of a Literature Survey and an Econometric Analysis, Policy and Operations Evaluation Unit, *Working Document,* the Netherlands, January 2003, pp. 9-10

Eaton and Fernandez[8] have opined that in the case of sovereign debt, there is an additional source of distortion. The fact that loans are contracted or guaranteed by governments of countries means that there is no collateral, and that creditors cannot go to court in case of failure to pay. Other sanctions and rewards are needed to induce countries to pay the debt.

The debt crisis is usually said to have begun when the government of Mexico announced that it could no longer service its international debt. Mexico was indeed was the first large country that did so in 1982, and from then on creditors became concerned about the risks they had taken. By the end of 1982, US banks had invested 187 per cent of their capital in developing countries and 119 per cent in Latin America. For the nine major banks, these percentages were 288 per cent and 177 per cent.[9] Hence, these banks could have been sick because the money was at risk. Since, banks all over the world also owe large amounts of money to each other; failure of some banks could have triggered a word-wide banking crisis and the collapse of the international financial system.[10]

The debt crisis of the 1980s broke out when interest rates suddenly rose and commodity prices fell. The debt crisis originated because of build-up of large debts in the 1970s, market failures and distortions on the supply side. The other reasons of debt crisis were high-risk lending of commercial banks, lack of

---

[8] Eaton, Jonathan, and Fernandez, Raquel, "Sovereign Debt", National Bureau of Economic Research, *Working Paper* No. 5131, Cambridge, MA, 1995

[9] Bowe, Michael, and Dean, James W.,"Has the Market Solved the Sovereign debt Crisis?" *Princeton Studies in International Finance* No. 83, Princeton, NJ: International Finance Section. Princeton University, 1997

[10] Hermes, C.L.M. "De internationale schuldencrisis, Groningen: Wolters- Noordhoff, 1992

supervision and regulation of overseas lending, bilateral governments' interests in stimulating exports and employment of their own countries, and high demand of borrowers' need without consideration of their repayment capacity. Moreover, the efficiency of borrowed funds decreased because of over supply of funds with low interest.

Rubens Ricupero, Secretary General of UNCTAD emphasized that since the 1980s, deregulation and liberalization of trade and capital flows undermined domestic policy efforts to support equitable and sustainable growth. He urged that debt relief and better conditions of debt repayment are necessary to ensure development of international trade and international finance.

Debt Relief and Media

Whether debt relief should be awarded to the HIPCs and other debtors, which are incapable to debt servicing or they are bound to pay both principal and interest, has assumed world debate by economists, planners, politicians, journalists, thinkers, international organizations, and world organizations. The arguments are both qualitative and lively. Both the options are justified and therefore the controversy in debt relief is more complicated. All the international, national and local newspapers have published volumes of articles, views and editorial comments on debt relief for a peaceful settlement of debt overhang in most of the low-income and IDA eligible countries. The world opinion on debt relief is as follows:

Guardian: The Highly Indebted Poor Countries Initiative (HIPC) has delivered only half the debt relief but it promised that it would force countries with huge humanitarian needs to shell out millions of dollars to international creditors. The Western creditors should adjust debt payment demands according to efforts to meet the Millennium Development Goals.

Washington Post: Bowing to the US Treasury and Wall Street, the IMF will remove a clause from its proposed bankruptcy mechanism that would have protected highly indebted countries from creditor lawsuits. Even with the concession, the US banking community remains opposed to the 'basic notion' of bankruptcy protection for countries with unsustainable debt.

Rabble: The corporate world is proposing a new debt repayment initiative, which would imply the exchange of territory for debt repayment. Critics view this as another way of giving the IMF and multilateral corporations more control over the debtor countries.

All Africa: Finance ministers from Commonwealth African countries suggested changes in the Heavily Indebted Poor Countries (HIPC) initiative. These ministers call for increased efforts to broaden the participation of creditors and for increased aid to HIPCs.

Observer: In reference to Big Food Group's decision not to pursue compensation from Guyana, the manager of the World Bank's HIPC unit argues that debt relief in fact encourages capital inflows to poor countries. His statement disputes the neo-liberal claim that debt forgiveness campaigns hurt poor countries by dissuading foreign investment.

Africa Action argues that the World Bank, IMF and the main creditors of Africa's debt can afford to write it off but refused to do so because they want to retain control over Africa's economies.

Washington Post: US Treasury Secretary John Snow urges France, Germany and Russia to cancel at least part of Iraq's billions of dollars in debt, which experts say Iraq cannot possibly pay in full. Debt relief advocates support the move, but blast Washington for hypocritically opposing the forgiveness of other impoverished countries' debt burden.

Washington Post: The editorial warns against politicizing international aid in the aftermath of the Iraqi war. This editorial satirizes the US double standard on urging debt forgiveness for Iraq while showing no enthusiasm for broadening debt relief for world's poorest countries.

Guardian: Charlotte Denny of the Guardian argues for an extension of the proposed debt deal for Iraq to poorer countries. Denny suggests creating an international tribunal to determine future loans to countries under the rule of a dictator.

Financial Times: In accordance with Washington and Wall Street's insistence on 'voluntary market-based' solutions to third world debt, Uruguay is seeking to ease its huge debt burden with a voluntary debt exchange deal with the IMF. Experts question the sustainability of this mechanism, arguing it does little to change the underlying economic problem in poor countries.

Jubilee Research: Jubilee Debt Campaign and CAFOD call in a joint report for an end to the privatization and liberalization conditions linked to debt relief that harm the poor and the creation of a fair procedure for poor countries if they become insolvent in the future.

Le Monde Diplomatique: Members of the Inter – American Development Bank will not loan Haiti the money to supply clean water and improve health infrastructure until the world's poorest country pays back the outstanding loans made to military dictators.

Los Angeles Times: Argentina's President Nestor Kirchner blames the IMF for its role in the Argentine financial disaster, urging the institution to grant the country a grace period to recover.

CAFOD, Christian Aid and EURODAD: They urge multilateral and bilateral donors to undertake policy actions to help achieve the Millennium Development Goals. The joint paper argues that without the requisite finance, low–income countries cannot meet the goals. It furthermore proposes specific aid and debt policy reforms. While admitting that "HIPC is no panacea" this IMF fact sheet does not respond to the critique of the HIPC mechanism as such Highly indebted poor countries can qualify for debt relief only if they implement IMF and World Bank – prescribed programs of "reform and sound policies," which in several cases caused poor countries' breakdown. This report analyzes achievements and failures of the IMF's HIPC-initiative to restore long-term debt sustainability to highly indebted poor countries.

Jubilee Research urges the IMF to evaluate debt sustainability according to the resources needed for achieving the Millennium Development Goals, rather than in relation to export incomes.

Vanguard, Nigeria: Nigeria's President Obasanjo urges the international community to tackle Africa's debt burden. The various initiatives of multilateral and bilateral creditors to relieve debt do not sufficiently address the problem.

Frontline (India): Droughts and diminishing institutional credits in agriculture have driven Indian farmers into debt. Moreover, agricultural globalization through the WTO regime forced the government to end subsidies and to withdraw safety nets. This evolution explains the rising number of suicides among poor Indian farmers.

Atlantic Monthly: Economist Joseph Stieglitz calls for an international set of laws governing the restructuring and relief of international debt. He particularly urges forgiveness of "odious debts" accumulated by dictatorial regimes in Iraq, Congo, Ethiopia, and elsewhere, to finance the oppression of its people – who are now asked to repay the debts.

Guardian: The US argues that the "Iraqi people should not be saddled with the debt of brutal regime". At the same time, it opposes all attempts of debt cancellation for Argentina, whose similarly cruel dictators accumulated an enormous debt with the complicity of Henry Kissinger. Naoimi Klein contends that US corporations expect only the profits from Iraq's reconstruction, which can explain this discrepancy.

UN Wire: Jose Antonio Ocampo, the UN Under-Secretary General for Economic and Social Affairs, argues that poor countries are "caught in a trap" where "slow growth reduces foreign investment, which in turn limits growth." Jose highlights that the heavy external debt burden of LDCs further inflames this situation.

Jubilee Research condemns the powerful creditors, largely the US, Germany and Japan, who are attempting to avoid increasing debt relief for poor countries. This situation reveals the hypocrisy in today's global economic system.

ERODAD Debt List serve: Rich nations argue over the amount of relief to give to highly indebted countries. In particular, the US Treasury, a key board member of the IMF and World Bank asserts that poor countries will use debt relief as a platform to borrow more from these international financial institutions.

Global Exchange: If rich countries were to forgive poor nations' debts, development would not necessarily follow. Cancellation would absolve debt created by local elites, without redistributing economic power to the population or guaranteeing that the deficits would not quickly recur. This article urges rich governments to implement ''proactive'' policies to address poor countries' need for capital and to empower their citizens' search for economic alternatives. Such policies would make a debt relief a sustainable development measure, rather than a temporary reprieve.

Globe and Mail: Many African countries are burdened by huge national debts that stifle development efforts. Leaders of selected African countries made an "emotional plea" to the G8 for debt cancellation so that limited finances could be directed toward economic and social issues. The G8 denied debt relief, and instead offered a moderate extension of the "heavily indebted poor countries "(HIPC) initiative.

A key policy paper from the **Foreign Policy in Focus** calls for:

(a) Immediate and comprehensive debt cancellation for impoverished countries,
(b) An international body, with strict requirements of fair representation, with authority to determine the legitimacy of debts and adjudicate their cancellation and reduction, and
(c) Annulment of debts incurred for failed economic programs and non-performing infrastructure projects.

The World Bank Group has classified 62 countries as low-income countries on the basis of 2005 GNI per capita, calculated using the World Bank Atlas method. Low-income countries are classified as GDP per capita US $875 or less.

Conclusion

Excessive debt burden of a country blocks economic progress, hampers social security, causes less investment in health and education sectors, increases corruption in public sectors, widens the rich-poor gap, makes politics a quick earning business proposition, increases number of hungry mouths and lawlessness in countries. Debts incurred for infrastructure development causes high political and administrative corruption and plunges the country into debt trap.

The poor countries suffer from unemployment, spiraling prices, migration of labour force from rural areas to urban centers, increase of slum dwellers in urban areas and shortage of farm-laborers for agricultural purposes. Natural resources like forests, mines and minerals are exhausted for industries for the benefits of industrialists and corrupt administrators.

Poor inhabitants' loss their dwelling houses and become nomads. Climate is changed and poor people are infected with chronic diseases. Internal security challenges the government because of hunger, poverty and corruption.

Debt increases internal crises including easy availability of arms and ammunitions. Even in the twenty-first century, millions of people of low-income countries are underfed, uneducated and without health care facilities. The Millennium Development Goals would not achieve targets. Debt relief is a right path for global peace and can assure peace to low-income countries and poor people.

+++++

Chapter II

RESEARCH STUDIES ON DEBT RELIEF

Man seeks peace because his earthly existence desperately needs it. Man welcomes peace because he feels that in peace alone is his life of achievement and fulfillment. Man spreads peace because he wants to transcend death.

Sri Chinmoy in 'Songs of the Soul'

The world can, and should, do better. Acceleration of progress requires a shared commitment to pursue this development agenda with greater vigor and urgency. It suggests that the world organizations, developed countries and governments of low-income countries have not paid due attention for reducing the number of poor people vis-à-vis solving 'hunger' problem of the world.

Poor countries always have the 'willingness to pay' but the fact that a large share of new multilateral disbursements is merely being recycled into multilateral debt service while demands of the development program are not met in full affecting their 'ability to pay'. The challenge facing the bilateral and international financial community is to extricate poor countries from the multilateral debt trap.

Borrowers persistently claim that lenders brought the crisis upon themselves and therefore advocate outright debt stock cancellation. However, lenders insist that borrowers committed themselves to international finance covenants that must be honoured; otherwise there is a moral hazard that new loans will not be repaid in future if current debts are cancelled. This fear should not be entertained, as borrowers did not pressurized the developed countries for high quantum of credits for infrastructure development; it was sanctioned by the developed countries for political and economic reasons that disturbed the very social fabric of the low-and-least developed countries.

Forgiveness is not a fundamental right. But the peace-lovers and borrowers request for 100 percent debt relief once for all for their survival, progress and peace.

This chapter has incorporated the suggestions and policy recommendations of the World Bank, IMF, UNDP, Universities, and economists on debt relief. It tries to explain the causes and effects of debt burden, debt trap, and debt relief. The background of HIPC initiative and its outcomes in the low-income-countries have also been discussed.

Research Findings

Bailey and Cohen (1987) have argued that the third world debt problem is not one of temporary liquidity but one of structural over indebtedness. They have proved Mexico's problems as a case study of mis-diagnosis by international monetary authorities. They examined the origins of the Mexican debt crisis of 1982, model of debtor responsibility, the exacerbation of problems from 1983 to 1986 including the decreasing political capacity of the country to sustain adjustment, and the failure of the model. They proposed that the third world debt crisis has entered a new phase characterized by erosion of the leverage of the monetary authorities and growing incentives for default among debtors and finally concluded that the only way Mexico can reduce its deficits and resume non-inflationary growth is with debt relief. Recommendations include: liberalization and rationalization of the Mexican economy, increased development funding, debt service limitation, and securitization of at least the private portion of the debt.[11]

Cline (1987) outlined the policy setting for increased mobilization of new financing to debtor countries from private banks as part of the strategy of debt management. He has drawn a proposal for new money packages that would choose the financing mechanism according to the preferences of different classes of banks including voluntary exit as well as the mechanism for enforcement. According to this package, meeting cash flow needs and equivalent burden sharing as well as monitoring requirements can be fulfilled. Cline has analyzed the domestic monetary implications of lending options, future direction of debt management, and debt strategy and proposals for relief.[12]

---

[11] Bailey, Norman A. and Cohen, Richard," The Mexican Time Bomb", ***Twentieth Century Fund Paper series***, New York, Priority Press, 1987, pages vi, 61.

[12] Cline, William R., "Mobilizing bank lending to debtor countries", Policy ***Analyses in International Economics*** series, no 18, Washington, D.C., Institute for International Economics, 1987, pages viii, 92

Fishlow (1987)[13] has analyzed the debt crises of Argentina and Brazil in the 1980s. The paper discusses the importance of domestic monetary policy versus external factors in provoking devaluation and establishes the differential role of reduced capital inflows in Argentina relative to Brazil. The paper emphasizes the different acceptance of Argentine and Brazilian securities on the London market and the consequences of market valuation for debt relief. It also contrasts the domestic adjustments required in the 1890s to achieve balance of payments equilibrium. The paper concludes by drawing parallels between the cyclical patterns of peripheral, externally financed development in the 1890s and developing country reliance on debt in the 1970s and 1980s.

Fischer (1987) has illustrated that since August 1982, the international debt crisis has dominated economic policymaking in the developing countries, economic relations between the debtor and creditor countries, and the attention of the multilateral institutions in their dealings with the debtor nations, and private sector decisions on lending to the developing countries. He has opined three solutions for resolving the international debt crisis. These are: Least radical are proposals for procedural reform and changes in the nature of the claims on the existing debt. The second type of solution is the creation of a facility, or new institution to deal with the overhang of existing debt. Finally, there are proposals for debt relief, either in direct negotiation between creditors and debtors and/or in conjunction with the creation of a facility.[14]

---

[13] Fishlow, Albert," Lessons of the 1890's for the 1980's", University of California at Berkeley, ***Working Paper in Economics***: 8724, January 1987, pages 56.

[14] Fischer, Stanley," Resolving the International Debt Crisis", National Bureau of Economic Research ***Working Paper***: 2373, September 1987.

Sachs and Huizinga (1987) have illustrated that commercial banks have weathered the debt crisis and have caused many debtor countries in economic paralysis. The growing consensus that much LDC debt will not be fully serviced in the future is reflected in at least two ways: discounts in secondary market prices for LDC debt and discounts in stock market pricing of banks with exposures in LDC. Since heavily exposed banks' share prices are already discounted, banks could absorb a significant book loss on their LDC exposure. Debt conversion schemes now under discussion could offer debt relief to debtor countries without causing further deterioration in market values of commercial banks.[15]

Corden (1988)[16] has opined that debt relief would increase the incentive of a debtor country to make an adjustment effort to invest and that for this reason creditors may benefit by granting relief. It is shown that there are actually opposing incentive effects of debt relief and that the argument could be valid in particular circumstances. A distinction is made between exogenous and endogenous relief, the latter compelled by low capacity to pay caused by low investment earlier.

Williamson (1988) examined proposals for debt relief that could be voluntarily conveyed by commercial banks. Some banks were prepared to grant substantial debt relief in order to secure exit from sovereign lending. By this, there could be gains to banks and debtors from facilitating the withdrawal of banks that were willing to pay a sufficiently high price. He Identified sources of potential gain from

---

[15] Sachs, Jeffrey and Huizinga, Harry," U.S. Commercial Banks and the Developing Country Debt Crisis", ***Brookings Papers on Economic Activity***; 0(2), 1987, pages 555-601.

[16] Corden, W. Max," Debt Relief and Adjustment Incentives", ***International Monetary Fund Staff Papers***, 35(4), December 1988, pages 628-43.

voluntary debt relief to both debtors and creditors, such as the positive incentive effect for debtor countries and the divergent interests of various banks. He also examined alternative mechanisms for the provision of voluntary debt relief including buybacks, exit bonds, and debt/equity swaps. He designed of a program of voluntary debt relief and estimated the impact that various specific initiatives would have on the debt problem.[17]

Corden (1988)[18] has analyzed "incentives" argument — why debt relief could be to the advantage of creditors collectively. Principal reasons analyzed are based on the "investment capacity" and the "default forestalling" arguments. Debt relief is defined as reduction of the present value of the contractual debt. The paper thus provides an analytical basis for various debt relief proposals that do not require finance or guarantees from creditor governments and for the considerable amount of relief in the form of rescheduling and concerted lending. The research paper also illustrates the free rider problem and the extent to which the market may overcome the debt burden.

Cohen (1988) has analyzed the optimal rescheduling strategy of lenders whose claims on a country showed a discount on the secondary markets. The paper illustrates that lenders should proceed as follows: They should split the debt into two components - performing and non-performing. They should act "as if" the debt amounted to the performing part and scale down how much money the borrower should service on that part only. The

---

[17] Williamson, John,"Voluntary Approaches to Debt Relief", Policy ***Analyses in International Economics series*** No 25 Washington, D.C: Institute for International Economics, 1988, pages x, 63.

[18] Corden, W. Max," Is Debt Relief in the Interests of the Creditors?" ***International Monetary Fund Working Paper***, WP/88/72 August 1988, pages 17.

optimal value of the "non-performing" part is shown to be strictly positive, while the equilibrium value of the "performing part" is shown to coincide with the market value of the debt. The paper relates this result to the "debt-overhang" argument (according to which too large a nominal claim may reduce the market value of the debt) and proposes an econometric estimate of the importance of this problem.[19]

Landskroner and Paroush (1988)[20] have used a model of the simultaneous optimal behavior of a lender with an outstanding claim and a borrower encountering debt-servicing difficulties. A third party, say, the IMF imposes a constraint in the form of an economic austerity program on the borrower. The borrower has to decide on the optimal economic policy while the lender has to decide about the optimal debt relief in the form of a new loan. The decisions of the two parties are related through the constraint, which affects the probability that the debtor will repay his debt to the creditor. Thus, the actions by the borrower are an incentive to the lender. They have used the model and the simultaneous optimal solutions of the borrower and the lender and have analyzed comparative static's of the effects of the different parameters of the model.

Dooley (1988)[21] analyzed debt relief that focuses on the behavior of debtors and existing creditors, which understate the incentives for collective action by

---

[19] Cohen, Daniel," Is the Discount on the Secondary Market a Case for LDC Debt Relief?" CEPREMAP ***Discussion Paper***: 8823, Oct 1988, pages28

[20] Landskroner, Yoram and Paroush, Jacob," Debt Relief and Adjustment Policies", New York University Salomon Brothers Center, ***Working Paper***: 501, December 1988, pages 24.

[21] Dooley, Michael P.," Debt Relief and Leveraged Buy-Outs", ***Internationa***l ***Monetary Fund Working Paper***: WP/88/103, November 1988, pages 6.

creditors. It is well known that debt relief could benefit existing creditors by providing incentives for domestic investment by residents of debtor countries. It is argued that relief could also make available additional profit opportunities to international investors. Under these circumstances, arrangements that would allow international investors to capture economic profits would make a leveraged buy-out of existing creditors, followed by relief, a profitable strategy for any investor or group of investors that could act collectively.

Aizenman (1988) has analyzed the factors determining the payment of outstanding debt in case of partial defaults, and the feasibility of renewed investment. It is observed that sectors with lower substitutability between domestic and foreign products will increase the resource transfer ceiling. Even with a partial default, investment in highly trade dependent sectors with high productivity may be warranted. This investment can be implemented by a marginal relief of the present debt service, in exchange for investment in the proper sector. A way to partially overcome some of the monitoring problems associated with renewed investment is possible through direct investment.[22]

Kamel (1988)[23] has analyzed the debt-growth model, which implicitly makes the assumption that the time rate of change of the country's exports and imports are equal. This paper presents an extended version of the model where this assumption is relaxed. The results of the investigation call for a re-examination of some widely accepted notions about sovereign

---

[22] Aizenman, Joshua, "Trade Dependency, Bargaining and External Debt", ***International Monetary Fund Working Paper***, WP/88/90, October 1988, pages 23

[23] Kamel, Nawal," Criteria for National Solvency", ***Oxford Applied Economics Discussion Paper***, 50, September 1988, pages 31.

international debt. A new approach to the evaluation of national solvency is presented taking explicitly into account national import growth as well as the inherited debt and the initial resource balance position. He has identified debt relief can put an insolvent country onto a solvency path and the minimum amount of such a relief can be established.

Krugman (1988) has examined the idea of reducing the debt of developing countries through a "menu approach" of schemes that attempt to harness the discounts on debt in the secondary market. This paper, after reviewing the rationale for the orthodox strategy of concerted lending and the case for debt forgiveness, examines the logic behind several market based debt reduction schemes. It shows that such schemes will ordinarily benefit both debtor and creditor only when the debtor is on the wrong side of the "debt relief Laffer curve"—that is, where a reduction in nominal claims actually increases expected payment. The paper elaborates that unilateral debt forgiveness is in the interest of creditors in any case. The implication is that there is no magic in market based debt reduction, as opposed to more straightforward approaches.[24]

Corden (1988) has designed a common proposal to deal with the developing countries' debt problem. The author has suggested setting up some kind of "international debt facility" which would buy up debt at a discount and then write down its contractual value, hence providing debt relief. There are three main parties to the proposed transaction, namely the debtor governments, the creditor banks, and the owners of the facility. The paper analyzes the central question of how each of the parties would be affected and, specifically, to what extent there would be some

---

[24] krugman, Paul R, "Market Based Debt Reduction Schemes", National Bureau of Economic Research Working Paper 2587, May 1988, Pages 41

redistribution between them as a result of the arrangement.[25]

Jorgensen and Sachs (1988)[26] have examined the patterns of defaults, renegotiations, and final settlements on foreign borrowing of several Latin American governments in the interwar period. One goal of the paper is to provide a detailed historical account of the borrowing and renegotiation experience of five Latin borrowers (Argentina, Bolivia, Chile, Colombia, and Peru). Another goal is to provide a quantitative assessment of the amount of debt relief that was implicit in the negotiated settlements of the defaults that were reached in the 1930s and 1940s. In general, the pattern of default and renegotiation resulted in substantial, though not complete, debt relief, in the sense of reducing the present value of debt repayments from the sovereign borrower to the bondholders.

Sachs (1988) raises several cautionary notes regarding high-conditionality lending by the International Monetary Fund and the World Bank in the context of international debt crisis. It is argued that the role for high-conditionality lending is more restricted than generally believed, because enforcement of conditionality is rather weak. Moreover, the incentives for a country to abide by conditionality terms are also likely to be reduced by a large overhang of external indebtedness. Given the limited ability to enforce conditionality agreements, modesty and realism should be a cornerstone of each program. The experience with conditionality suggests two major lessons for the design of high-

---

[25] Corden, W. Max," An International Debt Facility", ***International Monetary Fund Working Paper***: WP/88/16, February 1988, pages 19.

[26] Jorgensen, Erika and Sachs, Jeffrey D.," Default and Renegotiation of Latin American Foreign Bonds in the Interwar Period", ***National Bureau of Economic Research Working Paper***: 2636, June 1988.

conditionality lending. First, debt forgiveness rather than mere debt rescheduling may increase a debtor country's compliance with conditionality, and thereby increase the actual stream of repayments by the indebted countries. Second, given the complexity of the needed adjustments, and the difficulty of enforcing conditionality agreements, programs are most likely to be successful when macroeconomic stabilization is given priority over large-scale liberalization.[27]

Froot (1989)[28] compared different forms of market based debt relief with coordinated debt forgiveness by the creditors. Debtors benefit from these schemes to the extent of expected payments fall, but lose to the extent they sacrifice current resources. Creditors' benefit when the buyback resources are 'additional', and when debt reduction creates greater incentives for full repayment. The source of buyback resources is a critical determinant in assessing potential welfare gains. For liquidity-constrained debtors, debt reduction is not optimal for debtors or creditors. For these countries, the optimal debt relief package (from the creditors' perspective) will include an infusion of new lending.

Schwartz (1989) undertook a comparative study relating to foreign creditors and the politics of development in Australia and Argentina (1880-1913). The author has observed that most comparative studies of Australia and Argentina argue that the economic effects of concentrated landholdings impede development, and that Australia's greater development is thus attributable to landholders'

---

[27] Sachs, J. D. "Conditionality, Debt Relief, and the Developing Country Debt Crisis", NBER ***Working Paper No W 2644***, July 1988, Social Science Research Network, Tomorrow ' s Research Today, abstract No. 261258

[28] Froot, Kenneth A.," Buybacks, Exit Bonds and the Optimality of Debt and Liquidity Relief", ***International Economic Review***, 30(1), February 1989, pages 49-70.

political defeat at labor's hands. In contrast, this paper argues first that their creditors not labour; primarily destroyed Australians landholders and second that Argentina and Australian landholders behaved like productive capitalists, not renters. Landholders' political behaviour, not their economic behaviour, affected the later development of agriculture and industry, for large holders did make productive-enhancing investment. But in Australia, landholders' political weakness allowed investment markets to be distorted in favour of industry, accelerating industrial development. The Australian and Argentine experiences suggest that balances of market-led and market-distorting policies are needed to resolve the current Third World debt crisis.[29]

Dooley (1989) analyzed debt relief that focus on the behavior of debtors and existing creditors, who understate the incentives for collective action by creditors. It is well known that debt relief could benefit existing creditors by providing incentives for domestic investment by residents of debtor countries. It is argued here that relief could also make available additional profit opportunities to international investors. Under these circumstances, arrangements that would allow international investors to capture economic profits would make a leveraged buy-out of existing creditors, followed by relief, a profitable strategy for any investor or group of investors that could act collectively.[30]

Green (1989) has illustrated that the massive external debt burden of sub-Saharan Africa has

---

[29] Schwartz, Herman,"Foreign Creditors and the Politics of Development in Australia and Argentina, 1880-1913", ***International Studies Quarterly***, (1989), 33, pp. 281-301.

[30] Dooley, Michael P.," Debt Relief and Leveraged Buy Outs", ***International Economic Review***, 30(1), February 1989, pp. 71-75.

gained widespread attention as a serious policy issue during the past few years. This paper reviews recent trends in the debt levels and economic performance of sub-Saharan countries and assesses a number of proposals for reducing their external debt service obligations. There is also a discussion of the modalities of various debt relief proposals that have been advanced.[31]

Calvo (1989) has studied debt relief and penalties in connection with sovereign country loans. The author has narrated conditions for the existence of penalties that were too low for ensuring Pareto efficiency, and showed the possible time inconsistency of optimal debt contracts. Hence, a methodology for ascertaining debt relief implicit in international loans was outlined.[32]

Hajivassiliou (1989) has employed panel-data econometric techniques to explore the relations between measures of credit worthiness and the debt discounts on the secondary market. It investigates empirically whether the secondary market discounts reflect a history of past repayment problems or whether they anticipate future debt crises. The answer to this question has implications about the desirability of debt relief. The study concludes that the secondary markets do not seem rapidly to absorb economic information and they are still in their evolutionary stage and are not yet very efficient. The

---

[31] Greene, Joshua," The External Debt Problem of Sub-Saharan Africa", ***International Monetary Fund Working Paper***: WP/89/23, March 1989, pages 32.

[32] Calvo, Guillermo A.," A Delicate Equilibrium: Debt Relief and Default Penalties in an International Context", ***International Monetary Fund Working Paper***: WP/89/10, January 1989, pages 22.

estimated models are also used to analyze other issues in the international finance literature.[33]

Stymne (1989) analyzed the causes of growth of Africa's debt burden, and discussed the factors that induced African countries to seek external loans as well as the factors affecting the supply of external financing. The author studied the development of some measures of debt burden for different categories of African debtors, and arrived at a hypothesis regarding feasible levels of debt and debt service ratios. In a final section, the paper discusses the options for debt relief using a simulation of payments ability.[34]

Rauscher (1989) investigated the relationship between the indebtedness situation of a developing country and its production of renewable resources. It is shown that such a relationship exists if the capital market on which the country borrows and lends is imperfect. Additionally, it can be seen that under realistic assumptions about the type of the market imperfection, a debt relief has a resource conserving effect.[35]

Dornbusch et al (1989) have edited a book with twelve papers, based on the proceedings of the Alternative Solutions to Developing Country Debt Problems Conference held in April 1989. They have examined what should or can be done to face the crisis of debt obligations. The chapters of the book

---

[33] Hajivassiliou, Vassilis, " Do the Secondary Markets Believe in Life after Debt?" ***Yale Cowles Foundation Discussion Paper***: 911, May 1989, pages 40

[34] Stymne, Joakim," Debt Growth and the Prospects for Debt Reduction: The Case of Sub-Saharan African Countries", ***International Monetary Fund Working Paper***, WP/89/71, September 1989, pages 45.

[35] Rauscher, Michael," Foreign Debt and Renewable Resources", ***Metro-economica***, 40(1), February 1989, pp. 57-66

are: developing country debt problems after seven years; reducing transfers from debtor countries; market based approaches to debt reduction; institutional approaches to debt relief; capital flight and re-flight; bargaining; the need for debt concessions and forgiveness; the view of the banking community; the size of the debt problem; different treatment in different countries; debt reduction; debt service reduction and new money; and making the best use of resources.[36]

Husain and Diwan edited a book with sixteen papers, presented at a World Bank symposium held in January 1989, to examine the debt crisis in perspective, debt management in the late 1980s, and debt reduction and re-contracting. The chapters included in the book are: the extent and causes of the debt crisis of the 1980s, the external debt difficulties of low-income Africa, debt in the 1930s and 1980s, fiscal adjustment and deficit financing during the debt crisis, public debt both in North and South, the commercial bank claims on developing countries, the use of the market-based "menu" approach and its limitations, the 1988 Brazilian financing package, the Baker Plan and Brady reformulation, the future financing needs of the highly indebted countries, liquidity, debt relief, and conditionality; how to cope with a debt overhang, efficient debt reduction, market-based debt reduction, secondary markets, and alternative forms of financial growth.[37]

---

[36] Dornbusch, Rudiger, Makin, John H. and Zlowe, David," Alternative Solutions to Developing Country Debt Problems", ***AEI Studies***, No. 494, Washington, D.C., American Enterprise Institute for Public Policy Research distributed by University Press of America, Lanham, Md., 1989, pages 127.

[37] Husain, Ishrat; Diwan, Ishac, edited," Dealing with the debt crisis", ***A World Bank Symposium***, Washington, D.C.: World Bank, 1989, pages xiv, 30

Frenkel et al (1989) edited a book with eighteen papers. These papers deal with the conceptual issues involved in analyzing debt problems. Papers focus on an overview of issues in debt strategy; the external debt problem of sub-Saharan Africa; market valuation of external debt; investment, openness, and country risk; debt and conditionality under endogenous terms of trade adjustment; buy-backs, debt-equity swaps, asset exchanges, and market prices of external debt; an international debt facility; debt relief and default penalties in an international context; multilateral negotiations for rescheduling developing country debt; sovereign debt renegotiation under asymmetric information; debt relief and adjustment incentives; market based debt reduction schemes; voluntary debt reduction; debt-equity swaps; the strategy of debt buy-backs; Mexican debt exchange; a solution to the interest rate risk management problems of indebted developing countries; and methodological considerations and policy issues.[38]

Mrak (1989) published another edited book with ten papers. These papers analyze international management of the debt crisis and its consequences, as well as the prospects for overcoming the debt crisis. Papers focus on the good news and the bad news of the Brady Plan; the debt problem; the Brady initiative; the interconnection between international trade, finance, and debt, and the implications for North-South economic relations; capital drain, debt relief, and creditworthiness of developing countries; restoring resource flow to developing countries; debt conversion as a solution to the debt problem; the sub-Saharan African debt problem; options for a cooperative approach to African debt; and adjustment

[38] Frenkel, Jacob A., Dooley, Michael P. and Wickham, Peter, (edited)," Analytical Issues in Debt", Washington, D.C.: ***International Monetary Fund***, 1989, pages v, 415.

policies in Latin America and the role of the public and private international financial system.[39]

Adler (1990)[40] observed that in the debt crisis years, many governments have adopted foreign debts from their domestic private sectors. This paper uses a simple open economy version of "**Blanchard's overlapping generations** (1985)" model to demonstrate that such a policy encourages the accumulation of national foreign debt and can contribute to higher inflation. Because individuals have finite lives they fail to fully internalize the governments' inter-temporal budget constraint. Current generations therefore regard the debt relief as an increase in wealth. They raise consumption, which causes current account deficits. Future generations have to lower consumption to service the additional debt. The debt service takes the form of a higher inflation tax. If the government tries to stabilize exchange rates while nationalizing debt, both the debt and inflation problems are exacerbated.

Claessens and Diwan (1990) have studied investment incentives in debt crisis for developing countries. They have opined that external debt depresses investment and lowers economic growth below its potential through its negative effect on liquidity and expected profitability. These effects can pull a country into a downward spiral in which both the debtor country and creditors lose. This article considers the possibilities for revising contracts between a debtor and its creditors once a debt crisis has erupted. The framework that they have

---

[39]Mrak, Mojmir, ed.," External Debt Problem: Current Issues and Perspectives", Ljubljana, Yugoslavia: Centre for International Cooperation and Development, 1989, pages 219.

[40] Adler, Oliver," Some Macroeconomic Effects of Nationalizing Private Sector Foreign Debt", ***Journal of International Money and Finance***, 9(4), December 1990, pp. 388-401.

developed shows how various combinations of new money and cuts in debt and debt service affect a debtor country's welfare, its debt repayments, and the earnings of its creditors. The analysis distinguishes between debtor countries that are willing and able to pre-commit credibly to an adjustment program and those that are not. This distinction provides the basis for a discussion of conditional lending by the international financial institutions to provide incentives and sanctions that make credible a debtor's promises to invest.[41]

Cohen[42] (1990) has suggested that an efficient rescheduling of the debt must take into account the market value of the debt. He has argued that the appropriate approach is not to write down the debt to its value on the secondary market, but to scale the flows of payments on the debt. The key to an efficient rescheduling is to offer debt relief reflecting the market discount, where the relief is contingent upon the country's adjustment effort (rather than setting repayment terms once and for all as in the Brady plan). He proposed, as an example, that stabilization or adjustment programs under the aegis of the International Monetary Fund or the World Bank could include provisions allowing debt servicing or repurchase for a set duration at the secondary market rate. This would both reflect and provide incentives to increase a country's ability to repay.

Rausser and Brazelon (1990) investigated the effects of industrial country commodity policies, macroeconomic policies and external debt on world commodity prices of LDCs. A theoretical framework is

---

[41]Claessens, Stijn and Diwan, Ishac," Investment Incentives: New Money, Debt Relief, and the Critical Role of Conditionality in the Debt Crisis", ***World Bank Economic Review,*** 4(1), January 1990, pages 21-41.

[42] Cohen, Daniel," Debt Relief: Implications of Secondary Market Discounts and Debt Overhangs", ***World Bank Economic Review***, 4(1), January 1990, pp. 43-53.

developed to provide the foundation for an empirical model that is estimated, assessed and then simulated to isolate the effect of debt relief on commodity prices.[43]

Calvo and Kaminsky (1990) studied the role of bank syndicates and debtor countries, which entered debt contracts during the 1970's. Their approach rests on the assumption that loan contracts charged a risk premium because banks entertained the possibility of debt reduction. Contrary to the previous literature on sovereign debt and debt overhang, they assumed full coordination between banks and debtors in designing optimal debt contracts. In this respect, they found that debt relief might actually be consistent with full pre-commitment situations. They studied an application of the model to data from Argentina, Brazil, and Mexico.[44]

Klein (1990) has illustrated a brief survey of developments in the valuation of country risk. The observations are: the point of departure is the recognition that the valuation of country risk can be approached using techniques developed in the literature on option pricing. The basic setup distinguishes three concepts of debt service: total contractual debt service, debt-servicing capacity, and actual debt service. Insolvency occurs when debt-servicing capacity falls short of the contractual debt service. Based on observations of stylized facts of rescheduling, it is assumed that under insolvency the

---

[43] Rausser, Gordon C. and Brazelon, Coleman," LDC Debt and Policy Linkages in the Determination of World Commodity Prices", University of California at Berkeley Department of Agricultural and Resource Economics (CUDARE) ***Working Paper***, 538, June 1990, pages 17

[44] Calvo, Guillermo A. and Kaminsky, Graciela L.," Debt Relief and Debt Rescheduling: The Optimal Contract Approach", University of California, San Diego, ***Department of Economics Working Paper***: 90-37, September 1990, pages 31.

debtor country receives debt relief proportional to the difference between contractual debt service and debt servicing capacity. It is then shown that option-pricing theory leads to a closed form representation of the spread a country has to pay on its external borrowing.[45]

Sweder (1991)[46] analyzed three questions in this paper: Could external restraint and internal balance in Mexico have been reconciled at levels of savings and investment that allowed satisfactory growth in output without the 1989-90 restructuring of debt? What are the likely implications of Mexico's "Brady deal" on economic growth? What are the macroeconomic effects of debt-equity swaps? This article develops and estimates a model to address these issues. The analysis concludes that the 1989-90 agreement in Mexico would contribute materially to macroeconomic stability and the restoration of economic growth.

Aizenman[47] (1991) has analyzed the welfare effects of a conditional debt relief in the presence of partial defaults. The paper explains that even for an economy in a state of partial default, external finance for investment in highly trade dependent sectors may be warranted. A marginal relief of the present debt service, conditional on an equivalent increase in investment in the trade dependent sectors, will benefit the debtor and will increase the future repayment. Investment targeted towards highly

---

[45] Klein, Martin," The Option Pricing Approach to the Valuation of Country Risk", Universitat Bonn Sonderforschungsbereich 303 - ***Discussion Paper***: B-157, June 1990, pages 5.

[46] van Wijnbergen, Sweder," Debt Relief and Economic Growth in Mexico", ***World Bank Economic Review***, 5(3), September 1991, pp. 437-55.

[47] Aizenman, Joshua," Trade Dependency, Bargaining and External Debt", ***Journal of International Economics***, 31(1-2), August 1991, pp. 101-120.

productive trade dependent sectors will benefit both creditors and debtors. A marginal relief of the present debt service or through direct investment can implement the investment.

Lagae (1991) has opined that creditors are prepared to forgive a part of foreign debt of individual less developed countries. But can the changed attitude of creditors toward the international debt problem be explained by efficiency considerations? In order to analyze the conditions for a partial debt relief to be favorable for debtors and creditors, the author started from a basic model with investment incentives. Partial debt forgiveness makes the debtor country better off through the combination of the direct debt reduction effect and the investment incentive effect. Creditors gain when the investment incentive effect exceeds the direct effect of the debt reduction. It can be shown that creditors gain from debt reduction if the price elasticity of the nominal value of debt is smaller than -1. This elasticity was calculated for 15 highly indebted countries and in 11 of these countries debt reduction was expected to be favorable for creditors.[48]

Corden (1991) has analyzed some central issues relating to LDC debt relief. The article explains the meaning of debt relief, how creditors can gain from debt relief and the role of the official sector in debt relief. Debt relief may lead to no change, to a decline, or even to an increase in the actual repayments that are made. When there is uncertainty about capacity to pay, debt relief benefits the debtor country. There is a paradoxical possibility that debt relief would yield an increase in repayments. This provides the basis for the argument that creditors

---

[48] Lagae, W., "Efficientievoorwaarden Voor Partiele Kwijtschelding Van Buitenlandse Schuld", ***Cahiers Economiques de Bruxelles***, 0(131), 3rd Trimester 1991, pp. 319-341

may gain from some degree of debt relief. Finally, the study analyzes some of the costs and benefits of the Brady plan and the lending activities of the Bretton Woods institutions.[49]

Griffith Jones (1991) attempted to focus on creditor countries' tax and banking regulations and the possible positive role which certain specific modifications to them can encourage debt relief. A key area for regulatory changes is that of tax treatment of provisions and debt service relief. Changes in banking, fiscal and other regulations are particularly relevant in the context of the current phase of "officially supported, market based debt reduction", which the Brady plan implies. The author made some specific suggestions for treatment of loan-loss and proposed an ex-ante definition of tax treatment on international lending.[50]

Franke (1991) has compared different ways in which a debt relief can be effected, given a low probability of full debt service, so as to ascertain how the existing obstacles to a debt relief can be diminished. Criteria for the evaluation of debt relief instruments are developed. The instruments well suited for a relief exhibit a 'menu' of elements. The debt relief should be costly to the debtor; involve burden sharing by the beneficiaries of the debt relief; restrain the debtor's behavior in market-based debt relief; and make the debt relief contingent upon exogenous, easily observable, and hedge-able variables.[51]

---

[49] Corden, W. Max," The Theory of Debt Relief: Sorting Out Some Issues, ***Journal of Development Studies***, 27(3), April 1991, pp. 135-145.

[50] Griffith Jones, Stephany," Creditor Countries' Banking and Fiscal Regulations: Can Changes Encourage Debt Relief?" ***Journal of Development Studies***, 27(3), April 1991, pp. 167-191.

[51] Franke, Gunter," Avenues for the Reduction of LDC-Debt--An Institutional Analysis", ***Journal of Institutional and Theoretical Economics***, 147(2), June 1991, pp. 274-295.

Berthelemy and Girardin (1991) suggested that while progress seems to have been made with the Brady plan concerning a solution to the debt crisis, it is useful to review the extent to which progress in economic analysis has shared in this move. This paper first puts the new debt relief strategies in their historical, empirical and analytical contexts. The concept of debt overhang of developing countries plays a major role here. The study of market solutions shows that a buy-back can generate a gain for the debtor at the expense of the creditors and can only be Pareto-improving in sharp debt-overhang situations. Concerted strategies are also examined in this paper, which thus leads to an analysis of option-menus established within the Brady plan.[52]

Morisset (1991)[53] applied a macroeconomic framework to Argentina to examine the implications of debt reduction operations for highly indebted countries. The general conclusion is that such operations can be quite successful in restoring investment and, consequently, growth in a country like Argentina. The paper emphasizes the importance of the incentive effects of debt reduction programs, which may dominate the liquidity effects. The empirical results are that, although the direct effect of debt relief on private investment is relatively weak, the indirect effect causes the decline in domestic interest rates and the increase in domestic credit becomes stronger. These results are encouraging because the liquidity effect resulting from the reduction in the foreign debt service will be limited in the short run in countries like Argentina which are

---

[52] Berthelemy, Jean Claude and Girardin Eric," New Strategies for Developing Countries Debt Relief", ***Revue d' Economique Politique***, 101(4), July-Aug 1991, pp. 529-604

[53] Morisset, Jacques," Can Debt Reduction Restore Economic Growth in Highly Indebted Countries?" ***Revue d'Economique Politique***, 101(4), July-Aug. 1991, pp. 639-66.

running arrears and are unlikely to obtain much new foreign lending.

Mikkelsen (1991) studied the impact of deserved debt relief on outstanding debt and estimated on the basis of that part of earnings which was increased due to a higher rate of return than the cost of funds. Using data for net transfers between commercial banks and the highly indebted countries of Latin America, estimates of deserved debt relief provide interesting information about the profitability of long-term loans. It turns out that the commercial banks as a whole have not had any substantial losses on their loans to Latin America during 1970-87. Furthermore, the variation of deserved debt relief across countries is very large. It is suggested that the countries in question should be granted, as a minimum, debt relief according to estimates of reserved debt relief.[54]

Acharya and Diwan (1991) have inferred that debt overhang may lead debtor countries to forgo worthwhile investments unless debt relief is offered. But creditors face a problem of screening countries willing to invest and increase debt repayment in response to partial relief from those unwilling. Debt buybacks can credibly screen a debtor country's willingness to invest and increase repayment. They have observed countries buying back a part of their debt, receive positive debt relief and others do not. They have concluded: (a) creditors systematically grant debt relief to countries that have a buyback program in place and (b) the secondary market price of country debt is higher when a debt equity swap program is in operation than the debt price with no such program.[55]

---

[54] Michelson, Jan Giehm," Deserved Debt Relief: A Note", ***World Development***, 19(8), August 1991, pp. 1117-20.

[55] Acharya, Sankarshan and Diwan, Ishac," Debt Buybacks Signal Sovereign Countries' Creditworthiness: Theory and Tests", Board of Governors of the Federal Reserve System

Kaminsky and Pereira (1992) hypothesized that most economists and specialists in international finance believe that the debt crisis has hurt investment and growth in debtor countries and have proposed debt relief as a way of alleviating the debt crisis. However, the empirical evidence on this link between the debt crisis and the collapse in growth has been elusive. In particular, Arrau (1990) and Borensztein (1990) have challenged the conventional wisdom by suggesting that the debt crisis did not generate a crippling burden. But in this paper, Kaminsky and Pereira have observed the effect of the foreign debt crisis on investment and growth in Argentina by using numerical simulations of an endogenous growth model. Two effects are examined in detail: first, the effect of collapse in public investment; and second, the effect of near rational decisions. Simulation results suggest that when these effects are taken into consideration, the debt burden can explain a substantial part of the collapse in growth.[56]

Koren (1992) has estimated the costs that accrue to an international organization financing a debt buy-back in favor of Eastern Europe. Since these costs are accompanied by proceeds on behalf of the original creditors and the debtor countries, the distribution of these gains between the beneficiaries can also be investigated. Both costs and proceeds are measured in terms of changes in the expected flow of repayments, not in terms of the nominal amount of debt forgiven. The results indicate that the economic

---

Finance and Economics, ***Discussion Series***: 180, November 1991, pages 26.

[56] Kaminsky, Graciela L. and Pereira, Alfredo M. (1992)," The Growth and Collapse of Debtor Countries: Is it the Debt Burden?", University of California, San Diego, ***Department of Economics Working Paper:*** 92-06, January 1992, pages 24.

costs would remain within a magnitude that can be easily born by the industrializing countries.[57]

Pastor (1992) explored the behavior of private investment in Latin America in the 1970s and 1980s. It is argued that the investment slowdown of the last decade was the result of slow growth, increased macroeconomic instability, and high levels of external debt. The "debt overhangs" implied that increases in output might be siphoned off to resource-short states or international creditors and thereby reduced the expected rate of return and hence debt accumulation. The "overhang" thesis is tested with a reduced-form cross-section time series regression for the private investment rate in eight Latin American countries in the period 1975-87; the results indicate that expected growth, public investment, and IMF programs have positive effects on private investment while macroeconomic instability, workers' share, and the debt overhang have a negative effect. The article ends with policy recommendations, including a call for debt relief.[58]

Lagos (1992) undertook a study with the purpose to look at the effects of debt conversion transactions in case of Chile. The decision to center on Chile lies in the fact that Chile was considered to have the most successful program of debt conversion among debtor countries. However, the Chilean debt conversion program presented some shortcomings. In fact, the study shows, the conversion scheme may have

---

[57] Koren, Stephan, "Debt Relief for Eastern Europe--Its Costs and the Distribution of Proceeds: Some Preliminary Results", ***Weltwirtschaftliches Archiv***, 128(4), 1992, pp. 639-661

[58] Pastor, Manuel, Jr.," Inversion privaday 'efecto arrastre' de la deuda externa en la America Latina", ***El Trimestre Economico***, 59(233), Jan.-March 1992, pp. 107-51.

negative effects regarding direct foreign investment and the balance of payments.[59]

Helleiner (1992) has suggested that sub-Saharan African development in the 1990s would require significant increases in transfers and debt relief from external official sources. The author opines that negotiation of conditions for assistance imposes heavy costs upon recipients. Once gross macroeconomic distortions are overcome, the risk of program failure from uncertainty and under-funding typically exceeds that in absence of further policy reforms, the effects of which are unproven. The relative influence of the International Monetary Fund (IMF) and World Bank in African programs has grown too large. The IMF, transferring resources out of the region, should retreat to a technical advisory role. The World Bank should develop contingency financing and cooperation with other sources of advice and finance.[60]

Husain (1992) explained that concerted debt reduction might be welfare improving even when the investment disincentive effect of a debt overhang is not large enough to place the debtor country on the wrong side of the debt Laffer curve. Whether the appropriate relief scheme involves debt reduction or new money, however, depends on whether investment disincentives or liquidity constraints dominate. It is shown that, except under very special circumstances, mixed policy packages involving both

---

[59] Lagos, Ricardo A.," Debt Relief through Debt Conversion: A Critical Analysis of the Chilean Debt Conversion Programme", ***Journal of Development Studies***, 28(3), April 1992, pp. 473-499.

[60] Helleiner, G. K.," The IMF, the World Bank and Africa's Adjustment and External Debt Problems: An Unofficial View", ***World Development***, 20(6), June 1992, pp. 779-92.

debt and liquidity relief may not yield the desired results.[61]

Green (1992) analyzed the external debt problem of sub-Saharan Africa between 1980 and 1990 and observed that the region's external debt more than tripled, to US $171 billion, while debt service payments and rescheduling rose by more than 150 percent to US $20 billion. In addition, the region continues to qualify as severely debt-distressed. During the last few years the region has benefited from several new debt initiatives, including a substantial increase in debt cancellation by bilateral creditors and the general application of Toronto terms for debt rescheduling. There are also proposals for further debt assistance, including more liberal rescheduling terms, broader debt forgiveness, and consolidating debt relief and aid generation activities.[62]

Ghatak and Levine (1992) used a small macro model of the Indian economy to examine the cost of the adjustment required to secure national solvency. This is compared with the corresponding cost if India were to repudiate its debts and experience financial autarky as a consequence. Their empirical results suggest that a small drop in the trend of growth rate, resulting from a loss of foreign investment and lending to the domestic sector, is sufficient to deter reneging, if the government is sufficiently farsighted and chooses a discount rate of 5 per cent (or less) a year. Debt relief generally improves the relative attractiveness of debt repayment.[63]

---

[61] Husain, Aasim M., " Sovereign Debt Relief Schemes and Welfare", International Monetary Fund, ***Working Paper***, WP/92/25, March 1992, pages 12

[62] Greene, Joshua E.," The Sub-Saharan African Debt Problem: An Update", International Monetary Fund ***Working Paper***: 92/52, July 1992, pages 13.

[63] Ghatak, Subrata and Levine, Paul," The Adjustment towards National Solvency in Developing Countries: An

Cohen (1992) calculated the returns on debts obtained by the developing countries from their (private and public) creditors (when taking account of the transfers already generated and of the liquidities value of the debt) and showed that they were satisfactory. Then he evaluated the conflict of interest between private and public creditors and assessed the role of the Brady Plan as a vehicle to achieving a 'grand settlement' of debt crisis and found that they were not satisfactory. The paper also explains that the group of re-schedulers did suffer from lower growth in the 1980s and their rate of capital accumulation did not accelerate in the years before the debt crisis. It is concluded that sovereign risk, rather than low returns, explains the failure of foreign finance to accelerate capital accumulation in the large debtor countries.[64]

The United Nations Conferences on Trade and Development has assessed the economic performance of the least developed countries (LDCs) and has provided the background necessary for reviewing progress in the implementation of the United Nations' Programme of Action for the Least Developed Countries for the 1990s. It has analyzed demographic trends and population policies in LDCs and examined issues relating to food security, including food insecurity in the Horn of Africa. The report addressed the issue of domestic resource mobilization for development and reviewed progress in the implementation of support measures for the LDCs, including the mobilization of external resources to LDCs, debt relief schemes, and technical cooperation. It considered the impact of the Uruguay Round on trading opportunities for these countries

---

Application to India", ***CEPR Discussion Paper***: 647, May 1992, pages 19.

[64] Cohen, Daniel "The Debt Crisis: A Post Mortem", ***CEPR Discussion Paper Abstract***, Center for Economic Policy Research, Aug. 1992

and assessed the role of non-governmental organizations in the LDCs.[65]

Mullineux (1993)[66] has advised that the banks should be relieved of at least some of their inherited bad debts at an early stage in the transition of formerly centrally planned economies. This should eliminate all seemingly perverse banks lending behavior and ensure that banks allocate capital more efficiently than the former central planners. The financial restructuring of banks will be mirrored in a restructuring of state-owned enterprises, and hence will pave the way for an early launch of the privatization program. The restructured banks should be privatized and encouraged to develop an active role in corporate governance, so that privatization can proceed successfully. Partial relief of bank debt, involving some debt for equity swaps between banks and SOE's, is a way of, containing the costs resolving the bad debt problem and the enterprise debt overhang and giving banks a stake in active corporate governance. It should also, along with the establishment of an effective bank regulatory and supervisory system, help to curb any moral hazard arising out of "bailing out" the banks.

The World Bank (1993) examined the public sector and identified priority areas where the government should focus its limited resources to address Guyana's key development issues within the framework of the government's Economic Recovery Program. It considered macroeconomic policies, public sector finances, the 1993-96 Public Sector

---

[65] ------------- **"The least developed countries, 1992 report"**, United Nations Conference on Trade Development; Secretariat, United Nations Publications, 1993, pages ix, 128

[66]Mullineux, Andrew W.," Privatization and Banking Sector Reform: Lessons from Poland", University of Birmingham Department of Economics, ***Discussion Paper***: 93-07, 1993, pages 26.

Investment Program, the economic outlook, external financing requirements, and the need for debt relief. The World Bank emphasized on the improvement of public sector management and administration; advised on strategies and expenditures in various sectors covering agriculture, sea and river defenses, transportation, water supply and sanitation, and the social sector.[67]

Arora (1993)[68] undertook research studies pertaining to review of literature on sovereign debt that deals with the issues of a country's ability-to-pay, willingness-to-pay and the policy responses to the debt crisis of the 1980. The existence of an ability-to-pay problem suggests a need for debt reduction, but plans for debt relief face potential incentive problems, and sovereign debt repurchases are not always a welfare maximizing method of debt restructuring. He concludes that with a willingness-to-pay problem, the potential penalties for debt repudiation are important in the endogenous determination of the repayment outcome. In addition, the asymmetric distribution of the costs of default can lead to a recurrent cycle of debt accumulation and default.

Tideman and Lockwood (1993) suggest that there is a need for an impartial international tribunal to consider requests for approval of repudiations of developing nations' debts. At present, debt relief is available as largess from the "Paris Club" of creditor nations or the "London Club" of commercial banks, but a nation that is treated unfairly has only the recourse of unilateral repudiation, which is subject to bias from self-interest. There is no impartial forum in

---

[67] -----------, "***Guyana: Public Sector Review***", A World Bank Country Study -Guyana, World Bank, Washington, D.C., 1993, pages xii, 312

[68] Arora, Vivek B.," Sovereign Debt: A Survey of Some Theoretical and Policy Issues", ***International Monetary Fund Working Paper***: WP/93/56, July 1993, pages 20.

which disagreements can be adjudicated. This paper explores the legal principles that might justify approval of repudiations of such debts, thereby advancing both economic efficiency and social justice.[69]

Hussain (1993) believes that concerted debt reduction may be welfare-improving even when the investment disincentive effect of a debt overhang is not large enough to place the debtor country on the wrong side of the debt Laffer curve. Whether the appropriate relief scheme involves debt reduction or new money, however, depends on whether investment disincentives or liquidity constraints dominate. It is shown that, except under very special circumstances, mixed policy packages involving both debt and liquidity relief may not yield the desired results.[70]

Abbott (1993)[71] evaluated approaches to debt relief and structural adjustment in sub-Saharan Africa and suggested a new integrated strategy for growth and development in the region. He examined reasons for long-term deterioration in the macro economy of sub-Saharan African countries and studied the performance of agriculture, foreign trade, and the public sector. He analyzed the nature, causes, and present dimensions of the current debt crisis as well as the structure and composition of external debts and their servicing costs. The author contends that the current debt crisis is neither temporary nor self-

---

[69] Tideman Nicolaus and Lockwood, Sharon, "The Legitimate Repudiation of a Nation's Debts" ***Eastern Economic Journal***, 19 (3), summer 1993, pp. 251-256.

[70] Husain, Aasim M.," Debt Relief Schemes and Welfare", ***Journal of International Money and Finance***, 12(6), December 1993, pages 632-43.

[71] Abbott, George C.," Debt relief and sustainable development in sub-Saharan Africa", Aldershot, U.K., Elgar; distributed in the U.S. by Ashgate Brookfield, Vt., 1993, pages xvi, 189.

correcting and that it appears to be getting worse. He argues that conventional debt relief measures are largely ineffectual and inappropriate for dealing with the ongoing debt crisis in sub-Saharan Africa.

Andrabi et al (1994) have explained why banking regulations are crucial to the unfolding of the current international debt crisis. The interplay of deposit insurance and capital adequacy requirements may create strong disincentives against offering relief to debtor countries with solvency problems, in spite of the fact that granting relief would improve the worth of the claims held by creditor banks. Furthermore, it is shown that the negotiating stance of individual banks is not related to its exposure to troubled loans in any simple way. Whether highly exposed banks are tougher than those with limited exposure is also generally dependent on the features of the regulatory environment.[72]

Mistry (1994) analyzes the emerging problem of the pyramiding of multilateral debt in developing countries affected by the recent debt crisis. He argues that multilateral lenders, such as the IMF and the World Bank, have become the problem for most severely indebted low-income and lower-middle-income countries rather than being the solution as lenders of last resort. The paper explains how the multilateral debt problem has arisen and identifies the countries most troubled by multilateral debt and discusses the effects of the pyramiding of multilateral debt service; the scope and the prospects for multilateral debt relief; and the urgent problem of clearing existing multilateral arrears.[73]

---

[72] Andrabi, Tahir, di Meana, Andrea Ripa "Bank Regulation and Debt Overhang", ***Journal of Money, Credit, and Banking***, 26(3), Part 1, August 1994, pp. 460 - 478.
[73] Mistry, Percy S.," Multilateral Debt: An Emerging Crisis", ***The Hague: Forum on Debt and Development***, 1994, pages 76.

Fernandez (1995) has studied the relationship between the probability of default of lesser-developed country commercial bank debt and the level of debt reduction granted by commercial banks. The analysis tests this relationship by regressing debt reduction totals for 29 middle-income debtors on 11 default probability indicators over the years 1985 through 1993 and finds a statistically significant relationship between the expected probability of default and the level of debt reduction. However, the findings fail to determine clearly the overall direction of this relationship. Thus, the evidence is insufficient to support the conclusion that the banks have behaved systematically as if they believed a debt-relief Laffer curve existed.[74]

Egli (1995) has analyzed the impact of secondary market for Third-World external debts and has observed that relief has been granted to the extent of 95 per cent. The obvious idea is to use such relief for remedying the position of Third-World debtors with small financial outlays. It shows the assumptions on which debt relief would lead to real consequences for debtors and creditors. Crucial in this context is the assumption that positive relations exist between a country's output and debt repayments. This is followed by an analysis of the effects of market-based debt relief instruments where repayments are assumed that are unrelated to output.[75]

Armendariz and Armendariz (1995) have studied the foreign debt of Mexico to show that, prior to debt relief; the country was indebted both domestically and externally, but had an additional incentive not to

---

[74] Fernandez, Jorge," La teoria del alivio de la deuda", ***Estudios-Economicos***, 10(2), July-Dec. 1995, pp. 163-193.

[75]Egli, Dominik, "Marktorientierte Schuldenerlassinstrumente (Market Based Debt Relief Instruments)", ***Kredit-und-Kapital***, 28(4), 1995, pp. 569-600.

default on its external obligations. However, repayment of the external debt was shown to involve a delicate tradeoff between 'growth' and 'inflation'; the government increased its ability to keep domestic interest rates relatively low thereby promoting investment and growth; and on the other hand the government worsened the budget-deficit problem thereby introducing additional inflationary pressures. The way to improve this tradeoff was by negotiating a debt relief operation on the foreign debt.[76]

Cockburn (1995) has opined that the current debt relief mechanisms constitute a partial and sporadic response to the present crisis in many developing countries including Cameroon. In particular, they rarely take into account external shocks, which are often the principal cause of the need for debt relief. He has developed a simple macro-economic model, which takes these shocks explicitly into account in determining the level of debt relief required. Debt relief thus becomes a stabilizing mechanism, which contributes to growth in developing countries and to their long-term capacity to reimburse their debt.[77]

Boot and Kanatas (1995) have analyzed debt renegotiation between a lender and a sovereign borrower. A sovereign, endowed with tradable and non-tradable goods technologies and debt outstanding, may have the incentive to shift production to non-tradable goods, if lenders are able to seize foreign assets generated by the sale of tradable. An integrated rescheduling 'package' involving debt forgiveness, new money, and

---

[76] Armendariz de Aghion, Beatriz and Armendariz de Hinestrosa, Patricia, "Debt Relief, Growth and Price Stability in Mexico", ***Journal of Development Economics***, 48(1), October 1995, pp. 135 -149

[77] Cockburn, John, "Allegement de la dette et chocs externes: Un modele d'indexation applique au Cameroun", ***Canadian Journal of Development Studies;*** 16 (1), 1995, pp. 79-103.

sovereign pre-commitment of production shows that it Pareto-dominates pure debt relief. With asymmetric information between lender and sovereign, pre-commitment possibly becomes an even more important feature of the renegotiated agreement.[78]

Cline (1995) undertook an analytical study on the debt crisis of 1980s and early 1990s and has derived lessons for international debt policy and development strategy. With decomposition analysis of 1983-84 projections, he has opined that debtor countries could export and grow their way out of the debt crisis by examining whether model parameters and assumptions were consistent with what occurred subsequently. He has critically reviewed the debt theory literature arising in response to the 1980s debt crisis, particularly with regard to the question of debt relief. The evolution of U.S. debt strategy from the initial rescue packages to the Brady Plan was traced and the performance was evaluated. He has reviewed the experience of adjustment to the debt crisis in the seven largest Latin American countries and analyzed the degree to which Russia, Eastern Europe, and sub-Saharan African countries were experiencing debt problems in the 1990s and found the best way to address each problem. Cline has worked out the nature and sustainability of the resurgence in international capital flows to developing countries, especially the formerly troubled debtors, and considered whether a new debt crisis is likely.[79]

Egli (1997) hypothesizes that the theory of optimal debt relief hinges critically on the output of a defaulting debtor country, which can be partially

---

[78] Boot, Arnoud W. A. and Kanatas, George, "Rescheduling of Sovereign Debt: Forgiveness, Pre-commitment, and New Money", ***Journal of Money*, *Credit, and Banking***, 27(2), May 1995, pp. 363-377.

[79] Cline, William R.," International debt reexamined", Institute for International Economics, Washington, D.C., 1995, pages xv, 535.

confiscated by the creditors. This assumption is at odds with the crucial feature of international credit relationships. The present paper focuses on an alternative enforcement method, namely the impediment of international trade. It is shown that a similar result can be derived. Additionally, it can be rational to grant further credit to countries with very little initial endowment, even though it is clear to the creditors that they will grant debt relief afterwards.

Bowe and Dean (1997) have considered some central puzzles surrounding the developing country debt crisis in mid-1982, including why market forces did not prevent the crisis; why market forces were apparently unable to resolve the debt crisis once it was underway; and why non-market intervention was employed and whether such intervention was rational on ex-ante theoretical grounds and justifiable on ex-post empirical grounds. They have reviewed the history of the crisis and the main official strategies used to cope with it; examined the rationale for liquidity and debt relief as well as evidence regarding their effectiveness and compared market-based debt relief with an international debt facility. They assessed the performance of the Brady Plan and analyzed the conditions under which the burden of debt and liquidity relief is equitably shared between official and private creditors.[80]

Boote and Thugge (1997) have described the debt burden of low-income countries and the traditional mechanisms that have been implemented by the international community to alleviate this burden. While these mechanisms are sufficient to reduce the external debts of many heavily indebted poor

---

[80] Bowe, Michael and Dean, James W, "Has the market solved the sovereign debt crisis?" ***Princeton Studies in International Finance***, No 83 Princeton: Princeton University, Department of Economics, International Finance Section, 1997, pages 70

countries (HIPCs) to sustainable levels provided these countries implement sound economic policies. But a number of countries are unable to adopt progressive and sound economic policies for political reasons and other factors. To deal with these cases, the World Bank and the IMF have jointly proposed and implemented the HIPC Initiative. The paper describes this initiative and suggests that it should enable HIPCs to exit from the debt rescheduling process.[81]

Hayri (1997) has developed a model for pricing sovereign debt under continuous time uncertainty, allowing creditors to carry out debt reductions. Focusing on the sovereign's willingness to pay rather than on their ability to pay, it models debt reductions as a non-cooperative game. The formulae derived from the model successfully predict the outcomes of the Brady debt relief deals. The model also predicts that the sovereign will get a positive share of the surplus generated by debt reductions and that the country will be on the 'wrong' side of its Debt Laffer curve well before the debt reduction.[82]

Ghani and Zang (1997) have studied financial debt management in Ethiopia. The problem of debt overhang facing a number of low-income countries has received considerable international attention in recent times. The international development community has begun to recognize that options would need to be seriously explored for providing debt relief to those countries where debt is not sustainable. When is debt not sustainable? How does one examine debt sustainability in the broader context of macroeconomic management? This paper

---

[81] Boote, Anthony R. and Thugge, Kamau," Debt Relief for Low-Income Countries and the HIPC Initiative", ***International Monetary Fund Working Paper***: WP/97/24, March 1997, P 23.

[82] Hayri, Aydin," Debt Relief", Center for Economic Policy Research, ***Discussion Paper:*** 1701, October 1997, pages 44.

builds on the Branson (1990) model of debt sustainability and applies it to a severely indebted low-income country, Ethiopia. It provides a simplified framework where debt sustainability (both domestic and external) is an integral element of macroeconomic stability. Interactions between different policy variables (such as debt, fiscal and interest rate policies), and outcome variables (such as GDP growth), as well as international economic conditions (international interest rates) jointly define if the country is on a sustainable debt path. Equations on debt sustainability can be easily estimated under this framework, and this could be easily estimated for other countries and in this sense, it provides a good starting point for examining debt sustainability.[83]

Stephens (1998) has studied the causes of reduction in trade finance in South- East Asian countries during post-1997, with a particular focus on the role of export credit agencies. It concludes that while such agencies did not cause or prolong the problem, they did not contribute significantly to a solution. The paper also suggests some implications from events in South-East Asia for both traditional debt-relief mechanisms and for the architecture of the international financial system.[84]

Christou et al (1998) have studied the optimal path of foreign public debt that can support politically unanimous (Pareto welfare improving) economic growth under uncertainty. The feasibility of the plan depends on whether the maintenance of political consensus in the debtor country requires additional

---

[83] Ghani, Ejaz and Zang, Hyoungsoo (1997), "Fiscal and Debt Management in a Severely Indebted Low-Income Country", ***Journal of Economic Research***, 2(1), May 1997, pp. 135-48.

[84] Stephens, Malcolm (1998), "Export Credit Agencies, Trade Finance, and South East Asia", ***International Monetary Fund Working Paper***: WP/98/175, December 1998, pages 52.

loans that are high relative to the country's outstanding debt. If a program is feasible, the creditors will have an incentive to preserve political support for the plan but in case of adverse developments, they offer debt relief. In certainty cases, where only total debt matters but in uncertainty cases, the timing of debt repayments is made critical for economic development.[85]

Cutler and Horwitz (1998) have described that over the past twenty-five years; about 330 (7 percent) of the country's 5,000 not-for-profit hospitals were converted into for-profit form. This paper explores the causes and effects of conversions through two case studies, Wesley Medical Center in Wichita, Kansas and the Columbia/Health One system in Denver, Colorado. They have opined that financial concerns and board culture perceived mission have encouraged the profit motives in hospital management. Financial concerns are multifaceted and include expectations about future profits, anticipated problems, servicing debt, and pessimism regarding the future of government reimbursement policies. The effects of these conversions are mixed. There are some efficiency associated with conversions such as cost-cutting, increased access to capital, and debt-burden relief. However, profits are often derived from increasing reimbursement from the public sector. Further, conversions are likely to cause fragmentation of the hospital market between rich and poor. The results show that not-for-profit hospitals are likely to copy the undesirable behavior of for-profit hospitals in their markets.[86]

---

[85] Christou, Costas; Dellas, Harris and Belessakos, Elias," Foreign Debt and Economic Development", ***Review of International Economics***; 6(1), February 1998, pages 1-14.

[86] Cutler, David M.; Horwitz, Jill R, "Converting Hospitals from Not-For Profit to For-Profit Status: Why and What Effects?" ***National Bureau of Economic Research Working Paper***: 6672, August 1998, pages 30.

Dent and Peter (1999) described Jubilee 2000--a campaign aimed at releasing low-income countries from the burden of un-payable sovereign debt. It discusses the problem of debt and poverty; the genesis, history, and growth of Jubilee 2000; the debt situation of fifty-one low-income countries that are the focus of the Jubilee 2000 debt-remission campaign; efforts made so far by the World Bank and the Paris Club to deal with the problem of debt; the boundaries and criteria of Jubilee debt remission; conditional ties for remission; benefits and costs of the remission; case studies of the debt problem in Nigeria, Malawi, and Nicaragua; no economic benefits from cancellation for creditor as well as for debtor countries; a parallel between Jubilee 2000 and the anti-slavery movement in the nineteenth century; tactical considerations and means of implementing the Jubilee; the future of the campaign beyond the year 2000; the origin and development of the campaign for debt relief/cancellation and the critique of the international financial institutions, 1983-93; the approach to debt in faiths other than Judaism and Christianity; the international spread of the Jubilee 2000 campaign; a criticism of World Bank philosophies and policies; other areas of activity and management where the international financial institutions fall short; whether a grand concordat is possible between debtor and creditor countries; and the reform of United Nations, and Bretton Woods structures.[87]

Gracia Aldaz[88] (1999) has reviewed the aid provided by Spain for development of HIPC countries. The discussion paper addresses the activity of the various

---

[87] Dent, Martin; Peters, Bill," The crisis of poverty and debt in the third world", Aldershot, U.K.; Brookfield, Vt. and Sydney: Ashgate, 1999, pages xii, 284

[88] Gracia Aldaz, Jesus, "La cooperation no reembolsable(Non-reimbursable Co-operation)", ***Informacion Comercial Espanola Revista de Economia***; 0(778), May-June 1999, pp. 103-118.

agents and their responsibilities, along with non-reimbursable co-operation instruments, such as, humanitarian aid, food aid, technical co-operation programmes, investment projects and the operations in connection with debt relief. Finally, it suggests certain perspectives for non-reimbursable co-operation and points out that the enactment of the Act on International Co-operation for Development affords an excellent opportunity to make the modalities and instruments through which aid is channeled more consistently to ensure due co-ordination of the various management centers, under a single criterion for action.

OECD Development Assistance Committee (1999) reviewed the development cooperation policies and efforts of Ireland for expanding aid program including priority country programs, area-based programs, partnership with NGOs, sector aid, debt relief; public-opinion, information, and development efforts. The review includes independent monitoring, its relevance, efficiency, effectiveness, assistance through multilateral agencies, aid volume, composition of assistance through geographical and sectoral distribution of bilateral ODA, technical cooperation, procurement policies and aid tying, NGO and private sector financial flows from Ireland to developing and transition countries, and Ireland's statistical reporting to the DAC.[89]

OECD Development Assistance Committee (1999) reviewed the development cooperation policies and efforts of Japan for the overall framework of Japan's development cooperation and recent changes in the policy directions. The review includes organization, aid management, issues in the health, education,

---

[89] ----------, OECD Development Assistance Committee, ***Development Co-operation Review Series***, (35) Paris and Washington, Organization for Economic Co-operation and Development, 1999, pages 97

environment, water and sanitation, basic human needs, poverty, and gender equality, aid interventions aimed at issues of governance and corruption. The review also includes Japan's aid evaluation, aid effectiveness and the coherence between Japan's development assistance objective and its trade and investment regime. In short, it summarizes the volume of Japan's official development assistance (ODA), Japan's contribution to multilateral institutions, the instruments of Japan's ODA and its geographical, country income group, and sectoral distribution, Japan's tying and procurement policies, and its debt relief to poorer countries. The review report annexes official documents outlining Japan's development assistance policy and intended changes to that policy, the OECD Development Assistance Committee's field reports and supplementary material on Japan's aid to China and to Ghana, and statistics on aid and other flows.[90]

Elbadawi (1999) has hypothesized that African countries should start thinking through undertaking an orderly transition from the current high dependence on foreign aid for financing economic and social development. Aid dependency should be reduced not because the international development community believes it will eventually happen, but because such dependence on foreign aid could substantially impair Africa's export competitiveness and therefore derail the continent export oriented development strategies. A combination of further debt relief, reforms of the current aid regime and enhanced policy environment should allow a managed transition to a mixed menu of official development assistance (ODA) and private capital flows. However, the attempt by Africa to increase its share of

---

[90] OECD Development Assistance Committee, ***Development Co-operation Review Series***, (34) Paris and Washington, D.C., Organization for Economic Co-operation and Development, 1999, pages 109

investments from international private capital markets should be firmly anchored to the basic tenets of an export based development strategy. To provide the basis for these policy conclusions, they estimate the relationship between ODA, real exchange rates (RER) and non-traditional exports for a panel of 62 developing countries, including 28 from Africa. Unsustainable ODA flows were shown to have caused substantial partial RER overvaluation in many African and non-African countries. Moreover, exceptionally high aid-dependent African countries have either experienced, or are likely to experience, overall RER overvaluation. Conditional on absence of RER overvaluation—a proxy for good policy environment of relevance to export performance, a robust Laffer curve-type relationship exists between aid and non-traditional exports through the misalignment of RER relative to its equilibrium. The Laffer curve relationship justifies a "precise" concept of aid dependency, based on the extent to which excessive ODA flows exceeded the threshold beyond which more ODA actually hinders rather than helps export expansion. According to this concept, several African countries were characterized as being "aid dependent".[91]

Marchesi and Thomas (1999) have developed a theoretical model in which both buybacks and adoption of an IMF program can be used as screening devices that enable a creditor to discriminate between debtor countries that are willing to use debt relief in order to invest and repay and countries that are not. Asymmetric information is assumed. This problem can be solved if the country has sufficient resources to engage in a debt buyback and so gain the debt relief. When the country is credit constrained, an alternative screening mechanism is to

---

[91] Elbadawi, Ibrahim A. (1999), "External Aid: Help or Hindrance to Export Orientation in Africa?" ***Journal of African Economies***; 8(4), December 1999, pp. 578-616.

undertake an IMF program in return for debt reduction and possibly an IMF loan.[92]

Easterly (1999)[93] has observed that a set of theoretical models predict that countries with unchanged long long-run savings preferences will respond to debt relief with a mixture of asset dissimulation and new borrowing. A model also predicts that a high-discount-rate government will choose poor policies and impose its inter temporal preferences on the entire economy. The ratio of the net present value of debt to exports rose strongly over 1979-97 despite the debt relief efforts. The HIPCs have shifted credit sources from private and bilateral sources to IDA and multilateral concessional financing. The researcher observes that although debt relief is done in the name of the poor, the poor are worse off if debt relief creates incentives to delay reform process needed for growth.

Nasution (2000)[94] has reported that three sets of factors caused the economic meltdown in Indonesia in 1997: negative external shocks (financial contagion, adverse terms of trade), weak fundamentals (financially fragile banks, over-reliance on foreign loans by corporations), and incompetent management (overly-rigid exchange rate, inadequate prudential supervision). When the crisis unfolded, the government was paralyzed by indecision over adoption of a currency board, reduction of large state-guaranteed investments, and implementation of

---

[92] Marchesi, Silvia and Thomas, Jonathan P.," IMF Conditionality as a Screening Device", ***Economic Journal***, 109(454), March 1999, pp. C111-25

[93] Easterly, William, "How Did Highly Indebted Poor Countries Become Highly Indebted - Reviewing Two Decades of Debt Relief", September 1999, World Bank Policy Research Working Paper No. 2225

[94]Nasution, Anwar, "The Meltdown of the Indonesian Economy: Causes, Responses and Lessons", ***ASEAN Economic Bulletin***; 17(2), August 2000, pp. 148-162

economic deregulation. The IMF's insistence on abrupt bank closures accelerated the bank run, and its insistence on abrupt fiscal tightening deepened the output collapse. He has suggested that recovery to sustained growth would require re-capitalization of banks, improved monitoring of the financial system, and prudent regulation of capital inflows, external debt relief, and greater flexibility in the exchange rate comprehensive microeconomic deregulation, and better macroeconomic management.

Cheru (2000) has linked the HIPC initiative to the HIV/AIDS epidemic in Zambia. He has opined that the HIV / AIDS epidemic has become the foremost contemporary threat to the development of many African countries and has caused a global public health emergency. Past achievements in economic growth, improved life expectancy and decreasing child mortality have been reversed by the rapid spread of the HIV virus. It is estimated that each day more than 5,000 people die from AIDS or HIV related illness, with the figure expected to climb to almost 13,000 by 2005 in Africa. In the context of this unfolding humanitarian crisis, creditor nations and institutions should cancel outstanding debt immediately so that resources of affected countries can be directed towards containment of the epidemic, within broader strategies of poverty alleviation. Addressing this crisis should not be construed as an act of charity, but an obligation and a necessity. Linking debt relief to HIV/AIDS is one small but important step in the long march to eradicate poverty in the poorest developing countries.[95]

Hayri (2000) has developed pricing formulae for sovereign debt by incorporating strategic debt relief

---

[95] Cheru, Fantu, "Debt Relief and Social Investment: Linking the HIPC Initiative to the HIV/AIDS Epidemic in Africa: The Case of Zambia", ***Review of African Political Economy***; 27(86), December 2000, pp. 519-53

games into a model of debt pricing under continuous time uncertainty. Two types of debt relief for sovereign borrowers are considered: debt reductions and exit deals. The formulae provide a good fit to the data and generate plausible predictions in a simulation analysis. The paper also examines how the availability of credible commitment mechanism affects the amount of debt reduction. Compared with the time-consistent equilibrium, creditors would want to commit to a larger, later debt reduction while the debtor would rather have an earlier, smaller debt reduction.[96]

Cohen (2000) developed the view that the perspective on the HIPC initiative was distorted by the fact that – contrary to the Brady deal itself – it lacked all perspective on the 'market value' of the debt which was written down. The appropriate 'market value' is one that takes account of the risk of non-payment arrears, rescheduling and 'constrained' refinancing of various sorts. Building upon econometric evidence that relies on middle-income debtors in the eighties, the paper argues that the initiative is about ten times less generous than face value accounting would suggest.[97]

Artus (2001) built a model for borrowing countries, which receive both public and private loans. If the economic situation of a country worsens, the cancellation of a part of the public loans would enable it to avoid defaulting on its private loans. But intervention of public lenders leads to an excess of private lending compared to the socially optimal level. If there were no discrimination between private and public lenders, the same proportion of private and

---

[96] Hayri, Aydin, "Debt Relief", ***Journal of International Economics***; 52(1), October 2000, pp. 137-152

[97] Cohen Daniel, "The HIPC Initiative: True and False Promises", CEPR Discussion Paper Abstracts, Centre for Economic Policy Research, Dec. 2000.

public loans would be cancelled. In this case the effect of moral hazard would disappear, but the risk of default by lending banks would appear. The author opines that debt relief programs may be implemented in the event of difficulty in the borrowing country to avoid the above-mentioned shortcomings.[98]

Gensollen (2001) has examined the debt reduction schemes, which lead debtor countries to increase their adjustment effort and their solvency. These conditions depend on the debtor's situation, and notably, on the cost of the requested adjustment. Nevertheless, the optimal agreement is imposed by the debt reduction mechanism. He has compared direct forgiveness and buybacks on the secondary debt market, and has observed that these two modes of debt relief are equivalent if buybacks are financed by loans of IFI that are seniors. If loans of IFI are juniors, these operations are inconsistent with the situation of the debtor and lead private creditors to refuse all financing to a country with an important cost of the adjustment.[99]

Bulir and Hamann (2001) have examined the empirical evidence on the volatility and uncertainty of aid flow, and discussed the main policy implications for aid flow. In their opinion, aid is found to be more volatile than revenue, particularly in highly aid dependent countries and mildly pro-cyclical. Uncertainty about aid disbursements is large and the information content of commitments made by donors is either very small or statistically insignificant. These findings imply that the current pattern of aid

---

[98] Arthur, Patrick, "Which Is the Best Relief Policy for Emerging Markets? ***Review-Economique***, 52(2), March 2001, pp 303-317

[99] Gensollen, Anne, "Debt Relief for Developing Countries: Adjustment Incentives, and Intervention of International Financial Institutions", ***Revue-Economique***; 52(2), March 2001, pages 319-35

disbursements is welfare- reducing. Policies to reduce the volatility and pro-cyclicality of aid were discussed.[100]

Asiedu, Elizabeth (2001) studied dataset of measures of institutional quality in (up to) 150 countries. The researcher used twelve indicators to study institutional quality. These are corruption in government, risk of contract repudiation, risk of expropriation, bureaucracy quality, government regulation, property rights, rule of law, independence of courts, political rights, civil liberties, and independence of unions and the media. Basing on data on these measures of institutional quality, she concludes that on the average Heavily Indebted Poor Countries (HIPCs) have worse institutions than other developing countries. The paper draws from the literature on institutional quality and economic growth and argues that in order to achieve long-term debt sustainability; HIPCs need to improve their institutions. One way to promote good governance in HIPCs is to predicate debt relief on institutional reform. This policy will allow HIPCs to achieve both short-term and long-term debt sustainability.[101]

Morrissey (2001) undertook a DFID research project on 'Poverty Leverage of Aid'. The paper considers how conditionality inherent in HIPC debt relief should be constituted to promote pro-poor policies. The paper considers: (a) the extent to which the policy proposed is pro-poor and (b) the potential for releasing resources for pro-poor expenditures. The paper provides an analytical framework to describe the policy environment for poverty reduction, and

---

[100] Bulir, Ales and A. Javier Hamann, "How Volatile and Predictable Are Aid Flows, and What Are The Policy Implications?", ***International Monetary Fund***, (Revised version), July 25, 2001, Pages 35

[101] Asiedu, Elizabeth, "Should the HIPC Debt Relief be predicated on Institutional Reform?" UNU / WIDER Conference in Debt Relief in Helsinki, July 2001, pages 13

identifies where donor effort and influence are most likely to be effective. An illustrative application is made in a comparative study of PRSPs in three countries. Uganda, in the PRSP process, is already benefiting from HIPC debt relief and has achieved significant reductions in poverty. Tanzania has recently completed the PRSP process and hopes to qualify for debt relief. Kenya has also started on the PRSP process but has been much less successful in devising a poverty reduction strategy. The paper argues that the elements of debt relief conditionality should be tailored to the features of the poverty-reduction policy environment in each country and provides guidelines for the design of conditionality.[102]

Dagdeviren and Weeks (2001) have studied how much poverty could be reduced through debt relief. They have concluded that neither a distribution-neutral debt cancellation, nor transferring all debt payments to investment for faster growth would achieve the International Poverty Targets. Therefore, debt relief must be combined with redistribution measures to achieve those targets.[103]

Abrego and Ross (2001) have analyzed debt relief efforts by creditors to alleviate the debt burden of low-income countries. The paper illustrates how the Heavily Indebted Poor Countries (HIPC) Initiative builds on traditional debt relief, and for the first time involves relief on multilateral debt. It seeks to reduce debt to sustainable levels and eliminate any debt overhang that might hinder growth and investment. It provides substantial debt relief to eligible countries

---

[102] Morrissey, Oliver, "Pro-Poor Conditionality for Aid and Debt Relief in East Africa", ***WIDER Development Conference on Debt Relief***, Helsinki, 17-18 August 2001

[103] Dagdeviren, H and J. Weeks (2001), "How much poverty could HIPC reduce?" Wider Development Conference: Debt Relief, 17 –18 August 2001, Marina Congress Centre, Helsinki

by reducing overall debt stocks by about one-half, or, together with traditional relief over time, by some 80 percent. It lowers debt service payments of HIPCs substantially, provides room for increased social spending, and provides a solid basis for debt sustainability. The latter requires efforts by both debtors and creditors. To fund poverty reduction efforts, HIPC relief is important, but much broader international support is needed as external transfers to HIPCs in the past far exceeded debt service paid. Experience has shown that external support can only be effective if it reinforces sound policies implemented by HIPCs themselves. Thus debt relief and ODA are most important not in isolation, but as help for self-help.[104]

Dijkstra and Hermes (2001) investigated whether and to what extent the uncertainty with respect to the annual debt service payments might have affected economic growth of the group of Highly Indebted Poor countries (HIPCs). They found supportive evidence for this hypothesis. They concluded that debt relief may contribute to regaining growth by reducing uncertainty with respect to the debt service payments, which in turn may increase the effectiveness of government policies and consequently provide the private sector with positive signals about future profitability of their investment.[105]

Edwards (2002) developed a model to investigate the connection between debt relief and current account sustainability. This model can be used as a key input

---

[104] Abrego, Lisandro and Doris C. Ross, "Debt Relief under the Initiative: Context and Outlook for Debt Sustainability and Resource Flows", ***International Monetary Fund***, August 2001, 42 pages

[105] Dijkstra, G. and Niels Hermes, "The Uncertainty of Debt Service Payments and Economic Growth of Highly Indebted Poor Countries: Is There a Case for Debt Relief?" ***WIDER conference on Debt Relief***, 17-18 August, 2001, Helsinki

in assessing whether a HIPC country's real exchange rate is 'overvalued' and will thus need to go through devaluation. The model explicitly considers concessional and commercial external debt, existence of a well-defined demand for international reserves, forgiven concessional debt within the context of the HIPC initiative, role of grants and donations, foreign remittances and transitional sustainable path of the current account balance. The model explains that external sustainability of a country depends upon two additional sets of variables: the availability of concessional loans going forward and the future path of grants and donations. The researcher has suggested that Nicaragua needs devaluation for external sector adjustment.[106]

Cohen and Soto (2002) have attempted to explain why single factor explanations of the poverty of nations were usually found to be unsatisfactory. Poor countries outside Africa, for instance, have an income per head, which stands at about one-third of the rich countries per head. Yet each of the three items of the Solow model, namely human capital, physical capital (appropriate weighted) and total factor productivity, are each equal to about 70 per cent of the corresponding levels of the rich countries. But 70 per cent to the power of three is 35 per cent. Multiplying small or relatively benign handicaps can yield dramatic effects on a country's income. The paper then moves on to explain each of the three items. It argues that the Lucas paradox on why capital is scarce can readily be solved. Once market prices rather than PPP prices are used to assess the return to capital mobility, and on the same ground it argues that PPP calculation bias downwards the TFP of poor countries. It then argues that human capital is lower

---

[106] Edwards, S., "Debt Relief and the Current Account; An Analysis of the HIPC Initiative", Paper presented in a Conference in honour of W. Max Corden held in Washington D.C. in April 2002.

in poor countries because of the fact that the returns to human capital are non-concave, so that the marginal propensity to turn one additional year of life expectancy into higher education is lower in poor countries than in the rich. The message of hope is that "transpiration" strategies a la Singapore may work elsewhere.[107]

Cordella et al (2002) have analyzed whether debt relief is the best instrument to increase the consumption of the poor in HIPCs. They have presented a model of conditional aid as an implicit contract between altruistic donors (concerned about the consumption of the poor), and recipient government representing the interests of the well offs. This contract is played out over an infinite horizon, and is supported by punishment threats for deviation. In a constrained optimal conditional aid relationship, they showed that debt relief could reduce the welfare of the poor. Their framework also provides a new explanation of why aid flows can be pro-cyclic, and why donors who are also debt-holders keep providing aid without granting debt relief.[108]

Bird and Milne (2003) have observed that although a great deal of attention has been paid to IMF conditionality and to the effects of IMF programs, relatively little attention has been paid to their completion rate. However, the record is that the clear majority of Fund programs are uncompleted. They have expressed that the completion rate is low and is a cause of concern. In principle, a lot of factors could

---

[107] Cohen, Daniel and Soto Marcelo, "Why are Poor Countries Poor? A Message of Hope which involves the Resolution of a Becker / Lucas Paradox", CEPR ***Discussion Paper***, Center for Economic Policy Research, September 2002

[108] Cordella Tito et al, "Conditional Aid, Sovereign Debt, and Debt Relief", ***Preliminary Report***, Department of Economics, University of California, Santa Cruz, CA 95064, December 20, 2002, pages 29

be at work. The researchers hypothesize that there are some other factors, which are responsible for program completion. If the researchers know all factors, they could be able to delineate the broad direction that policy should take.[109]

Stewart and Wang (2003) have reported that the World Bank and the IMF have introduced Poverty Reduction Strategy Papers (PRSPs) as a necessary tool for HIPC debt relief and access to other funds. The PRSPs are intended to increase national 'ownership' of programs, through extensive participation. This paper assesses whether they actually do empower poor countries, by exploring the process and content of the PRSPs. It finds that as far as civil society is concerned, the PRSPs currently permit little significant contribution to program design. Governments appear to take a bigger role, but are also heavily constrained, especially with respect to macro-policy. The facts that the content of PRSPs is very similar to previous adjustment packages suggest that little real change has occurred through this process. Moreover, some large IFI programs are unaffected by the process. Hence PRSPs do not significantly empower poor countries. They may give the appearance of greater ownership, but so long as there is no significant underlying change, such a change in perceptions about ownership, which could make IFI designed programs more effective and thereby empower them, is likely to be short lived.[110]

---

[109] Bird, Graham and A. Milne, "Debt Relief for Low Income Countries: Is It Effective and Efficient?" ***The World Economy***, January 2003, 26 (1), p.43

[110] Stewart Frances and Michael Wang, "Do PRSPs Empower Poor Countries And Dis-empower The World Bank, Or Is It The Other Way Round?", ***Working Paper*** Number 108, Queen Elizabeth House, University of Oxford, May 2003, pages 27

Arslanalp and Henry (2003) have concluded that when less developed countries (LDCs) announce debt relief agreements under the Brady Plan, their stock markets appreciate by an average of 60 per cent in real dollar terms – a $42 billion increase in shareholder value. In contrast, there is no significant stock market increase for a control group of LDCs that do not sign Brady agreements. The result persists after controlling for IMF programs, trade liberalization, capital account liberalization, and privatization programs. The stock market appreciation successfully forecast higher future net resource transfers, investment and growth. Creditors also benefit from the Brady Plan. Controlling for other factors, stock prices of US commercial banks with significant LDC loan exposure rise by 35 per cent - a $13 billion increase in shareholder value. The results suggest that debt relief can generate large efficiency gains when the borrower suffers from debt overhang.[111]

Arslanalp and Henry (2004) suggest that debt relief is unlikely to stimulate investment and growth in the world's highly indebted poor countries (HIPCs). This is because the HIPCs do not suffer from debt overhang. The principal obstacle to investment and growth in the world's poorest countries is a lack of basic economic institutions that provide the foundation for profitable economic activity. If the goal is to help poor countries build the institutions that best suit their development needs, then the energy and resources currently devoted to the HIPC initiative could be more effectively employed as direct foreign aid.[112]

---

[111] Arslanalp, S. and Henry, Peter B,"Is Debt Relief Efficient?" Department of Economics, Stanford University, Research Paper Series, November 2003, pages 35

[112] Arslanalp, S. and Henry, Peter B., "Helping the Poor to Help Themselves: Debt Relief or Aid?" ***Sovereign Debt at the Crossroads***, Oxford University Press, 2004

Marchesi and Missale (2004) examined both grants and net loans made to low income countries during the last two decades (1980s and 1990s) to understand the main reasons that motivated the behaviour of both donors and creditors. They found that the total amount of net transfers to HIPCs, as compared to non-HIPCs, have been increasing with their debt level. Greater net transfers have taken the form of net loans from multilateral organizations and grants in exchange for loans from bilateral institutions. This evidence thus suggests that HIPCs have kept receiving large amounts of resources just because of their high indebtedness, thereby supporting both the hypothesis of defensive lending and defensive granting.[113]

Berthelemy (2004)[114] has provided an overall empirical assessment of the motivations of official development assistance granted by rich countries to developing countries, as revealed by their aid allocation behaviour. The study explains that such behaviour results from a combination of self-interest purposes and of more altruistic development objectives. He used three-dimensional panel data set, combining the donor, recipient dimensions and time dimension. The data revealed a lot of heterogeneity in donor behaviour and varying degrees of altruism of different donors.

Benn Eifert and Alan Gelb (2005) have considered approaches towards improving the predictability of aid to low income countries with a special focus on budget support. In order to accelerate progress

---

[113] Marcesi, S and Missale, A., "What does motivate lending and aid to the HIPCs?" ***University of Siena and University of Milano***, Debt Relief Conference, 10 August 2004, Hamburg

[114] Berthelemy, JC,"Bilateral donors' interest vs. recipients' motives in aid allocation: do all donors behave the same?" ***University Paris***, Conf. on Political Economy of Aid, Hamburg, 9-11 Dec. 2004

towards the Millennium Development Goals, the donor community is increasing aid flows while pushing for more coordination and tighter performance based activity. However, these factors may increase the unpredictability of aid, from current levels, which are already high enough to impose significant costs. Predictability is a particular challenge in the area of budget support, which will continue to increase in importance as aid is sought to underpin longer-term recurrent spending commitments. They have suggested that donors must extend their funding horizons to improve predictability. The countries can buffer public spending against short-run fluctuations in aid disbursements through simple saving and spending rules built around a buffer reserve fund of 2-4 months of import cover. Guidelines can be set to limit the volatility of budget support while keeping it performance-based, and past experience can be used more systematically to develop "outcome" norms to better guide aid allocation. They have emphasized that in-depth assessment of progress in key areas, buttressed by output, financial management and service delivery indicators is required every three years or so.[115]

Conclusion

Debt problem, debt overhang or high indebtedness is caused by:

(a) Political and bureaucratic corruption,
(b) Mismanagement of borrowed funds,
(c) Wrong policies adopted by inefficient and corrupt government,
(d) Unnecessary investment in unproductive sectors,

---

[115] Benn Eifert and Alan Gelb, "Improving the Dynamics of Aid towards More Predictable Budget Support" World Bank Policy Research Paper 3732, October 2005, pp. 1- 39

(e) Devaluation of home currency,
(f) Inflation,
(g) Interference of state planning by multilateral organizations,
(h) Unnecessary ambitious projects,
(i) Long-term low-interest loans by foreign banks, and
(j) Failure of installments of outstanding debts.

Even asking for reduction of nominal claims would invite more loans and more burdens. High indebtedness of low-income countries results in further credit. Moreover, the World Bank officials offer more certificates to the borrowing states/ countries in press conferences to ask for more debts by these indebted countries/ states.

An abysmal percentage of the foreign fund is mis-utilized and misappropriated by politicians, bureaucrats and contractors.

As a result, urbanization gets boost and peasants commit suicides. The rich-poor gap widens and there is increase of Terrorists, Maoists and Naxalites.

The state borrows more funds because the amount is to be diverted into personal accounts of political leaders and government employees; the borrowed fund is to be used in election purposes. This results in higher percentage of budget for debt repayments to the creditor countries and reduction in expenditure in healthcare and education sectors of debtor countries. Foreign funding encourages investment in mega industries, national highways, rural roads, massive buildings, and researches on diseases and agriculture. But the state governments neglect in farmers and farming; farmers commit suicide; government reduces employees; corruption increases in all sectors; Maoists, Naxalites and Terrorists challenge the administration; there occurs massive unemployment; and migration of youths from rural areas to urban slums increases. In short, the administration runs on false promises, corruption and foreign debt.

Therefore, the world is facing more problems today than it was facing in the twentieth century. The unmanageable debt crises could be managed through increased development funding, debt service limitations, offering security of at least to the private portion of debt; debt strategy and proposals for relief; direct negotiation between creditors and debtors; debt conversion schemes; debt relief by banks, country, and institutions; voluntary debt relief including debt buy-backs; rescheduling and concerted lending; macro-economic stabilization; unilateral debt forgiveness; setting of international debt facility; market-led and market-distorting policies; sovereign debt renegotiations under asymmetric information; contingency financing by the World Bank; and by effective bank regulatory and supervisory system. Moreover, the following factors could be applied to help the low-income and low-middle-income countries to drag them out of poverty and debt overhang. These are:

(a) The 'Paris Club' for creditor nations and the 'London Club' for commercial banks can help the debtor countries.
(b) The IMF and the World Bank can undertake debt servicing and re-purchase for a set duration at the secondary market rate for liberalization and rationalization of LDCs
(c) Optimal debt contracts with full pre-commitment situations
(d) Broader debt forgiveness, more liberal rescheduling terms and consolidating debt relief
(e) Linking debt relief to HIV/AIDS
(f) Economic status of debtor countries

(g) Good governance and sound policies practiced by HIPCs
(h) Priority in clearing multilateral arrears
(i) Sound economic policies and Pareto welfare improving economic growth
(j) Campaign for debt relief
(k) Option pricing theory for external borrowing
(l) Performance based budget and Current account sustainability

Debt relief improves the relative attractiveness of debt repayment. Debt relief has a resource conserving effect. Debt relief can mitigate the sufferings of the low-income countries and solve debt overhang and poverty.

In short, the developed countries and multilateral organizations should prioritize 100 percent debt relief to all indebted low-income countries once for all for a world free of hunger and starvation. Debt relief can promote and strengthen WORLD PEACE in the twenty-first century.

+++++

Chapter III

INDEBTED COUNTRIES APPEAL FOR DEBT RELIEF

Every child in Africa is born with a financial burden, which a lifetime's work cannot repay. The debt is a new form of slavery as vicious as the slave trade. ---All Africa Council of Churches

Poverty is darkness. Poverty is deprivation, destitution, oppression and denial of entitlement. Poverty reflects poor health, malnutrition and causes endemic diseases. In the Twenty-first century, 1 billion poor people are living in slums, and 60 per cent of children die from diseases and malnutrition and never attend their first birthday in Islamic States. Nearly half of the children of Angola are severely malnourished and a high percentage of them in the heavily land-mined central highlands are stunted. In Cote d'Ivoire, yellow fever has posed a serious problem as this virus is generally transmitted to humans through mosquitoes, which cause mild flu-like symptoms to high fever, death and the fatality rate can exceed 50 per cent in unprotected populations. In poor countries, humanitarian crisis stemming from drought and locust, malaria, malnutrition, hunger of poor people and nomadic herders, genocide and extermination, civil strife, violence, corruption and drug trafficking have been activated in virulent forms. Food shortage is common in most of the developing countries. But the paradox is that at the same time, 1 billion people are overweight and 17 millions deaths are caused with largely preventable obesity and overweight and it is estimated that the number may increase to 1.5 billion by 2015. However, the World leaders have been partially successful in fighting poverty and terrorism, boosting security and protecting human rights.

The world organizations and debtor countries are aware of the economic problems of the African, Latin American, South Asian and Middle East countries. They too know how these low-income countries have utilized their credit. The debt problem of the low-income countries is alarming. The World Bank Group has reported that in 2002, the internal debt of low-income countries stood at about US $ 523 billion. Out of which, US $ 399 billion was public and publicly guaranteed debt. Low-income countries owed US $104 billion to the World Bank. Of this, US $ 82 billion was owed to the International Development Association, the part of the World Bank that provides zero interest loans and direct grants to the poorest nations. The International Bank for Reconstruction and Development was owed US $ 22 billion. Under the heavily indebted poor countries (HIPC) Initiative, 27 low-income countries have qualified for debt relief of more than US $ 54 billion out of US $110 billion of total outstanding.

The World Bank's contribution to HIPC will be about US $ 13 billion;

Debt service to export ratios also have been substantially reduced to an average of 10 per cent; and

In African countries receiving debt relief, poverty reduction spending (such as allocations to education and health) has increased from about 38.6 per cent of government revenue in 1999 to 47.8 percent in 2003.

In 2002, the external debt of middle-income countries was about US$ 1,817 billion, of this public and publicly guaranteed debt stood at US $983 billion. Middle-income countries owed about $ 107 billion to the World Bank. Of this, US $18 billion was owed to the International development Association and US $ 89 billion was owed to the International Bank for Reconstruction and Development.

In 2006, the debt burden of poor countries has increased because of liberal sanction of credit by the developing countries and multilateral banks. The debt skyrocketed in all the low-income countries during the first decade of the Twenty- First Century as follows:

(a) Total external debt of 54 low-income countries = US $523 billion
(b) Total loans made to oppressive regimes (low and middle-income countries) = $500 billion
(c) Africa's total external debt = US $300 billion
(d) Loans to South Africa's apartheid regime (being repaid by current government) = $22 billion
(e) Total debt service being paid every day by low-income countries = US $100 million
(f) For every $1 received in grant aid, low-income countries pay = $2.30 in debt service.

This chapter comprises three sub-sections illustrating (A) Country Classification, (B) Indebted Countries, and (C) Unsolved Problems Can Be Solved.

(A).Country Classification

For operational and analytical purposes, the World Bank's main criterion for classifying economies is gross national income (GNI) per capita. In previous editions, this term was referred to as gross national product, or GNP. Based on its GNI per capita, every economy is classified as low income, middle income (subdivided into lower middle and upper middle), or high income. Other analytical groups based on geographic regions are also used.

The Bank's analytical income categories (low, middle, high income) are based on the Bank's operational lending categories (civil works preferences, IDA eligibility, etc.).[116]

The World Bank has classified different countries as per geographical regions, income groups, and atlas methodology or as ICP and PPP category, and lending category. These are as follows:

Geographic region: Classifications and data reported for geographic regions are for low-income and middle-income economies only. Low-income and middle-income economies are sometimes referred to as developing economies. The use of the term is convenient; it is not intended to imply that all economies in the group are experiencing similar development or that other economies have reached a preferred or final stage of development. Classification by income does not necessarily reflect development status.

---

[116] Notes: Classifications are set each year on 1 July. These official analytical classifications are fixed during the World Bank's fiscal year (ending on 30 June), thus countries remain in the categories in which they are classified irrespective of any revisions to their per capita income data. Taiwan, China is also included in high income. Source: http://web.worldbank.org

Income group: Economies are divided according to 2005 GNI per capita, calculated using the World Bank Atlas method. The groups are:

Low income = $875 or less;
Lower middle income = $876 - $3,465;
Upper middle income = $3,466 - $10,725; and
High income = $10,726 or more.

There are 35 high-income countries with more than US $ 10,726 per capita income, 28 upper-middle income countries in the range of $3,466 to $ 10,725 per capita income, 59 lower-middle income countries in the range of $876 to $ 3,465 per capita income and 52 low-income countries with less than $ 875 per capita income. Moreover, there are other 20 countries for which income statistics are not available or unreliable. (194 countries)

Atlas methodology classification: There are 39 high-income countries with more than US $ 10,726 per capita income, 35 upper-middle income countries in the range of $3,466 to $ 10,725 per capita income, 55 lower-middle income countries in the range of $876 to $ 3,465 per capita income and 50 low-income countries with less than $ 875 per capita income. Moreover, there are other 29 countries for which income statistics are either unavailable or unreliable. (208 countries)

Categories of countries: If we analyze the world scenario on categories of countries, the World Bank has reported that as per atlas methodology classification, GNI per capita was US $ 580 in low-income countries, US $ 2,640 in middle-income countries, US $ 1918 in lower-middle income countries, US $ 5625 in upper middle-income countries, US $ 1746 in low and middle-income countries, US $ 1627 in East Asia and Pacific countries, US $ 4113 in Europe and Central Asia, US $ 4008 in Latin America and Caribbean countries, US

$ 2241 in middle east and north Africa, US $ 684 in South Asia, US $ 745 in sub-Saharan Africa in 2005. But the GNI per capita was US $ 35, 131 in high-income countries and US $ 31,914 in European Monetary Union in 2005.

International Comparison Program (ICP) and Purchasing Power Parity (PPP):

International comparable data are crucial to forming sustainable policies and monitoring progress. Purchasing Power Parities account for differences between countries and to measure real quantities.

There are 55 high-income countries with more than US $ 10,726 per capita income, 56 upper-middle income countries in the range of $3,466 to $ 10,725 per capita income, 48 lower-middle income countries in the range of $876 to $ 3,465 per capita income and 8 low-income countries with less than $ 875 per capita income. Moreover, there are other 41 countries for which income statistics are either unavailable or unreliable. (208 countries)

GDP per capita and Purchasing Power Parity (PPP) classification:

If we analyze the world scenario on categories of countries, the World Bank has reported that as per Purchasing Power Parity (PPP) classification, GNI per capita in low-income countries was 2,486 international dollars in 2005. Similarly, GNI per capita was 7195 international dollars in middle-income countries, 6313 international dollars in lower middle-income countries, 10,924 international dollars in upper middle income countries, 5,151 international dollars in low and middle-income countries, 5,914 international dollars in East Asia and Pacific countries, 9,142 international dollars for Europe and Central Asia, 8,111 international dollars in Latin America and Caribbean countries, 6,076 international dollars in middle east and north Africa, 3142 international dollars in South Asia, 1,981 international dollars in sub-Saharan Africa in 2005. The GNI per capita was 32, 524 international dollars in high-income countries and 28,958 international dollars in European Monetary Union in 2005.

There are 85 high-income countries with more than US $ 10,726 per capita income, 71 upper-middle income countries in the range of $3,466 to $ 10,725 per capita income, 65 lower-middle income countries in the range of $876 to $ 3,465 per capita income and 12 low-income countries with less than $ 875 per capita income. (233 countries)

So it is evident that there is huge income disparity among the nations. The GDP per capita (PPP) of Bermuda is $69,900 and for Luxembourg it is $65,900 in 2005, while the GDP per capita (PPP) of Solomon Islands, Comoros, Somalia, Malawi and Gaza Strip is only $600 in 2005. The ratio of GDP per capita - Purchasing Power Parity (PPP) between the lowest and highest income generating country is 1: 116.5. The reasons of such variations in income are many but we have to find out the solutions of this challenge. We are citing other examples: the GNI per capita of Norway is $59,590 as against $270 for Nepal and $470 for Bangladesh. Similarly, the above facts explain that the low-income countries particularly the South Asia and sub-Saharan Africa are the worst sufferers as more than three-fourths of world poverty population reside in these parts of the world. But the World Bank, International Monetary Fund and developed countries focus their attention to sub-Saharan Africa and neglect the South Asia. A hungry man of any country should be treated equally. A hungry man is alive because he wants to die; he is alive because he anticipates that his children would earn food for the family and construct a dwelling house in future.

Lending category: IDA countries are those that had a per capita income in 2005 of less than $1,025 and lack the financial ability to borrow from IBRD. IDA loans are deeply concessional—interest-free loans and grants for programs aimed at boosting economic growth and improving living conditions. IBRD loans are non-concessional. Blend countries are eligible for IDA loans because of their low per capita incomes but are also eligible for IBRD loans because they are financially creditworthy.

There are more than 60 IDA countries with per capita income of less than $1,025 in 2005 and lack the financial ability to borrow from IBRD. All other countries can borrow from IBRD, as they are financially creditworthy.

The present system of poverty reduction programs cannot eradicate poverty; cannot solve poverty problems; cannot reduce rich-poor gap and cannot reduce the number of poor people. But it is possible through the 'good wishes' of those, who have sympathy for the poor brethrens. The first step to assist the poor countries is debt relief. It is to be followed by transparency in administration, anti-corruption drive, sound macro-economic policies and a good budget preferably a pro-poor, pro-rural and pro-agricultural budget.

(B) Country Reports

In this section, various country reports such as Burkina Faso, Ethiopia, Mozambique, Uganda, Bangladesh and India have been analyzed to indicate the poverty - related issues and human welfare measures available in these low-income-countries. Out of 54 low-income-countries only six countries have been identified to represent the economic status of these countries. India, which produces atomic energy for peaceful purposes, is the highest indebted country in the world and the highest numbers of hungry people reside in this country. If the largest democracy in the world cannot check child sale, human trafficking and starvation deaths, the international forums and organizations should find suitable measures to advise the country for preserving democracy and peace through suitable debt management and debt relief.[117]

Burkina Faso

Burkina Faso (formerly Upper Volta) achieved independence from France in 1960. Repeated military coups during the 1970s and 1980s were followed by multiparty elections in the early 1990s.

Burkina Faso's high population density and limited natural resources result in poor economic prospects for the majority of its citizens. Recent unrest in Cote d'Ivoire and northern Ghana has hindered the ability of several hundred thousand seasonal Burkinabe farm workers to find employment in neighboring countries.

Burkina Faso is situated in Western Africa, north of Ghana. Its total area is 274,200 sq km, land area is 273,800 sq km and water area is 400 sq km. Its natural resources are: manganese, limestone, marble; small deposits of gold, phosphates, pumice, salt. Its arable land is only 17.66 per cent, permanent crops 0.22 per cent and other 82.12 per cent. Burkina Faso has irrigation facility for an area of 250 sq km. The country faces recurring droughts. Deforestation, over grazing, soil erosion, desertification, and water shortage are the major issues in Burkina Faso. Hence, the country has signed international agreements for conserving biodiversity, climatic change, desertification, endangered species, and utilization of

[117] Maps of Burkina Faso, Ethiopia, Mozambique, Uganda, Bangladesh and India are collected from www.worldatlas.com and country reports are collected from World Bank, IMF and UNDP Publications

hazardous wastes, protection of ozone layer, law of the sea, and for marine life conservation.

Population of Burkina Faso is 13,902,972 and growth of population is 2.31 per cent. Life expectancy is 48.85 years and fertility rate is 6.47 children born / woman. HIV / AIDS prevalence is 4.2 per cent and 300,000 of people are affected by this diseases. Already 29,000 persons have died though HIV/AIDS. Major infectious diseases are hepatitis A, hepatitis E, typhoid, malaria and meningitis. Literacy is 26.6 per cent.

Economy

One of the poorest countries in the world, landlocked Burkina Faso has few natural resources and a weak industrial base. About 90 percent of the population is engaged in subsistence agriculture, which is vulnerable to harsh climatic conditions. Cotton is the key crop and the government has joined with other cotton producing countries in the region to lobby for improved access to Western markets.

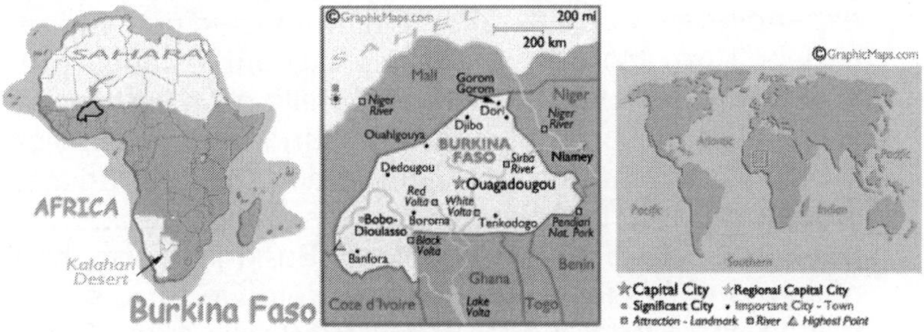

Burkina Faso

GDP growth has largely been driven by increases in world cotton prices. Industry remains dominated by unprofitable government-controlled corporations. Following the CFA franc currency devaluation in January 1994, the government updated its development program in conjunction with international agencies; exports and economic growth have increased. The government devolved macroeconomic policy and inflation targeting to the West African Regional Central Bank (BCEAO), but maintains control over fiscal and microeconomic policies, including implementing reforms to encourage private investment. The bitter internal crisis in neighboring Cote d'Ivoire continues to hurt trade and industrial prospects and deepens the need for international assistance.

In 2005, GDP (PPP) of Burkina Faso was $ 16.66 billion; GDP real growth rate was 3.5 per cent, GDP per capita (purchasing power parity) was $ 1200 and GNI per capita was $ 400. Agriculture contributed 32.2 percent, industry 19.6 per cent and services 48.2 per cent of Gross Domestic Product of Burkina Faso. The country has labour force of 5 million and 90 per cent of them are engaged in agriculture. Population below poverty line is 45 per cent.

Inflation rate was 6.4 per cent in 2005. In that year, investment was 20.7 per cent of GDP in gross fixed assets, revenue budget was $1.033 billion and expenditure was $1.382 billion including capital expenditure. Moreover, current account balance was $ 460 million; export was $ 395 million f.o.b.; import was $ 992 million f.o.b. (2005). Burkina Faso exports cotton, livestock and gold and imports capital goods, foodstuffs and petroleum. Burkina Faso spends 1.3 per cent of GDP in defense. Burkina Faso had reserves of foreign exchange and gold worth of $ 764 million and external debt was $ 1850 million in 2005.

Burkina Faso remains one of the poorest countries in the world, ranking 180th out of 208 countries in the World Development Indicators database, World Bank, 1 July 2006. In this context, Burkina Faso has made determined efforts to address key social areas, such as primary education and basic health care. Over the past ten years, for instance, the share of the education budget allocated to basic education increased from 45 percent to about 58 percent. This budgetary reprioritization has been complemented by the construction of additional school facilities, with an average of 800 additional classrooms added each of the past several years. Progress in improving health indicators in Burkina Faso has been equally difficult, though substantial steps forward have been made in building more health centers, training more health personnel and increasing the availability of essential generic drugs.

Burkina Faso has also devoted attention to implementing crucial economic reforms, with tangible results. Despite deterioration in the terms of trade, real GDP between 1996 and 1999 grew on average by 5.6 percent annually, owing mainly to the 1994 CFA franc devaluation, a large public investment program, and financial and structural policies aimed at maintaining macroeconomic stability. Inflation has dropped in recent years to 2 percent, and public finances have improved markedly, with government revenue increasing to 15 percent of GDP in 1999. Translating improving economic performance into broad poverty reduction is the primary aim of IMF and IDA program support.

The economy of Burkina Faso proved resilient in 2008 despite a difficult national and international economic and financial climate. Prudent economic policy and pragmatic and targeted structural measures supported this outcome. GDP (Gross Domestic Product) growth for 2008 is estimated at 4.2 per cent - short of earlier forecasts for 4.7 per cent - but up from 3.6 per cent in 2007. The economy should continue to be resilient in 2009, with projected growth of 6 per cent and 4.2 per cent in 2010. Growth will be driven by two factors — a decline in raw material prices, which should lead to a drop in production costs and thus spur investment, and a significant shift of revenue to rural areas due to specific support measures for agricultural production and small producers.

Inflation rose sharply due to the steep rise in consumer prices, especially food costs, during the first half of 2008. This occurred despite the suspension of customs duties and taxes on staple products. The inflation rate, near zero in 2007, rose to 9.3 per cent in 2008. Farm production support, consisting of inputs for small producers, should help ease shortages in the domestic market in 2009 by significantly increasing the supply of food-crops. At the same time, prices will be supported as efforts get underway to rebuild stocks in line with national food safety policy objectives. Inflation is expected to drop from 5.4 per cent in 2009 to 3.5 per cent in 2010.

Despite the growing strength of the mining sector, the Burkina Faso economy is still structurally and excessively dependent on cotton, which remains the country's main export earner. Steps must be taken to diversify production by supporting domestic processing so as to create added value and generate employment.

Debt Relief

The International Monetary Fund (IMF) and the World Bank Group's International Development Association (IDA) agreed that Burkina Faso has satisfied the requirements to reach its completion point under the original Heavily Indebted Poor Countries (HIPC) Initiative, and is thereby eligible to begin receiving around US$400 million in debt service relief, or US $229 million in net present value (NPV) terms. Burkina Faso was one of the initial countries to qualify for assistance under the original HIPC framework when it reached its decision point in September 1997.The IMF and IDA also agreed that based on its determined efforts in social and structural reform, the policy commitment presented in the Poverty

Reduction Strategy Paper, and the implementation of IMF and IDA programs, Burkina Faso has qualified for additional assistance under the enhanced framework (adopted in September 1999) amounting to US$300 million in debt service relief over time (US$169 million NPV). Together with the debt service reduction obtained under the original framework, total savings on IDA debt service is estimated at about US$282 million, with the IMF providing an additional US$49 million. The combined debt service savings from all Burkina Faso's creditors under the HIPC Initiative of US$700 million effectively cuts in half Burkina Faso's debt service obligations over the coming years. [118]

All creditors are expected to proceed speedily with providing debt relief under the original framework. Regarding the enhanced assistance, the IMF and IDA will start providing interim debt relief under the enhanced framework. Burkina Faso will reach its completion point under the enhanced Initiative and receive the remainder of its debt relief from all creditors once it has it fulfilled a number of steps designed to improve key policies in the education and health sectors. Country authorities have outlined many of these measures in a Poverty Reduction Strategy Paper (PRSP), drafted in consultation with a broad cross section of local civil society and with the support of international partners. Burkina Faso's completion point under the original HIPC Initiative and eligibility under the enhanced HIPC Initiative is recognition by the international community of the progress made in implementing economic reforms and in the social sectors. The resources freed by the HIPC Initiative will help support the continuation and strengthening of this progress.

---

[118] West African country completes original HIPC Initiative and qualifies for additional relief under enhanced framework, African Economic Outlook / CIA–the World Fact Book

ETHIOPIA

Unique among African countries, the ancient Ethiopian monarchy maintained its freedom from colonial rule with the exception of the 1936-41 Italian occupations during World War II. In 1974, a military junta, the Derg, deposed Emperor Haile SELASSIE (who had ruled since 1930) and established a socialist state. Torn by bloody coups, uprisings, wide-scale drought, and massive refugee problems, the regime was finally toppled in 1991 by a coalition of rebel forces, the Ethiopian People's Revolutionary Democratic Front (EPRDF). A constitution was adopted in 1994, and Ethiopia's first multiparty elections were held in 1995. A border war with Eritrea late in the 1990's ended with a peace treaty in December 2000. Final demarcation of the boundary is currently on hold due to Ethiopian objections to an international commission's finding requiring it to surrender territory considered sensitive to Ethiopia.[119]

Ethiopia is situated in Eastern Africa. Its total area is 1127,127 sq km, land area is 1119,683 sq km and water area is 7,444 sq km. Its natural resources are: small reserves of gold, platinum, copper, potash, natural gas and hydropower. Its arable land is only 10.01 per cent, permanent crops 0.65 per cent and other 89.34 per cent. Ethiopia faces earthquakes, volcanic eruptions in geographically active Great Rift Valley and faces frequent droughts. Deforestation, over grazing, soil erosion, desertification, and water shortage are the major issues in Ethiopia. Hence, Ethiopia has signed international agreements for conserving biodiversity, climatic change, desertification, endangered species, and utilization of hazardous wastes and protection of ozone layer.

---

[119] CIA–the World Fact Book –Ethiopia, www. Harvardhumanaitarian.org / www.oxfamamerica.org/

Population of Ethiopia is 74.77 million and growth of population is 2.31. Life expectancy is 49.3 years and fertility rate is 5.22 children born/woman. HIV / AIDS prevalence is 4.4 per cent and 1.5 million of people are affected by these diseases. Already 120,000 persons have died though HIV/AIDS. Major infectious diseases are diarrhea, hepatitis A, hepatitis E, typhoid, malaria, meningitis and rabies. Literacy is 42.7 per cent.

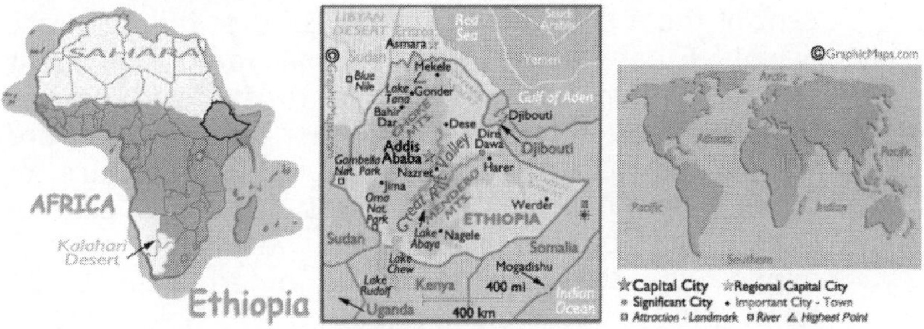

Ethiopia

Economy: Ethiopia's poverty-stricken economy is based on agriculture, accounting for half of GDP, 60 per cent of exports, and 80 per cent of total employment. The agricultural sector suffers from frequent drought and poor cultivation practices. Coffee is critical to the Ethiopian economy with exports of some $156 million in 2002, but historically low prices have seen many farmers switching to supplement income. The war with Eritrea in 1998-2000 and recurrent drought have buffeted the economy, in particular coffee production. In November 2001, Ethiopia qualified for debt relief from the Highly Indebted Poor Countries (HIPC) initiative, and in December 2005 the International Monetary Fund voted to forgive Ethiopia's debt to the body. Under Ethiopia's land tenure system, the government owns all land and provides long-term leases to the tenants; the system continues to hamper growth in the industrial sector, as entrepreneurs are unable to use land as collateral for loans. Normal weather patterns late in 2003 helped agricultural and GDP growth recover in 2004-05.

In 2005, GDP (PPP) of Ethiopia was $64.73 billion; GDP real growth rate was 8.9 per cent, GDP per capita (purchasing power parity) was $900 and GNI per capita was $ 160. Agriculture contributed 47.5 percent, industry 9.9 per cent and services 42.6 per cent of Gross Domestic Product of Ethiopia. The country has labour force of 27.27 million and 80 per cent of them are engaged in agriculture. Inflation rate was 11.6 per cent in 2005. In that year, investment was 21.9 per cent of GDP in gross fixed assets, revenue budget was $2.338 billion and expenditure was $2.88 billion including capital expenditure of $788. Moreover, public debt was 106.2 per cent of GDP. Current account balance was $844 million; export was $612 million f.o.b.; import was $2.722 f.o.b. (2005). Ethiopia exports coffee, gold, leather products, live animals, oilseeds and imports food and live animals, petroleum and petroleum products, chemicals, machinery, motor vehicles, cereals and textiles. Ethiopia spends 3.4 per cent of GDP in defense. Ethiopia had reserve of foreign exchange and gold worth of $1226 million and external debt was $5101 million in 2005. It received economic aid of $308 million in 2000/01.

The PPP (purchasing power parity) of Ethiopia was $ 54.99 billion in 2006, $61.09 billion in 2007 and $66.29 billion in 2008. The GDP (official exchange rate) was $25.08 billion in 2008. The GDP per capita increased from $700 in 2006 to $800 in 2007 and 2008. Agriculture contributed 45.9 percent, industry 12.9 percent, and services 41.2 percent as estimated in 2008. Employment constituted 80.2 percent in agriculture, 6.6 percent in industry, and 13.2 percent in services sector in 2005.

Ethiopia earned revenue of $4.586 billion and incurs an expenditure of $5.729 billion in 2008. Public debt was 34.4 percent of GDP in 2008 and inflation rate of consumer prices was 41 percent in the same year. Ethiopia had a stock of domestic money of $3.651 billion and stock of domestic credit of $6.694 billion as on December 31, 2006. However, stock of quasi money was $3.258 billion as on 31 December 2007. Ethiopia had reserves of foreign exchange and gold of $1.008 billion and external debt of $3.158 billion as on 31 December 2008.

Ethiopia produces cereals, pulses, coffee, oilseed, cotton, sugarcane, potato, cut flowers; hides, cattle, sheep, goats; and fish in agriculture sector.

The country possesses food processing, beverages, textiles, leather, leather, chemicals, metals processing and cement industries. The industrial production growth rate was 6 percent in 2008.

The electricity production was 3.268 billion kWh and consumption was 2.941 billion kWh in 2006. The oil (proved reserves) was 428,000 bbl and natural gas (proved reserves) was 24.92 billion cu m as on January 1, 2008.

The country exports coffee, gold, leather products, live animals and oilseeds. The export partners are Germany 8.2 percent, Saudi Arabia 7 percent, US 6.9 percent, Djibouti 6.6 percent, China 6.5 percent, Italy 6.5 percent, Japan 5.9 percent and Netherlands 4.8 percent. The import partners are: Saudi Arabia 17 percent, China 15.9 percent, India 7.8 percent and Italy 5.1 percent (2007).

Ethiopians struggle with an array of challenges such as droughts, floods, and erratic weather cycles. It cause food crisis almost each year. Landlocked and almost twice the size of Texas, Ethiopia is a country of contrasts. Great fluctuations in climate across a terrain that covers 698,818 square miles help explain why Ethiopia is so often the victim of natural disasters that swing between drought and flood. From the cool, wet highlands to the scorching Danakil Depression—a basin so low and so hot that it has the highest average temperature of any place on the planet—the variations in topography help produce rainfall patterns that range from 87 inches a year to less than 8 inches annually. Sometimes, in some places, the rain doesn't seem to stop. And sometimes, in other places, it doesn't come at all.

2006 has been one of those ruinous years when erratic weather cycles—starting with drought—triggered a food crisis for more than 2 million people across the southern reaches of the country. Then the floods devastated crops; left 900 people dead, 1,000 missing, and displaced 48,000 others in pockets around the country. It is reported that flood affected the lives of 140,000 people in areas around Dire Dawa, West Shewa, and South Omo, and in the regions of Amhara, Afar, Gambella, and Tigray. Natural disasters cause crises, calamities, sufferings and diseases in Ethiopia each year. As a result, Ethiopians are facing extreme poverty with which they struggle for the entire life. People who have few assets or savings can't bounce back quickly when trouble strikes.

Poverty

According to the United Nations Human Development Index, Ethiopia and its 75 million residents sit almost at the bottom of a ranking that measures standards of living, education levels, and life expectancy. Out of 208 countries, Ethiopia received an HDI ranking of 202 in 2006. What does poverty look like in this Horn of Africa country? Agriculture is by far the largest activity, providing 80 percent of Ethiopia's employment and contributing 42 percent to the country's gross domestic product. Yet, coffee farmers are among some of the country's poorest people, earning little for their efforts while shouldering price fluctuations that leave them struggling to feed their families. Poverty also plagues countless herders, many of whom live in the more arid zones where irregular weather wreaks havoc on their pastureland and water sources. Almost 81 percent of Ethiopia's people live on less than $2 a day. That in turn limits their access to a whole range of necessities and critical services such as clean water and health care. The UN's Human Development Report notes that in 2002, 78 percent of the population did not have sustainable access to an improved source of water. In 2006, one of the consequences of lack of clean water hit home: an outbreak of acute watery diarrhea left 279 Ethiopians dead and sickened 28,880 others. Dirty water carries the microorganism that can cause that illness.

Also in 2002, only 2.6 percent of Ethiopia's gross domestic product (GDP) was spent on public health. Between 1990 and 2004, the country had just three doctors for very 100,000 people. Women suffer particularly from this shortage, delivering the vast majority of their babies without the benefit of medical care. Between 1992 and 2003, skilled health providers attended only 6 percent of births. The consequences of this broad neglect are devastating. The average life expectancy for an Ethiopian is just shy of 48 years.

When natural disasters repeatedly strike a vulnerable population, robbing people of their sources of food and income and destroying their homes, the setbacks can be long-term and for some people, insurmountable. They quickly exhaust whatever savings they may have had and sap to depletion the support of family and friends, who may well be in equally hard straights. In any given year, 5 million Ethiopians face chronic food shortages and depend on aid to survive. Shortages of the basics—food, water, and pastureland—can spark conflict. Ethiopia has witnessed bursts of violence this year, too, triggered by politicized relationships among herders in the Borena and Guji zones and a dispute over land—so critical in a harsh environment where people need every patch of pasture and pocket of water to survive. The conflict forced the displacement of more than 90,000 people.

Solutions to all of this are challenging, particularly in a country where half the GDP is based on agriculture—much of it relying on increasingly erratic rainfall and poor cultivation practices. Compounding Ethiopia's economic problems is the country's system of land tenure by which the government owns the land and leases it to tenants. The system discourages entrepreneurial enterprise because the land can't be used as collateral for loans. Oxfam affiliates have been working for more than 40 years in Ethiopia through its cycles of drought, flood, and conflict. Besides providing emergency support to people weathering these crises, Oxfam aims to help them find long-term solutions that will allow their communities to become both resilient and self-sustaining. Among the programs, Oxfam works on peace building, drought management and strengthening of livelihoods.

Humanitarian crisis

A humanitarian crisis is developing in Southern Ethiopia with tens of thousands of people internally displaced due to the recent conflict in the Guji and Borena Zones of the Oromiya region. The Borena and Guji Zones are approximately 300 miles (480 km) and 250 miles (400 km) from Addis Ababa, respectively. The Oromiya region with a population of 25 million (1/3 of the national population) is the largest and most diverse region of Ethiopia. The woredas (districts) affected by the Southern Ethiopia conflict are located in both lowland and highland regions where agro-pastoralist and pastoralist communities co-exist.

Woreda officials estimate up to 150,000 people have been displaced since the outbreak of violence on May 30th, 2006 (the actual number may be closer to 100,000.) The intra-ethnic and inter-ethnic violence represents a marked change in the pattern of an ongoing low-level conflict. As a result, large populations have been displaced over thousands of square kilometers between the Guji and Borena Zones with internally displaced persons (IDPs) moving towards areas where their clans predominate. The movement has resulted in severe disruptions of livelihoods and thousands of people left without food, shelter and essential non-food items such as water carrying containers, blankets and materials for cooking. In several locations people have been displaced for over a month and are beginning to show signs of under-nourishment and illnesses associated with exposure to harsh environments and degraded living conditions. Many fled for their lives leaving behind all assets; others have had their assets taken during their displacement. Others have brought livestock with them although looting; lack of access to water and heavy pressure on grazing lands in their new locations has contributed to severe losses of livelihoods.

An immediate response plan is needed to meet the emergency relief needs of this population including food aid, blankets, jerry cans and plastic sheeting for temporary shelter construction. Technical assistance will likely be needed in the areas of water and sanitation, especially for IDPs settled in or near urban areas. Many IDP communities are currently at critically low survival levels of water consumption (2-3L/person/day). Excreta disposal remains a problem for populations that are in close quarters with their animals. Although no outbreaks of disease were observed, risks for communicable diseases are a real risk. Protection will be a crucial issue for IDPs, both in their current locations as well as in their home villages. There is a perception by many that they are being pressured by the Ethiopian government to return to their villages; most remain fearful of violence and state that they don't feel adequate measures have been taken to ensure their safety upon return. Peace-building efforts have not yet begun and it is clear that the displacement will last for weeks to months.

Plan for Action

Oxfam America (OA), its affiliates and its local partners, already working in the area, are well positioned to take a lead in assisting this vulnerable population. The Rapid Public Health Assessment (RPHA) developed by the *Harvard Humanitarian Initiative (HHI) for OA highlights the most pressing needs of these communities and of vulnerable sub-groups within them The Rapid Public Health Assessment (RPHA) team comprised of physicians and public health professionals from the Harvard Humanitarian Initiative (HHI), along with humanitarian coordinators from Oxfam America (OA) and their local partner the Research Center for Civic and Human Rights Education (RCCHE) were dispatched to the four woredas where IDPs reportedly settled. Initial reports gave wide-ranging numbers for the total displaced population and little information was available regarding the specific humanitarian needs or state of health of the IDPs.

The results of this rapid public health assessment of the internally displaced populations in the Borena and Guji Zones of Southern Ethiopia, conducted by Harvard Humanitarian Initiative for Oxfam America, confirms that there has been a large scale displacement of people fleeing conflict in their home villages. The immediate needs of the population are primarily food aid, reliable water sources and adequate sanitation, provision of shelter as many are still without any form of shelter one month into their displacement, and non-food items. Oxfam America and its partners should act urgently to address the immediate needs of this population as well as to implement on-going monitoring to assess their changing location, health status and humanitarian needs.

Mozambique

Almost five centuries as a Portuguese colony came to a close with independence in 1975. Large-scale emigration by whites, economic dependence on South Africa, a severe drought, and a prolonged civil war hindered the country's development.

Mozambique is situated southeastern Africa, bordering the Mozambique Channel, between South Africa and Tanzania. Its total area is 801,590 sq km, land area is 784,090 sq km and water area is 17,500 sq km. Its natural resources are: coal, titanium, natural gas, hydropower, tantalum, and graphite. Its arable land is only 5.43 per cent, permanent crops 0.29 per cent and other 94.28 per cent. Mozambique has irrigation facility for an area of 1,180 sq km.

The country faces severe droughts; devastating cyclones and floods in central and southern provinces. The current issues of Mozambique are: a long civil war and recurrent drought in the hinterlands have resulted in increased migration of the population to urban and coastal areas with adverse environmental consequences; desertification; pollution of surface and coastal waters; elephant poaching for ivory is a problem. Hence, the country has signed international agreements for conserving biodiversity, climate change, climate change-Kyoto Protocol, desertification, endangered species, hazardous wastes, and law of the sea, ozone layer protection.

Population of Mozambique is 16,099,246 and growth of population is 1.38 per cent. Life expectancy is 39.82 years and fertility rate is 4.62 children born /

woman. HIV/AIDS prevalence is 12.2 per cent and this disease affected 1.3 million of people by 2001. Already 110,000 persons have died though HIV/AIDS. Major infectious diseases are hepatitis A, hepatitis E, typhoid, malaria and plague. Literacy is 47.8 per cent.

Economy: In 2005, GDP (PPP) of Mozambique was $ 26.18 billion; GDP real growth rate was 7.5 per cent, GDP per capita (purchasing power parity) was $ 1300, and GNI per capita was $ 310. Agriculture contributed 26.2 percent, industry 34.8 per cent and services 39 per cent of Gross Domestic Product of Mozambique. The country has labour force of 9.2 million and 81 per cent of them are engaged in agriculture, 6 per cent in industry and 13 per cent in services sector. Population below poverty line is 70 per cent.

Mozambique

Inflation rate was 6.5 per cent in 2005. In that year, investment was 29.6 per cent of GDP in gross fixed assets, revenue budget was $ 1.031 billion and expenditure was $1.93 billion including capital expenditure. Moreover, current account balance was $ 639 million; export was $ 1690 million f.o.b.; import was $ 2041 million f.o.b. (2005). Mozambique exports aluminum, prawn, cashew, cotton, sugar, citrus, timber, and electricity and imports machinery and equipment, vehicles, fuel, chemicals, metal products, foodstuffs, textiles. Mozambique spends 1.3

per cent of GDP in defense. Mozambique had reserves of foreign exchange and gold worth of $1.051 billion and external debt was $ $5.456 billion in 2005. It received economic aid of $632.8 million in 2001.

Poverty Alleviation

At the end of the civil war in 1992, Mozambique ranked among the poorest countries in the world. It still ranks among the least developed nations with very low socioeconomic indicators. In the last decade, however, it has experienced a notable economic recovery. Per capita GDP in 2004 was estimated at U.S. $276, a significant increase over the mid-1980s level of U.S. $120. With a high foreign debt (originally $5.7 billion at 1998 net present value) and a good track record on economic reform, Mozambique was the first African country to receive debt relief under the initial HIPC (Heavily Indebted Poor Countries) Initiative. In April 2000, Mozambique qualified for the Enhanced HIPC program as well and attained its completion point in September 2001. This led to the Paris Club members agreeing in November 2001 to substantially reduce the remaining bilateral debt. This led to the complete forgiveness of a considerable volume of bilateral debt. The United States has finished this process and forgiven Mozambique's debt. During their summit in Scotland in July 2005, the G8 nations agreed to significant multilateral debt relief for the world's least developed nations. On December 21, 2005, the IMF formalized the complete cancellation of all Mozambican IMF debt contracted prior to January 1, 2005.

Macroeconomic Review

Rebounding growth: The resettlement of civil war refugees, political stability and continuing economic reforms have led to a high economic growth rate. Between 1994 and 2004 average annual GDP growth was 8.2 per cent. Mozambique achieved this growth rate even though the devastating floods of 2000 slowed GDP growth to 2.1 per cent. The economy bounced back and consistent GDP growth rates between 7 per cent and 8 per cent are expected again in 2005 and 2006, with the World Bank predicting average growth of 7 per cent from 2004 through 2008. The Government of the Republic of Mozambique projects similar growth expansion (between 7 per cent-10 per cent a year over the next five years), but future strong expansion requires continued economic reforms, major foreign direct investment, and the resurrection of the agriculture, transportation and tourism sectors. Focusing on economic growth in the agricultural sector is a major challenge for the government. Although more than 80 per cent of the population engages in small-scale agriculture, the sector suffers from inadequate infrastructure, commercial networks and investment. However a majority of Mozambique's arable land is still uncultivated, leaving room for considerable growth.

Low inflation: The government's tight control of spending and the money supply, combined with financial sector reform, successfully reduced inflation from 70per cent in 1994 to less than 5 per cent in 1998-1999. Economic disruptions resulting from the devastating floods of 2000 caused inflation to jump to 12.7 per cent that year. The government is still working to bring inflation down to those lower numbers. In 2003 inflation reached 13.5 per cent; in 2004 it decreased slightly to 12.6 per cent (consumer price index used to measure inflation rates). The exchange rate of home currency was fluctuated drastically in 2005 and in 2006; decimal system of currency was adopted.

Extensive economic reform: Economic reform has been extensive. More than 1,200 state-owned enterprises (mostly small) have been privatized. Preparations for privatization and/or sector liberalization are underway for the remaining parastatals, including telecommunications, electricity, ports, and the railroads. The government frequently selects a strategic foreign investor when privatizing a parastatal. Additionally, customs duties have been reduced, and customs management has been streamlined and reformed. The government introduced a highly successful value-added tax in 1999 as part of its efforts to increase domestic revenues. The 2005-06 Plan included Commercial Code reform, revision of the labor law, comprehensive judicial reform, financial sector strengthening, continued civil service reform, and improved government budget, audit, and inspection capability.

Improving trade imbalance: Mozambique exported $1.26 billion worth of goods and imported $1.4 billion worth of goods in 2004. The ratio of exports to imports has increased significantly from the immediate-postwar years, when it was 1 to 4. Support programs provided by foreign donors and private financing of foreign direct investment mega-projects and their associated raw materials have largely compensated for balance-of-payment shortfalls. The medium-term outlook for exports is encouraging, as a number of recent foreign investment projects have improved the trade balance. This export growth is expected to continue. MOZAL I, a large aluminum smelter that commenced production in mid-2000, greatly expanded Mozambique's trade volume. In April 2001, the IFC approved financing assistance for MOZAL II, which doubled overall production capacity. Phase two went online in April 2003, five months ahead of schedule, using primarily Mozambican workers during construction. Traditional Mozambican exports include cashews, shrimp, fish, copra, sugar, cotton, tea and citrus and exotic fruits. Most of these industries are being rehabilitated. In addition, Mozambique is less dependent upon imports for basic food and manufactured goods as the result of steady increases in local production.

SADC trade protocol: In December 1999, the Mozambican Council of Ministers approved the southern African Development Community (SADC) Trade Protocol. The Protocol will create a free trade zone among more than 200 million consumers in the SADC region. Implementation of the Protocol began in 2002 and has an overall zero-tariff target set for 2008; however Mozambique's country-specific zero-tariff goal is currently 2015. Mozambique joined the WTO on August 26, 1995.

The country is still in transition, with a large number of social and economic challenges, including unemployment, low agricultural production, and limited infrastructure and social services. Due to these and many other problems, Mozambique is still considered one of the poorest countries in the world. In 2003-2005 per capita income was $290, the prevalence of AIDS was 16.2 percent, and infant mortality was 101 per 1,000. Still, over the last couple of years Mozambique has made some substantial progress in fighting poverty and improving human development. Sustained growth and increased spending in the social sectors contributed to a 16 percent decline in poverty in the six years from 1997, reaching 54 percent in 2003. Inequality remained low by regional standards, and progress was made toward the key Millennium Development Goals (MDGs) of infant mortality and primary enrolment.

The performance of Mozambique's economy at the macro level has been impressive: real GDP growth since 1993 has averaged 8.1 percent, and was 7.5 percent in 2004, 7.7 in 2005, and 10 percent in 2006. Annual inflation decreased from over 54 percent in 1995 to 13.5 percent in 2003, 12.6 percent in 2004, and a substantial decrease to 6.3 in 2005.

The Bank and other donors fully endorse Mozambique's poverty reduction agenda defined in the Action Plan for Reduction of Absolute Poverty (PARPA), Mozambique's PRSP, which was presented to the Bank and the International Monetary Fund (IMF) Boards in 2001. Since then the PRSP has been updated in the first PRSP Progress Report of March 2004. The Government of Mozambique has recently finalized the preparation of its second PRSP/PARPA. One of the key challenges is the rising rate of morbidity and mortality from HIV/AIDS. The national HIV prevalence among adults (15–49 years olds) is estimated at 16.2 percent in the period 2003–05. Economic models indicate that AIDS has reduced per capita GDP growth by as much as 1 percent per annum because of reduced productivity growth, lower human capital accumulation, and reduced physical accumulation, not to mention the social burden of the disease.

World Bank Assistance

Mozambique joined the World Bank Group in 1984, and assistance began in 1985 with a credit from the World Bank's International Development Association (IDA) for reconstruction and economic rehabilitation. Since the early 1990s World Bank assistance to Mozambique has been defined in its Country Assistance Strategy (CAS). The current World Bank CAS was prepared in November 2003, and covers the four-year period 2004–07. The CAS is aligned with the government priorities set forth in the PARPA, and has three main areas of focus:

(a) strengthening governance;
(b) spurring broad-based economic growth by improving the business environment; and
(c) Improving the provision of services, particularly to the poor.

A CAS review has been conducted and the finding contained in its progress report FY04-06 reiterates the Bank's commitment to work along the three pillars above.

This is the first country assistance strategy prepared by the World Bank as a joint effort of IDA, IFC, and MIGA, which confirms the strong emphasis of the CAS on strengthening the investment climate. It includes an evaluation of achievements under the previous CAS, as well as a set of monitoring indicators for the coming four years to determine to what extent the CAS's outcomes are achieved. The World Bank has started preparatory work leading to the designing of an updated CAS.

In 2004, the World Bank joined a group of donors, now known as the Group of 18 or G18, which directly funds Mozambique's state budget. The G18 uses government procedures and processes in accordance with government operational cycles as the basis for direct budget support. The government reviews progress of the PARPA through a Performance Assessment Framework (PAF), which is the main instrument for policy reform. The use of government procedures and processes for direct budget support makes donor assistance more predictable and transparent, and better harmonized and aligned with Mozambique's priorities and its planning and budgeting cycles. Budget support is al located to the PARPA's priority sectors, on which the government spends about 65 percent of its total resources. About half of the Mozambican government's revenue comes from donors, via budgetary and other forms of support. IDA, IFC, and MIGA activities in Mozambique are consistent with and supportive of the policy and investment goals of the PARPA, and the broad objectives, programs, and processes of other donors.

Mozambique benefits from Word Bank debt cancellation under both the Highly Indebted Poor

Country (HIPC) initiative, and the Multilateral Debt Relief Initiative (MDRI). Resources made available by debt relief provided under the HIPC and the MDRI initiatives are being allocated to key anti-poverty programs, as outlined in the PRSP/PARPA. At present, the accumulated debt relief from the World Bank for Mozambique amounts to US$2,361 million. This is composed of US$1,306 million under the MDRI, and US$1,055 million under the HIPC.

Debt Relief

In April 1998, Mozambique was the sixth country in the world to be declared eligible for debt relief under the World Bank and IMF Heavily Indebted Poor Countries Initiative, ensuring some US$1.4 billion (in nominal terms) in debt relief. In September 2001, Mozambique reached the completion point under the enhanced HIPC initiative. Of the total estimated debt-service relief under HIPC of some US$4.3 billion, the World Bank provided about US$1,055 million ($444 million in net present value terms). This approximately halved Mozambique's debt service payments, from over $100 million before 1999 to an average of $56 million from 2002 to 2010. It reduced Mozambique's debt service-to-export ratio from around 20 percent to less than 5 percent on average.

The G-8 Summit 2005 in Gleneagles, Scotland and G8 leaders pledged to cancel the debt of the world's most indebted countries, most of which are located in Africa, including Mozambique. Starting on July 1, 2006, the World Bank canceled the International Development Association (IDA) debt of Mozambique under the Multilateral Debt Relief Initiative (MDRI). Through this initiative Mozambique received an estimated debt relief amounting to US$1,306 million. Before the MDRI, Mozambique was to pay US$32 million as debt service to IDA in 2007-08, and a further US$97 million in 2009-11. The MDRI is an extension and a deepening of the HIPC Debt Relief

Initiative. The eligibility criteria for MDRI reflect the HIPC completion point criteria. These include:

(a) Satisfactory macro-economic performance under the IMF Poverty Reduction and Growth Facility Program;
(b) Satisfactory progress in implementing a Poverty Reduction Strategy; and
(c) The existence of a Public Expenditure Management mechanism that meets minimum standards for governance and transparency in the use of public resources.

IDA non-lending activities include technical assistance and studies, which are prepared in collaboration with government, donors and other stakeholders, and are disseminated on completion. The resources for these studies come from IDA's administrative budget, often complemented by support from other donors. One of the most important and recently approved of these studies is the Country Economic Memorandum (CEM), completed in August 2005. The CEM outlines and analyzes the major challenges ahead for the country at all major sectors. IDA lending supports government development projects through either concessional credits or grants. As of August 2006, IDA lending to ongoing projects totaled US $ 1011.86, distributed by sector as follows:

(a) Human Development (US $ 165.8 million)- 16 percent;
(b) Public Sector and Decentralization (US$231.2 million): 23 percent
(c) Agriculture and Rural Development (US$79.7 million): 8 percent
(d) Infrastructure (US$ 517.16 million):51 percent
(e) Private Sector Development & mining (US$ 18 million): 2 percent

Recently approved projects include credits for Market Led Smallholder Development in the Zambezi Valley

(US$20); Technical and Vocational Education (US$30 million), Trans-frontier Conservation Areas and Tourism Development (US$20 million), Financial Sector Technical Assistance (US$10.5 million), and for the Second Poverty Reduction Support Credit (US$120 million). Five investment projects are under preparation: all are scheduled for Board presentation in the course of the current fiscal year. The investment operations are: Roads and Bridges Management Project II; Health Service Delivery Project, Legal Sector Capacity Building Project; Maputo Urban Development Project; and PRSC III. The World Bank works in close collaboration with the IMF on the macroeconomic program.

IFC Support: As of August 2006, International Finance Commission committed portfolio totals US$120.5million and consists of nine projects in finance, agribusiness, primary metals production, oil & gas, and general manufacturing sectors, including four operations in the small- and medium-sized enterprise sector. IFC's main investment has been in the Mozal aluminum smelter near Maputo. IFC support ($120 million) for the first phase in FY97 was crucial to the US$1.3 billion project, and was IFC's largest single investment at the time. Mozal entered production in June 2000, six months ahead of schedule, and its production more than doubled Mozambique's total exports in 2001 from 1999 levels. IFC also provided $25 million to the second phase of Mozal, which doubled production capacity. IFC has further supported Mozal's HIV/AIDS programs, and is assisting the company with an SME linkage program to expand its local sourcing to Mozambican firms.

In FY05, IFC approved $3 million in the form of grant funding for the creation of the Mozambique SME financing and technical assistance facility. The facility was established on a pilot basis as an IFC-administered program to provide an integrated package of risk capital and technical assistance (TA) to selected SMEs. One SME project under the responsibility of the facility was approved and committed during FY05. The Private Enterprise Partnership for Africa (PEP Africa) is in the process of setting up a Tourism Sector Development Initiative, and an SME HIV/AIDS Program. IFC is currently working on four potential projects for investment potential of $18 million, and its SME facility is also analyzing five high probability SME projects for direct investment and technical assistance. In addition, the PEP Africa program is considering several interventions that would help improve the investment climate.

MIGA Program

Mozambique is MIGA's fourth-largest host country and the largest in Africa. The portfolio consists of twenty-one guarantees totaling $264 million in gross exposure ($148 mllllon in net exposure), including $72 million for Sasol, $20.8 million for the Moma mining project, and $13.9 million for the Maputo Port. In FY06, MIGA's work focused on providing advice and assistance to the Investment Promotion Centre to advance the free zone work program initiated in coordination with the now closed IDA funded Enterprise Development Project (PoDE). MIGA is currently working on several applications for investment with a potential of over $100 million in increased coverage. With regard to the newest program in Mozambique, MIGA has a new small investors program (SIP) for investments of less than $5 million.

The World Bank Institute (WBI) engages in several distance-learning activities in Mozambique. Training for local government officials was the most popular of these activities, followed by health, and journalism during 2002. This level of activity is likely to be increased. The WBI recently included Mozambique among its group of focus countries, and committed to expanding its program of activities. Currently, WBI is participating in the preparation of the Maputo Urban Development Program.[120]

Mozambique has continued its record of strong macroeconomic performance since the mid-1990s and its performance compares well with other countries in the region. Output growth in Mozambique over the past decade averaged almost 8 percent. Growth has been sustained by investment financed by large aid and private capital inflows, mainly into the natural resource sector. It has also been sustained by a strong trade sector—merchandise exports' share of Gross Domestic Product (GDP) more than tripled to nearly 30 percent of GDP, eliminating a trade deficit of about 30 percent of GDP.

However, even before the current global crisis, growth had been weakening, with projections about 1 percentage point lower than in the past decade. In recent years, these flows contributed to an appreciation of currency in real effective terms. Growth has also been unevenly distributed and a recent survey suggests that poverty may have increased in recent years, particularly in rural areas.

Against a backdrop of a highly uncertain global economic environment, Mozambique's macroeconomic prospects remain positive, but have weakened. Mozambique's growth in 2009 could fall several percentage points below trend. In view of the World Economic Outlook projections for a slow global recovery, growth is projected to strengthen in 2010, but will probably remain below 6 percent until 2011. Similarly, the external overall balance is projected to turn negative in both 2009; before returning positive in 2011 and stabilizing external reserves around 3.4 months of imports.

---

[120] CIA – The World Fact book – Mozambique / International Monetary Fund

The scope for supportive macroeconomic policies to offset the impact of the global economic slowdown is curtailed by the large projected decline in external reserves. Most of the deterioration in the external overall balance is the direct result of the external shock; the fiscal expansion is estimated to account for only US$42 million of the reserve loss in 2009 through higher import demand.[121]

UGANDA

The colonial boundaries created by Britain to delimit Uganda grouped together a wide range of ethnic groups with different political systems and cultures. These differences prevented the establishment of a working political community after independence was achieved in 1962. The dictatorial regime of ID-AMIN (1971-79) was responsible for the deaths of some 300,000 opponents; guerrilla war and human rights abuses under MIlton OBOTE (1980-85) claimed at least another 100,000 lives. The rule of YOWERI MUSEVENI since 1986 has brought relative stability and economic growth to Uganda. During the 1990s, the government promulgated non-party presidential and legislative elections.

Uganda is situated in Eastern Africa, west of Kenya, bordering Sudan, Kenya, Tanzania, Rwanda and Democratic Republic of Congo. Its total area is 236,040 sq km, land area is 199,710 sq km and water area is 36,330 sq km. Its natural resources are: copper, cobalt, hydropower, limestone, salt, and arable land. Its arable land is only 21.57 per cent; permanent crops 8.92 per cent and other 69.51 per cent. Uganda has irrigation facility for an area of 90 sq km. The country faces current issues of environment such as: draining of wetlands for

---

[121] IMF Executive Board Concludes 2009 Article IV Consultation with Mozambique, Public Information Notice (PIN) No. 09/85, July 16, 2009

agricultural use; deforestation; overgrazing; soil erosion; water hyacinth infestation in Lake Victoria; poaching is widespread. Uganda is a landlocked and fertile and well-watered country with many lakes and rivers. The country has signed international agreements for conserving biodiversity, climate change, climate change-Kyoto Protocol, desertification, endangered species, hazardous wastes, and law of the sea, ozone layer protection and wetlands

Population of Uganda is 28,195,754 and growth of population is 3.37 per cent and infant mortality rate is 66.15 deaths / 1000 live births. Life expectancy is 52.67 years and fertility rate is 6.71 children born / woman. HIV/AIDS prevalence is 4.1 per cent and 530,000 of people are affected by this disease. Already 78,000 persons have died through HIV/AIDS. Major infectious diseases are hepatitis A, typhoid, and malaria. Literacy is 69.9 per cent.[122]

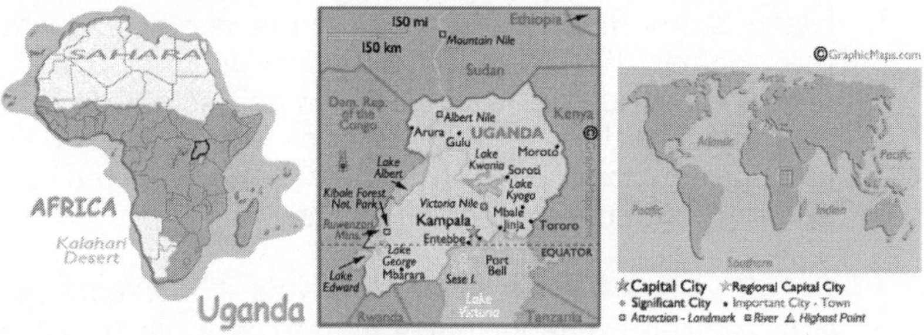

Uganda

Economy: Uganda has substantial natural resources, including fertile soils, regular rainfall, and sizable mineral deposits of copper and cobalt. Agriculture is

---

[122] Note: estimates for this country explicitly take into account the effects of excess mortality due to AIDS; this can result in lower life expectancy, higher infant mortality and death rates, lower population and growth rates, and changes in the distribution of population by age and sex than would otherwise be expected (July 2006 est.)

the most important sector of the economy, employing over 80 percent of the work force. Coffee accounts for the bulk of export revenues. Since 1986, the government - with the support of foreign countries and international agencies - has acted to rehabilitate and stabilize the economy by undertaking currency reform, raising producer prices on export crops, increasing prices of petroleum products, and improving civil service wages.

The policy changes are especially aimed at dampening inflation and boosting production and export earnings. During 1990-2001, the economy turned in a solid performance based on continued investment in the rehabilitation of infrastructure, improved incentives for production and exports, reduced inflation, gradually improved domestic security, and the return of exiled Indian-Ugandan entrepreneurs. In 2000, Uganda qualified for enhanced HIghly Indebted Poor Countries (HIPC) debt relief worth $1.3 billion and Paris Club debt relief worth $145 million. These amounts combined with the original HIPC debt relief added up to about $2 billion. Growth for 2001-02 was solid despite continued decline in the price of coffee, Uganda's principal export. Growth in 2003-05 reflected an upturn in Uganda's export markets.

In 2005, GDP (PPP) of Uganda was $ 47.76billion; GDP (official exchange rate) was $7.909 billion, GDP real growth rate was 4 per cent, GDP per capita (purchasing power parity) was $ 1800, GNI per capita was $ 280. Agriculture contributed 31.1 percent, industry 22.2 per cent and services 46.9 per cent of Gross Domestic Product of Uganda. The country has labour force of 13.17million and 82 per cent of them are engaged in agriculture, 5 per cent in industry and 13 per cent in services sector. Population below poverty line is 35 per cent.

Inflation rate was 8.1 per cent in 2005. In that year, investment was 23.4 per cent of GDP in gross fixed assets, revenue budget was $ 1.845 billion and expenditure was $1.904 billion including capital expenditure. Moreover, current account balance was $ -355 million; export was $ 768 million f.o.b.; import was $ 1608 million f.o.b. (2005). Uganda exports coffee, fish and fish products, tea, cotton, flowers, horticultural products and gold. The country imports capital equipment, vehicles, petroleum, medical supplies; cereals. Uganda Mozambique spends 2.2 per cent of GDP in defense.

Uganda had reserves of foreign exchange and gold worth of $1.286 billion and external debt was $ 4.973 billion in 2005. It received economic aid of $ 959 million in 2003. Uganda is subject to armed fighting among hostile ethnic groups, rebels, armed gangs, militias, and various government forces; Ugandan refugees have fled the Lord's Resistance Army (LRA) into the southern Sudan and the Democratic Republic of the Congo; LRA forces have attacked Kenyan villages across the border.

Refugees (country of origin): 214,673 (Sudan) 18,902 (Rwanda) 14,982 (Democratic Republic of Congo), IDPs: 1,330,000-2,000,000 note - ongoing Lord's Resistance Army (LRA) rebellion, mainly in the north; LRA frequently attacks IDP camps (2005)[123]

BANGLADESH

Europeans began to set up trading posts in the area of Bangladesh in the 16th century; eventually the British came to dominate the region and it became part of British India. In 1947, West Pakistan and East Bengal (both primarily Muslim) separated from India (largely Hindu) and jointly became the new country of

---

[123] CIA – The World Fact book – Mozambique / International Monetary Fund

Pakistan. East Bengal became East Pakistan in 1955, but the awkward arrangement of a two-part country with its territorial units separated by 1,600 km left the Bengalis marginalized and dissatisfied. East Pakistan seceded from its union with West Pakistan in 1971 and was renamed Bangladesh. About a third of this extremely poor country floods annually during the monsoon rainy season, hampering economic development.

Bangladesh is situated in Southern Asia, bordering the Bay of Bengal, between Burma and India Its total area is 144,000 sq km, land area is 133,910 sq km and water area is 10,090 sq km. Its natural resources are: natural gas, arable land, timber and coal. Its arable land is only 55.39 per cent; permanent crops 3.08 per cent and other 41.53 per cent. Bangladesh has irrigation facility for an area of 47,250 sq km. The country faces severe droughts, devastating cyclones, much of the country inundated during summer monsoon season. Bangladesh has 4246 km of land boundaries, Burma 193 km and India 4,053 km and the coastline measures 580 km. The current issues of Bangladesh are: many people are landless and forced to live on and cultivate flood-prone land; water-borne diseases prevalent in surface water; water pollution, especially of fishing areas, results from the use of commercial pesticides; ground water contaminated by naturally occurring arsenic; intermittent water shortages because of falling water tables in the northern and central parts of the country; soil degradation and erosion; deforestation; severe overpopulation Hence, the country has signed international agreements for conserving Biodiversity, Climate Change, Climate Change-Kyoto Protocol, Desertification, Endangered Species, Environmental Modification, Hazardous Wastes, Law of the Sea, Ozone Layer Protection, Wetlands

Population of Bangladesh is 147,365,352 (July 2006) and growth of population is 2.09 per cent. Life expectancy is 62.46 years and fertility rate is 3.11 children born / woman. HIV/AIDS prevalence is 0.1 per cent of population and 13,000 people are living with HIV / AIDS. Already 110,000 persons have died through HIV/AIDS. Major infectious diseases are diarrhea, hepatitis A, hepatitis E, typhoid, malaria and dengue. Literacy is 53.9 per cent.

Economy

Despite sustained domestic and international efforts to improve economic and demographic prospects, Bangladesh remains a poor, overpopulated, and inefficiently governed nation. Although half of GDP is generated through the service sector, nearly two-thirds of Bangladeshis are employed in the agriculture sector, with rice as the single-most-important product. Major impediments to growth include frequent cyclones and floods, inefficient state-owned enterprises, inadequate port facilities, a rapidly growing labor force that cannot be absorbed by agriculture, delays in exploiting energy resources (natural gas), insufficient power supplies, and slow implementation of economic reforms. Reform is stalled in many instances by political infighting and corruption at all levels of government. The opposition, the bureaucracy, public sector unions, and other vested interest groups also have blocked progress in Bangladesh. The BNP government, led by Prime Minister Khaleda ZIA, has the parliamentary strength to push through needed reforms, but the party's political will to do so have been lacking in key areas. One encouraging note: growth has been a steady 5 percent for the past several years.

In 2005, GDP (PPP) of Bangladesh was $ 305.9 billion; GDP (official exchange rate) was $ 63.56 billion, GDP real growth rate was 6.4 per cent, GDP per capita (purchasing power parity) was $ 2100, GNI per capita was $470 and public debt was 44.5 per cent of GDP. Agriculture contributed 19.9 percent, industry 19.8 per cent and services 60.3 per cent of Gross Domestic Product of Bangladesh. The country has labour force of 66.6 million and 63 per cent of them are engaged in agriculture, 11 per cent in industry and 26 per cent in services sector. Population below poverty line is 45 per cent.

External Debt

In 2007, Bangladesh spent almost 25 percent of its Revenue for external debt servicing while spending 15.65 percent and 5.89 percent of its revenue expenditure on education and health respectively. Every year Bangladesh pays, on an average $ 1070 million, to its foreign creditors. To address the problems of global recession,

Bangladesh needs unconditional debt cancellation.

In 2008, the country's annual debt servicing swelled to a record US$1.97 billion, making it the biggest chunk of expenditure in the national budget. The amount was up by $414 million compared to the previous fiscal year and it made up 15.7 per cent of the total budgetary expenditure — higher than the spending in education and health. The debt service payment represented 15.53 per cent of country's total merchandise exports, 9.2 per cent of exports of goods and services including remittances and 2.5 per cent of the gross domestic products (GDP).

Increasing receipt of foreign loans, start of repayment period of big loans due to expiry of grace period and un-favourable exchange rate are the major reasons for higher debt payment. Large trade deficit, widening gap between savings and investment, slow growth of revenues and a rapid growth of public expenditure have also contributed to the soaring amount of debt servicing.

The government statistics showed that after the payment of $1.965 billion principals and interests against all the public sector loans, the outstanding debt of the country has stood at $21.26 billion till June last year 2008. Per capita debt obligation of the country stood at $149.54 in the last FY2008.

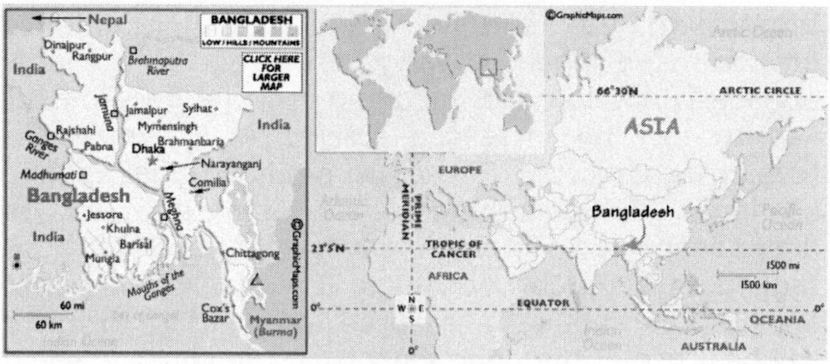

Bangladesh

Every year the government meets its mounting development expenditure by taking medium and long-term loans from donors such as the World Bank, Asian Development Bank and Islamic Development Bank (IDB). It also borrows from bilateral donors such as Japan government, the United States, Saudi Arabia for executing projects and purchasing items such as aircraft, ship and food grains on deferred payment. The debt servicing has crossed the one-billion-dollar-mark in FY 2004 due to higher borrowing over the last decade.

The debt repayment could have been much higher than the present amount if the Japan government did not write off principal and interests on 36 Japanese loans signed before June 1989. If Japan did not waive the aids and interests, we had to repay $1.46 billion additional money to the donors. Grant or donation by donors has been shrinking fast in the total aid package since 2000, worsening the debt status of the country. Till late 1990s donors' grant accounted for more than 45 per cent of the total aid. But it started to decline significantly from earlier this decade. Last year, the government received $658.11 million worth of grant from different multilateral and bilateral donors while loan was $1.4 billion. The total debt liability would worsen in the near future, pushing the country towards a "debt-trap."

Investment has shrunk, exports and remittance growth have been slowing down and the global outlook is not so good, meaning that the government has to rely on increased foreign aid to meet its bulging expenditure. These are ominous signs for the economy. The government must act fast to cut its dependence on foreign loans, particularly those tagged with tough conditions. The quality of public expenditure should be ensured in an effort to make the best use of the debt. Only then the country would get better return from the loans and the debt repayment will be easier.[124]

Inflation rate was 7 per cent in 2005. In that year, investment was 24.4 per cent of GDP in gross fixed assets, revenue budget was $ 5.993 billion and expenditure was $ 8.598 billion including capital expenditure. Moreover, current account balance of Bangladesh was $ 37 million in 2005. The export of merchandise was $ 9.37 billion f.o.b.; import was $ 12.97 billion f.o.b. (2005). Bangladesh exports garments, jute and jute goods, leather, frozen fish and seafoods. The country imports machinery and equipment, chemicals, iron and steel, textile, foodstuffs, petroleum products and cement. Bangladesh spends 1.8 per cent of GDP in defense. Bangladesh had reserves of foreign exchange and gold worth of $2.825 billion and external debt was $ 20.63 billion in 2005. It received economic aid of $ 1.575 billion in 2000.

---

[124] Financial Express, June 29, 2009

Discussions with India remain stalled to delimit a small section of river boundary, exchange 162 miniscule enclaves in both countries, allocate divided villages, and stop illegal cross-border trade, migration, violence, and transit of terrorists through the porous border; Bangladesh resists India's attempts to fence or wall off high-traffic sections of the porous boundary; a joint Bangladesh-India boundary inspection in 2005 revealed 92 pillars are missing; dispute with India over New Moore /South Talpatty / Purbasha Island in the Bay of Bengal deters maritime boundary delimitation; Burmese Muslim refugees strain Bangladesh's meager resources. The Bangladesh inhabitants are entering into the coastal area of Orissa state profusely over the years and are settled in Kendrapara district without authorization. The super cyclone washed away thousands of refugees into the sea in 1999.

Refugees: Refugees (country of origin): 20,402 (Burma), IDPs*:* 61,000 (land conflicts, religious persecution) (2005). Elicit drugs: Bangladesh acts as transit country for illegal drugs produced in neighboring countries.[125]

INDIA

The Indus Valley civilization, one of the oldest in the world, dates back at least 5,000 years. Aryan tribes from the northwest infiltrated onto Indian lands about 1500 B.C.; their merger with the earlier Dravidian inhabitants created the classical Indian culture. Arab incursions starting in the 8th century, Turkish in the 12th century and European traders, beginning in the late 15th century invaded India. By the 19th century, Britain had assumed political control of virtually all-Indian lands. Indian armed forces in the British army played a vital role in both World Wars. Nonviolent resistance to British colonialism led by Mahatma M. K.

---

[125] CIA – The World Fact book – Mozambique / International Monetary Fund

GANDHI brought independence in 1947. The subcontinent was divided into the secular state of India and the smaller Muslim state of Pakistan. A third war between the two countries in 1971 resulted in East Pakistan becoming the separate nation of Bangladesh. Despite impressive gains in economic investment and output, India faces pressing problems such as the ongoing dispute with Pakistan over Kashmir, massive overpopulation, environmental degradation, extensive poverty, and ethnic and religious strife.

India is situated in Southern Asia, bordering the Arabian Sea and the Bay of Bengal, between Burma and Pakistan. Its total area is 3,287,590 sq km, land area is 2,973,190 sq km and water area is 314,400 sq km. Its natural resources are: coal (fourth-largest reserves in the world), iron ore, manganese, mica, bauxite, titanium ore, chromites, natural gas, diamonds, petroleum, limestone, arable land. Its arable land is only 48.83 per cent; permanent crops 2.8 per cent and other 48.37 per cent. India has irrigation facility for an area of 558,080 sq km. The country faces severe droughts; flash floods, as well as widespread and destructive flooding from monsoon rains; severe thunderstorms; earthquakes. India has 14,103 km *border countries:* Bangladesh 4,053 km, Bhutan 605 km, Burma 1,463 km, China 3,380 km, Nepal 1,690 km, Pakistan 2,912 km and the coastline measures 7,000 km. The current issues of environment in India are: deforestation; soil erosion; overgrazing; desertification; air pollution from industrial effluents and vehicle emissions; water pollution from raw sewage and runoff of agricultural pesticides; tap water is not potable throughout the country; huge and growing population is overstraining natural resources.

Hence, the country has signed international agreements for conserving environment. These are: Antarctic-Environmental Protocol, Antarctic-Marine

Living Resources, Antarctic Treaty, Biodiversity, Climate Change, Climate Change-Kyoto Protocol, Desertification, Endangered Species, Environmental Modification, Hazardous Wastes, and Law of the Sea, Ozone Layer Protection, Ship Pollution, Tropical Timber 83, Tropical Timber 94, Wetlands and Whaling.

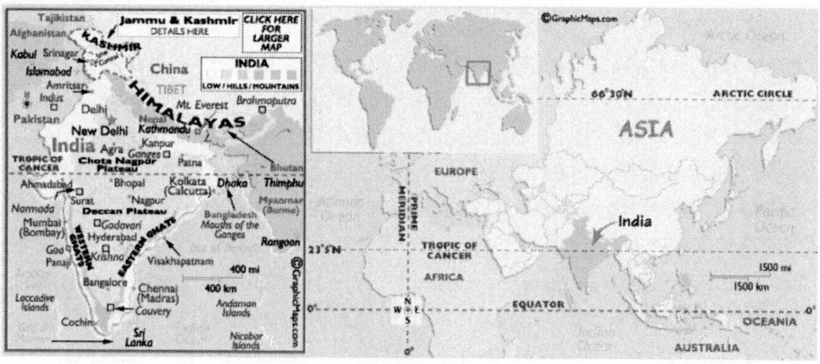

India

Population of India is more than 1.21 billion in 2012. Growth of population is 1.38 per cent. Life expectancy is 64.71 years and fertility rate is 2.73 children born / woman. HIV/AIDS prevalence is 0.9 per cent of population and 5.1 million people are living with HIV / AIDS. Already 310,000 persons have died through HIV/AIDS. Major infectious diseases are diarrhea, hepatitis A, hepatitis E, typhoid, malaria, dengue and rabies. Literacy is 59.5 per cent.

Economy

India's diverse economy encompasses traditional village farming, modern agriculture, handicrafts, a wide range of modern industries, and a multitude of services. Services are the major source of economic growth, accounting for half of India's output with less than one quarter of its labor force. About three-fifths of the work force is in agriculture, leading the UPA government to articulate an economic reform program that includes developing basic infrastructure to improve the lives of the rural poor and boost economic performance. Government controls on foreign trade and investment have been reduced in some areas, but high tariffs (averaging 20 percent on non-agricultural items in 2004) and limits on foreign direct investment are still in place.

The government in 2005 liberalized investment in the civil aviation, telecom, and construction sectors. Privatization of government-owned industries essentially came to a halt in 2005, and continues to generate political debate; continued social, political, and economic rigidities hold back needed initiatives. The economy has posted an average growth rate of more than 7per cent in the decade since 1994, reducing poverty by about 10 percentage points. India achieved 7per cent GDP growth in 2005, significantly expanding manufacturing. India is capitalizing on its large numbers of well-educated people skilled in the English language to become a major exporter of software services and software workers. Despite strong growth, the World Bank and others worry about the combined state and federal budget deficit, running at approximately 9 per cent of GDP; government borrowing has kept interest rates high. Economic deregulation would help attract additional foreign capital and lower interest rates. The huge and growing population pose social, economic, and environmental problem.

In 2005, GDP (PPP) of India was $ 3.666 trillion; GDP (official exchange rate) was $ 719.8 billion, GDP real growth rate was 8.4 per cent, GDP per capita (purchasing power parity) was $ 3,400 and GNI per capita was $ 720. Agriculture contributed 18.6 percent, industry 27.6 per cent and services 53.8 per cent of Gross Domestic Product of India. The country has labour force of 496.4 million and 60 per cent of them are engaged in agriculture, 17 per cent in industry and 23 per cent in services sector. Population below poverty line is 25 per cent.

Inflation rate was 4.2 per cent in 2005. In that year, investment was 28.1 per cent of GDP in gross fixed assets, revenue budget was $ 111.2 billion and expenditure was $ 135.8 billion including capital expenditure of $15 billion. Moreover, public debt was 53.8 per cent of GDP (federal and state debt combined in 2005) and current account balance was $ - 12.95 (in 2005). The export earnings amounted to $ 76.23 billion f.o.b.; import earnings amounted to US $ 113.1 billion f.o.b. (2005). India exports textile goods, gems and jewelry, engineering goods, chemicals, leather manufactures. The country imports crude oil, machinery, gems, fertilizer, and chemicals. India spends 2.5 per cent of GDP in defense. India had reserves of foreign exchange and gold worth of $ 136 billion and external debt was $ 125.5 billion in 2005. It received economic aid of $ 2.9 billion in financial year 1998- 99.

Major Highlights of External Debt in 2009

(a) India's external debt as at end March 2009 was placed at US $229.9 billion (22.0 percent of GDP) recording an increase of US $5.3 billion or 2.4 percent over the level of the previous year, mainly due to the increase in trade credits.
(b) As per international comparison of external debt of the twenty most indebted countries, India was the fifth most indebted country in 2007.
(c) By way of composition of external debt, the share of commercial borrowings was the highest at 27.3 per cent as at end March 2009 followed by short-term debt (21.5 per cent), NRI deposits (18.1 per cent), and multilateral debt (17.2 per cent).
(d) The debt service ratio has declined steadily over the years and stood at 4.6 per cent as at end March 2009.

(e) (v) Excluding the valuation effects due to appreciation of US dollars against other major currencies and Indian rupee. The stock of external debt would have increased by US $ 18.7 billion as compared with the stock as at end March 2008.

(f) The share of short-term debt in total debt increase to 21.5 per cent at end March 2009 from 20.9 per cent at end March 2008 primarily on account of rise in short-term trade credits.

(g) Based on residual maturity, the short-term debt accounted for 40.6 per cent of the total external debt at end-March 2009.

(h) The ratio of short-term debt to foreign exchange reserves at 19.6 per cent in March 2009 was higher as compared with 15.2 per cent in March 2008.

(i) The US dollar continues to remain the dominant currency accounting for 57.1 per cent of the total external debt stock as at end-March 2009.

(j) India's foreign exchange reserves provided a cover of 109.6 per cent to the external debt stock at the end of March 2009 as compared with 137.9 per cent as at end-March 2008.

External Debt of India (expressed in US $)

The Long-term Debt of India was US $75,257 million in 1991, $ 88,485 million in 1998, $ 1,07,214 million in 2004, $ 115,250 million in 2005, $ 118,594 million in 2006,$ 143,201 million in 2007, $ 177,574 million in 2008 and $ 180,514 million in 2009 (p).

The Short-term debit was $ 8544 million in 1991, $ 5046 million in 1998, $ 4431 million in 2004, $ 17,723 million in 2005, $ 19,539 million in 2006, $ 28,130 million in 2007, $ 46, 999 million in 2008, and $ 49,373 million in 2009 (p).

The total external debt (including both Short-term and Long-term debt) was $ 83,801 million in 1991, $ 93,531 million in 1998, $ 1,11,645 million in 2004, $ 132,973 million in 2005, $ 138,133 million in 2006, $ 171,331 million in 2007, $ 224,573 million in 2008, and $ 229,887 million in 2009 (p).

The external debt consists of Multilateral, Bilateral, IMF, Trade Credit, ECBs, NRI deposits, and Rupee debt. The government of India is availing credit from the International Monetary Fund since 2004.

Moreover, Government of India is utilizing US$ 180,514 million (78.5 percent) of debt on long-term basis and US$ 49,373 million (21.5 per cent) of total debt as short-term debt as on March 31, 2009. The total outstanding debt of India is $229,887 million as on March 31, 2009.

Of the total external debt, the share of commercial borrowings was the highest at 27.3 percent followed by short-term debt at 21.5 percent, Non-Resident Indian deposits accounted for 18.1 percent and multilateral debt was 17.2 percent of the total debt by March 2009.

India is the fifth most-indebted country in the world after China, Russia, Turkey and Brazil.

India's foreign exchange provided a cover of 109.6 percent to the external debt stock at the end of March 2009 against 140 percent at the end of March 2008. The share of concessional debt in the total stock declined to 18.2 percent from 19.7 percent in the previous fiscal reflecting the continuing increase in non-concessional private debt. (Pioneer News Service, July 1, 2009, p.10). The World Bank would finance India to the extent of US $ 14 billion from 2009 to 2012.

It was borrowing about US $2.3 billion per year for the last four years (2005–2008). But the World Bank is now expecting to award credit to the extent of US$ 7 billion to India in 2010. The Bank expects that India would get US $18 billion from IBRD, US $ 5 to 6 billion from IDA and US $3.5 from IMF during 2010 – 2012 (three years). India is the biggest debtor country in the World Bank and has already borrowed US $19.57 billion from the World Bank. The World Bank finances 68 low-income countries too.

India's external debt rises at 2.55 percent and reached US $244 billion by March 31, 2012. India becomes a permanent debtor country of the World Bank as evidenced from its track records.

The World Bank fully knows that its credit is being mis-utilized in Orissa state (India), but it praises the government. The President of World Bank visited integrated coastal zone management area in Orissa in March 2012. Why this scheme is financed, while farmers are committing suicides in the state?

Refugees (country of origin): 92,394 (Tibet/China) 57,274 (Sri Lanka) 9,761 (Afghanistan), IDPs: 600,000 (resulting from 26 December 2004 tsunami); 500,000 (Jammu and Kashmir conflicts; most IDPs are Kashmiri Hindus) (2005)

Trafficking in persons: India is a source, destination, and transit country for men, women, and children trafficked for the purposes of forced or bonded labor and commercial sexual exploitation; the large population of men, women, and children - numbering in the millions - in debt bondage face involuntary servitude in brick kilns, rice mills, and embroidery factories, while some children endure involuntary servitude as domestic servants; internal trafficking of women and girls for the purposes of commercial sexual exploitation and forced marriage also occurs; the government estimates that 90 percent of India's sex trafficking is internal. [126]

India Today

Even after 65 years of independence, large-scale poverty remains the most shameful blot on the face of India. India still has the world's largest number of poor people in a single country. Of its nearly 1.21 billion inhabitants, an estimated 350-400 million are below the poverty line, 75 per cent of them in the rural areas. More than 40 per cent of the population is illiterate, with women, tribal and scheduled castes particularly affected. It would be incorrect to say that all poverty reduction programmes have failed.

The growth of the middle class (which was virtually non-existent when India became a free nation in August 1947) indicates that economic prosperity has indeed been very impressive in India, but the distribution of wealth has been very uneven. The main causes of poverty are illiteracy, a population growth rate by far exceeding the economic growth rate for the better part of the past 50 years, protectionist policies pursued since 1947 to 1991, which prevented large amounts of foreign investment in the country.

Poverty alleviation is expected to make better progress in the next 50 years than in the past, as a trickle-down effect of the growing middle class. Increasing stress on education, reservation of seats in government jobs and the increasing empowerment of women and the economically weaker sections of society, are also expected to contribute to the

---

[126] CIA – The World Fact book – Mozambique / International Monetary Fund

alleviation of poverty. Eradication of poverty can only be a long-term goal in India.[127]

Farmers' Suicides in India

A report of the Reserve Bank of India says that as against RBI norms, only seven out of 27 PSU banks could achieve the stipulated target of distributing 18 per cent of the net bank credit to the agriculture sector as on November 2008. Hence, the percentage of agriculture in the GDP declined to 30.5 percent in 1988 to 17.5 percent in 2008, and growth in agriculture declined from 3.1 percent in 1988 to 1.6 percent in 2008.

The paradox is that even farmers in apparently prosperous states like Punjab, Andhra, and Maharashtra, are committing suicides. In a decade since 1997, about 200,000 farmers committed suicide due to indebtedness following crop shifting from traditional crop to cash crops - and slapdash trade liberalization and corporate globalization agenda of the government.

The World Bank led structural adjustment policies have brought new imperialism in the farm sector forcing poor Indian peasants to buy new seeds for every planting season from the global corporate. Perhaps there may be a link between farmers' deaths and the 'reform' agenda. The highest level of farmers' suicide in India is the Virdharbha region in Maharashtra state; it faces 4000 suicides per year or 10 suicides per day. And this is the reason with the highest acreage of Monsanto's GMO Bt. Cotton.

The Arjun Sengupta Committee report says that 836 million Indians live on less than 20 INR (Indian rupees) a day. The NSSO estimated that 19 percent of Indian rural people lived on less than 12 INR a

---

[127] A Synopsis by IndiaOneStop.Com

day. About 1.9 million people in India suffer from tuberculosis.[128]

Every third hungry person in the world is an Indian and one in three Indians (340 million) go to bed hungry. India is now a republic of hunger, a republic of dynasty and a republic of corruption.

In short, the important indicators are:

(a) Number of people living below $1 a day: 34.7 per cent (World Development Indicator, 2005)
(b) Less than $2 a day: 79.9 percent (World Development Indicator, 2005)
(c) GDP per capita – US$ 613 (World Bank)
(d) Life expectancy: 63 years (Census of India, 2001)
(e) Malnutrition: 21 per cent of India's total population (Human Development Report, 2004)
(f) Untraced Children: Each year 45,000 children are untraced in India (National Human Rights Commission)
(g) HIV / AIDs infected: 5.7 million (Government, India)

High Incidence of Poverty in Ten Indian States

A number of states in India are experiencing acute poverty problems. Mother sells her son; senior citizens and young graduates try to commit suicide including burning themselves for poverty. Farmers commit suicide for crop failure or low rate of return. The government machinery is corrupt. Justice is delayed.

The government of India has accepted pro-rich policies of FDI, SEZ, private capital, reforms and

---

[128] Swarna kumar Anand, "Resurgent India, Hungry Indians" The Pioneer, Bhubaneswar, March 6, 2010.P.9

protection to small industries from MNCs for the benefits of the rich people. For example, the concept of Special Economic Zone (SEZ) is that it tantamount to hijacking of public resources for private enrichment. When such enrichment turns into land speculation (including in SEZ) and the enrichment ushers in structural change in pursuit of the consumerist life style of western affluent, there is cause of concern. FDI should not enter into retail trade in India.

There are at least 10 states in India, which can be compared with African countries in respect of per capita income, unemployment of youths, low agricultural income, incidence of poverty, school dropouts, life expectancy at birth, infant mortality, and maternal mortality, unavailability of healthcare and per capita state burden of debt. These states are: Orissa, Jharkhand, Bihar, Chhattisgarh, Madhya Pradesh, SIkkim, Assam, Meghalaya, Tripura, and Arunachal Pradesh, where 34 per cent to 57 per cent of the people belong to the BPL category (below poverty line). As per the World Bank indicators, percentage of families under the BPL category in different states touches up to 75 per cent of total population.

(C) Problems Can Be Solved

Let us study the history of Greece civilization to solve the problems of hunger, poverty and debt overhang, which hinders world peace. In the past the Greek philosophers searched for solutions of unsolved problems and they were successful. Today's civilizations must acknowledge their achievements. If we try sincerely, we can also achieve laurels in more areas of unsolved problems.

We are confident that only a small number of free thinkers can make it possible – a world free of hunger, a world of peace and a world of humanity.

William Harris has reported the growth of civilization in our planet; and this endeavor has made men as human beings.

"After the last glacial retreat, which occurred some twelve thousand years ago, humankind went into a remarkable fast escalation in a dozen directions, which produced the whole fabric we call Civilization. The first step was probably the documental selection and hybridization of certain plants, which in a developed form because what we call the "grain plants". Seed amaranth and rice in Asia, maize in South America, wheat in the Near East, and cultivation of fruit and nut plants made possible a much larger food supply and naturally a much larger population. The availability of multitudes of human hands made feasible textiles made from cotton or wool, the cotton and wool trades, mines and the metals with their accompanying technologies, and in the wake of all this hustle and bustle, warfare as the earliest of the systems of transfer of goods from one set of hands to another.

When large numbers of people begin to over-produce, that is, make more that what they personally need, we begin to accrue surpluses, which immediately lead to trade. Barter may be complex in its processes, but it is intellectually simple, since it proceeds with what are arbitrary but always balanced equations.

But when we begin to evolve complex economic situations, in which the equations are balanced by considerations, which lie outside the items, which are being exchanged, we enter the world of true economics. Shortages of food or cloth, the need for tin from England to alloy copper from Cyprus to make bronze which will be sold in Denmark, opportunities to accrue capital in cash from deals prompted by famine, greed and a self-growing set of economic parameters - - -these are factors which began to emerge by the fifth millennium B.C., and changed the whole notion of what a society and a nation and an empire could be like.

Nothing like this had ever occurred before, in all the hundreds of millennia since man appeared as a Human Being. Now for the first time Man the hunter and gatherer is hard pressed by Homo Faber, man the fabricator and engineer. And they are both eclipsed in the fast ensuing millennia by a new breed of clever, useful, effective and often unscrupulous fellow, who can best be called Homo Economicus. He is clearly the man of the present world we live in, like him or not, we seem to be unable to do without him, and apparently we desperately need the skills he has. He is certainly in terms of the civilizations we have put up throughout the world, the man of the future.

All in all, an analytic study of the Greek mythological lore would seem to be inextricably tied up with the history of previous millennia, with the early history of the Middle East, and with the development of that special and novel breed of human behavior, which we call Civilization".[129]

Conclusion

To day, one billion people are hungry. They are devoid of minimum standard of living, health care facility, education for children, houses and two square meals a day. The poor has not committed any mistake to become poor. The country, the administration, the kings, the monarchs, and particularly the present governments of all the low-income countries are responsible for the wretchedness of people. Democracy has taught 'corruption theory and practice' to the elected representatives and the voters.

---

[129] William Harris, Prof. Em. Middlebury College, www.middlebury.edu/~harris

It is necessary that the World organizations, developed countries, international organizations, international funding institutions, Universities and religious pundits should organize or appoint **'Think Tanks'** for solving poverty, hunger and debts that faces most of the countries and find ways for ensuring **'world peace'**.

All the low-income countries need 100 per cent debt relief to push their economy to a higher position for better utilization of their own resources for the benefits of the people. There are 54 low-income countries and 58 low-middle-income countries, which need debt relief. In other words, 112 countries face acute shortage of funds for development process. Therefore, creditors should grant 100 percent debt relief to these 54 low-income countries once for all on December 31, 2014 and decide the fate of 58 low-middle-income countries on December 31, 2015.

The donor countries, international funding institutions, international banks have already realized more than the amount of capital invested in the low-income countries. Therefore, it is presumed that debt relief refers to the interest component of the transaction. Moreover, debt relief ensures the good will of the developed countries towards the developing and other HIPC countries

The world organizations, donor countries, and G-8 countries should initiate for the formation of **"United Nations Anti-corruption Organization"** to check corruption through out the entire globe. It is assumed that poverty is directly proportional to corruption. So the number of corruption cases in low-income countries is more than developed countries and can be identified easily and quickly.

If corruption is restricted or abandoned, the societies can ensure peaceful life for each individual and it can be achieved by amending:

(a) **The service code;**
(b) **The anti-corruption Act; and**
(c) **Prompt judgement by the courts**

The donor countries and organizations may cancel future donations, aids, and grants to developing countries for five years. They should also cancel all grants to the NGOs and Civil Societies for five years, as these grants encourage corruption in low-income countries.

But their humanitarian grants and donations during natural calamities should continue to save the poor.

The UN country organizations should empanel more number of specialists to assist in the preparation of the state budget of low-income countries. The specialists can prepare development strategies, evaluation reports for low-income countries and can act as advisers of government organizations. The services of specialists in different countries can create a new world order.

The influential churches and other religious groups should influence the donor countries to declare **'Full Debt Relief'** on or before 31st December, 2016 for extending cooperation to the poor people of low-income countries and for low-middle-income countries as on or before 31st December, 2017.

In short, awarding debt relief to the loaned countries would result in World Peace.

+++++

Chapter-IV

NECESSITY OF DEBT RELIEF

I encourage you in your advocacy for total debt cancellation for poor countries because, frankly speaking, it is a scandal that we are forced to choose between basic health and education for our people and repaying historical debt.

President Mkapa of Tanzania – 2005

The poor countries face unending debt crises because of huge amount of unproductive and underutilized external and internal obligations. Debt of poor countries rises despite ever increasing payments, while aid of developed countries is falling. So the question is: Can the Millennium Development Goals (MDGs) adopted by the international community be fulfilled by the year 2015? The MDGs can be achieved, if the developing countries follow pro-poor, pro-rural and pro-agricultural policies. The poor countries need total debt relief, more aid, free and fair trade and investment in productive projects.

People of poor countries can be benefited through corruption-free administration. They suffer as immoral politicians control politics and administer the state. The excess borrowed fund has made all the low-income countries increase of unemployment, income disparity, rich-poor divide, and social disequilibria.

The developed countries and world organizations should study the severity of poverty of the poor and corrupt activities of the politicians–administrators-business men in the low-income countries. This knowledge would help these coveted organizations to formulate plans, programs and sanction of funds for the states/countries. The funds released by the funding organizations should be properly utilized for fulfilling the targets fixed by the funding organizations to achieve the Millennium Development Goals. Duplication of programs by different donor organizations results in corruption both by the officials of the funding organizations and the recipient institutions. There is lack of transparency in accounts, stocks, investments, quality, procurement and proper utilization of funds.

The donor countries should declare the amount of debt relief, aid or grants they can provide annually, and the pattern of bilateral trade and rate of simple interest for long-term investments for infrastructure investments. Necessarily the grants, aid and loan of the donors could be bettered accounted for in the budgets of the developing countries. Till today, a number of countries don't include donors' grants in their budgets. This practice causes corruption both at field level and by the governments. The recipient countries can better utilize aids; grants, donations, and credit amounts released by the developed countries provided they assure the amount before the budget session.

The burden of debts, payment of annual installments, sanction of new projects, infrastructure development such as concretization of village roads, new ports, railways, national high ways, massive buildings, forceful acquisition of agricultural land for non-agricultural purposes have increased foreign debt but these debts have neglected the hungry people. There has been massive migration from rural to urban areas; innocent unemployed youths have accepted Terrorism, Naxalism or Maoism as a way of life. Most of the progress in work is confined to advice of foreign delegates, report preparation, and newspaper reports.

So the need of the people is 100 per cent debt relief. But they hesitate to sanction debt relief in full and they make debt relief complicated by adding more conditionality, more reports, more promises and more advices.

The poverty reduction strategy paper (PRSP) of each poor country is necessary for consideration debt relief. This chapter comprises four sub-sections such as (A) the necessity of Debt Relief, (B) Poverty Reduction Strategy Papers (PRSP), (C) Engagement of UNDP in PRSP Process and (D) Review of PRSP.

(A) Necessity of Debt Relief

(1) Debt relief promotes economic efficiency when there is debt overhang.

(a) It is a good accounting practice to write off debts that cannot be collected. (Summers, 2000)[130]

---

[130] Summers, L. "Moving Forward with Millennial Debt Relief" Remarks at Reception to Celebrate HIPC, House Banking Committee Room, United States Congress, Washington DC, February 1, 2000

(b) Debt relief can benefit both creditors and debtors (Krugman, 1989)[131]
(c) Debt relief can solve debt overhang (Myers, 1977)[132]

(2) Debt overhang is not the principal problem in HIPCs

(a) The principal problem in the HIPCs is poor social infrastructure
(b) The HIPCs need aid as the most efficient policy instrument for investment in social infrastructure as poor countries do not have the tax base to raise the resources. (Bulow and Rogoff 1988[133]; Bulow, 2002[134])

(3) HIPC needs aid, as debt relief is not equivalent to aid.

The goal is to improve economic development and reduce poverty. Hence, aid is necessary in poor countries. Debt relief crowds out existing aid flows. In an effort to increase resource transfer to the HIPCs, proponents of the HIPC Initiative have been pushing for a reduction in debt servicing. Ironically, debt relief has actually reduced the net resource transfer to the world's poor countries.

Debt relief may change the composition of aid. Debt relief may result in an adverse shift in the

---

[131] Krugman, P. "Market-Based Debt Reduction Schemes" Analytical Issues in Debt edited by Jacob Frenkel et al , Washington, IMF.
[132] Myers, Stewart "Determinants of Corporate Borrowing" *Journal of Financial Economics,* 5, 147-175
[133] Bulow, J. and David Dollar, "Cleaning up Third World Debt Without Getting take t the Cleaners" Journal of Economic Perspectives, 4(1) Winter 1990, pp. 31-42
[134] Bulow, Jeremy " First World Governments ad Third World Debt", Brookings Papers on Economic Activity, No.1: 2000, pp. 229-55

composition of aid – away from multilateral inflows and towards bilateral inflows. Bilateral aid is like direct cash flow to the recipient government.

(4) Aid should be properly invested for economic growth.

(a) Aid should be given only to countries with good economic policies
(b) Aid should be managed multilaterally (Burnside and Dollar, 2000)[135]
(c) There should be more focus on the productivity of aid projects.
(d) Aid, not debt relief, should be the policy instrument best suited for achieving high social rates of return through investment in public goods.[136]

Debt Relief under HIPC Initiative

The IMF and World Bank first launched the HIPC Initiative in 1996 with the aim of ensuring that no poor country faces a debt burden it cannot manage. The Initiative entails coordinated action by the international financial community, including multilateral organizations and governments, to reduce to sustainable levels the external debt burdens of the most heavily indebted poor countries. Following a comprehensive review in September 1999, a number of modifications were approved to provide faster, deeper and broader debt relief and to strengthen the links between debt relief, poverty reduction and social policies. In 2005, in the context of accelerating progress toward the Millennium

---

[135] Burnside, C and Kenneth, R. "Aid, Policies, and Growth", America Economic Review, September 2000, 90(4), pp.847-868

[136] Arslanalp, S. and Peter Blair Henry (2003), "The world's poorest countries: Debt Relief or Aid? Research Paper Series No. 1809, Stanford Graduate School of Business, 1-28 pages

Development Goals, the Multilateral Debt Relief Initiative has supplemented the HIPC Initiative. The MDRI allows for 100 percent debt relief by three multilateral institutions—the IMF, the International Development Association (IDA) of the World Bank, and the African Development Fund (AfDF)—for countries completing the HIPC process.

Yet the HIPC Initiative, even supplemented by the MDRI, is not a panacea. Even if all of the external debts of these countries were forgiven, most would still depend on significant levels of concessional external assistance, since their receipts of such assistance have been much larger than their debt-service payments for many years.

Conditionality of HIPC Initiative

The HIPC Initiative assistance is considered if country / countries:

(a) Face an unsustainable debt burden, beyond traditionally available debt-relief mechanisms;
(b) Establish a track record of reform and sound policies through IMF and World Bank supported programs; and
(c) Prepare a Poverty Reduction Strategy Paper (PRSP) through a broad-based participatory process (an interim strategy is sufficient to begin the process).

The mechanism eventually created for countries to qualify for and benefit from the HIPC initiative involved a complex web of criteria, conditions and phases. Under the first HIPC Initiative the criteria for eligibility consisted of three elements. In other words, indebted countries must satisfy the following conditions.[137]

---

[137] Dagdeviren, H and J. Weeks (2001), "How much poverty could HIPC reduce?" Wider Development Conference: Debt

(a) Be eligible for concessional assistance from 'IDA – only',
(b) Have their indebtedness at an unsustainable level, which cannot be remedied by traditional debt-relief mechanisms,
(c) Implement sustained economic reform and poverty reduction programs approved by the WB and the IMF

The first step is to carry out a debt sustainability analysis to determine the country's debt relief needs. If a country's external debt ratio after traditional debt relief mechanisms is above a threshold for the value of debt to exports (or, in special cases, the value of debt to fiscal revenues), it qualifies for assistance under the Initiative. Once a country has made sufficient progress in meeting the criteria for debt relief, the Executive Boards of the IMF and World Bank formally decide on a country's eligibility, and the international community commits to reducing debt to the sustainability threshold. This is called the decision point. Once a country reaches its decision point, it may immediately begin receiving interim relief on its debt service falling due. In order to receive the full and irrevocable reduction in debt available under the HIPC Initiative, however, the country must establish a further track record of good performance under IMF- and World Bank-supported programs. The length of this second period depends on three factors. These are:

(a) Satisfactory implementation of key policy reforms agreed at the decision point,
(b) Maintenance of macroeconomic stability, and
(c) Adoption and implementation for at least one year of the PRSP

Relief, 17 –18 August 2001, Marina Congress Center, Helsinki

Once a country has met these criteria, it can reach its completion point, after which, lenders are expected to provide the full relief committed at the decision point.

Financing through HIPC Initiative

The total cost of providing assistance to the 29 countries that have reached the decision point and the 13 countries potentially eligible for debt relief under the enhanced HIPC Initiative is estimated to be about $61 billion in 2004 net present value terms. The bilateral creditors will provide more than half of this and the rest will come from multilateral lenders. The IMF's share of the cost is financed primarily by the investment income on the net proceeds from off-market gold sales in 1999 that were deposited to the PRGF-HIPC Trust. Member countries have provided additional contributions to this trust.

Benefits through HIPC Initiative

Debt service has dropped by more than half in relation to both exports and government revenue between 1998 and 2004 for the 29 countries for which packages have already been approved. Yet for debt reduction to have a tangible impact on poverty, the additional resources need to be targeted at the poor. Before the HIPC Initiative, eligible countries were, on average, spending slightly more on debt service than on health and education combined. Now, under their recent IMF and World Bank-supported programs, these countries have increased markedly their expenditures on health, education and other social services and, on average, such spending is now almost four times the amount of debt service payments.

While country-by-country data demonstrate that these countries are seeing clear gains, it has taken time and effort to ensure that money is redirected to aid the poor in ways that most reduce poverty. And difficult problems remain. For example, in war-ravaged Rwanda and Ethiopia, pressing reconstruction needs may mean large new loans at the same time that old debt is being reduced.

Difficult problems also remain in HIPCs that have not yet been able to reach their decision points. Some of these countries are plagued by uneven policy records or poor governance, which in turn may be caused by serious problems such as civil conflict. Some others have debts too large to write off given current funding for the Initiative. This is true, for example, in Liberia and Sudan, which are both afflicted by civil conflict. The IMF and the World Bank agreed to extend for an additional two years up to the end of 2006. This "sunset clause" would be applicable for remaining HIPCs to adopt an IMF or World Bank supported program of adjustment and reform that would allow their consideration for debt relief under the enhanced HIPC Initiative. Maintaining a sustainable debt position while seeking the additional financing needed to make progress towards the MDGs remains a serious challenge for countries, even after debt relief under the HIPC Initiative. None of these are easy problems. But the IMF and World Bank are looking for solutions, with poverty reduction as the central focus.[138]

Stages of Debt relief

Debt relief under the HIPC Initiative is provided in two stages. In the first stage, the debtor country needs to demonstrate the capacity to use prudently whatever debt relief is granted by adhering to IMF and World Bank supported economic adjustment programs. During this period, the country will receive debt relief from Paris Club creditors under traditional mechanisms (usually a flow rescheduling on Naples

---

[138] IMF External Relations Department, December 2005

term) and concessional financing from multilateral institutions and bilateral donors. At the beginning of the second stage, the decision point under the Initiative is reached. The Executive Boards of the IMF and World Bank determine whether the full application of traditional debt relief mechanisms would be sufficient for the country to reach sustainable levels of external debt, or whether additional assistance would be required under the Initiative. The IMF and World Bank commit to grant debt relief, provided the country continues implementing macroeconomic reforms and structural adjustment policies, including strengthened social policies aimed at reducing poverty. At this point, Paris Club creditors provide additional debt relief through a flow rescheduling, and commit to provide at the end of the second stage a stock of debt operation, when the completion point has been reached. The full amount of debt relief by the IMF and the World Bank are provided at the completion point. The multilateral development banks, commercial creditors and non-Paris Club official bilateral creditors also participate in the debt relief operation on comparable terms.[139]

The Enhanced HIPC Initiative builds on traditional external debt reduction mechanisms over the last two decades, to provide additional external debt relief from wider international community to countries requiring HIPC relief. It provides a solid basis for HIPCs to achieve debt sustainability and to exit the rescheduling cycle. This is a major achievement, but maintaining debt at sustainable levels over time is a more complex undertaking – which requires efforts both by debtors, and creditors / donors. For this, it is essential that debtors pursue sound economic policies, including good debt management. The HIPC

---

[139] Gilman Martin and Wayne Mitchell (2004), "Achievements to Date Challenges Ahead: A View from the IMF" HIPC Debt Relief: Myths and Reality, FONDAD, The Hague, February 2004, pp.72 - 96

relief is provided on a voluntary basis and depends on the concern and goodwill of each participating creditor for these heavily indebted poor countries.

(B) Poverty Reduction Strategy Papers

The Poverty Reduction Strategy Papers (PRSPs) were first introduced in 1996 and were modified in 1999. These reports form the basis of multilateral lending to the heavily indebted poor countries and other developing countries that are unable for debt servicing. These reports are the policy documents of borrower countries where in the policies relating to economic, social and structural programmes are chalked out explicitly for reducing poverty.

PRSPs explicitly incorporate participation into the IMF/WB lending framework for poor countries. These multilateral organizations follow a long history of concern with participation in the development community, spanning nearly four decades. Starting with a series of high-level declarations of support for 'popular participation' by international development organizations in the 1970's, to the re-orientation of bilateral aid projects towards 'customer focus' and 'stakeholder participation' in the 1990s, the concept of participation has increasingly been mainstreamed in the policy dialogue.[140]

Policy reforms imposed on developing countries through conditionality have greatly weakened the autonomy of recipient countries. The vast majority of poor countries in Africa, and many in Latin America and Asia, have been subject to a series of IMF and World Bank adjustment packages, especially over the last twenty years. These reforms cover all the major

---

[140]Cornwall, A. (2000), "Beneficiary, Consumer, Citizen: Perspectives on Participation for Poverty Reduction", ***SIDA Studies*** No. 2, Stockholm, Swedish International Development Cooperation Agency

economic decisions - budgets, tax, expenditure policies, exchange rates, trade and tariff policies, price policies, privatization, and credit policies - such that countries subject to them have very little control over their economic policies. Moreover, sectoral adjustment policies additionally expand the scope of conditionalities - including education and health policies for example. The Comprehensive Development Strategy of the World Bank further extends the realm of potential conditionality into the law and matters of governance. Conditionality thus has been a major source of disempowerment whether or not the policy reforms are in the recipient countries longer-term interests.[141]

The poverty economists, international volunteer organizations, non-government organizations (NGOs) are waging mass rally, conventions, mass appeal to the G8 countries and other funding institutions for 100 per cent debt relief.

Great celebrities and personalities like the Pope, the Prime minister of UK, Nelson Mandela, and Nicholas Brady, and renowned activists like Bono, Brad Pitt, Kylie Minogue, Cameron Diaz and Jesse Helms have suggested the funding institutions to undertake debt relief to the poorest and developing countries.

The PRSP is the essential document for award of debt relief under HIPC Initiative, concessional IDA lending and grants through the IMF's Poverty Reduction Growth Facility (PRGF). The reports are designed for implementation by the debtor countries for a period of three years. Necessarily the borrower countries

---

[141]Stewart Frances and Michael Wang, "Do PRSPs Empower Poor Countries And Dis-empower The World Bank, Or Is It The Other Way Round?", ***Working Paper*** Number 108, Queen Elizabeth House, University of Oxford, May 2003, pages 27

with participation of the governments and civil societies with active direction of the World Bank and the International Monetary Fund prepare PRSPs. Then the Poverty Reduction Strategy Paper (PRSP) is revised, modified and accepted by the Bank and the Fund for award of debt relief. In short, PRSPs aim at poverty reduction of the debtor countries and award of debt relief by the creditors. For availing debt relief, a country needs strong economic performance of macroeconomic policies together with structural and social reforms. Once the country qualifies for debt relief, it has to make considerable progress in poverty alleviation through social sector reforms. The country should also spend the savings from debt relief on social sectors. The social sector reforms include:

(a) Improving Quality of Life of the Poor
(b) Reforms in the Education Sector
(c) Reforms in the Health Sector

Increasing the Income of the Poor

(a) Rural Development
(b) Micro Finance
(c) Road Infrastructure
(d) Rural Electrification
(e) Governance and Security
(f) General Poverty Situations

Principles Underlying the PRSP Approach

Country-Driven: Country-ownership of a poverty reduction strategy is paramount. Broad based participation of civil societies in the adoption and monitoring of the poverty reduction strategy tailored to country circumstances will enhance its sustained implementation.

Result-oriented

(a) An understanding of the nature and determinants of poverty, and the public actions that can help reduce it, is required for the formation of an effective strategy.
(b) Medium and long term goals for poverty reduction, including key outcome and intermediate indicators, are needed to ensure that policies are well designed, effectively implemented and carefully monitored.

Comprehensive

(a) Sustained poverty reduction will not be possible without rapid economic growth; macroeconomic stability, structural reforms and social stability are required to move countries to a higher path of sustainable growth.
(b) Poverty is multidimensional; specific actions are needed to enable the poor to share the benefits of growth, increase their capabilities and well being, and reduce their vulnerabilities to risks.
(c) A poverty reduction strategy should integrate institutional, structural, and sectoral interventions into a consistent macroeconomic framework.

Partnerships

Development of a strategy by Government can provide the context for improved coordination of the work of the Bank and the Fund, as well as that of regional development banks and other multi-laterals, bilateral assistance agencies, NGOs, academia, think tanks, and private sector organizations.

Long-term perspective

(a) A medium and long term perspective is needed, recognizing that poverty reduction will require institutional changes and capacity building including efforts to strengthen governance and accountability and is therefore a long term process.

(b) National and international partners' willingness to make medium term commitments will enhance the effectiveness of their support for a poverty reduction strategy.[142]

Preparation of PRSP of Country/ Countries

Obstacles to poverty reduction

(a) What are the key patterns of poverty in its various dimensions?
(b) How are these influenced by the level and pattern of growth: public policy, public service provision, social and institutional functioning and by exogenous shocks?
(c) What are the main obstacles to more rapid growth and to spreading the benefits of growth to the poor?

Objectives and Targets

(a) What targets for various dimensions of poverty reduction have been established?
(b) What are the targets for selected intermediate indicators?

Strategies and Action Plan

(a) What are the priority public policies to increase growth and reduce poverty?
(b) What institutional changes are needed to implement the strategy?
(c) How can public spending and institutions be made more efficient and responsive to the needs of the poor?

---

[142] International Monetary Fund

Monitoring and Evaluation Systems

(a) What is the framework for monitoring progress of the strategy and what is the involvement of civil society in the process of evaluation?
(b) What safeguards ensure the transparency and accountability of public budgeting and expenditure?

External Assistance and External Environment

(a) What level of external assistance is expected to be available to support the country's efforts?
(b) Could more assistance be effectively absorbed, and if it were, what would be the likely impact on poverty reduction goals?
(c) How does technical assistance, from all sources, support implementation of the strategy?
(d) What would be the effect of greater success to partner country markets on growth and poverty reduction

Participatory Process

(a) What was the nature of the participatory process and how were the views and interests of the poor incorporated?
(b) What impact did the process have on the formulation and content of the strategy?

Benefits of PRSP to Encourage and Track Country Progress

(a) The development of appropriate diagnostics that help national authorities understand better the major obstacles to poverty reduction and growth in the context of their own countries and the related identification and availability of good indicators of progress in poverty reduction;

(b) The deepening of a shared vision across civil society regarding desired poverty reduction goals;
(c) The setting of priorities and design of public actions to achieve desired poverty reduction outcomes; and
(d) The development of participatory processes used for the setting of poverty reduction goals and the monitoring of implementation and progress.[143]

(C) Engagement of UNDP in PRSP Process

- A Policy Note

The UN instruments are also highly relevant to the PRSP process. A high quality Common Country Assessment (CCA) is an important analytical building bloc for the Government to formulate its PRSP. Moreover, other reports such as MDG report, and other financial reports are prepared either by individual agencies or jointly. And just as the CAS may be perceived as the World Bank's 'business plan' for support to the PRSP, the UN Development Assistance Framework (UNDAF) can be seen as the basis on which the UN system supports poverty reduction in each country. The CCA and UNDAF guidelines, which are currently being updated, will indicate the linkages with the PRSP. Moreover, the planned outcomes in the Country Program Outline (CPO) will be aligned with the objectives of the UNDAF, and therefore with the PRSP too. Policy Notes are intended to strengthen UNDP's upstream policy advice on key issues and priority themes. This note recognizes the fact that a growing number of Country Offices (currently over 60) are engaged in supporting the preparation; implementation and monitoring of PRSPs. PRSPs offer improved prospects for real

---

[143]Poverty Reduction Strategy Papers – Operational Issues, Prepared by the Staffs of the IMF and the World Bank, December 10, 1999 – Email: prsp@imf.org

progress on poverty reduction provided that the appropriate conditions are in place. The key messages that emerged related to both process and content of PRSPs are:

(a) Allow for flexibility in lie with different country circumstances
(b) Temper expectations ad set realistic targets
(c) Priorities policies and actions, and develop capacity and systems to enable this
(d) Keep an openness to alternate policy choices in the PRSP process
(e) Sustain efforts over the long term, with a corresponding commitment by countries and development partners; and
(f) Restructure and harmonize donor assistance, including multi-year budget support

UNDP's view of PRSP

Addressing a World Bank-sponsored Seminar on International Development Targets in March 2001 in Washington, the UNDP Administrator stated that the UN must applaud and support the PRSPs. The UNDP uses traditional strengths to help vest deep country ownership in providing support for civil society consultation. It ensures that the poverty reduction goals are given maximum space in the macro-economic envelope and its technical assistance is used to help developing countries develop real choices, and where appropriate, real alternative views or analysis as they seek to map out their own development strategies.

The Administrator highlighted the important role played by the World Bank in respect of the PRSPs and the leadership of UNDP in supporting the monitoring of the Millennium Development Goals (MDGs), drawing on the unprecedented mandate given to the UN system by the Millennium Declaration of September 2000. UNDP's convening power and aid co-ordination role, its multi-sectoral approach, its normative role and its country presence are recognized as significant to secure country-level ownership of the PRSP and country-level monitoring of the MDGs. For country level reporting on the MDGs, UNDP is leading the UN Country Team's effort as 'scorekeeper' of the MDGs. UNDG has issued a Guidance Note on MDG reporting at the country level. UNDP expects to play a major role in maximizing the potential of PRSPs to contributing to poverty reduction. Indeed, a recent review of UNDP Support to Poverty Reduction Strategies in PRSP Countries details support to the design, implementation and monitoring of poverty reduction strategies in 60 countries. In order to maximize the potential contribution of PRSPs two principles of engagement derive from UNDP's role as the 'development agency of the developing countries'. These are:

(a) Engage at the behest of Government and national partners in civil society, and
(b) Help to elaborate real choices, and where appropriate, alternative views and analyses, based on criteria of equity and human development.

UNDP's potential contributions

PRSPs have raised the priority of poverty reduction in a growing number of countries, and have had a valuable influence on policy-making by stressing pro-poor consequences. It has helped sharpen the focus on the poor and given a new urgency to reducing poverty by seeking to establish time frames, benchmarks and monitorable outcomes. The extent to which PRSPs are able to make a real contribution to poverty reduction depends on a range of factors, including coherence with long-term human development criteria. UNDP support is essential in helping to create the right conditions by addressing substantive issues related to poverty reduction. Some of the important issues are outlined below:

Build on existing work and previous experience:

Many Governments have been engaged in the formulation of national poverty reduction strategies during the 1990s. In over 100 countries, UNDP has played a key role in raising awareness of poverty in all its dimensions and intensifying the policy debate on poverty eradication, especially through its National Human Development Reports (NHDRs). PRSPs need to build on this prior experience, even where (perhaps especially where) the PRSP counterparts in Government—usually Finance Ministries—are different from the Ministries, which had been previously working on national poverty reduction strategies. While the PRSP process has in many cases enhanced the budgetary rigors of pre-existing national poverty strategies, it should ensure the collaboration of those parts of the public (and in some cases non-governmental) sector, which had been previously engaged. Also, comprehensiveness must be balanced with realism, taking into account national capacities.

Provide adequate time for consultation:

Because of its links to debt relief and IDA lending, PRSP preparations are often undertaken with haste, limiting the time given to consultation with stakeholders, and inhibiting broad national ownership. Poverty reduction is a political challenge. It touches on critical but sensitive issues involving rights and entitlements. It is likely that pro-poor policies will meet opposition. Contrary to common belief, poverty reduction is not universally perceived as a common good. Pro-poor policies are likely to interfere with the interests of groups in society that exert more power and influence than what the poor can muster. Patient and inclusive dialogue is needed, not necessarily as a road to consensus, but in order to promote understanding of the hard choices involved. Thus, national ownership implies that key stakeholders are consulted and have an understanding of the trade-off involved, even if they are not necessarily in agreement with the policy choices. It is necessary to reconcile Government's desire for haste for debt relief and IDA lending with an adequate social dialogue.

Ensure coherence and pursue a longer-term perspective:

In building on past experience, UNDP support can also help ensure coherence between PRSPs and other planning instruments, such as five-year Development Plans, longer-term Vision Statements, National Long-term Planning Strategies (NLTPS) and National Strategies for Sustainable Development. UNDP, which has been a partner for many countries in the development of frameworks and instruments of planning, can help to ensure that PRSPs are compatible with these instruments, and in this way also bring in the longer-term perspective necessary for the achievement of the MDGs. While a three-year period of the PRSP corresponds to the time frame of World Bank and IMF lending, it is manifestly too short to engender significant progress in poverty reduction. To address coherence and ensure a longer-term perspective, some countries will seek to develop an effective planning framework, which responds to the challenge of poverty reduction. In most others, there will be several instruments. This different framework is mutually consistent in terms of policy prescription, and that they promote, rather than detract from, institutional harmony in implementation.

Promote macro-economic policies for poverty reduction:

The PRSP needs to take account of a country's macro-economic context, including the positive and negative consequences of globalization. Equally, the PRSP's impact on poverty will be limited unless the macroeconomic framework, including monetary and fiscal policies, are re-examined in light of their impact on the poor. It is not uncommon to find PRSPs that do not explicitly link the macro-economic framework to poverty reduction. Targets are set for inflation, budget deficit and current account deficit without assessing how they will impact on the poor, or whether different targets would impact differently on poverty reduction.

Incorporate equity as a core anti-poverty strategy:

An anti-poverty strategy that overlooks equity concerns is deeply flawed. This is not an argument against growth; economic growth has an obvious role to play in poverty reduction. Equity not only matters for poverty reduction, but also for growth. Recent research makes it increasingly difficult to build a case that inequality is good for growth. On balance, an evidence offer more support for the view that inequality is harmful to growth than the opposite view, which has prevailed in development economics for decades. The growing consensus that high inequality slows economic growth invalidates the conventional argument that an equity-driven anti-poverty strategy will merely lead to the sharing of poverty—not of wealth. Equity is good for the poor because it is good for growth and for distributing its benefits across the population, including the poor. High inequality inhibits growth, contributes to poor policy-making and delays pro-poor reforms.

Address trade issues as they relate to poverty:

It is also vital to incorporate into PRSPs, considerations of trade and the external economic environment. In most PRSP countries, exports account for more than a quarter of GDP (and imports for a higher proportion). Trade is often a key determining factor of the pace and pattern of economic growth and distribution. In recent years, however, many poor countries have been caught in the scissors of declining primary commodity export prices and rising import costs. There are other concerns associated with the globalization process, including the volatility of external capital flows and the uneven spread of foreign direct investment and technologies. UNDP works to 'mainstream' trade concerns into PRSPs under the Integrated Framework (cosponsored by UNDP, WB, IMF, ITC and WTO). A major UNDP / UNCTAD project is addressing the concerns of programme countries with respect to globalization issues.

Translate anti-poverty strategies into operational programs:

Time and efforts invested in the preparation of a full PRSP should be managed carefully. Their opportunity cost in terms of formulating sectoral development plans (such as SWAps—Sector-wise approaches) will be high. Sectoral plans offer more space for analytical work and discussions about specific policy options and trade-off.

General statement of intent that can address trade-off in terms of priority setting and policy-making; but it is unlikely to turn into a specific plan with detailed policy measures. Swaps are the channels through which the PRSP will eventually be implemented. Indeed, the term 'poverty reduction' is not an operational concept; is has to be broken down in meaningful and practical programmes backed by appropriate resources allocations and policy reforms. That can only happen at the sectoral level, not at the aggregate level in the abstract. Swaps should be developed for the priority areas that will yield the greatest impact on poverty—such as agriculture, transport, education and health. More sectors may need to be covered but it is unlikely that the civil service will have the capacity to handle more than 3-5 SWAPs simultaneously.

UNDP services and interventions: UNDP Country Offices are best placed to determine the precise nature of the services and interventions, which can help to improve the coverage and quality of the issues addressed in the PRSP. Below are suggested areas of support in defining both the PRSP process and its contents. The Thematic Trust Fund on Poverty Reduction is available to cover part of the costs associated with UNDP's support to PRSPs.

(a) Poverty assessments: It is indispensable that each PRSP be predicated on a sound analysis of poverty in its many dimensions and causes. UNDP has a strong track record in supporting poverty surveys and participatory assessments. It also needs to help ensure that in the formulation process; the many dimensions of human poverty as well as the considerations of key stakeholders are taken fully into account. Among the poverty-related concerns that UNDP considers as critical are respect for and promotion of human rights; equity and gender equality; and the vulnerability of specific groups. Therefore, dis-aggregated data are essential to identify the main characteristics of the poor and the vulnerable, such as gender, ethnicity, location, education, etc. and any combination thereof.

Generally, assessment of poverty in a country is based on macro level studies on the basis of government reports, which is also questionable. Poverty assessments can be made successful by surveying rural households with local economists.

(b) Pro-poor policy options: UNDP must encourage a pro-poor focus in the policies that lie at the heart of PRSPs. This means advocating public finance policies (covering both revenue and expenditure and in line with the 20/20 Initiative) that favour human development concerns and are not entirely driven by short term economic expediency; access to land, credit, and other key assets that favour the poor; policies that enhance empowerment. Gender issues are integral to policy analysis and the resultant strategies to eradicate it. Gender sensitivity implies the need for positive provisions for women's rights and the elimination of gender discrimination, and the securing of their sustainable livelihoods and social protection.

(c) Consultation with key stakeholders: Building on our political neutrality and the breadth of our mandate, many UNDP Country Offices already enjoy close interaction, on both operational and policy matters, with civil society and NGOs. Consultations cannot be done in haste. UNDP has helped to establish new forums and consultation mechanisms, by building on existing institutional mechanisms, including Parliaments, regional and local assemblies where they exist. UNDP deals with civil societies through separate policy notes. UNDP can help to foster dialogue on poverty reduction. A recent example is the National Poverty Forum in Uganda—which UNDP helped to create, and which it co-chairs with the Government. A principal objective is to open opportunities for civil society—including women's and indigenous peoples' organizations—as well as the private sector, to participate in public debates, to ensure that the interests of the poor are taken into account in the design of poverty strategies. The Secretary General's 2000 Global Compact also provides opportunities for further strengthening ties with the private sector. In fragile situations, UNDP should help to ensure that PRSPs are sensitive to conflict prevention, and contribute to building social cohesion. But it does not contact the real beneficiaries such as the poor farmers, peasants and landless labourers.

(d) Monitoring PRSP implementation: UNDP can support the monitoring of the impact of national poverty reduction strategies. In its role of MDG scorekeeper, UNDP can help build local monitoring capacity, and stress the use of the MDGs, but which are conceptualized in line with national priorities and dis-aggregated by gender, ethnic, geographical, rural/urban and other distinctions that characterize the poor. The National Human Development Report is a relevant depository of data. Since the purpose of monitoring PRSPs is to determine their short-term impact and effectiveness, periodic national household surveys will not be sufficient. In addition to detail household surveys (which UNDP is actively supporting in the Latin America and other regions), UNDP should encourage the development of more frequent surveys and rapid assessments of the poor and by the poor themselves. UNDP ensures that the results of these surveys are fed back in a timely way to policy-makers and community leaders. This is one of the goals of the poverty 'observatories' in some francophone African countries. The active involvement of NGOs and local community organizations in the monitoring of PRSP performance is an area where UNDP can make a difference.

(e) UN Country Team Support: UNDP has a clear mandate to provide leadership on poverty reduction within the UN Country Team. Individual agencies contribute to poverty reduction in their respective areas of specialization: UNICEF for the welfare and rights of children; WHO on health issues; FAO and WFP on food security; UNFPA on maternal health, and so on. As they have already demonstrated in several countries, UN Country Teams—and UN Theme Groups—offer the opportunity to combine expertise in support of PRSPs that are truly integrated and gender-sensitive. The principal vehicles for this support are the Common Country Assessments (CCAs), which can feed directly into the process of PRSP formulation, and the UNDAF, which should be the main programming framework for UN support in the implementation of the PRSP. The UNDG Guidance Note on PRSPs outlines the relationship among these different instruments, as well as with the MDG reports.

(f) Resource mobilization: UNDP can play an important role in helping Government to mobilize resources in support of PRSPs. Some Country Offices already made poverty reduction strategies the focus of Round Tables and in-country donor consultation meetings. These exercises must not be centered on a list of specific project proposals, but on realistic projections of the resource needs—domestic and external— required to accomplish the goals of PRSPs. This matching of resources, moreover, must take into account future obligations as well as present needs. UNDP should caution against a new round debt accumulation.

(g) Country experiences: UNDP supports in the formulation of PRSPs:

1.Supporting national PRS and development plans upon which the I/PRSP are based: Central African Republic; the Gambia; Ghana; Guinea-Bissau; Madagascar; Malawi; Mozambique; Senegal; Uganda; Zambia; Cambodia; Mongolia; Sri Lanka; Bolivia; Yemen; Georgia

2.Provision of technical assistance in PRSP preparation, integrating lessons from pilots, commenting on drafts: Angola; Benin; Bangladesh; Cameroon; Madagascar; Mauritania; Niger; Rwanda; Sierra Leone; Tanzania; Cambodia; Lao PDR; Viet Nam; Honduras; Nicaragua; Yemen; Armenia; Kyrgyz Stan

3. Studies linked to preparation of PRSP (e.g., expenditures on basic social services, determinants of poverty/inequality; review of previous PRS): Guinea-

Bissau; Malawi; Rwanda; Viet Nam; Bolivia; Honduras; Nicaragua

4. Enabling the incorporating of various thematic linkages for effective PRS, such as governance, gender, environment, HIV/AIDS - Burkina Faso, the Gambia, Mauritania, Uganda

Human development and pro-poor policy

5. Ensuring that human poverty and human development – including rights-based approaches - are taken into consideration and encouraging pro-poor policies. Lesotho; Madagascar

Macro-economic policy framework

6. Developing macroeconomic framework, preparation of guidelines and background studies: Angola; Benin; Ghana; Lesotho; Cambodia; Lao PDR; Viet Nam; Bolivia; Nicaragua; Georgia; Kyrgyz Stan
Trade

7. Incorporating international trade considerations (including the Integrated Trade Framework) into PRSPs: Burundi, Ghana

Promoting consultation, stakeholder participation in the PRSP process

8.Fostering stakeholder awareness and inputs through Poverty Forums, seminars and workshops: Angola; Cameroon; Guinea; Lesotho; Niger; Tanzania; Uganda; Zambia; Bangladesh; Cambodia; Nepal; Pakistan; Bolivia; Honduras

9. Creating high-level institutional mechanisms for participation such as multi-stakeholder advisory committees. Lesotho; Tanzania; Honduras

PRSP Monitoring Indicators and Assessments

10.Strengthening PRSP monitoring capacity - development of disaggregated indicators, data, training at national and local levels as well as poverty observatories: Benin; Burkina Faso; Cameroon; Chad; Ethiopia; Guinea; Lesotho; Examples: Malawi; Rwanda; Tanzania; Uganda; Cambodia; Mongolia; Nepal; Bolivia; Haiti;/ Honduras; Nicaragua; Armenia; Tajikistan

11. Facilitating poverty surveys and assessments, especially at grassroots level, to feed into policy formulation: Benin; Chad; Ghana; Malawi; Mauritania; Niger; São Tomé and Principe; Tanzania; Pakistan; Viet Nam; Bolivia

12. Monitoring progress towards MDGs as benchmarks in determining progress in poverty reduction: Viet Nam

Co-ordination and Implementation Capacity

13. Co-coordinating UN Country inputs into PRSP formulation and ensuring consistency and closer linkages between PRSPs and the CCA/UNDAF: Ghana; Guinea-Bissau; Kenya; Malawi; Mauritania; Tanzania; Uganda, Armenia

14. Improving alignment of the principal planning bodies and instruments, and ensuring PRSP compatibility with other PRS, development plans: Ghana; Kenya; Lesotho; Mozambique; Cambodia; Viet Nam; Bolivia, Guyana

15.Advising government on strategy and processes for PRSP formulation and implementation: Angola; Burundi; Chad; Côte d'Ivoire; Ghana; Kenya; Lesotho; Madagascar; São Tomé and Principe; Bangladesh; Cambodia; Pakistan, Viet Nam; Haiti; Djibouti

16. Strengthening institutional (national government) capacity for PRSP implementation: Madagascar;

Malawi; Mauritania; Tanzania; Zambia; Cambodia; / Mongolia; Nepal; Viet Nam; Nicaragua

17. Strengthening local government capacity for PRSP implementation: Lesotho; Uganda; Cambodia; Lao PDR;

Resource mobilization

18. Helping governments mobilize resources in support of PRSPs through Round Tables and other in-country donor consultation meetings such as Angola, Mali and Laos. [144]

The UNDP could have made all PRSPs with consultation of local economists, administration and people.

In all low-income countries, pro-poor, pro-rural and pro-agricultural policies could have been chalked out to benefit the maximum number of people in the countryside. Imposing reforms for faster growth in low-income countries has caused development, but has increased poverty, hunger, migration, corruption and diseases. All these countries have fallen into debt trap, and these countries could never be able to repay the amount in future. The funding institutions can solve this situation.

(D)

Review of P R S P

(1)WB Operation Evaluation Department (OED)

July 22, 2004

The Bank and the IMF launched the Poverty Reduction Strategy (PRS) Initiative in 1999 to improve the planning, implementation, and monitoring of public actions geared toward reducing poverty. Low-income borrower countries are required

---

[144] UNDP' s engagement in Poverty Reduction Strategy, August 2002, Web: http://www.undp.org/poverty/practicenotes/prsp.pdf

to complete a PRS paper, or PRSP, for access to Bank and Fund concessional lending and to HIPC debt relief. PRSPs are also to serve as the framework for external assistance. This evaluation reviews progress against these aims, and assesses the effectiveness of the Bank's support. It was conducted in collaboration with the Independent Evaluation Office of the IMF, which is producing a parallel evaluation focused on the Fund's support to the Initiative. The World Bank carries independent evaluation work through Operation Evaluation Department (OED).[145] The Poverty Reduction Strategy Initiative: An independent Evaluation of the World Bank's support is based on:

1. The PRS Initiative has begun to orient stakeholders in low-income countries toward a focus on poverty, attention to results, and an overarching framework for aid management

2.The tension in designing a Bank/IMF-driven initiative involving conditionality that is simultaneously meant to foster a country-driven process has hampered customization of the Initiative to country conditions and caused limited focus on domestic planning and implementation processes; and

3. To enhance second generation PRSPs in difficult country environments; which have not yet produced an initial PRSP. The Bank should foster better customization, assist in exploring a wider range of policy options including attention to growth, and help define clearer partnership frameworks around PRSPs with accountabilities for both countries and partners.

Main Findings:

---

[145] OED REACH, World Bank Operations Evaluation Department @http://worldbank.org/oed

The Initiative is relevant but benefits vary: The Initiative has improved the poverty focus of national strategies. The process of gathering sector programs under one strategic umbrella has helped policymakers better appreciate the links between sector strategies and poverty reduction. But progress has depended on each country's public sector capacity, Government-partner relationships, and relations among donors. The Initiative has added the most value in countries where government leadership and aid management processes were already strong.

Tensions in the Initiative's design have caused problems during implementation: There is an inherent tension in the design of a Bank/IMF-driven initiative-involving conditionality that is simultaneously meant to foster a country-driven process. The perception of ownership varies among stakeholders (see figure 1). This has led to two problems during implementation. First, there is no mechanism or guidance to adapt the Initiative's processes and requirements to differing country conditions, especially weak public sector capacity. Countries have focused more on completing documents, which give them access to resources, than on improving domestic processes. Secondly, there are no intermediate milestones for what the principles are expected to achieve, which makes it difficult to assess progress. This lack of clarity has led to different and sometimes incompatible expectations among stakeholders.

Key areas need strengthening: Alternate options and growth policies: Most PRSPs to date have not considered the full range of policy actions required for growth and poverty reduction. They focus largely on public expenditures, and pay more attention to social sector spending than to infrastructure, rural development, and other areas with poverty reduction potential. More analytical work is needed about how development policies and programs can best lead to poverty reduction.

Alignment: External partners have supported PRSP formulation, but neither donors nor the Bank have defined specifically whether or how they should change the content of their programs to reflect PRSPs. Donors have changed their processes through increased participation in budget support and streamlining performance monitoring.

Results focus: The development of country-specific indicators and monitoring systems to track them is still at a preliminary stage in most countries. The information gathered is generally not linked to decision making.

The Bank has effectively supported PRSP formulation, but alignment has not entailed major changes in Bank programs. Bank lending since the launch of the Initiative has increased for countries with PRSPs completed through 2003. The content of Bank assistance strategies formulated subsequent to PRSPs overlaps with the content of PRSPs. But since PRSP programs are broad and not well prioritized, this overlap has not entailed major changes for the Bank. The Bank has conducted more economic and sector work in PRSP countries than it did before the Initiative. But this additional work largely takes the form of fiduciary diagnostic studies. Critical gaps remain in linking policies and programs to poverty impact.

The Bank management's process for presenting a PRSP to the Board undermines ownership. Stakeholders perceive this practice as "Washington signing off" on a supposedly country-owned strategy. Joint Staff Assessments' analytical quality and coverage are mixed, and they are not widely shared with national stakeholders. These shortcomings limit their usefulness both as assessments of the PRSP as a basis for Bank support and as a feedback tool for the country.

Recommendations

To deepen the PRS process in existing PRSP countries—and its expansion to countries with more difficult policy environments—the Initiative requires reorientation along the lines noted below.

The Bank should emphasize ways of improving country processes for planning, implementing, and monitoring public actions geared toward poverty reduction, and place less emphasis on completion of documents. It should encourage countries to establish appropriate goals that are within current country capacity to monitor and use.

The Bank should develop a review procedure that is more supportive of ownership and more effectively linked to decisions about the Bank's program. Feedback to countries on their PRS processes should be transparent, comprehensive, and candid.

The Bank should help countries address key analytical gaps about the poverty impact of policies and programs. Analysis should address areas such as sources of growth, the quality of non-social- sector strategies, and the integration of the macro framework and structural and social reforms.

The Bank should assist countries in using the PRSP as a partnership framework by encouraging government-led aid management and selectivity, and should better integrate its own assistance with the efforts of other partners. The Bank should assist countries in improving the prioritization of their PRSPs, and demonstrate how the content of its programs has changed in light of these improved PRSPs.

(2) Evaluation of PRSP and PRGF by the IMF and the World Bank, January 31, 2003

The International Monetary Fund (IMF) and the World Bank (WB) adopted a new strategy to enhance the contribution of their interventions to international poverty reduction efforts for their assistance to low-income countries in 1999.

The main planks of this strategy were twofold:

(a) Both institutions were to base their concessional lending and debt relief to low-income countries on Poverty Reduction Strategy Papers (PRSPs) prepared by the countries themselves; and
(b) IMF concessional lending was to be provided through a revised lending facility, the Poverty Reduction and Growth Facility (PRGF) with a stronger poverty reduction focus.

Of the 77 countries that are eligible for the PRGF, 28 have produced interim PRSPs and another 23 have produced a full PRSP. Almost all of the latter countries are currently engaged in PRGF-supported programs. There should now be sufficient evidence on how the approach is working in practice for an independent evaluation to be undertaken, so as to allow at a still relatively early stage for any adaptations of the approach that might appear desirable. The evaluation was undertaken and will be undertaken by the Independent Evaluation Office (IEO) of the IMF and the Operations Evaluation Department (OED) of the World Bank.

The procedure for evaluation of Poverty Reduction Strategy Papers (PRSP) and Poverty Reduction and Growth Facility (PRGF) must include (a) background information, (b) main questions to be addressed for evaluation purposes and (c) methodological approaches. Necessarily the World Bank and the

International Monetary Fund have formulated a set of questions for the evaluators for the evaluation purposes.

Background Information

Objectives of PRSP and PRGF initiatives:

From 1987 to 1999, the bulk of IMF concessional lending was provided under the Enhanced Structural Adjustment Facility (ESAF). Internal and external evaluations conducted in 1997 and 1998, respectively, identified a number of problems that hindered the effectiveness of programs supported by this facility.

The external evaluation highlighted the following as major problem areas:

(a) Lack of national ownership;
(b) Weaknesses in the analytical and empirical bases of the social policy content of programs; and
(c) Insufficient attention to tradeoffs involving policy choices that imply significantly different paths for growth and social welfare.

Initially, after considering the lessons from the two reviews, the Executive Board endorsed several recommendations of IMF staff and the external evaluators aimed at strengthening the effectiveness of ESAF-supported programs. Subsequently, it became clear that bolder and broader steps were needed, in particular to ensure that debt relief under the enhanced HIPC Initiative—which was also agreed upon at that time—had a significant poverty reduction impact.

A new approach to supporting reform and adjustment programs in low-income countries was therefore developed by the staffs of the World Bank and the

IMF and subsequently endorsed by their respective Boards. The key element was to be the development by countries themselves of poverty reduction strategies, set out in a new vehicle: the Poverty Reduction Strategy Paper (PRSP). While stating clearly that the ultimate goal of the new policy was poverty reduction and the achievement of related international development goals, the initial policy framework did not spell out explicitly the objectives of PRSPs. The PRSP should aim at expected outputs and intermediate outcomes.

Primary outputs:

(a) Focused document laying out realistic but challenging poverty objectives, along with the policies needed to achieve them
(b) Suitable basis for IMF and World Bank concessional lending;
(c) Key instrument for low-income countries' relationships with the donor community

Intermediate outcomes:

(a) Development of participatory processes for the setting of poverty reduction goals and the monitoring of the implementation of poverty reduction strategies
(b) Improved understanding of links between policies and poverty reduction outcomes
(c) Setting of priorities and design of public actions to achieve poverty goals
(d) Development of appropriate diagnostics and indicators of progress in poverty reduction
(e) Deepening of a shared vision across civil society regarding poverty reduction strategy

The IMF Executive Board endorsed the Managing Director's proposal to transform the ESAF into the PRGF to complement this new tool. Prominent features that were to distinguish PRGF from ESAF-supported programs included:

(a) Broad participation and greater country ownership;
(b) Embedding the PRGF-supported program in a broader set of measures set out in an overall strategy for growth and poverty reduction;
(c) Government budgets that are more pro-poor and pro-growth
(d) Ensuring appropriate flexibility in fiscal targets;
(e) More selective structural conditionality;
(f) Emphasis on measures to improve public resource management /accountability; and
(g) Social impact analysis of macroeconomic adjustment and structural reforms

Regarding the PRSP

(a) Broad agreement among all stakeholders involved on the validity of the objectives of the PRSP approach and its usefulness in tackling poverty;
(b) General recognition that there have been improvements over time in PRSP process and content;
(c) Widespread agreements that the four key achievements of the PRSP approach to date are: A stronger sense of ownership among most governments; a more open dialogue; a prominent place for poverty reduction in policy debates; and an acceptance by the donor community of the principles of the PRSP approach.
(d) Focus should now shift beyond process to content and implementation; Hence the importance of improving knowledge of the linkages between policies and poverty outcomes; and Utilizing and building local capacity in core areas.

Areas that will need continuing attention are:

(a) Realism in the setting of goals and targets as well as in managing expectations;
(b) The importance of openness and transparency;
(c) The importance of flexibility, to allow for different country circumstances;
(d) The desirability of debate about alternative policy choices; and
(e) The importance of patience and perseverance with implementation

Problems identified in a significant number of cases include:

(a) The lack of involvement of specific groups, including Parliaments, in the participatory process;
(b) Unsatisfactory modalities for donor involvement (apart from the Bretton Woods Institutions);
(c) Lingering weaknesses in poverty data and analysis and in target setting;
(d) Lack of adequate poverty and social impact analyses;
(e) Lack of satisfactory monitoring indicators and/or institutional arrangements;
(f) Insufficient prioritization and specificity of public actions identified in PRSPs;
(g) Uneven coverage of cross-cutting issues such as gender, HIV/AIDS, good governance and rural development;
(h) Persistent weaknesses in public expenditure management systems and accountability in general;
(i) Uneven integration of the PRSP process into existing decision-making processes; and
(j) Need for more opportunities for learning and disseminating lessons and good practices.

While still refraining from providing strict directives as to the content of PRSPs and the implementation of the process, these internal reviews nonetheless identified a number of "good practices" in all the areas of the PRSP process.
Regarding the PRGF

In all three fundamental areas for change, namely program content, country ownership and the IMF' s role, there has been substantial progress, but more can be done. Areas of progress include consistency between the policy goals and macroeconomic frameworks of PRGF-supported programs and PRSPs, increased allocation of resources toward poverty reduction spending, streamlined structural conditionality and better coordination with the World Bank. More systematic incorporation of poverty and social impact assessments (PSIAs) into program design, increased efforts towards improving the quality and management of public spending, and a perceived need to encourage deeper and broader discussion and analysis of the macroeconomic framework and the policies in PRGF-supported programs with increasing focus on the analysis of the sources of growth are necessary to increase the scope for further improvements.

(3) Broad Questions for Preparation of PRSP

PRSP Process and IMF Inputs into It

1. To what extent are PRSPs country-driven documents in the areas of the IMF's primary responsibility? Specifically, does IMF involvement strike the right balance between providing need support and allowing the process to be genuinely driven by country authorities? Do the methodological tools provided by the IMF in its areas of expertise (e.g. the relevant sections of the PRSP Sourcebook) provide adequate guidance and allow sufficient scope for country-driven choices between alternative

policies? Is IMF policy advice (including in the Sourcebook) based on concrete evidence of the links between policies and growth/poverty reduction?

2. What is the nature of the IMF' s contribution to the participatory process, in particular, in terms of: (i) provision of information to the various stakeholders groups (ii) Interaction with the donor community and civil society. Is the process by which the macroeconomic framework of PRSPs is formulated participatory and, if not, what are the practical obstacles to a participatory approach on such issues?

3. In the areas within its mandate, does the IMF adequately assess the ability of countries to undertake an effective PRSP process? Does it include poverty and social impact analyses and what steps does it take—either directly or in coordination with other providers of technical assistance—to help countries strengthen their capacity for domestic policy formulation, implementation and monitoring?

PRGF process

4. Has the process of program formulation changed under the PRGF? Does it study (i) the IMF's own internal procedures (including the cycle of missions); (ii) the scope, depth, and transparency of IMF staff interactions with various stakeholders (including line ministries, parliaments, private sector, the poor, CSOs, and donors); and (iii) the analytical basis of the macroeconomic framework? In particular, how are poverty/social impact assessments (PSIA) incorporated into the design of the policy framework and what are the obstacles to greater uses of PSIA? Where the PRGF program was preceded by a PRSP, was it clearly derived from the former?

PRSP Contents

5. In the areas of the IMF' s primary responsibility, to what extent do PRSPs have the general components expected from them, including an analysis of the impact on growth and income distribution of past macroeconomic and related structural policies, a robust macroeconomic framework, along with related priority public actions and a credible financing plan?

6. Do PRSPs improve the clarity of policy choices in the macroeconomic and budgetary areas by providing realistic goals and projections, an analysis of the costs and benefits of alternative policy options and the tradeoffs between them, and a suitable prioritized plan of actions?

7. In the areas of the IMF's primary responsibility, do PRSPs provide a framework suitably linked to implementation, including monitoring arrangements and feedback mechanisms? While taking into account the expanded time horizon over which their results will be seen, are PRSPs also sufficiently connected to shorter-term policy-making instruments (in particular the budget and the medium-term expenditure framework), so as to provide a framework within which a PRGF-supported program can be derived?

Joint Staff Assessment

8. Are JSAs clear and candid in their assessments of suitability of PRSPs as a basis for IMF concessional lending? How are inputs from other stakeholders handled in making such assessments?

9. What is the assessment of the usefulness of JSAs by: (i) country authorities? (ii) The Executive Board? (iii) Other PRSP stakeholders? To what extent do JSAs play a signaling role of their own to aid donors?
PRGF-Supported Program Design / content

10. To what extent do PRGF-supported programs incorporate the key features intended to differentiate

them from ESAF-supported ones? In particular, to what extent are these programs aligned on PRSPs, in terms of their macroeconomic framework, targets and policy objectives, linkage and support to budgetary processes, and use of monitoring indicators? Is program design influenced by PSIAs?

11. Is streamlined structural conditionality suitably prioritized in PRGF-supported programs to those actions judged critical to successful implementation of macroeconomic policy? Is the World Bank's conditionality taken into account in that process? What has happened to the aggregate level of conditionality and how are gaps and overlaps between the agendas and priorities of both institutions handled?

12. Are program targets and underlying projections realistic (and consistent with the World Bank's assumptions)? Are they set in sufficiently flexible terms for timely adaptation in case of unexpected shocks (be they positive or negative)?

13. How are external financing requirements derived in PRGF-supported programs? How are these estimates linked to the longer-term objectives set out in PRSPs, including debt sustainability? How is the tradeoff between accommodating the higher spending plans embedded in PRSPs and preserving/progressing toward macroeconomic stability being handled in PRGF-supported programs?

Institutional Effects

14. In macroeconomic and related areas, are PRSPs contributing to substantial improvements in domestic policy formulation and implementation? For example, are they contributing to improvements in the analytical bases (including relationships between macroeconomic and related structural policies and poverty outcomes, monitoring tools etc.) for policy

debates and economic policy decisions? In particular, do the monitoring and evaluation arrangements provided for in PRSPs effectively feed back to policy formulation in these areas?

15. Are PRSPs linked to countries' budgets and public expenditure management frameworks on a permanent, institutionalized basis, as an integral part of domestic policy formulation?

16. Have the various institutional arrangements surrounding PRSPs brought about a closer, more effective collaboration between the IMF and the World Bank (including in their analytical work and setting of priorities for their respective country operations)? What has been the performance of the Joint Implementation Committee (JIC) in that respect?

Impact on Economic Policy and Preliminary Evidence on Outcomes

17. How has the PRSP process affected the nature and scope of the policy debate, within the country and between the country and the IMF, as well as policy outcomes on key issues that are in the IMF's primary area of responsibility? How has PRGF-supported program implementation been affected? For example, what changes in policies have resulted from a more country-driven process?

18. What can be said of the evolution of expenditure composition parameter vis-à-vis suitable comparing group(s), looking at both budget allocations and actual spending? What has been the impact on tax structure/budgetary process and public expenditure management frameworks? What do the intermediate indicators used to monitor progress towards the MDGs suggest (focusing on those indicators that are most relevant to the IMF's role)?

19. While it is too early for a systematic assessment of the impact of the PRSP/PRGF on final objectives, the evaluation will collect what evidence is available on the evolution of various program outcomes (e.g. GDP growth and key macro indicators) compared, for example, with earlier ESAF-supported programs.

Architecture and design of the PRSP/PRGF initiatives

The evaluation will also address several issues involving the design and architecture of the PRSP/PRGF approach, in order to assess its relevance and sustainability with respect to the ultimate objectives. Taking into account the parallel evaluation by the OED the goal would not be to examine all questions involving the overall architecture, but to address some specific questions concerning the IMF's role:

20. Does IMF staffs receive sufficiently clear guidance from both internal and public policy documents regarding: (i) their involvement in the PRSP process? (ii) For formulation of PRGF-supported program (iii) the depth and modalities of their collaboration with World Bank staff? Is staff consistent with a uniform face the supporting institutional arrangements and the incentives and effective delivery of the promises embedded in the PRSP/PRGF approach as far as the IMF is concerned?

21. Are the IFI's expectations regarding the PRSP spelled out clearly enough for PRSPs to provide an effective, operational strategic policy framework for poverty reduction and a vehicle for effective donor coordination?

22. Are the functions of the JSA process and the IMF's role in it appropriate? In particular, does the need to gain JSA endorsement lead to a form of self-censorship on the part of countries? Should changes be envisaged to the JSAs, e.g., by making them more

inclusive of other stakeholders' views, so as to make judgments on PRSPs less of a "Washington thing" while providing a frank and clear assessment?

23. What actions could/should the IMF take, within its mandate and area of expertise (e.g., as part of its broader surveillance role), to link the PRSP objectives with policies in the advanced economies that would improve the external economic environment faced by the PRSP countries?

24.What does the evaluation suggest regarding what should be the long-run role of the IMF—and the PRGF in particular—in relation to the PRSP process in countries: (i) with no immediate short term balance of payments need? (ii) With clear short-term balance of payments needs but where the poverty reduction strategy or its implementation is judged inadequate? In those cases, what suggestions emerge from the evaluation about what would be a suitable strategy for IMF involvement and what functions should the IMF perform in those cases, based on its comparative advantage?

(4) Envisaged Methodological Approach

The evaluation will follow a three-tier approach consisting of:

(a) In-depth cases studies
(b) Crosscutting analyses of the full sample of countries with a full PRSP
(c) Control-type analyses.

The case studies will contribute to answering all the questions, while cross country or institution-wide analyses will be undertaken to test how generalized findings from the case studies are, and to provide additional evidence on each set of issues. The matrix presented in provides a summary mapping of key tasks and methodologies envisaged tackling them.

The case studies would involve both deskwork (including reviews of relevant IMF documentation, both published and unpublished, as well as reviews of external evaluative evidence) and field work. They would seek the views of all relevant stakeholders (country authorities including line ministries and parliaments, civil society, donors and IMF and World Bank staff) through a combination of interviews and surveys. They would place particular emphasis on analyzing changes in the nature of the policy debate by following through a few critical policy issues in each country and assessing how their treatment has evolved under the PRSP/PRGF initiative

Control-type analyses are also envisaged, essentially of two sorts: first, broad-based statistical analyses of the full sample of PRGF-eligible countries, in order to compare the performance of program versus non program countries, PRSP versus non PRSP countries and ESAF versus PRGF-programs. Second, tentatively, a desk review of a small number of PRGF-eligible countries that chose not to engage in the PRSP process may be undertaken, in order to highlight any differences in the process of policy formulation and in actual policy choices and outcomes compared to PRSP countries. There are obvious problems of sample-selection bias in any choice of such a limited control group, but it may highlight some useful qualitative messages.

The modalities for cooperation between the IEO and the OED on their respective evaluations will be guided by the following broad principles. These are:

(a). Each institution will produce its own evaluation report in keeping with its own procedures, and these reports will be presented to their respective Boards; and

(b) The inputs to the evaluations will be organized in such a way as to avoid duplication of demands on member countries (with respect to country case studies). Joint case studies are expected to involve, inter alias, joint country missions and a common stakeholder survey, as well as single country reports.[146]

(5) Joint World Bank and IMF Report on PRSP
Progress in Implementation, February 2, 2005

The PRS approach was intended to be country-driven, results-oriented, comprehensive, partnership-based and with a long-term perspective on development and poverty reduction. The aim of the 2005 PRS Review is to provide a framework for more systematically considering progress in PRS implementation and undertake an analysis to assess progress to date. The 2005 PRS Review focused on five themes identified through discussion with stakeholders and reviewed the literature that is central to the effectiveness of the PRS approach. The key questions included for addressing the review were necessary for considering the progress, challenges and good practice related to a set of note outlines for conducting the review. This exercise was made for the UN Summit on implementing the Millennium Declaration. The PRS Review established direct causal links between poverty outcomes and the PRS approach, given the vulnerability of most PRS countries to exogenous factors and the persistent shortcomings of monitoring and evaluation systems.

These themes are:

(a) Strengthening the medium term orientation of the PRS
(b) Framing development goals
(c) Setting the stage for increased aid

---

[146]IMF – Independent Evaluation Office of the IMF (January 31, 2003)

(d) Building systems to support evidence-based decision making
(e) Possible areas for recommendations / future action

Utilizing the PRS as a mutual accountability frame work between countries and donors

(a) Building capacity
(b) Supporting analysis
(c) Improving aid alignment, conditionality and volume
(d) Architecture changes
(e) Assisting in coordination
(f) Possible areas for recommendations / future action
(g) Broadening and deepening meaningful participation
(h) Involving stakeholders
(i) Opening up the space for dialogue
(j) Sustaining participation
(k) Influencing programs
(l) Possible areas for recommendations / future action

Enhancing linkages between the PRS, the MTEF, and budgets

(a) Using domestic processes
(b) Allocating resources
(c) Defining financing plans
(d) Building capacity
(e) Possible areas for recommendations / future action
(f) Tailoring the PRS approach to conflict-affected and fragile states
(g) Assessing relevance
(h) Tailoring content
(i) Applying PRS principles

Possible areas for recommendations/ future action[147]

Of the countries engaged in the PRSP, the World Bank considers 25 as conflict-affected, while many others have social and economic conditions that put them at risk of conflicts escalating into large-scale violence. The World Bank, in collaboration with the British Department for International Development (DFID) and other partners, has embarked on a working program aiming to ensure effective poverty reduction in conflict-affected countries. All reports should include the possibility of reducing poverty and hunger within a specified period.

(6) The World Bank:

Full Debt Cancellation Approved for Some of the World's Poorest Countries, July 2005

At the July 2005, G8 Summit in Gleneagles, Scotland, and the G8 leaders pledged to cancel the debt of the world's most indebted countries, most of which are located in Africa. The International Development Association (IDA) of the World Bank, the International Monetary Fund and the African Development Fund will provide debt cancellation to countries that have reached completion point from the Enhanced Heavily Indebted Poor Countries (HIPC) Initiative. Initially, 17 HIPC countries will be eligible for 100 percent debt cancellation: Benin, Bolivia, Burkina Faso, Ethiopia, Ghana, Guyana, Honduras, Madagascar, Mali, Mozambique, Nicaragua, Niger, Rwanda, Senegal, Tanzania, Uganda and Zambia. Mauritania has completed the HIPC program, but will qualify for relief after implementing key public-expenditure management reforms. The remaining HIPC countries will be eligible for debt cancellation

[147]Concept Note, Joint World Bank and IMF Report on: Poverty Reduction Strategy Papers – Progress in Implementation, 2005 PRS Review, February 2, 2005

once they have completed the requirements of the HIPC Initiative.

Donors have agreed to a financing package that calls for additional donor contributions over time to ensure delivery of fresh resources for poverty reduction. Compensatory financing over the duration of the cancelled loans will be based on strong indicative pledges already made, and donors are undertaking the necessary steps in their home countries to provide their financing commitments. The World Bank has provided debt relief to low-income countries through the joint World Bank and IMF Debt Initiative for Heavily Indebted Poor Countries (HIPC Initiative), which started in 1996. Two-thirds of Heavily Indebted Poor Countries (HIPCs, 29 countries) are receiving debt relief, which will amount to US$59 billion in lower debt service payments over time. The World Bank's contribution to the HIPC Initiative for the 29 countries approved so far is expected to be about US$14 billion over time.[148]

Through the 1980s and early 1990s, lending continued to fund policy reforms in the hope these countries could grow their way out of trouble. But, for a number of reasons, including policy decisions of the governments involved, the expectations of increased growth failed to materialize. By 1992, the 33 nations identified as the most severely indebted low-income countries faced a massive debt-servicing crisis. In 1992, the net present value (NPV) of debt-to-export ratio – a measure of a country's ability to repay foreign borrowings - had increased to 620 percent from 266 percent 10 years earlier. The current threshold for debt relief under the HIPC Initiative is an NPV of debt-to-export ratio of 150 percent or NPV of debt-to-revenue ratio of 250 percent.

---

[148] For more information on debt, see http://www.worldbank.org/debt, Updated April 2006

The original scheme called for an eligible country to have a three-year track record of strong performance on a series of measures – such as economic stabilization programs, public sector reforms (including restructuring or privatization of loss-making state enterprises), and targeting of public spending toward poverty reduction, health, and education – before it would qualify for debt relief. Analysis used to project debt and growth levels. It also noted the need to manage the expectations of what the Initiative can achieve directly and how it relates to the broader efforts of the Bank and the international community to help these countries to achieve sustained growth and poverty reduction.

(7) HIPC Initiative Progress Report

The HIPC Initiative provides a comprehensive debt relief to the 40 (of which 33 are in Africa) most heavily indebted countries pursuing adjustment and reform programs, after they have reached their decision and completion points. The overall cost of the HIPC debt relief committed for the 29 African countries that have already reached decision or completion point, is estimated to US $35.7 billon, in NPV terms. The Bank Group's share is US$3.6 billion, equivalent to 10.2 percent of the total HIPC debt relief from all creditors. Debt relief from World Bank and IMF are respectively US $9.3 billion and US $2.1 billion in NPV terms, accounting for 25.9 percent and 6.0 percent of the total debt relief respectively.

Completion Point Countries (20)

As at end March 2009, twenty (20) Regional Member Countries (RMCs) such as Benin, Burkina Faso, Burundi, Cameroon, Ethiopia, Gambia, Ghana, Madagascar, Malawi, Mali, Mauritania, Mozambique, Niger, Sao Tome & Principe, Senegal, Sierra Leone, Rwanda, Tanzania, Uganda, and Zambia had reached their completion points under the HIPC initiative. A total of US$19.2 billion of irrevocable debt relief has been committed to these countries. The Bank Group's share of the HIPC assistance is US $2.0 billion, while that of the World Bank is US $6.8 billion. Central African Republic is expected to reach its completion points by end December 2009.

Decision –point Countries (9)

Nine decision-point countries, such as Central African Republic, Chad, Congo Republic, Cote d'Ivoire, Democratic Republic of Congo, Guinea, Guinea Bissau, Liberia, and Togo are in the interim period, ie, between the completion and decision point. Cote d'Ivoire is the latest RMC to reach decision point in March 2009. As a result, the Bank Group's debt relief assistance to Cote d'Ivoire is estimated to US$199.5 million, in end-December 2007 NPV terms. The Bank Group has already delivered its full share of HIPC assistance through its arrears clearance operation in March 2009. As such, there will be no further interim debt relief from the Bank Group under the HIPC initiative.

The Bank Group's interim assistance limit is normally capped at 40 percent of the relief committed at the decision point. Under exceptional circumstances, the HIPC debt relief limit during the interim period could be increased to provide incentives for the timely implementation of reform programs. For example, the interim debt relief limits for Guinea Bissau and Guinea have been increased on their provision of relief by the Boards in July 2008. The interim debt relief assistance was raised to 50 percent and to 60 percent of the relief committed at the decision point for Guinea and Guinea-Bissau, respectively.

Pre-decision point countries (4)

Furthermore, four pre-decision point countries, such as Comoros, Eritrea, Somalia, and Sudan are eligible, but they have not yet qualified for HIPC initiative. The Bank Group provides an opportunity for arrears clearance operation for pre-decision-point RMCs through its Fragile States Facility (FSF, previously PCCF) under the HIPC Initiative. The arrears cleared through the FSF are counted as the Bank Group's expected debt relief. Since 2000, the Bank Group has cleared the arrears for Burundi, Central African Republic, Comoros, Cote d'Ivoire, Republic of Congo, Democratic Republic of Congo, Liberia, and Togo prior to their decision points.

In short, as at March 2009, the total debt relief cost due to the 33 Regional Member Countries (RMCs) eligible to the HIPC Initiative from the Bank Group is estimated at US$3.9 billion in NPV terms, equivalent to about US$5.8 billion, in nominal terms. Nearly half of the cost (US$2.0 billion, in NPV terms) represents irrevocable debt relief to the 20 post-completion-point countries. The cost for the 9 interim countries amounts to US$1.7 billion. The estimated cost of the HIPC Initiative debt relief to the remaining 4 pre-decision-point HIPCs is estimated to be US$0.2 billion.

With regard to the financing of the HIPC debt relief initiative, the Bank Group has agreed with the HIPC Trust Fund on the following arrangements. The HIPC Trust Fund will fund the entire interim relief. The HIPC Trust Fund makes annual payments to the special account opened for this purpose by the Bank from which the debt relief payments are made. The contribution from the Bank Group HIPC account and the HIPC Trust Fund represents respectively 20 percent and 80 percent of the estimated debt relief assistance to the beneficiary countries. At end-December 2008, the total resources mobilized for the Bank Group through the HIPC Trust Fund amounted to US$2.5 billion.

To date, the HIPC Trust Fund has adequate resources to meet entire contribution for irrevocable and interim debt relief assistance to the countries that have reached their completion and decision points, respectively. However, the HIPC Trust Fund will need about US$1.4 billion of new cash inflows to cover its contribution for overall debt relief to the 33 HIPC African countries.[149]

(8) Sunset Clause of December 31, 2007

In 2004, when the deadline was extended to end-2006, the Executive Boards of the Bank and IMF decided the initiative to new entrants by 'ring fencing' a final list of countries potentially eligible for assistance under the initiative. In September 2005, eight (8) more potentially eligible low-income countries were identified in addition to 38 countries enlisted earlier. In addition, three countries that technically meet the income and indebtedness criteria at end-2004 have indicated that they do not want to avail themselves of the Initiative. These countries are: Bhutan, Lao PDR and Sri Lanka. The Boards on a case-by-case basis, whose data are verified to meet the relevant 2004 thresholds, can extend the Sunset Clause.

(9) Debt-Forgiveness as Imperialism

The G8 relief deal is actually a paltry and niggardly reduction of a small part of a debt that has to grow to gigantic proportions more because of adding on unpaid interest than because of any recent flows of fresh resources. And this pathetic amount is being traded for yet more concession made by the debtor countries, in terms of sweeping and extensive privatisation of public services and utilities, which is about all that is left for governments to sell in these

---

[149] IMF External Relations Department

countries, as well as large increase in indirect taxes which fall disproportionately on the poor.

Some analysts write '**aid as imperialism',** some say '**debt-forgiveness as imperialism'**, yet some others say that it is not naked as violence, but disguised as **charity and empathy for the oppressed**, and when the rest of the world is made to applaud the benevolent concern expressed by the great powers.

The G8 countries decided a continuance of HIPC initiative, which insisted upon the imposition and intensification of heavily neo-liberal policies that have ravaged poor debtor countries.

Privatization of natural resources and strategic economic sectors are for the benefit of large multinational corporations; it simply divides the world.

Higher cost of health care and education, directly affects the access of the poor to these basic socio-economic rights.

Increase in VAT, a regressive tax, which means increased costs and lower real incomes of common people.

Free flow of capital leads to great volatility of exchange rates and capital flight by the elite.

Lower tariff protection leads to thousands of small and middle producers losing their livelihoods as they cannot compete with imported goods.

It is not hard to see that this is a deal designed to further the economic interests of imperialism, which has once again been sold across the world as a huge concession made to the worlds poor. A poet said, "After such knowledge, what forgiveness?"[150]

Conclusion

Debt servicing absorbs budgetary and foreign exchange reserves. It reduces government spending on agriculture, health, education and social services. Moreover, the servicing of debt by the Heavily Indebted Poor Countries forces the government to squeeze the number of employees as it fails to pay their salary. Further, this causes corruption to flourish in all government departments. There is moral breakdown of government machinery and among citizens of debtor countries. The external debt, which aims at welfare and economic development of LDCs, results in debt overhang, devaluation, corruption, high child mortality, morality degradation, and unemployment, increase of rich–poor gap, terrorism and administrative failure. However, HIPC Initiative is a step not only to reduce debt burden but also to foster sustainable growth of low-income countries.

Debt relief seems to be a dubious and politically motivated program.

The IMF and the World Bank[151] assess the following conditions for awarding debt relief. These are:

(a) The country must face unsustainable debt burden
(b) It has to establish a tract record of reforms and sound policies through IMF and World Bank supported programs, and
(c) Must prepare a PRSP through a broad-based participatory process.

---

[150] Jayati Ghosh, 'Debt Forgiveness as Imperialism", IDEAS, News Analysis, July 28, 2005
[151] Press Release No: 2006 / 370 / PREM Contacts, WASHINGTON, April 21, 2006

The sanction of debt relief is based up on a report, which includes debt sustainability, policy performance, poverty reduction, and credit participation, future debt relief measures for the recipient country. Moreover, the applicant country submits reports on background information of the country, human development, macro-economic policy, trade, and stakeholder participation, PRSP monitoring indicators and assessment, and resource mobilization. The funding institutions need information on PRSP status, policy performance, and creditor participation, social and structural completion triggers and reports on decision and completion points.

The World Bank announced on April 21, 2006 that the Multilateral Debt Relief Initiative has been approved, clearing the way for cancellation of International Development Association (IDA) debt to some of the world's poorest countries. Starting on July 1, 2006, IDA is expected to provide more than US $37 billion in debt relief over 40 years.

Countries are now able to put more resources into programs that directly help those who need it most – the poor who need better education, better health services and greater access to clean water. This press release clearly explains that debt relief would continue for 40 years. Debt relief program is daily covered in newspapers, media, and speeches, Internets through out the entire globe as people of 54 low-income countries and 58 low-middle-income countries are in extreme need of debt relief. The HIPC program has started since the last 11 years, yet the reports are being written each year to know the status of progress of implementation. The IMF and World Bank prepare separate Joint Staff Assessments (JSAs) of the poor countries, which desire IMF / World Bank credit. The IMF and World Bank have participated in 148 Poverty Reduction Strategy Papers (PRSPs) and Interim PRSPs. Both organizations have also produced 26 related policy papers and 11 other PRSP related documents till November 11, 2004. Within the last five years, many more reports have also been prepared. Moreover, the World Bank regularly publishes PRSP newsletter. As the debt relief program would continue for a minimum period of 40 years (may be further extended to a half-century?).

In short, Debt relief program covers from grandfather to grandson.

If the donors, bilateral organizations, multilateral organizations, and G-8 are really interested to assist the hungry mouths of the world, they can individually and/or jointly issue a 'White Paper' on debt accrued to the low-income countries as on **December 31, 2015** and declare 100 percent debt relief as 'One Time Settlement' for these 54 countries. (Annex – 1)

Similarly, as a second proposal, the creditor countries and organizations should consider debt accrued to the low-middle-income countries as on **December 31, 2016** and declare 100 percent debt relief as **'One Time Settlement'** for these 58 countries. By the process of granting DEBT RELIEF, the developed countries would really assist the poor countries economically, politically and legally; and would not indirectly encourage terrorism, and a war among rich and poor countries.

DEBT RELIEF is a peaceful and the most effective attempt for achieving global peace.

When the G8 countries bear farming subsidies of $350 billion to their farmers and spend $900 billion on defense expenditure annually, the G8 can safely award 100 percent debt relief to the low-income countries. These countries should also consider debt relief to 58 low-middle-income countries. The debtor countries opine that the creditor countries would sacrifice only the interest portion of the borrowed funds provided they consider the amounts paid through installments for debt service as principal amounts. This should be the right approach and right time to assist the poor people of the low and least developed countries.

Justice Delayed is Justice Denied.

Each developed country, creditor organization, international funding institution, and members of Paris club or London club, or multilateral funding institution can take a decision separately or jointly on debt relief for the benefit of more than ONE BILLION PEOPLE, who are hungry, and another TWO BILLION PEOPLE, who are poor.

Debt Relief should not be used as a political propaganda; it is simply a humanitarian approach to solve the greatest problem of the world.

100 percent debt relief by the rich countries and rich organizations would not hamper their economic strength as they have already received back their invested capital through installments. The donors would loose only the cumulative interest amount on the principal.

Now, the ball is in the court of the rich nations. Let them affirm 100 percent debt relief.

+++++

Chapter- V

INTERNATIONAL FORUMS FAVOUR DEBT RELIEF

We will spare no effort to free our fellow men, women and children from the abject and dehumanizing conditions of extreme poverty, to which more than a billion of them are currently subjected. We are committed to making the right to development a reality for every one and to freeing the entire human race from want.

United Nations Millennium Declaration

World peace is trampled through hunger; poverty and debt overhang in most of the low-income and lower-middle-income countries. So the United Nations General Assembly set out a new global vision for humanity and recognized 'collective responsibility to uphold the principles of human dignity, equality and equity at the global level. They pledged to 'spare no effort to free our fellow men, women and children from abject and dehumanizing conditions of extreme poverty.[152]

The Millennium Development Goals aims to halve world poverty by the year 2015; to achieve universal primary education; to promote gender equality and empower women; to reduce child mortality; improve maternal health; to combat HIV / AIDs and other diseases; and to ensure environmental sustainability. Since then the MDGs have been adopted by all major donor agencies as guiding principles for their strategies for poverty eradication. The UN Millennium Declaration was not the only remarkable event of the year 2000. Equally notable – though perhaps more poignant – was the winding down of the Jubilee 2000 campaign, described by Kofi Annan as 'the voice of the world's conscience and indefatigable fighters for justice'. The Jubilee 2000 coalition had campaigned for the cancellation of the un-payable debts of the poorest countries by the end of 2000, under a fair and transparent process. Their petition – the largest ever – had been signed by 24 million people worldwide.[153]

In this chapter, the suggestions of the Peoples Millennium Forum, South Asian Association for Regional Cooperation Commonwealth Civil Society, Commonwealth HIPC Ministerial Forum, Bangkok Recommendations, and Commonwealth Ministerial Debt Sustainability Forum have been incorporated for the purpose eradicating poverty and hunger. The representatives of World Bank, International Monetary Fund, and UK also participated in the deliberations. All of these international forums have advocated and emphasized the need of debt relief for

---

[152] United Nations Millennium Declaration, Resolution 55/2
[153] Greenhill, R (2002), "The unbreakable link – debt relief and the millennium development goals", Jubilee Research, at the New Economics Foundation, London, pp29

fighting against hunger and poverty. These are as follows:

(A). Peoples Millennium Forum:

Declaration and Agenda for Action Strengthening the United Nations for the 21st Century, 22-26 May 2000

The United Nations organized the Peoples Millennium Forum at the UN headquarters in New York from 22 – 26 May 2000. 1,350 representatives of over 1,000 non-governmental organizations (NGOs) and other civil society organizations from more than 100 countries attended the conference to build upon a common vision. The resolutions adopted at civil society conferences in 1990's and the UN world conferences of the 1990's were again discussed to draw the attention of governments to the urgency of implementing the commitments they have made, and to channel collective energies by reclaiming globalization for and by the people.

The representatives of People's Millennium Forum adopted their vision of a world that is human-centered and genuinely democratic, where all human beings are full participants and determine their own destinies. All the people of the world belong to one human family, in all diversity, living on one common homeland and sharing a just, sustainable and peaceful world, guided by universal principles of democracy, equality, inclusion, voluntarism, non-discrimination and participation by all persons, men and women, young and old, regardless of race, faith, disability, sexual orientation, ethnicity or nationality. It is a world where peace and human security, as envisioned in the principles of the United Nations Charter, replace armaments, violent conflict and wars. It is a world where everyone lives in a clean environment with a fair distribution of the earth's resources. The vision includes a special role for the dynamism of young people and the experience of the elderly and reaffirms the universality, indivisibility and interdependence of all human rights – civil, political, economic, social and cultural.

The Challenges:

The people begin the new millennium facing grave and interconnected challenges. As actors in the struggle for peace, justice and the eradication of poverty, NGOs encounter daily the human impact of rising violence and armed conflicts, widespread violations of human rights, and unacceptably large numbers of people who are denied the means of a minimal human existence. At the same time, new and emerging diseases such as HIV/AIDS threaten to devastate entire societies.

Globalization and advances in technology create significant opportunities for people to connect, share and learn from each other. At the same time, corporate-driven globalization increases inequities between and within countries, undermines local traditions and cultures, and escalates disparities between rich and poor, thereby marginalizing large numbers of people in urban and rural areas. Women, indigenous peoples, youth, boys and girls, and people with disabilities suffer disproportionately from the effects of globalization. Massive debt repayments are still made by the poorest nations to the richest, at the expense of basic healthcare, education and children's lives. Trafficking in women, sexual exploitation, drug trafficking, money laundering, corruption and the flow of small arms promote insecurity. States are becoming weaker, while an unaccountable, transnational private sector grows stronger. A single-minded focus on economic growth through uncontrolled free markets, combined with the adjustment and stabilization policies of international financial institutions controlled by the rich creditor nations are crippling many national economies, exacerbating poverty, eroding human values and destroying the natural environment.

Globalization should be made to work for the benefit of everyone: eradicate poverty and hunger globally; establish peace globally; ensure the protection and promotion of human rights globally; ensure the protection of global environment; enforce social standards in the workplace globally.... This can happen only if global corporations, international financial and trade institutions and governments are subject to effective democratic control by the people. The Peoples Millennium Forum sees a strengthened and democratized United Nations and a vibrant civil society as guarantors of this accountability. And they issue a warning: if the architects of globalization are not held to account, this will not simply be unjust; the edifice will crumble with dire consequences for everyone. In the end, the wealthy will find no refuge, as intolerance, disease, environmental devastation, war, social disintegration and political instability spread.

The Peoples Millennium Forum wishes to put forward a series of concrete steps to strengthen cooperation among all actors at the international, national, regional and local levels to make this vision a reality. Their Agenda for Action includes steps that should be taken by civil society, governments, and the United Nations.

These are as follows:

(a) Eradication of Poverty: including social development and debt cancellation
(b) Peace, Security, and Disarmament
(c) Facing the challenge of globalization: equity, justice and diversity
(d) Human Rights
(e) Sustainable development and the Environment
(f) Strengthening and Democratizing the United Nations and International organizations

However, in this chapter only the first important objective has been presented as this section refers to Eradication of Poverty: including social development and debt cancellation.

Eradication of Poverty

Poverty is a violation of human rights. With 1.3 billion people living in extreme poverty, it is the biggest widespread violation of human rights in the world. Poverty exists not only in the developing countries, but is also a dramatic and hidden reality in the industrialized countries. Particularly affected are disadvantaged and underrepresented groups - indigenous people, people with disabilities, women, children, youth, and the elderly. Hunger and the HIV/AIDS pandemic are also highly related to poverty. Processes of impoverishment inherent in the global economic system are resulting in increasing inequity, social injustice and violence worldwide.

Eradication of poverty has become a matter of urgency. Poverty eradication is not an automatic consequence of economic growth; it requires purposeful action to redistribute wealth and land, to construct a safety net and to provide universal free access to education. The Peoples Millennium Forum calls on all governments, and the United Nations to make poverty eradication a top political priority.

The Forum urges the United Nations to take up the following suggestions:

(a). To act as an independent arbitrator to balance the interest of debtor and creditor nations and to monitor how debt cancellation funds are spent.

(b)To introduce binding codes of conduct for transnational companies, and effective tax regulation on the international financial markets, investing this money in programs for poverty eradication.

(c). To immediately establish at the United Nations, a Global Poverty Eradication Fund, which will ensure that poor people have access to credit, with contributions from governments, corporations, and the World Bank and other sources

(d). To adopt cultural development as the focus theme of one of the remaining years of the International Decade for the Eradication of Poverty (1996-2007)

The Forum urges **the Governments** to take up the following suggestions. These are:

To implement fully the commitments made at the World Summit for Social Development in 1995, in partnership with all actors of civil society in an integrated and holistic framework. Governments should focus their efforts and policies on addressing the root causes of poverty and providing for the basic needs of all, giving special priority to the needs and rights of disadvantaged and underrepresented. We further call on the governments to anchor the Copenhagen goals in their national statutes and to introduce national anti-poverty strategies that provide safety nets and basic livelihood allocation as a right.

(a) To strengthen the entrepreneurial capacity of women, indigenous people and people in the informal productive sector, ensuring access to credit, to enable them to become self-employed. This is the sure way of creating jobs for all and a sustainable way of eradicating poverty.

(b) To support the efforts of the poor to keep families together, with particular attention to disadvantaged and underrepresented groups including indigenous people, people with disabilities, women, children, youth, and the elderly. Effective action and resources are essential for those affected by migration.

(c) To address the incidence, impact and continuing human costs of HIV/AIDS. To increase spending for health research and to ensure that the fruits of this research reach the people

(d) To recognize the special potential of people with disabilities and ensure their full participation and equal role in political, economic, social and cultural fields

(e). To further recognize and meet their special needs, introduce inclusive policies and programs for their empowerment, and ensure that they take a leading role in poverty eradication. To urge all states to apply the UN standard rules on the equalization of opportunities for persons with disabilities.

(f) To review, adopt and maintain macro-economic policies and development strategies that address the needs and efforts of women in poverty, particularly those with disabilities. To develop gender-based methodologies to address the feminization of poverty and to recognize the leading role of women in eradicating poverty, as outlined in the declaration of the Fourth World Conference on Women in Beijing.

(g) To provide universal access to "education for all," prioritizing free basic education and skills training for poor communities to improve their productive capacities. We call on governments to increase budgets for education, to reduce the technology gap, and to restructure educational policy to ensure that all children (girls and boys) receive moral, spiritual, peace and human rights education, while acknowledging, through programs for families, adult literacy and the elderly, that education is a lifelong process. Special attention must be paid to the girl child. And higher education must be attainable on merit and not only on ability to pay.

(h). To move towards economic reforms aimed at equity: in particular, to construct macro economic policies that combine growth with the goal of human development and social justice; to prevent the impoverishment of groups that emerged from poverty but are still vulnerable to social risks and exclusion; to improve legislation on labor standards including the provision of a minimum legal wage and an effective social system; and to restore people's control over primary productive resources as a key strategy for poverty eradication.

(i) To introduce and implement programs to eradicate corruption in governments and civil society at large, and to promote good governance, accountability, democracy and transparency as the foundation for public ethics.

(j) To adopt comprehensive, integrated policies so that priorities of such government departments as trade and defense are in line with the policies for international sustainable development.

(k) To promote the use of indigenous crops and traditional production skills to produce goods and services

(l) To explore the feasibility of a legally binding Convention for Overcoming Poverty, to be drafted in effective consultation and partnership with people living in poverty themselves.

(m) To cancel the debts of developing countries, including odious debts, the repayment of which diverts funds from basic needs.

(n) To improve measures to ensure that funds from debt cancellation are spent in consultation with the impoverished sections of society within the indebted nations. To direct international financial institutions to cancel 100 per cent of the debt owed to them and to establish an arbitration process that balances the interests of debtor and creditor nations, with an independent arbitrator who will ensure discipline and transparency.

(o). To call the World Trade Organization (WTO) to rectify urgently, the agriculture agreements that put pressure on developing countries to liberalize food imports, threatening their rural livelihoods, employment, natural resources, indigenous knowledge and food production and security in general.

The Forum urges **Civil Society** to take up the following suggestions:

(a) To monitor and pressure governments to ensure that all the ten commitments made at the World Summit on Social Development become a reality for all.
(b) To assume responsibilities to help formulate and implement the national strategies for poverty eradication and to ensure the participation of the poor and marginalized communities
(c) To create or strengthen mechanisms to monitor organizations that work against the interests of the poor.
(d) To develop new relations and partnerships among community institutions, educators, scientists, researchers, local authorities, businesses, labor and NGOs in a constructive dialogue and planning process so that all can contribute their best. To pay special attention to those who have suffered most from poverty and to those who have the least opportunity to be heard by others. The poor must see themselves as real partners and must be empowered to enhance and employ their own abilities and resources in order to be of service

to themselves, their families, their communities and their common home.

(e) To exert our best efforts to implement the Universal Declaration of Human Rights - affirming the universality, indivisibility and interdependence of ALL rights, civil, political, social, economic and cultural - and to join the global movement for human dignity.

(f) To improve conditions for decent work, capacity building and participation

(g) To encourage the media to help monitor the commitments that governments have made.

(h) To dedicate attention to the special needs of the young and the elderly, especially those from the South, and to provide opportunities for them, including access to information, and all forms of health care and education, which are essential to the eradication of poverty.

(i) To direct special action to decrease high levels of youth unemployment to all global stake-holders at local, national, regional and international levels.[154]

(B) South Asian Association for Regional Cooperation (SAARC) January 4-6, 2004

The South Asian Association for Regional Cooperation recognized that the problem of poverty in South Asia needed to be tackled from a multi-dimensional aspect and agreed that a focused and action-oriented plan is the need of the hour. The Finance and Planning Ministers of the SAARC countries, united in their determination to reduce poverty, drawing upon the experience of the member countries and committed to achieve the Millennium Development Goals (MDGs), resolved to pursue the following policies of the Plan of Action:

---

[154] Peoples Millennium Forum, Declaration and Agenda for Action Strengthening the United Nations for the 21st Century, New York, 22 – 26 May 2000

Internal Policies

(1) Recognize that poverty reduction requires good governance through

(a) Improved public sector management and delivery system, particularly in areas that affect the poor {land administration, police and judiciary).
(b) Effective monitoring of public expenditure to prevent leakages
(c) Transparent and cost effective public procurement practices
(d) To take steps to prevent domestic money laundering.
(e) Development of IT

(2) Pursue sound macro-economic management policies through

(a) Focus on quality and pattern of growth
(b) Fiscal discipline, domestic resource mobilization and reduced internal and external borrowing
(c) Outcome-based spending on poverty reduction programs
(d) Economically viable projects in the productive sector

(3) enrich the concept of Human Development through adoption of Bhutan's philosophy of promoting **'Gross National Happiness'** through

(a) Equitable socio-economic development
(b) Preservation of environment
(c) Promotion of cultural heritage
(d) Good responsible governance.

(4) Recognize the importance of combating both rural and urban poverty through

(a) Better targeting of poor in both rural and urban areas
(b) Appropriate agriculture, livestock and fisheries policies, including pricing, tenure, water and watershed development
(c) Promoting employment through rural non-farm enterprise
(d) Access to micro-finance.
(e) Small and medium enterprise development
(f) Creation of rural infrastructure
(g) Development of service sector, including tourism

(5) Promote multi-cultural, pluralism and mass education through

(a) Removal of social and cultural barriers to the pursuit of human development goals
(b) Representative and participatory institution building
(c) Gender equality and empowerment of women
(d) Extension of coverage of education, improvement of its quality and reduction of dropouts by school feeding programs and introduction of other incentives
(e) Vocational and technical training and skill up-gradation

(6) Expand Social Safety Nets through

(a) Food assistance for vulnerable groups
(b) Schemes targeting the poorest and the most vulnerable by providing old age benefits, disability and benefits on the death of primary bread earner.
(c) Affordable health packages
(d) Provision of safe drinking water and sanitation
(e) Incentives to preserve the strength of traditional family structures

(7) Invest in human capital and social sectors through

(a) Outcome-driven allocations to social sectors
(b) Encouragement of private sector investment in education and health

(8) Exercise prudence in allocating public resources and strengthen domestic resource mobilization through

(a) Prioritization of public expenditure
(b) Increased domestic revenue to reduce the dependence on ODA
(c) Fewer but well targeted subsidies.
(d) Coordinated improvement of revenue collection agencies

(9) Empower local communities and governments through

(a) Decentralization
(b)Financial devolution
(c)Community participation

(10) Strengthening poverty alleviation programs through

(a) Building up the physical assets of the poor, including grant assistance to the indigent for purchase of small capital assets
(b) Significant budgetary and credit allocations
(c) Supportive policies for social mobilization
(d) Associating non-governmental and civil society organizations (CSOs).

(11) Expand intra-regional trade and capital flows as decided by the Eleventh SAARC Summit through

(a) Early completion and full operative ness of SAPTA
(b) Faster movement towards SAFTA

(c) Facilitation of intra-regional capital flows.

(l2) Learning from each other's experience through

(a) Exchange of best practices
(b) Frequent interactions among scholars, practitioners and policy makers at all levels.

External Policies

(1).Work with developed countries to increase ODA to 0.7 per cent of GNP through
(a) Formulating common positions at relevant international forum
(b) Frequent consultations among member states on issues of finance and international investment.

(2). Seek increased market access in developed countries through:

(a) Joint positions to address the biases against developing countries in WTO related issues
(b) Removal of tariff and non-tariff barriers
(c) Joint positions against creeping protectionism against the exports of developing countries
(d) Flexibility for developing countries in Intellectual Property Rights

(3) Reduce the burden of multi-lateral borrowing and external debt through

(a) More selective multi-lateral borrowing
(b) Debt swaps for human development.
(c) Debt relief for poverty reduction
(d) Debt relief for non-HIPC developing countries
(e) Increased grant assistance for investment in social sector development.

(4) Discuss with developed countries ways to unearth past inflows of illegal and tax-evaded money

originating from SAARC countries and control them in future through

(a) Instituting mechanisms, wherever required, to prevent corrupt practices in international trade and service transactions.
(b) Disallowance of illegal capital flows into International Banking Systems.

The SAARC resolved that this Plan of Action would be pursued in the framework of balanced and sustainable development. It further resolved that the Finance and Planning Ministers meet regularly in future to review policies and programs on poverty alleviation and progress on objectives outlined in the Plan of Action.[155]

(C) The Commonwealth Civil Society Communiqué on the Heavily Indebted Poor Countries Initiative (HIPC)

1-2 March 2004

The representatives of civil society from Ghana, Mozambique, Sierra Leone, Uganda, and the regional network, the African Forum and Network on Debt and Development (AFRODAD), met in Freetown, Sierra Leone from 1 to 2 March 2004.

The following persistent problems need to be redressed if debt sustainability and poverty reductions are to become realities in the Commonwealth countries:

---

[155] The Plan of Action on Poverty Alleviation was recommended by the Third Meeting of the SAARC Finance/Planning Ministers on Poverty Alleviation (Islamabad, 8-9 April 2002) and was approved by the Twelfth SAARC Summit (Islamabad, 4-6 January 2004), SAARC Secretariat, PO Box 4222, Tridevi Marg, Kathmandu, Nepal.

(a) Debt sustainability remains a mirage among the HIPC graduates. The World Bank and IMF definition of debt sustainability is not achievable as it fails to take cognizance of the sufficiency of resources in HIPC countries to adequately finance social services. The sustainability ratios are too narrow and too high to attain. The failure of Uganda and Mozambique, both HIPC II graduates, to attain sustainable debt levels and ratios due to exogenous factors such as natural disasters, falling commodity prices and HIV/AIDS is a case in point. Indeed, HIPCs have limited capacity to deal with external shocks.

(b) Lack of non-Paris Club creditors participation in debt relief. The fact that HIPCs are still obliged to repay debts to non-HIPC participating creditors continues to put severe strain on HIPCs, causing them to slide back into the debt cycle.

(c) The experience of the HIPC initiative and its implementation process has exposed a capacity gap which is obviously growing and greatly undermines effectiveness and efficiency in both civil society and government. Fundamentally, partnership between civil society and government should be complementary and mutually reinforcing of each other's efforts towards poverty reduction and national development.

(d) The inflexibility of the HIPC process, in particular the preparation of the PRSPs, has led to shallow analyses of poverty and lack of national consensus for the implementation of those strategies. In some cases, they have clearly undermined national democratic processes, such as parliamentary approval, which are essential for consensus building. In the majority of countries implementing HIPC, citizen participation in the preparation of the PRSPs was limited to selective consultation, which did not reflect meaningful engagement. The result of this situation is lack of broad awareness of the process, widespread disagreement with the process and a lack of a pragmatic strategy to address poverty. Additionally, the inflexibility of the time-scale and conditions for reaching decision point places constraints on governments and impedes meaningful engagement with citizens.

(e) The economic policy conditions attached to the HIPC process mirrors the prescriptions imposed on these countries during the era of structural adjustment. The HIPC conditions on privatization, lowering tariffs and trade liberalization have led to increased poverty, asset stripping and job losses that cause social unrest. There is need to de-link debt relief and poverty reduction.

(f) Partial intervention in quality social service delivery: They note with great concern that much investment has gone into infrastructure development, but there is a lack of resources to make them fully functional and beneficial to local communities.

The representatives of civil society urge their ministers, under the auspices of the Commonwealth, to promote the following:

The Commonwealth

(a) Non-HIPC creditors who are members of the Commonwealth should offer debt relief to HIPC members. Indeed, Commonwealth creditor countries should take a lead role in granting total debt cancellation to Commonwealth HIPC countries.

(b) The Commonwealth should lead an international call for fair and transparent assessment of debt sustainability in HIPC countries. An assessment team agreed upon between creditors and debtors should be established. Those countries that continue to have unsustainable debt levels even after reaching HIPC completion point should receive total cancellation of their debt.

(c) HIPC creditors need a compensation strategy to enable them to cancel the debt of other HIPC countries, as their resource base may not allow them to undertake such action without correlated relief from their own creditors.

(d) Measures should be taken by the Commonwealth to help member states with fiscal and debt management training.

(e). The Commonwealth Foundation should work with member countries to enhance the capacity of governments and civil society to fully engage as partners in policymaking and facilitate information sharing on such international initiatives as HIPC.

National governments

(a) In their use of HIPC funds governments should adopt a rights-based approach that respects the ability of local communities to identify and prioritize their needs. Their communities should be respected as claim-holders while their governments remain as duty-bearers.

(b) The involvement and effective participation of civil society organizations (CSOs) in national economic policy matters especially debt procurement, management and monitoring should be facilitated.

c) Information sharing is a prerequisite for inter-sectoral approaches; fora that promote dialogue between government and CSOs at national, regional, Commonwealth and international level should be formalized and institutionalized if partnerships are to be effective and meaningful.

(d) HIPC governments need to develop and present an acceptable working definition of debt sustainability to guide donors and investors on priority investment need to facilitate national development. These governments should propose their urgent needs for the benefits of their people. If they do not explain the purpose, the donors' grant would be utilized in less important sectors.

Donors and International Financial Institutions

(i) Donor governments should ensure that HIPC funds are not used as a substitute for overseas development assistance obligations.

(ii) Donors should consider establishing a HIPC Disaster Recovery Fund for compensation, rehabilitation, reconstruction and investment in lasting preventive measures to minimize vulnerability. Local communities should be involved in mitigation strategies as part of a combined effort.

(iii) HIPC governments' sovereignty to make decisions about national needs and requirements must be maintained, as they best understand their local context; otherwise they will continue to suffer consequences like those of the premature introduction of Structural Adjustment Programmes.

(iv). Decision and completion points should be de-linked from the Poverty Reduction Growth Facility and a consultative group involving civil society should do the determination of such points.

(v) Development partners should support building the capacity of governments and civil society to fully engage as partners in policymaking and facilitate information sharing.

In short, the civil societies will continue their work to ensure that poverty reduction and total and unconditional debt cancellation are attained for HIPCs to serve the interests of the Commonwealth people. CSOs will exert pressure for accountability and sustainable expenditure patterns from their governments. CSOs will intensify civic education efforts, emphasizing citizen ownership of development programmes, and their financing and resource management. In this regard the representatives of civil society call on Commonwealth governments to build on the recognition of the role of their civil society and citizens in Diaspora in promoting development and democracy. The Commonwealth governments need to enhance the space and opportunities for interaction with Civil Societies Organizations (CSOs) on issues related to HIPCs, PRSPs, and debt crisis and poverty reduction.[156]

(D) Commonwealth HIPC Ministerial Forum

Maputo, Mozambique, 15 – 16 March 2005

The representatives of civil society from Cameroon, Ghana, Guyana, Kenya, Malawi, Mozambique, Uganda, Sierra Leone, Zambia and the regional network, the African Forum and Network on Debt and Development (AFRODAD) suggested the following for debt relief.

Issues

1. The HIPC initiative has failed to provide low-income countries a 'permanent and robust exist' from indebtedness and no participating country has achieved debt sustainability. Low-income countries owe a total of US$523 billion in debt to all creditors. Of this, the African Continent alone has a debt stock of $330 billion and still spends US$15 billion every year in debt service to rich countries and the

[156] Commonwealth HIPC Ministerial Forum, Commonwealth Secretariat, Freetown, Sierra Leone, 1-2nd March 2004

international financial institutions. Continued debt service by sub-Saharan African countries constitutes a reverse transfer of resources to wealthy creditor countries by those that can least afford it. Moreover, a number of severely indebted countries, such as Nigeria, have been excluded from the HIPC initiative altogether.

2 The international community now recognizes that such unbearably high levels of debt are incompatible with attaining the internationally agreed Millennium Development Goals (MDGs) by 2015. Even those countries that have successfully reached completion point under the HIPC initiative, and have received some debt write-off, have quickly found their debts unsustainable once again. This is the case for Uganda and Mozambique, among others.

3. The HIPC initiative does not address domestic debt; notwithstanding that many participating countries are experiencing increases in their domestic debt to GDP ratio.

4. The creditor-led framework of the HIPC initiative has contributed to changing rules of the game, most notably with regard to the criteria for reaching completion point; this can have negative consequences for participating countries. Countries that are judged to have failed to meet the requirements of the Poverty Reduction and Growth Facility (PRGF) and are suspended from the HIPC initiative, for example, are forced to resort to the domestic market for resources to meet their obligations, and thereby increase their domestic debt stock.

5. The World Bank / IMF debt sustainability analysis does not include domestic debt and is not linked with a country's ability to achieve the MDGs. As argued in the report of the Africa Commission, debt relief and aid made available to countries should be analyzed

against the backdrop of the financing needed to reach the MDGs, rather than the present narrow economic indicators to determine debt sustainability.

6. They recognize the efforts of the governments to tackle poverty in their countries. In this context, they would like to work with the governments to ensure that debt relief takes into account the financing needed to attain the MDGs and addresses the burden of domestic debt in all impoverished nations. The representatives appreciate that governments have tried to address some of these concerns in both domestic and international forums and the representatives are committed to working with the governments to find lasting and sustainable solutions to the poverty ridden and debt trap countries of the commonwealth countries.

Recommendations

7. It is against this backdrop that the representatives make the following recommendations, which they called on their governments to support.

i. Domestic debt should be considered in all debt sustainability analyses as servicing; it can also impede economic growth and governments' ability to provide public goods and services. Debtor governments should be given the support required to manage domestic debt.

ii. Financing of priority expenditures and the MDGs must be ring-fenced. HIPC eligibility should be de-linked from the PRGF in order to limit the need for countries to resort to the domestic market to make up resource shortfalls.

iii. Equal participation in the design of frameworks and in decision-making processes about debt resolution should be introduced to ensure that these initiatives respond to the needs of the countries they are intended to benefit and result in a decrease in indebtedness and support poverty reduction. Creditor-designed and led debt resolution exercises have failed.

iv. Private sector involvement in the provision of social services must not only be determined by commercial interests, but should also be driven by social responsibility, in particular in the sharing of risks associated with the provision of public goods, such as water. The concept of public private partnerships should be expanded to include the participation of people, in order to design and deliver essential service solutions that guarantee access for all and are compatible with the achievement of the MDGs.

v. Cent percent unconditional cancellations of debts should be extended to all the low and middle-income countries where debt service payments are seriously hindering efforts towards achieving the Millennium Development Goals.

vi. Any debt relief initiatives should ensure additional, sustained and positive net financial flows to these countries in order to release resources for investment in poverty reduction.

Proposal for enhanced debt relief

8. The representatives welcome the efforts of some creditor countries to address the debt crisis. Of the current proposals tabled by creditor nations, the UK Government proposal for 100 per cent debt service cancellation over 10 years is a welcome step forward. It could, however, be more comprehensive if it were expanded to include more countries. The fact that the proposal extends to a limited number of countries that meet certain criteria and conditions as decided by creditors is of concern. There is also concern that only using bilateral contributions for multi-lateral debt

payments effectively serve to convert grants into loans and increases moral hazard for institutional lending. There is further unease that this proposal might divert resources away from overseas development assistance to debt cancellation, when what is needed is for debt cancellation to complement rather than substitute aid

9. It is in this context that the representatives propose the following:

(a) Cent per cent multilateral debt cancellation should be implemented for all poor countries. Additional funding should be provided to meet the MDGs.
(b) The required funding should be generated in a tiered manner, as outlined below, with each of three tiers being exhausted before the next one is used.
(c) The first source of funding would be the sale of IMF gold, which could mobilize up to $35 billion. This money should be used for the cancellation of multilateral debt owed to the IMF and other institutions such as the World Bank.
(d) If these resources prove insufficient, additional bilateral contributions of the kind pledged by the UK can be used to make up the shortfall.
(e) If additional funds are still needed, a third source of funding of up $17.5 billion could be made available through the World Bank's non-concessional lending arm, the International Development Association (IDA).

10. Given the recurrent nature of debt and in order to bring about a permanent exit from debt, the international community needs to energetically support the creation of an alternative debt restructuring mechanism to address grossly unequal debtor-creditor relations in international debt negotiations. We believe that proposal for a Fair and

Transparent Arbitration Process (FTAP) and International Arbitration Courts represent strong and viable options for a fair debt work out mechanism. Such a mechanism should address complaints of odious and illegitimate debt. It should be open to all countries, involve civil society organizations and address multilateral, bilateral and commercial debts. Additionally, the governments need to adopt legislation that limits their debt service to not more than 10 per cent of government revenue in order to allow sufficient investments in the social and productive sectors of debtor countries.[157]

(E) Bangkok Recommendations

10 – 11 May 2005

The Special Body on Least Developed and Landlocked Developing Countries endorsed the following recommendations to enable the Asia-Pacific Least Developed Countries (LDCs) attain the Millennium Development Goals (MDGs) at its Seventh Session, held in Bangkok, 10 and 11 May 2005. It is significant that these include five key recommendations where the Asia-Pacific LDCs are expected to take specific actions at the national level and seek complementary international support. There is an explicit acceptance of the importance of appropriate domestic policies, institutions and governance in order to make this global partnership most productive. Out of which one recommendation on 'Aid and Debt Relief' is illustrated in this chapter.

Aid and Debt Relief to achieve the MDGs:
Actions at the national level

(a) Aid works for development only if proper policies and institutions are in place. Good governance at all

---

[157] Statement by Representatives of Civil Society, Commonwealth HIPC Ministerial Forum, Maputo, Mozambique, 15 – 16 March 2005

levels is a prerequisite for effective use of aid. People and communities are both participants in and beneficiaries of such assistance.[158]

(b) Making aid effective calls for better aid harmonization and coordination. Since each country is different, with its own set of challenges, development goals and strategies, a country-based approach, which enables each country to reach its development goals, is necessary. Such an approach promotes country-based ownership and channels aid to sectors where its impact is the greatest by requiring recipient countries to prepare their own development programmes. Development also requires financing not merely of initial investments but also of the many forms of current expenditure. In order to ensure that aid is harmonized, recipient countries need to prepare a coherent aid policy in the spirit of the Rome Declaration and in consultation with donors. Greater discussion of these issues at the national level is also essential.

(c) For effective aid utilization, assessment of outcomes is more important than assessment of available inputs. However, it is important for governments to undertake appropriate costing and analyze paths for achieving their development goals.

---

[158] Voices of the Least Developed Countries of Asia and the Pacific: Achieving the Millennium Development Goals through a Global Partnership, United Nations Development Program, 2005, published by ELSEVIER, New Delhi-110024, pp.32 - 34
Note: The Special Body on Least Developed and Landlocked Developing Countries is an inter-governmental body established to review the economic and social developments in these groups of countries and to give high priority to their concerns. The recommendations contained in the Report were endorsed at the inter-governmental level at the Seventh Session of the Special Body on Least Developed and Landlocked Developing Countries, Bangkok, 10-11 May 2005

Emphasis needs to be placed on enhancing the efficiency of utilization of such aid assistance. From that perspective, recipient countries could strengthen their domestic capacities for planning and project implementation, improve monitoring and evaluation, ensure better institutional coordination among various government agencies involved in negotiating and utilizing aid, and achieve greater decentralization of project implementation where feasible and desirable. Countries could benefit from the experiences of other countries in similar situations. Resources available from other developing countries of the region could also be tapped.

Actions by the international community

(a) The international community was urged to meet the targets in the Brussels Programme of Action, the Almaty Programme of Action and the Mauritius Strategy. Aid should be determined by economic and social concerns and directed to addressing fundamental causes of poverty, especially in countries with internal conflicts and countries battered by natural disasters. Given the limited capacity of these countries to incur financial obligations, external assistance to them should primarily be in the form of grants. Aid should also be front-loaded.

(b) Steps should be taken for greater coherence among donors in areas such as policy conditionality and ODA practices; trade regimes and technology transfer from donor countries. Efforts should also be made to ensure that policy conditionality converge with recipient country priorities, thus promoting national ownership. Independent monitoring and evaluation of aid performance at the level of the recipient country should be considered. The fostering of national ownership should be based on genuine dialogue and conducted in a spirit of partnership between donors and recipients.

(c) The international community should continue its dialogue with recipient countries on issues such as grant components in aid, tied purchases and financing of recurring costs to bring about improvements in these areas. Donors should consider 'programme budget support' as the main long-term strategy to assist these countries and indicate their long-term commitment to assist these countries.

(d) Regional solutions could enable smaller countries to address issues that would have been too costly to implement at the country level by introducing economies of scale.

(e) The priority needs and concerns of least developed and landlocked developing countries change over the years. The international community should therefore ensure that their assistance continues to address the changing needs of these countries.

(F) Commonwealth Ministerial Debt Sustainability Forum, Washington April 22, 2009

The Commonwealth Ministerial Debt Sustainability Forum (CMDSF) consisting of Cameroon, The Gambia, Ghana, Guyana, Lesotho, Malawi, Mozambique, Nigeria, Sierra Leone, United Republic of Tanzania, Uganda, and Zambia discussed the implications of the economic and financial crisis for low income and debt vulnerable countries; progress in improving creditor participation in providing HIPC debt relief, reducing creditor litigation and in enhancing information exchange to improve debtor negotiation capacities; country needs for and efforts to build debt management capacity; and assistance with debt management being provided by the Commonwealth Secretariat.[159]

---

[159] Commonwealth secretariat Press release, Washington D.C., USA 22 April 2009

Implications of the economic and financial crisis

1. Ministers noted the serious implications of the crisis for low income and debt vulnerable countries. The sharp contraction in world output and trade combined with lower inflows of remittances and investment has increased the financing gap such countries face at a time when fiscal positions in many countries had been weakened by high food and fuel prices. In parallel, deteriorating financing conditions make access to external finance even more difficult. Without sharply increased concessional assistance and action to protect critical expenditures including on social safety nets, human development and key infrastructure projects, progress in poverty reduction will be seriously set back.

2. They exchanged views on the impact of the crisis on their respective economies and the policies they had put in place. In considering the reaction of the international community, they welcomed increases in concessional assistance that have already taken place, and noting the current pressures on donor country budgets Ministers called for a further increase in concessional financing flows: with increasing needs and progress towards the MDGs under great threat donors should make a concerted effort to meet and if possible go beyond their Gleneagles commitments to increase the quantity and quality of their development assistance.

3. In this context Ministers welcomed the commitments made by G20 leaders in London and the options to mobilise significant additional International Financial Institutions (IFI) resources to meet countries' financing needs. They welcomed in particular the commitments to substantial additional concessional finance from the IFIs over the next two or three years, including extra resources for social protection in the poorest countries and further support for the World Bank's Vulnerability Framework

and the commitment to accelerate work on reform of the IFIs and securing a stronger voice for developing countries. However, they noted that IFI estimates of financing needs in low income countries were much greater than the commitments by donors. They stressed the importance of donors delivering fully on these new commitments as a first step and being willing to enhance them if additional finance is required.

4. They noted the long standing concern of the forum regarding the need for greater flexibility in the application by the IFIs of the non concessional borrowing policy and the Debt Sustainability Framework. Consequently, they welcomed the commitment to review the flexibility of the Debt Sustainability Framework and the commitment to increase the use of non concessional lending for countries with sound policies, to be completed by the Annual meetings. They emphasised the importance of ensuring that the views of borrowing members are fully integrated into any revised policy and urged the Commonwealth Secretariat to work with the new Chair of the Forum to influence the development of the policy.

5. They noted the steps being taken by the World Bank to meet pressing needs of low income countries by accelerated IDA disbursements, and by the IMF to discontinue structural performance requirements, but urged both institutions to make further progress in reducing the number of conditions in their programmes.

Creditor Participation and Litigation

6. Ministers expressed their continuing concern at the failure of many non-Paris Club and commercial creditors to participate in debt relief under the Enhanced HIPC Initiative on an equal burden sharing basis, and the continuing action by some non-Paris

Club bilateral creditors and many commercial creditors to seek full repayment through litigation.

7. Ministers urged indebted countries to make full use of the IDA Debt Reduction Facility and technical assistance provided by the Commonwealth Legal Clinic, and called for rapid activation of the African Legal Support Facility. The Clinic has been in consultation with the African Legal Support Facility for the signing of a MOU in order to enable relevant Commonwealth members to obtain funding facility to meet with the costs of defending any litigation from vulture funds. They also encouraged HIPCs with significant remaining commercial debt to explore the prospects for a repeat IDA debt reduction facility, and asked the Commonwealth secretariat to commission a feasibility study of how remaining debts to small multilateral creditors could be extinguished.

8. They also called on Commonwealth, G8 and other major official creditors and donors:

- (a) To raise the issue of debt relief forcefully with non-Paris Club creditors;
- (b) To urge non-Paris Club and commercial creditors to agree not to sell debts to potential litigants;
- (c) To consider how to amend creditor legislation to prevent litigation being launched in their jurisdictions.
- (d) In addition they asked Commonwealth donors to provide funding to help cancel debts between low income countries, and wealthier Commonwealth developing country creditors to provide debt relief.

9. Improving Information Exchange: To improve information exchange Ministers recognised the importance of pooling information amongst low income countries to assist their efforts to secure debt relief and future access to finance. They urged

international and regional organizations to work together to compile by October 2009 more detailed information for HIPCs on creditor participation, best possible relief terms and litigation experiences, in a format designed to assist negotiations. They asked for donor support for this effort, including help with translation to make information available in relevant languages and electronic form. They recognised the responsibility countries themselves had to provide information on these issues to make it a success and committed themselves to provide all information needed for this joint effort in a timely way. They called on the new Chair of the Forum to work with the Secretariat to find ways to take this initiative forward.

10. Capacity Building: Ministers agreed on the need for a major effort to strengthen country capacity for debt strategy formulation and execution which must be complemented by efforts to strengthen legal, institutional and organisational frameworks for debt management. They committed their governments to act as needed to improve legal and institutional frameworks, and to use national capacity rather than external technical assistance. In particular they committed to: Ensuring legal frameworks are in place to give debt management staff a clear mandate. Recruiting and training professional debt management staff, and reducing dependency on external technical assistance. Comprehensive and objective assessments of country capacity building need for discussion with potential donors. Such needs are likely to include capacity for domestic debt market development as well as external financing strategies, for budget forecasting, and for portfolio and risk management.

11. Ministers called on donors and the IFIs to provide stronger financial and training support in these capacity building efforts for all members of the Forum, noting that all such support should be based on countries' own plans and designed to strengthen

country capacity, avoiding the use of external technical expertise wherever possible. They welcomed all efforts by the international community to strengthen public debt management work including the work of HIPC Capacity Building Programme, the regional institutions and the work programme of the World Bank and International Monetary Fund and urged all institutions to work closely together to meet the needs of these countries. Ministers stressed the importance of the active participation of countries in the use and development of these tools to ensure full ownership of the policy outcomes of using these tools and building capacity to implement agreed policy.

12. Commonwealth Assistance: Ministers recognized the valuable role of the Commonwealth Secretariat in capacity building at the national level and more recently at the sub-national level. They welcomed the refocusing of the Secretariat's work to build capacity on comprehensive debt analysis recognising that such holistic analysis can inform the choice of new financing instruments and markets, especially in the current uncertain times. Ministers commended efforts by the Secretariat to build debt management capacity through e learning, targeted secondments and in this context urged that the second phase of the Regional Adviser project be initiated. They also welcomed and supported the timely efforts by the Secretariat to complete work to create integrated debt databases in member countries and to strengthen data recording of both domestic debt and the increasingly important issue of private external debt liabilities. The Ministers specifically urged the Secretariat to join the Debt Management Facility initiative of the World Bank.

13. Ministers strongly commended the work of the Commonwealth Legal Clinic in assisting Commonwealth, and other, HIPCs handle creditor lawsuits, improve national systems to remove the possibility of such litigation in respect of future loans, and in advocacy, for example on the need for

legislation in creditor countries to prevent litigation by vulture funds. Looking forward, they welcomed the commitment of the Commonwealth Secretariat to build on the experience of the Legal Clinic as part of an effort to strengthen the capacity of the Secretariat to support countries in their efforts to access finance. They called on donors to provide the funding needed for this work.

Conclusion

The international forums offered the following suggestions for reduction of poverty and 100 per cent debt relief. These are:

As most of the commonwealth countries are classified as least developed countries or less developed countries and face debt overhang, the Common Wealth Countries should adopt united efforts and impress upon the UK to convince the Paris Club, Non-Paris Club, and the G-8 countries to accept debt relief for relieving these countries from financial crises.

The amount of ODA should be increased to $ 100 billion.

The conventions express that non-Paris club, bilateral, multilateral and commercial creditors should participate in HIPC Initiative.

The commonwealth desires private participation in infrastructure development through Build, Operate, and Transfer (BOT) projects or through private - public partnerships.

The HIPC Initiative has failed to provide low-income countries a 'permanent and robust exit' from indebtedness and no participating country has achieved debt sustainability'. Low-income countries owe a total of US $ 523 billion in debt sustainability. Of this African continent has a debt stock of $330 billion and still spends US $ 15 billion every year in debt service. Similarly, the non-African countries owe $189 billion and spend $8.7 billion every year on debt service.

These conventions suggest **100 percent multilateral debt cancellation** for all poor countries.

The international community was urged to meet the targets in the Brussels Program of Action, Almaty Program of Action and the Mauritius Strategy. Moreover, the recipient countries in consultation with donors need to prepare a coherent aid policy in the spirit of the Rome Declaration.

The SAARC countries must recognize that poverty reduction requires good governance, macro-economic management policies, and co-operation among themselves.

The SAARC countries should adopt **'Suresh Pritam philosophy'** of promoting 'Gross Domestic Peace of a country' by studying the status of food security, debt sustainability, capacity to meet household expenses, area free from rebellion, war and terrorism, corruption free administration and politics, clean environment, families without court cases, share of state budget in budget expenditure proposal and factors contributing peace. (Ref: World Peace Volume One – Poverty and Peace).

Additional funds should be provided to meet the MDGs of all the low-income and low-middle-income countries.

LDCs should be accorded stable and predictable market access through WTO bound duty-and-quota free access for all exports.

Good governance is a pre-requisite for effective use of aid.

The LDCs should expand intra-regional trade and capital flows, empower local communities and strengthen poverty alleviation programs. These countries must try to reduce external debts and multilateral debts.

The developed countries should keep their promises by increasing ODA to 0.7 percent of GDP.

Globalization should be made to work for the benefits of every one: eradicate poverty and hunger globally and establish peace globally; and

The developed countries should cancel the debts of developing countries including odious debts.

The planners must attempt for reduction of poverty and hunger in rural areas of low-income countries.

The planners must see that suicide of farmers and sale of children must be stopped at all costs.

+++++

Chapter-VI

INTERNATIONAL ADVOCACY FOR DEBT RELIEF

When no political leader can claim ignorance of what is happening in the poorest part of the world – we are asking for the richest part of the humanity to reach out in all humanity and conscience to the poorest. We are asking for the cancellation of the un-payable debts of the world's impoverished countries. We are in a position to demand justice. We want nothing less than to enter the new millennium as one world. ---- Mulima Kufekisa Akapelwa in Birmingham during the G8 Summit on 16 May 1998

The low-income countries are heavily indebted and bonded. There is acute problem of mass poverty, illiteracy and immature deaths through starvation or diseases in most of the sub-Saharan countries, South Asia, Latin American countries and Caribbean countries. As a result, the international activists of both North and South are organizing 'debt relief' campaigns to arise awareness through global protests, meetings, e-mails and seminars. The influential churches, development agencies and non-government organizations of developed countries started the movement on moral and ethical grounds to save the bonded poor and debt overhang of low-income countries. The Jubilee 2000 internationalized this movement and made it mass-based. The 'Third World Debt Issue' is not confined to researchers and politicians; it has puzzled the UNO, donor countries, the World Bank, International Monetary Fund, OECD, International banks and other global institutions.

The procedure adopted by the World Bank and International Monetary Fund delays the granting of debt relief to the low-income countries and debars fundamental human rights of the people of indebted countries for generations. The HIPC Initiative, Poverty Reduction Strategy Papers (PRSP), Poverty Reduction Growth Facility (PRGF), Multilateral Debt Relief Initiative (MDRI), Evaluation, Participatory process, rescheduling, refinancing, restructuring, conditionality, Joint Staff Assessment and completion point are the different exercises of a magic show. These instruments cannot allow 100 per cent debt relief. The donor countries, World Bank, IMF, G-8, and International Banks should declare their intentions for 100 per cent debt relief to all low-income countries on the total outstanding debts as on June 30, 2010.

Debts should be cancelled because these debts increased the number of hungry persons in all the indebted countries.

In July 2000, Anglican Archbishop Ndungane issued an urgent call to the world's highly indebted poor countries to close ranks and to refuse to service their debts to the G8 countries. He said, "If the wealthy G-8 countries lack the will to cross the Rubicon, we must take the initiative. It is the time for us to recognize that we are dealing with the same colonialists who have never acted voluntarily in our interest."

In this chapter, the activities of AFRODAD, Jubilee Debt Campaign (UK), Liberal Democrat Youths and Students, Catholic Agency for Overseas Development (CAFOD), Churches and Religious Organizations, OXFAM, Women's Organization and Make Poverty History have been discussed to highlight their contributions for a hunger-free, debt-free and a peaceful world.

(A) African Forum and Network on Debt and Development (AFRODAD)

AFRODAD is a research, lobby and advocacy regional organization seeking to secure positive policy changes to redress Africa's Debt and Development crisis in order to achieve equitable and sustainable development that will lead to an African and worldwide prosperous society.

AFRODAD[160] is a civil society organization born of a desire to secure lasting solutions to Africa's mounting debt problem, which has impacted negatively on the continent's development process. The organization aspires for an equitable development process, leading to a prosperous African society. The mission of the organization is to secure policies that will redress the African Debt Crisis based on a human rights value system.

Africa is burdened with an unmanageable debt, which is hampering the continent's economic growth. The continent's debt has been attributed to several factors. These include the oil crisis of the 1970s, the deteriorating terms of trade, low export growth, misuse of borrowed funds and corruption, and poor

---

160 AFRODAD E-mail Subscribe

governance. The answer probably lies in a combination of all these. But wherever the reason, it cannot be denied that Africa's debt crisis is one of the major causes for the economic crisis facing the continent today. Africa needs to increase economic growth to improve the standard of living for the majority of its people but the whole continent is in bondage of debt of the western countries. Africa's total external debt stood at US $231 billion in 1999 and annual debt service payment amounted to US $15.2 billion per year. In Africa, 51 per cent of people are living in absolute poverty, 40 per cent of revenue is allocated for debt servicing and 33 countries (out of 41) are classified as heavily indebted poor countries.

AFRODAD makes database of country profiles, which covers political, economic and social analysis and suggests solutions for sustainable exit of debt problems of each African poor countries. Unless debt cancellation is activated, the process of sustainable development is not feasible in African countries. The specific objectives of the database are:

(a) To provide ongoing basis on the experience of PRSP process with the intention of moving towards monitoring PRSP process
(b) To show from these processes the development policy issues and evaluate the content of country PRSPs in terms of their consistency with the main development goals especially, poverty reduction as well as the similarities and differences in methodology of the process of PRSPs.
(c) To stimulate engagement with civil society organizations (CSOs) in discussions and understanding of the policy issues in PRSPs.

Research and policy analysis forms the core business of AFRODAD to gain a deeper understanding of the underlying causes of the debt problem, institutional mechanisms contributing to the problem and the responsibilities of stakeholders - that are the creditors, the debtors' institutions and the beneficiaries. This organization has studied various research projects on African Debt Profiles, Arbitration on Debt, Regional Integration and Debt, Public Guaranteed Debt, Reality of Debt etc. AFRODAD has submitted a joint statement of African NGOs and trade unions prior to the 2004 summit, Sea Islands, USA on 8 -12 June 2004. The statement has included justifications for debt relief, trade justice, and continental integration and for immediate steps for HIV/AIDS, Malaria and Tuberculosis.

But the West's response to the debt problem has been to hatch up plan after plan, initiative after initiative. But none of these has adequately addressed the whole problem and the bulk of the crisis remains unresolved. Calls have been made for the total cancellation of the debts, without success. African leaders need to provide effective leadership to end this slavery; so far, there has not been an effective response to the continent's predicament, in the face of the escalating health and social crisis in many countries.

(B) Jubilee Debt Campaign (UK)

Jubilee 2000 grew from small beginnings to become an international campaign that brought great pressure on G7 leaders to cancel the un-payable debts of the poorest countries by the year 2000, under a fair and transparent process. 24 million signatures had been gathered for the Jubilee 2000 petition, the first-ever global petition, by the end of the campaign. There were Jubilee 2000 campaigns in more than 60 countries around the world. G7 leaders had committed to writing off $100 billion of poor country debts, and debt had been pushed on to the global political agenda. The Jubilee Framework has evolved as a result of debate, over many years, in both the north and the south, on the most appropriate and most democratic mechanism for resolving debt crises.

Framework

The very existence of a framework, enabling any indebted nation to file for a standstill on debt payments; or for her creditors to declare her insolvent, will be a form of regulation of international capital flows; and will discipline both lax lenders and reckless borrowers.

(a) The Jubilee Framework could apply to all indebted countries, not just those IMF deems insolvent.

(b) The criteria for petitioning for a standstill would be determined by the debtor nation. For the Jubilee movement, debts that can only be repaid at a cost to the fundamental human rights of the population are deemed un-payable debts.

(c) The Jubilee Framework would remove international creditors, like the IMF, from playing the role of plaintiff, judge and jury in the event of international debt crises. Central to the framework would be the independence of the insolvency court.

(d) The court would be an ad-hoc body, appointed to deal with each individual petition for insolvency. It would not require an international treaty.

(e) The Jubilee Framework would accept the IMF as a 'portal' or 'gateway' to the process, given the vital role that the Fund will play in assembling working capital for the sovereign debtor during the debt standstill period.

(f) However under the Jubilee Framework, the IMF would not be able to influence the appointment or the proceedings of the ad-hoc, independent panel. The role of ensuring the independence of the panel should be assigned to the Secretary General of the United Nations.

(g) The sovereign debtor and creditors would determine the composition of the court. Both sides would nominate one representative each; the two representatives would then choose a third, in whom they both have confidence – to act as the judge.

(h) Within the Jubilee Framework, the proceedings of the court will be transparent and accountable both to creditors; but most importantly, to the citizens of debtor nations.

(i) The court will assess all debts; and ascertain if they were contracted legitimately.

(j) Fundamental to the Jubilee Framework is public participation in the proceedings of the court, and in the resolution of crises involving public money. Accountability to the electorate of government officials responsible for reckless borrowing in debtor nations; and for lax and corrupt lending in creditor nations, we believe, will introduce discipline into the lending and borrowing process, and challenge corruption.

(k) The Jubilee Framework, like Chapter 9 of the US legal code, will give rights to citizens to comment on the economic soundness of the court's 'composition plan'; and give taxpayers the right to object to the plan.

(l) The Jubilee Framework is the first vital step towards democratizing international capital markets, and thereby, the project known as 'globalization'.

(m) The International Jubilee 2000 movement mobilized, protested and pushed third-world-debt to the top of the global agenda in just four years of campaigning; and forced the world's most powerful creditors, the G7, to agree to cancel $100 billion of the debts of the poorest countries. The ordinary people of Argentina have deposed a President and a powerful finance minister in just a few days by using pots and pans and without political leadership. They unsettled international markets; imposed losses on international creditors; reversed long-standing economic policies; weakened the authority of the IMF; and are now demanding democratic elections of reluctant politicians. How much more can a global movement of ordinary citizens achieve?

(n) The International Jubilee 2000 movement is seeking to reverse the malign influence of neo-liberal economists who have embarked on what the Austrian economist Karl Polanyi described as a starkly utopian project: the disembodying of the 'globalize' economy from society, from the environment and from democratic institutions. They are determined to transform the international financial system into one that is embedded – in democratic, social, environmental and political relations. That is the ambition of the wider Jubilee 2000 movement and of the 'the Jubilee Framework.'

International insolvency: key principles

An international insolvency process would have to begin by adopting the key legal principles underlying all insolvency procedures.

(a) The first principle is that any process should be based on the application of justice and reason. The process should not be viewed as an act of mercy.
(b) The second principle is that any process should protect the human rights, and the human dignity of the debtor, as well as the rights of creditors.
(c) The third principle is fundamental to the Rule of Law; namely that it is not possible to be

judge in one's own court. In other words, neither creditors nor the debtor can control the court of bankruptcy, or decide on their own claims or payments. The judge has to be independent of both debtor and creditors, and to resolve the crisis within a framework of justice that recognizes the human rights of the debtor.

(d) Fourthly, the movement would add a vital principle, central to bankruptcy law for governmental organizations in the US; namely that citizens affected by a debt crisis, have a legal right to have their voices heard in the resolution of that crisis. In other words freedom of information, transparency of process and accountability to the public must be central to an international insolvency framework.

The Jubilee movement[161] is promoting a new international insolvency framework – a Jubilee Framework – because the purpose of all insolvency law is defined as granting the debtor a new financial life. The US legal code under section 101 (note 63) states: 'the opportunity to accumulate new wealth unhampered by pressure and discouragement of pre-existing debts. The movement is concerned with public sovereign debtors. The movement is promoting this new framework to strengthen democratic participation in (a) the resolution of a crisis, (b) the prevention of future crises and (c) the development of a 'new financial life' for the country as a whole. A just, transparent and democratically accountable framework for resolving debt crises would contrast

[161] Note: The British movement has worked closely with campaigns in Europe, Asia, Africa and Latin America. This movement is supported by the UN Secretary-General, Dr. Yilmaz Akyuz, chief economist of UNCTAD and his staff, and works with academics including Professors Kunibert Raffer of the University of Vienna and Prof. Jeffrey Sachs of Harvard – in developing the concept.

dramatically with the reality faced by hundreds of millions of people living in more than 80 sovereign debtor nations, as they struggle to deal with powerful creditors in forums dominated by creditors".[162]

The Jubilee Research submitted a proposal the 'UN financing for Development Conference' to remind the UN's Millennium Summit in 2000 to **'free the entire world from want'**. The report concludes with the following suggestions.

The British Chancellor's welcome proposal for an increase in OECD aid by $50 billion a year will prove ineffective in achieving the Millennium Development Goals in the HIPC countries, unless there is 100 per cent cancellation of debts of these countries;

A high proportion of aid flows are currently being directed towards unproductive debt repayments to institutions like the IMF and World Bank, and not genuine aid for the poorest people of the world. We believe that this will not be welcome news to OECD taxpayers;

To achieve the first MDG of halving the proportion of people living in extreme poverty in the HIPC countries will not only require 100 percent debt cancellation; but also an increase in the current level of aid to the HIPCs from $15 billion to $46 billion a year;

This is less than the increase in US military spending in one year, 2003, and would cost each person in the developed world only $1 per week, or $50 a year;

The world would be a much more secure place if these resources were used for development, rather than for destruction;

---

[162] Ann Pettifor (2002), "Resolving International Debt Crisis – The Jubilee Framework for International Solvency", ***New Economic Foundation***, Supp Jubilee Research

Even if the first goal is not achieved, protecting the human rights of million of people in the HIPC countries will require spending on health, education, water and other social services in order to meet the other Millennium Development Goals;

These expenditures alone will require 100 per cent debt cancellation, plus additional aid of $16.5 billion. [163]

The UK government and Jubilee Debt Campaign:

The UK government published a formal proposal for 100 per cent multilateral debt cancellation for a number of countries in late 2004. This is a welcome step - but differs in many respects from what Jubilee Debt Campaign is calling for. The un-payable debts of the world's poorest countries should be cancelled in full, by fair and transparent means. Jubilee Debt Campaign believes that, for purposes of halving extreme poverty and meeting the MDGs, HIPCs and HIPC-like countries should not be required to service their debts until at least 2015. Private creditors should also grant debt relief. Full un-payable debt cancellation is needed as a matter of justice and eliminating poverty: the poorest countries should not have to make any further repayments of such debts. This applies to private as well as official debt. Any resources necessary to achieve such cancellation should be in addition to, and not drawn from, the funds required meeting existing targets for overseas aid.

The international definition of overseas aid, which all creditor countries adopt, allows debt relief to count as aid. It all comes from the same pot of money and is

---

[163] Greenhill, R (2002), "The unbreakable link – debt relief and the millennium development goals", A report from Jubilee Research at the New Economics Foundation, 29 pages

all intended, at least for the poorest countries, to be spent on poverty-reducing measures (direct and indirect). Although debt cancellation is a newer pledge, it should still count towards meeting the pre-existing 0.7 per cent target for aid rather than being additional to it. Debt cancellation is a matter of justice, not aid; we need to end the perpetual indebtedness of poor countries and the damage this continues to cause, as well as improve relations between North and South. Debt relief must not count towards the pre-existing target that aid should reach 0.7 per cent of national income. In any case, both debt cancellation and aid levels of at least this proportion are needed to eradicate poverty. The international financial institutions must stop requiring poor countries to implement harmful economic policies, such as privatization and liberalization, as a condition for granting debt relief. Jubilee Debt Campaign accepts that some economic policy conditions have been harmful in the past. Sympathetic to the idea those poor countries must be allowed greater independence. Still wants to use some economic conditions to determine which non-HIPCs benefit from debt cancellation. Jubilee Debt Campaign wants conditions to be streamlined, but still wants creditor / donor - led impact assessments of potential conditions to determine whether or not they are applied (i.e. the starting point is that privatizations and fiscal constraints are desirable unless proven otherwise).

No economic policy conditions should be attached to debt relief – they are proven to be damaging in many cases and undermine the independence of poor countries. The only conditions should be ones that ensure transparency and good financial accounting in the use of debt cancellation proceeds (with the assumption that these will be spent on poverty reduction). Full multilateral debt cancellation should be rapidly delivered, particularly given that many countries have already demonstrated the ability to ensure that the proceeds of debt cancellation already received under HIPC are properly targeted at poverty reduction. Jubilee Debt Campaign recognizes that debt cancellation is an important means of financing development. Not adopting a full 'human development' approach, but believes that poor countries' multilateral debt service should be met by bilateral donors until debt 'sustainability' is achieved 'within the context of meeting the MDGs'.

Debt cancellation should be through writing off 100 per cent of multilateral debts and for a range of countries. The World Bank and IMF need to play their full part by canceling 100 per cent of the 'multilateral' debt owed to them by poor countries. Moreover, such cancellation is an essential (if insufficient) means of meeting the existing development targets, such as the MDGs, en route to ultimately eliminating poverty. A fair, transparent and comprehensive international insolvency process should be created to allow creditor and debtor countries to resolve debt crises without compromising the ability of poor countries. To meet the basic social needs of their peoples and without forcing poor countries to repay what the insolvency process determines to be odious debts. A just means of dealing with national insolvency is required; it is needed now for low / middle income countries (i.e. those for whom JDC is not advocating an immediate 100 per cent write-off, but who nonetheless clearly exhibit massive problems of indebtedness). It would also arbitrate on odious (e.g. 'dictator' debts) debts. Future development funding for the world's poorest countries should have a strong bias towards grants, until such a time as they can reasonably be expected to bear low-interest loans. Grants should effectively and efficiently target poverty, without compromising environmental and human rights standards, and be free of undemocratic and economically damaging conditionalities. Supportive of the current World Bank and IMF proposals on 'debt sustainability', which could actually lead to poor countries being asked to shoulder more debt in mid / long term. Jubilee Debt Campaign position rejects World Bank and IMF proposals.

Jubilee Debt Campaign advocates a 'human development' approach, reasoning that the poorest countries cannot sustain any debts at all whilst striving:

(a) Millennium Development Goals, including halving global extreme poverty by 2015.

(b) Heavily Indebted Poor Countries, those officially classified as such, are eligible for the current international debt relief programme, or 'HIPC Initiative'. Jubilee Debt Campaign believes there are many non-HIPCs whose debts should also be cancelled.

Debt relief with strings: Many African countries spent more on debt servicing than either health or education. Cameroon, Ethiopia, Gambia, Guinea, Madagascar, Malawi, Mauritania, Senegal, Uganda and Zambia spent more on debt than health in 2002. The Heavily Indebted Poor Countries (HIPC) initiative is the international debt relief scheme. 18 Countries that have received debt cancellation through HIPC (Between 1996 - 2005) amounted to $30 billion. Debt cancellation granted in one day to Iraq by the 'Paris Club' was $31 billion (November 04, 2005).

Zambia's debt repayments to the IMF alone cost $25 million, more than the country's education despite 40 per cent of rural women being unable to read and write. Zambia was unable to employ 9,000 qualified teachers because of a public sector wage freeze imposed by the IMF in 2004 as a condition of receiving HIPC debt relief. Sub-Saharan Africa receives $10 billion in aid every year - but has to pay back at least this amount in debt repayments. Malawi spends more on servicing its debt than on health, despite nearly one in five Malawi's being HIV positive. Bolivia still spends more on debt servicing than on health, even though its infant mortality rate is 10 times that of the UK although it is the second country to be granted debt cancellation after Uganda.

In Benin, 54 per cent of the money saved through debt relief has been spent on health, including on rural primary health care and HIV programmes. In Tanzania, debt relief enabled the government to abolish primary school fees, leading to a 66 per cent increase in attendance. Mozambique was able to offer all children free immunization after it was granted debt relief. In Uganda, debt relief led to 2.2 million people gaining access to water.

Jubilee Research: Jubilee Research is a successor to Jubilee 2000 UK and a part of the Global and National Economics (GNE) programme at New Economic Foundation, London. It is a radical "think-and-do" tank, founded in 1986 by the people who led the first Other Economic Summit – a forerunner to the World Social Forum. It is based on the principles of new economics, and was voted Prospect Magazine's UK Think Tank of the Year in 2002/3. Working on the UK and international economies and the environment, it seeks to promote welfare, human rights and environmental sustainability, and to resolve tensions between these objectives. Its GNE team coordinates work on markets and climate change with Jubilee Research's programme of international financial reform building on the work of the hugely successful Jubilee 2000 debt cancellation campaign.

Jubilee Research continues to provide up-to-date, accurate research, analyses, news and data on international debt. More broadly, it works to establish an international financial system, which fosters and supports the achievement of economic and social rights, including the eradication of poverty, in a framework of sustainability, equity and self-reliance.

Many of the components of such a program have already been largely developed, and have widespread support in civil society. They include:

(a) Criteria for sustainable levels of debt based on human development needs
(b) The Tobin tax and other forms of taxation at the global level
(c) Alternative ways of preventing and resolving financial crises
(d) Appropriate use of capital controls
(e) Democratization of international financial institutions
(f) Improvements in the level and quality of aid
(g) Reform of policy conditionality
(h) International insolvency mechanisms

Jubilee Research seeks to bring these various proposals together into a coherent overall program through an extensive process of consultation with Northern and Southern civil society groups. It is committed to challenging the present economic system by:

(a) Demonstrating the need for and benefits of such a program
(b) Developing a strong global constituency of support.
(c) Resolving technical problems and answering criticisms of the project

It also aims to establish global and regional networks of NGOs and CSOs as a two-way channel of communication to provide input to the formulation of the reform proposal, and to stimulate consistent advocacy on a global scale.[164]

---

[164] Supporting Economic Justice Campaigns World Wide, Web: www.jubileeresearch.org

(C) Liberal Democrat Youth and Students (L D Y S)

The Liberal Democrat Youth and Students[165] organization is the wing of the Liberal Democrat party of all-young people and students in the U.K. They are linked to the main party but this is an autonomous organization because they run their campaigns and speak their mind. This forum possesses executive and various committees to propose and approve policies. The young students are perturbed with the problem of poor countries around the world. This organization suggests that debt of the poorest countries should be completely cancelled and debt of the major countries by 50 per cent. The Third World Debt Conference was held in spring 1991. The observations are:

(a) That according to UNICEF, 500,000 children die every year as a direct result of the debt crisis
(b) That of the 17 most highly indebted countries, 14 are suffering rapid loss of rainforest
(c) That since 1983, net flow of capital has been from the deprived world to the developed world
(d) That last year the Third World transferred $51 billion more to the west in debt payments than it received in new loans and aid combined.
(e) That the British Banks have played a major role in the debt crisis
(f) That over the 1980's the British Banks received an average of over £2 billion in debt repayments each year
(g) That the British Banks have also received considerable tax benefits by creating provisions against their bad debts, but have considerable tax benefits by creating provisions against their bad debts, but have

---

[165] Liberal Democrat Youth and Students, 4 Cowley Street, London

consistently failed to turn these provisions into actual debt relief

(h) That it is estimated that the British Banks have now received over £3 billion in taxpayers' money against provisions; this is equivalent to 3 years entire government aid budget

Conference believes:

(a) That, without substantial debt relief, development in the Third World is impossible
(b) That the debts of the poorest countries should be completely cancelled
(c) That the debts of the other major countries should be cut by at least a half
(d) That legislation should be introduced to ensure tax relief is clawed back if provisions are not converted into actual debt relief.
(e) That future aid should be supplied with the provision that development takes full account of its impact on the environment and be targeted at improving social and economic conditions in the country.

Conference instructs the executives to:

(a) Launch a joint campaign on debt with "Third World First", the student movement against underdevelopment, and to cultivate strong links with this organization.
(b) Organize a day of action targeting British Banks.
(c) Organize a fundraising event to benefit this campaign and anti-debt organization in the Third World.
(d) Make the views of the Student Liberal Democrats known to the Liberal Democrats Federal Policy Committee and the relevant policy-working group.
(e) Work towards protest around the Group of Seven Meeting in July 1991.

(D) Catholic Agency for Overseas Development (C A F O D)

CAFOD had its beginnings in 1961 and believes that all human beings have a right to dignity and respect, and that the world's resources are a gift to be shared equally by all men and women, whatever their race, nationality or religion. Hundreds of thousands of people campaign with CAFOD for fairer trade, for cancellation of third world debt or for an end to the use of anti-personnel landmines have been carried out by people who want to change the way the world works – for the better. CAFOD campaigns for challenging the root causes of poverty. CAFOD[166] shares in the Catholic Church's tasks of proclaiming the good news of the Kingdom of God, bearing witness to love, truth and justice and building bridges of hope with the poor. The Vision is:

(a) The good things of creation are cherished, developed and shared by all;
(b) The rights and of each person are respected, discrimination is ended and all are gathered into a single human family from which no one is excluded;
(c) The voice of the poor is heard and heeded by all, and lives are no longer dominated by greed; and
(d) All have access to food, shelter and clean water; to a livelihood, health and education.

Mission

(a) Empower people in regardless of their race, gender, religion or politics to bring about change through development and relief programmes overseas;

---

[166] Catholic Agency for Overseas Development, Romero Close, London, Registered Charity No. 285776, Email: cafod@cafod.org.uk

(b) Raise public awareness of poverty and injustice, increasing understanding of the world-wide interdependence of rich and poor, and creating the will to change unjust structures and lifestyles; and

(c) Act as an advocate for the poor, articulating a clear analysis of the underlying causes of poverty and challenging governments and international bodies to adopt policies, which incorporate the principles of social justice.

CAFOD fights poverty through love, truth and justice. Hence, the work of CAFOD bears values of compassion, solidarity, partnership, integrity of creation, stewardship and hope. The organization seeks to stand alongside suffering communities in solidarity; it recognizes the importance of hearing the problems of poor to solve with partnership; and utilizes resources most effectively. It hopes that the lives of poor women and men can still improve. The world's richest countries are betraying promises made to help the poor in Africa according to a new CAFOD report, "**Justice Not Charity**".

(a) Rich countries committed in 2000 to the Millennium Development Goals aimed at reducing poverty by 2015, but they have produced neither the necessary financing nor policies to achieve them.

(b) Tony Blair has promised to make Africa a priority during UK presidency of Group of Eight (G8) most industrialized nations in 2005, but action does correspond to promises.

Gap between rich and poor widening

(a) CAFOD Director Chris Bain said, "The gap between the rich and poor is widening. At least 300 million Africans live on less than 50 pence a day. The cost of tackling poverty would not hurt us. The £30 billion spent on

Christmas shopping in the UK could halve global poverty".

(b) Millions of lives depend on the world's richest countries coming up with the money and changing the way they trade. Britain can take the lead to reduce poverty of low-income countries.

(c) CAFOD estimates that Africa needs at least $40 billion per year in aid from the world's richest countries if it is to meet the Millennium Development Goals by 2015.

(d) Currently the continent only receives $18 billion per year from donor countries - about as much as they spend on pet food.

(e) Adding insult to injury, the aid conditions often keep Africans from investing in their economic productivity.

(f) As a result, Africa is way off track in meeting the MDGs by the 2015 target. For example, Africa will, according to projections, only halve the numbers of people living in absolute poverty by 2147.

Betrayal of debts

Although world leaders promised $100 billion in debt relief in 1999 at the G8 Summit in Cologne, only $31 billion has been delivered to date. And the scheme for debt relief for poor countries is so flawed that many countries are worse off than before.

Over a half of the Heavily Indebted Poor Countries (or HIPCs) spend 15 percent of their government revenue on debt servicing. The government of Zambia can't afford to pay schoolteachers enough for survival.

CAFOD argues that in 2005 the G8 must come up with a new framework for debt relief based on a poor country's ability to meet the Millennium Development Goals. Under this regime, almost all HIPCs and some other poor countries like Nigeria would require total debt cancellation and additional aid.

Trade justice needed

Increases in resources are not enough. Without changes to international trade rules, Africa will be caught in a commodity trap. African markets in places like Zambia and Mozambique are more liberalized than many European markets. Meanwhile, the US and EU paid their farmers billions to overproduce goods that were dumped on the unprotected Third World markets. The result is the pauperization of African farmers.

CAFOD wants a reform of northern agricultural subsidies and for African countries to be able to protect their markets. Agriculture is Africa's best chance but its farmers are being shackled by unfair trade rules.

Financial Aspects of CAFOD

The cornerstone of CAFOD' s finances is the funding that it receives from the Catholic Community - an expression of that community's concern and commitment to promote human development and social justice. In 2003 - 2004, CAFOD received contributions more than 19 million pounds from Catholic Community as individuals, and through groups and parishes. CAFOD also received more than 8 million pounds from governments, institutional donors and other aid agencies. Moreover, it received more than 4 million pounds in partnership and programme funding from Department for International Development (DFID) of UK. Their overseas programmes received backing from a wide range of organizations including the European Union, the governments of the Channel Isles, Ireland and the Isle of Man, Comic Relief and members of the Caritas worldwide network of Catholic development and relief agencies. CAFOD practices accountability, uses funds effectively and makes a measurable impact on poverty reduction. In 2002 - 03, CAFOD raised more than 30 million pounds and supported development and emergency relief projects in more than 60 countries particularly in programmes related to poverty reduction, conflict and natural disaster.

Campaigning

CAFOD challenges the root causes of poverty and hopes that 2005 is a year of unprecedented opportunity for rich countries to tackle some of the root causes of poverty. It is behind a massive rallying call for trade justice, debt cancellation and more and better aid. CAFOD criticizes the injustice of European Union farming subsidies and questions, "Would you fly a herd of cows round the world on an all-expenses-paid holiday? CAFOD works with local communities in 64 countries to help them to meet their own needs. It does this through more than 500 partner organizations – trusted, local organizations staffed by local people who are working to reduce poverty.

(E) The Churches and Religious Organizations

The churches and religious organizations of United States of America have requested the congressional leaders and members of the foreign operations conference committee to craft foreign aid legislation that proves the government to be compassionate and caring. These organizations lament for the low levels allocated to debt reduction. Especially in this Jubilee year, we must not abandon our poorest neighbors who are struggling to overcome poverty, consolidate democratic governance and revitalize their economies while burdened with un-payable foreign debts.

The suggestions are:

1. To fund debt relief fully at the level needed to fulfill the US share of the Cologne debt initiative - $225 million for FY 2001, and $210 for FY 2000. They are concerned that any report language on user fees or a moratorium on future borrowing not negatively impact further on the most impoverished citizens in the most impoverished countries;

2. To fund for Global Health and HIV/AIDS response programs at the highest possible levels and to accept House report language detailing the explanation of eligible programs under these categories. As communities that have been actively involved in responding to these crises for some time, the organization urged the members not to exclude the faith community as an appropriate partner, especially in responding to the global AIDS crisis

3. Migration and Refugee Assistance should be at least $700 million. Even the Administration request of $658 million means a reduction of $14 million in temporary protection assistance for African refugees and as a result 9000 refugees cannot take admissions in the U.S.:

(a) To fund adequately for the African Development Foundation at the House level for $16 million, and $10 million for the Inter-American Foundation at the House level
(b) To fund $5 million for the International Fund for Agriculture and Development at the House level;
(c) To support $90 million for the UN Development Programme; and
(d) To fund the International Development Association (at the Senate level) of $750 million

In general the organizations ask the members to fund bilateral and multilateral development assistance, disaster assistance and refugee assistance at the highest possible levels. If it is necessary to find offsets for the recommendations, it is suggested that reducing allocations to international anti-narcotics funding, foreign military financing, and International Military Education and Training can be undertaken to fulfill the target.[167]

(F) Oxford Committee for Famine Relief (OXFAM)

Oxfam was the original postal abbreviation for the Oxford Committee for Famine Relief (OXFAM), which was started in England during World War II to provide relief to war victims in Europe. Since then, Oxfam have been established in 12 countries. In 1942, a group of Quaker intellectuals, social activists, and Oxford academics formed the Oxford Committee for Famine Relief in response to the plight of refugees in Greece. After the war, Oxfam (a name derived from its postal code abbreviation) continued its work, sending materials and financial aid to groups aiding the poor throughout Europe.

As the situation in Europe improved, Oxfam's attention shifted to the needs of people in developing countries. Twenty-eight years later, a group of volunteers founded Oxfam America in 1970 in response to the humanitarian crisis created by the fight for independence in Bangladesh. Oxfam Great Britain provided a loan for the group and, at first; Oxfam America funneled funds exclusively through Oxfam Great Britain. Originally located in Washington, DC, Oxfam America relocated to Boston in 1973.

---

[167] The Washington Office on Africa, "The Washington Office on Africa, July 25, 2000

Oxfam America[168] relies almost exclusively on private funding, and is fortunate to have more than 225,000 individual donors. Among leading humanitarian organizations, it stands alone in its refusal of US government funds, declining support from any sources that might compromise its independence. As conscientious stewards of donors' money, Oxfam America operates efficiently and aims to minimize fundraising and administrative costs. In 2005, it allocated 84 percent of its expenditures for development programs and emergency relief. Between 1999 and 2005, Oxfam allocated an average of nearly 80 percent of its expenditures for those activities, and at least 90 percent of funds designated by donors for humanitarian emergencies directly supported its relief efforts for emergencies. Oxfam strives to exceed or maintain these standards each year.

Oxfam America creates lasting solutions to poverty, hunger, and social injustice. Because it is not tied to any specific political, economic, or religious interests, it is able to independently develop, fund, and support effective programs that help people overcome poverty and secure their rights. To protect its ability to speak out on behalf of those who most need it and to preserve its independence, Oxfam America does not accept funds from organizations involved in industries in which it is campaigning or from the US government. Additionally, Oxfam does not accept product donations because they could compromise the effectiveness of Oxfam programs.

Oxfam America seeks to operate efficiently and to minimize fundraising and administrative costs. In 2005, Oxfam America allocated 84 percent of its

---

[168] The Washington Office on Africa, July 25, 2000, "The Washington Office on Africa Endorses OXFAM Appeal on Debt Relief March 23, 2001" / July 10, 2009, www.oxfamamerica.org

expenditures for development programs and emergency relief. Between 1999 and 2005, Oxfam America allocated an average of nearly 80 percent of its expenditures for those activities. During this period, at least 90 percent of funds designated by donors for humanitarian emergencies directly supported its relief efforts for those emergencies. Oxfam strives to exceed or maintain these standards each year. Oxfam America is one of the top charities rated by leading charitable watchdog organizations, including the American Institute of Philanthropy.

Oxfam America is not able to provide financial aid to individuals, nor can arrange, organize, or fund study-abroad programs. However, to find answers to financial aid questions, Oxfam partners with local communities to address their needs directly and to create solutions that will be sustainable over time. Due to its limited funds, Oxfam can only support organizations that are working in approximately 30 countries in which it has programs. Here are some additional details on how Oxfam America allocates funds:

(a) The majority of grants are for one year.
(b) In 2004, Oxfam funded over 244 partner organizations.
(c) Grants usually range from $10,000 to $40,000, and in a few cases up to $60,000.
(d) In general, grant proposals are developed in cooperation between Oxfam's regional staff and potential partner organizations. While Oxfam usually refers unsolicited requests to regional staff (if the proposal is in line with the regional strategy), such proposals are rarely funded.
(e) Oxfam does not fund individuals (education, health, livelihoods etc.).
(f) Oxfam does not fund government projects, churches, clinics/health centers, schools, and government bodies.

Employment: Volunteers and interns play a vital role in helping Oxfam America achieve its goals. The nature of work often requires very specific knowledge and skills, and it can sometimes be dangerous. Anyone can participate in Oxfam's online community and receive our monthly e-newsletter and occasional action alerts. While many of email campaigns are targeted to US-based organizations and authorities, Oxfam also coordinates with groups all over the world.

General: Oxfam is constantly in need of dedicated individuals to mobilize their communities in the fight against hunger, poverty, and social injustice. Here are just a few suggested ways to channel individuals' energies to help:

(a) Learn more about what Oxfam does, the fundamental rights that Oxfam America defends and which underlies the issues Oxfam works on.
(b) Address the root causes of poverty by taking action online.
(c) Help in education and outreach efforts by holding an Oxfam Hunger Banquet.
(d) Become a monthly Pledge Partner.

The headquarters is in Boston and its Policy and Advocacy Office is in Washington, DC. Oxfam works, campaigns, and takes action in the fight against poverty, hunger and social injustice. The OXFAM urged the support for $ 240 million in debt relief for the world's poorest countries to fulfill the United States pledge to an international debt relief plan. The Foreign Operations Authorization and Appropriations bills included $ 240 million in FY 2002 and an additional $ 135 million would be added in FY 2003. The OXFAM is convinced that the USA administration believes that debt relief has already been put to good use, for example:

Uganda has enrolled over two million new students in school and significantly reduced the rate of HIV transmission.

Tanzania and Benin will end public school fees, a major obstacle for poor families.

Honduras has committed to expand schooling up to the 9th grade and will hire 1,000 new teachers.

Senegal will hire 2,000 teachers per year for three years (6,000 totals).

Mali, Mozambique and Senegal are planning to use the savings from debt relief to increase their spending on HIV / AIDS prevention.

Debt relief does make a difference in people's lives. Hence, the congress took crucial steps for debt relief by authorizing and funding bilateral debt cancellation, authorizing and funding multilateral debt relief, and authorizing the IMF to revalue part of its gold reserves to write off a portion its debt. It also affirmed a new process for debt relief and lending at the World Bank and IMF that includes greater transparency, participation, and poverty reduction.

The US shoulders only 4 per cent of the total $27 billion cost of debt relief for over 30 countries. The US has authorized and appropriated $545 million out of $ 920 million and has specified the following conditions for debt relief:

(a) The countries must perform satisfactorily under an economic reform program.
(b) Promote civil society participation
(c) Implement anti-corruption measures and transparent policy making
(d) Adopt strategies for poverty reduction including civil society input

(e) Strengthen private sector growth, trade and investment and
(f) Prohibits those countries, which violate human rights, support terrorism or undertake excessive military spending.

But US have the capacity to support debt relief for the poorest countries through implementation of international agreement worth of billions of dollars.

Crisis in Africa

On July 10, 2009 OXFAM informed that this is a state of emergency with the economic crisis costing Africa $245 billion in 2009. The G8 promised an emergency plan of $25 billions for 2009, but the amount has not yet been sanctioned till date. The G8 offers broken promises and photo opportunities for Africa.

Oxfam welcomes the G8 joint statement that commits leaders to focus on hunger and the needs of small farmers. However, G8 has committed $20 billion over 3 years for agriculture development. The new money makes a down payment on eliminating hunger. With a billion people facing hunger, more new money is still needed.

Canada 2010 is the end of the road for the G8 - all the promises they have made are due. They have 12 short months to avoid being remembered as the ones who let the poor and the planet die.

With the 2-degree limit, the G8 effectively agreed that the floodwaters shouldn't reach the ceiling. But they did nothing about the water already swirling around African necks. The G8 must deliver action now to counter and cope with climate chaos. This means that developed countries to deliver more than $150 billion per year for developing country action on adaptation and emissions.

The G8 are leaving today with a huge unfinished agenda. Millions of children are out of school, millions more dying from curable diseases. This is shameful and the Canadians must move fast to fix it. There won't be any second chances.

(G). Women's Environment and Development Organization October 15-19, 2001

The Women's Environment and Development Organization of United Nations Financing for Development (FfD) held its third preparatory meeting in New York on October 15-19, 2001 and recommended the following suggestions for the international community. These are as follows:

(a) Recognize that debt financing is an integral part of a country's development efforts
(b) Demand unconditional debt cancellation based on credible economic, social, moral, legal and historical arguments, including the illegitimate debts of all Southern countries, such as those that cannot be serviced without causing harm to people and communities, those incurred by corruption and fraud and those incurred by exorbitant interest rates
(c) Establish an independent, transparent arbitration process for debt cancellation and an ethical lending and borrowing mechanism to prevent future recurrence of the debt crisis
(d) Eliminate all conditionalities attached to new loans and debt relief
(e) Initiate public hearings for stakeholders to articulate coherent strategies and propose alternatives for debt relief. Establish an independent and transparent arbitration process for debt cancellation,
(f) Build civil society capacity to enable its effective participation in such debt relief discourse, in the monitoring of current debt

relief processes and in the acquisition of new loans by governments; and

(g) Develop an ethical lending-borrowing process, which would involve civil society as well as national parliaments.[169]

(H) Make Poverty History
August 2006

The Make Poverty History campaign (MPH) in Australia comprises more than 70 non-government development agencies, faith groups and community-based organizations. It comes under the auspices of the Australian Council for International Development (ACFID) and is a part of the Global Call to Action against Poverty. The common objective of all groups involved in the campaign is to encourage the Australian Government to take a leadership role in achieving the Millennium Development Goals by committing to more and better aid, fair trade and dropping the debt of poor countries.

1. Reduction of Poverty: The White Paper of the Australian Government commits to maintaining a focus on the Mekong region, which includes least developed countries such as Cambodia and Laos. Given that the majority of the least developed countries are in Africa, there is a compelling case for the Australian Government to apply some of the aid increase to Africa. While Australia's focus on the Asia-Pacific region is understandable, the sheer scale of development challenges facing Africa renders it worthy of greater, albeit carefully targeted, attention. To address these concerns, Make Poverty History is asking the Australian Government to:

---

[169] Gail Lerner, World Council of Churches Ecumenical Team (WCC/ET) Rebecca Desiree Lozada, Freedom from Debt Coalition, Philippines, Women's Environment and Development Organization.

(a) Commit to, and provide a timetable for, increasing Australia's overseas development assistance to 0.5 per cent of GNI by 2010, and 0.7 per cent by 2015.

(b) Demonstrate its commitment to the MDGs by: (a) Incorporating them in Aus-AID's planning and evaluation approaches; (b) Providing an annual progress report to Parliament on Australia's efforts to achieve the MDGs.

(c) Provide sufficient resources and assistance for developing countries to implement well-designed MDG-based national development strategies and structure bilateral assistance around these strategies.

(d) Continue to significantly increase the level of investment in people, through the provision of funding directed at achieving the MDGs, for example basic health and education programs.

(e) Actively participate in the UN Financing for Development process, including supporting consideration of new international development financing options.

(f) Revise Aus-AID's monitoring and evaluation processes to reflect the central role of the poverty reduction agenda.

(g) Contribute Australia's fair share (around 1.5 per cent) of the total costs of the Global Fund for AIDS, TB and Malaria, and the Education for All Fast Track Initiative.

(h) Continue to implement its commitments to untie all Australian aid (both formally and in practice) and maximize capacity development, control and participation by developing countries.

(i) Expand assistance to the poorest countries in our region and allocate at least 0.20 per cent of GNI to the Least Developed Countries.

(j) Consult with the NGO sector on strategies to improve the MDGs and the role of the Australian aid program in achieving them.

2. Trade in Services (GATS): The Australian Government is a leading proponent of liberalization in the services sector because it accounts for over 70 per cent of Australia's national output and employs four out of every five Australian workers. Exports of services account for about one-quarter of our total exports and are growing fast. While tourism and education services make up the bulk of these, Australia also exports architectural, engineering, legal, accounting, financial, insurance and medical services.

The Productivity Commission has estimated that Australia could gain up to US$ 2 billion a year from the global liberalization of trade in services. When the WTO negotiations on services were first launched, it was agreed that countries would only have to participate on a voluntary basis, offering to liberalize sectors if they decided it would be beneficial. However, over the last year developing countries have been under increasing pressure to engage in the negotiations and open their markets to Foreign Service providers. It has even been suggested that responding to requests to liberalize services is effectively an unofficial condition of promised agricultural reform. Australia has joined with other countries to make requests to developing countries – particularly ASEAN countries – regarding the liberalization of relevant services. It is crucially important that these countries are not pressured into agreements, which have irreversible implications for them. There must be no coercion in this process – developing countries must be given more time and greater flexibility to negotiate fair agreements on services.

The Make Poverty History campaign urges the Australian Government to continue to play a leadership role by advocating for fairer trade at the international level. In particular, the campaign asking the Government for the following objectives:

(a) To maintain its pressure on rich countries, such as the US, EU and Japan, to significantly reduce or eliminate agricultural subsidies, and advocate for a genuine opening of markets in developed countries to agricultural exports from developing countries.
(b) To advocate for greater international recognition of the principle that developing countries should be given the power to decide the pace and extent of their trade liberalization
(c) To ensure that food security, rural development or the livelihoods of poor and vulnerable people are protected in any liberalization of developing country agricultural markets, including through appropriate provision for the use of 'Special Products'.
(d) To respect the principles of 'special and differential treatment' and 'less than full reclprocIty' for developing countries in NAMA negotiations, including through modification of the tariff formula to reduce its disproportionate impact on developing countries, and through the inclusion of a 'Special Safeguard Mechanism'.
(e) To preserve the voluntary nature of the GATS negotiations
(f) To ensure that governments retain the right to regulate foreign companies operating in the services sector, and support the exemption of essential services (including health, education, water, sanitation and electricity) from liberalization.
(g) To increase funding for trade-related capacity building and the broader development of skills and infrastructure in developing countries
(h) To support initiatives aimed at helping small producers in developing countries in areas such as meeting quality standards, marketing, labeling, and accessing appropriate price hedging and insurance schemes;

(i) To establish a scheme enabling residents of Pacific countries to undertake seasonal work in Australia as a major support to poverty reduction within the region.

(j) To support initiatives aimed at improving labour conditions in developing countries and encouraging clear labeling and certification so that Australian consumers can reward companies that provide fair working conditions. And

(k) To Work towards international and domestic legal arrangements which minimize corruption in trade and require Australian companies to adhere to human rights, labour and environmental standards when they operate in other countries.

3. Debt Relief: The Australian Government has supported debt relief for the world's poorest countries as part of the Heavily Indebted Poor Countries (HIPC) initiative. Specifically, the Government has given $122 million in multilateral support for the initiative and cancelled the bilateral debts of Ethiopia and Nicaragua. The G8 Meeting in July 2005 agreed to the Multilateral Debt Relief Initiative (MDRI) - an extension of the HIPC initiative, worth US $37 billion, whereby 100 per cent of the debt owed by the world's 18 poorest countries would be immediately cancelled. The Australian Government has pledged a financial commitment to this initiative. While the Government's support of the HIPC and MDRI initiatives has been welcome, there is a need a genuine need to extend debt relief to additional countries. 31 of the 59 countries identified by the United Nations Development Program as least likely to achieve the MDGs are HIPC countries. Although a small creditor in global terms, Australia has a strong economy, a credible international voice and relatively little bilateral debt owed to it by poor countries. Thus we would urge the Australian Government to take a positive approach to the extension of debt relief to other poor countries.

The United Kingdom Government has committed to pay its share of the debt service costs for all 66 IDA-only countries and has challenged other countries to do the same. The Australian Government is yet to respond to this challenge. Major bilateral and multilateral creditors have acknowledged the lack of an effective sovereign bankruptcy system, but have failed to agree on the form such a system should take. Australia could provide fresh leadership to address this major gap in the international financial system.

The Make Poverty History Campaign is asking the Australian Government to:

(a) Advocate that debt relief programs be broadened to incorporate all the 66 developing countries, which are eligible only for loans from the World Bank's International Development Association.
(b) Advocate for debt relief programs like the HIPC initiative and the Multilateral Debt Relief Initiative to be provided without harmful economic conditions.
(c) Immediately address the issue of the bilateral debts owed to it by its two largest debtor countries, Indonesia and The Philippines, by exploring debt relief options such as debt-for-poverty-reduction swaps.
(d) Advocate for the immediate cancellation of all debts found to be odious.

The Jubilee Debt Campaign has been successful in placing the need for a sovereign debt bankruptcy mechanism on the global economic agenda. The IMF and its members are examining what the IMF calls a 'sovereign debt restructuring mechanism'. Many academic articles have been published on this topic.

(a) Support the adoption of a fair and transparent Arbitration Process for "bankrupt" poor countries.
(b) Actively pursue reforms to increase democratic and accountable governance within international financial institutions.

4. Good Governance: The Australian aid program, like many other aid programs, has a strong emphasis on supporting good governance projects. Improved governance is essential to achieve the MDGs, however the Goals will not be achieved if aid program focuses solely on good governance at the expense of poverty reduction – both are essential. While many middle-income countries could afford to achieve the MDGs if they improved the effectiveness of their current programs, the poorest countries suffer from an absolute shortage of resources. These countries will not achieve the Goals without assistance from developed countries.

The OECD Development Assistance Committee (DAC) Peer Review of Australian aid highlighted the importance of Australia maintaining a focus on building the capacity of developing country governments to reduce poverty. Similarly, the group of experts (the 'Core Group'), commissioned by the Government to make recommendations for the White Paper on aid, emphasized the need for Australia's aid program to adopt a stronger focus on 'investing in people'.

Make Poverty History welcomed the Government's decision to implement this recommendation. The White Paper identifies "investing in people" as one of four key themes for the Australian aid program over the next decade and foreshadows significant funding increases for education and health services. The widespread failure of many developing country governments to adequately supply public services, such as clean water, primary healthcare, education and other services vital to the livelihood of poor people, has been well documented. For example, this formed the core theme of the 2004 World Development Report.

Many Make Poverty History member organizations have extensive experience in the provision of essential services to poor communities. Their strong view is that improving the performance of these public services is critical for good governance, as well as for poverty reduction. Civil society also has an important role to play in improving governance. In particular, civil society empowerment to ensure the accountability of government service providers is vital for improving the effectiveness of services to poor communities. There are more than 50 social accountability programs being developed or implemented in the Asia-Pacific alone. Such programs that develop the capacity of civil society require continued and new support. For this reason, Make Poverty History welcomes the "Building Demand for Better Governance" program outlined in the White Paper on Australia's aid program.

5. Combating Corruption: Corruption is a serious and widespread problem in many developing countries – it reduces economic development and minimizes domestic resources, diverts aid and hurts the poor most. The causes of corruption are complex and must be tackled by comprehensive and multi-strategy approaches. Effective anticorruption strategies can take many years and flexibility is required to learn from what has and has not worked. Significantly, however, aid can work despite corruption. Aid can and does help reduce suffering in even the most corrupt societies. The global development experience demonstrates that particular aid programs can be further improved to make them more effective in corrupt environments. Instead of cutting aid to corrupt countries, aid delivery mechanisms and strategies should be modified to take account of corrupt practices. If we are to reduce corruption and help the poor we need to provide corruption immune and corruption busting aid as part of a range of actions to boost development and reduce poverty. Aid should not be suspended because of corruption. Suspending aid is unlikely to reduce corruption; however it will most certainly increase the suffering of the poor and increase the risks of global problems such as infectious disease and terrorism impacting on Australia. However aid in seriously corrupt contexts will need to be constrained, well targeted and have specific conditionalities imposed.

Aus AID has a strong focus on anticorruption an activity in its programs and this focus is maintained in the White Paper on aid. It has provided support for a number of Transparency International national integrity studies and has funded ombudsman and anti-corruption mechanisms. It has sought to improve police, judicial and parliamentary accountability in several countries and supported the Asian Development Bank / OECD Anti-Corruption Initiative for the Asia-Pacific. Australia was also one of the first countries to ratify the UN Convention against Corruption and has recently announced its support for the Extractive Industries Transparency Initiative. This positive work provides a base for Australia to expand its support for and integration of anti-corruption measures in the aid program. The challenge for the Australian Government is to enhance the effectiveness of aid in corrupt contexts while supporting partner nations in efforts to reduce corruption.

Make Poverty History (MPH) welcomes the Government's commitment, outlined in the White Paper, to mainstream anti-corruption efforts in Australia's aid program, develop a whole of-government anti-corruption strategy and continue to provide support for regional and global anti-corruption initiatives. We also welcome the commitment to provide support to build demand for transparency and anti-corruption within countries.

MPH asks the Government as follows:

(a) Train all staff in Government agencies, which are responsible for aid program planning, implementation and evaluation, in knowledge of the relevant law, conventions and effective anti-corruption strategies.
(b) Provide long-term and consistent support to partner countries, and anticorruption reformers within those countries, in their efforts to reduce corruption and, as foreshadowed in the White Paper, provide support for international and regional approaches which provide a common voice when dealing with corrupt governments.
(c) Provide strong support and funding for both institutional good governance and, as the White Paper outlines, grass roots or demand-led anti corruption strategies.
(d) Implement and provide active support for the international promotion of key transparency initiatives such as (i) The Global Transparency Initiative, (ii) The Global Reporting Initiative, (iii) The IMF Code of Good Practice on Fiscal Transparency and (iv) The OECD Guidelines for Multinational Enterprises.
(e) Improve Aus AID's openness and accountability and adopt an information disclosure policy based on that of the World Bank.
(f) Increase penalties for Australian companies found guilty of bribing foreign governments and implement better systems for detecting foreign bribery transactions when conducting ATO tax audits.
(g) Actively support initiatives designed to maximize repatriation of corruptly obtained money, including an International Convention

to facilitate this, and give this issue the same level of priority that has been given to tracking terrorism related funds.

(h) Establish an independent extractive industry complaints mechanism for Australian companies.

6. Access to Technology: Access to modern technologies for both health needs and sustainable economic growth are critical for reducing poverty. Australia has some of the most effective health technology to combat poverty-related illnesses and is a world leader in other fields such as agriculture, water services, remote communications and waste treatment. The Australian Government does fund and make relevant research available to developing countries. It is also a supporter of the Declaration on the Trade-Related Aspects of Intellectual Property Rights (TRIPS) Agreement and Public Health, which allows developing countries to produce and import generic drugs in emergency situations. Nevertheless, there is much potential for Australia to take a greater leadership role in making relevant technologies available to developing countries. Make Poverty History encourages the Australian Government to:

(a) Provide its fair share (1.5 per cent) of the cost of international initiatives to develop vaccines and treatments for the major developing world diseases, including HIV and AIDS, tuberculosis, malaria and diarrhea diseases.

(b) Actively support global initiatives to provide greater incentives for private sector research into HIV and AIDS, tuberculosis, malaria and diarrhea diseases.

(c) Develop ways in which Australian research expertise could be increasingly applied to developing world needs.

(d) Provide information technology support to developing country partners to enhance their capacity to monitor and implement their MDG plans.

7. Peace-Keeping and Conflict Resolution: Conflict within and between countries presents a major threat to development and the achievement of the MDGs. The Australian Government's intervention in Timor-Leste and its participation in the Regional Assistance Mission to the Solomon Islands and Enhanced Cooperation Program with Papua New Guinea demonstrate the regional leadership role, which the Government has taken in seeking to prevent and minimize conflict. It is important that conflict reduction programs are based on both institution building, such as policing and legal structures, as well as investment in community-level conflict resolution and the enhancement of human rights. The Australian Government already supports a number of peace and human rights initiatives. An enhancement of this approach could be a cost effective and beneficial means of conflict prevention in neighbouring fragile states.

Make Poverty History encourages the Australian Government to:

(a) Promote community-based conflict resolution programs and programs which enhance the observance of human rights.
(b) Support regional and global security through national security funds, preserving the use of ODA for poverty-focused initiatives.

In short, the Millennium Development Goals present an unprecedented opportunity for the international community to work together in a united effort to make poverty history. If the international community fulfils its commitment to meet the MDGs, literally millions and millions of lives will be saved. The purpose of the Make Poverty History campaign is to remind the world leaders to achieve these goals for a hunger-free world. Rich countries, like Australia, can play a crucial role by giving more and better aid, insisting on fair trade and canceling the massive debts of poor countries. Moreover, the MDGs offer a useful planning for coordinating Australian aid in low-income countries. Not only will they serve to increase the focus of Australia's program on poverty reduction, but they will also enable Australia to act in concert with virtually every other OECD country.

Australia has already taken significant steps to improve aid quality and coordination and to build sustainable economic growth throughout its immediate region. It is now time for the Government to bring its substantial experience and skills to a broader poverty effort, particularly across the whole Asia-Pacific region. The recommendations in this platform are intended to help the Australian Government, not simply meet its international obligations, but blaze a trail of leadership in the global fight against poverty.[170]

2009 Campaign:

Make Poverty History continued to campaign for significant policy changes that improves the lives of people living in extreme poverty. The MDGs would remain central to the campaign. The organization focuses on maternal health, child mortality, climate change and development. Climate change seriously threatens the lives and livelihoods of poor people around the world and severely hinders developing countries efforts to reach their objectives of poverty reduction and sustainable development. Both of these campaigns would continue to raise awareness throughout the Australian population and inspire action amongst the community and political leaders.

---

[170] Make Poverty History -Policy Platform, August 2006/ 2009

Conclusion

Debt was caused and multiplied in all the least and low developed countries because of foreign rule for centuries, odious debts, mismanaged spending and lending, rampant corruption, internal conflicts, wars at the borders, natural calamities, easy availability and long period loan and lack of foresight of political leaders.

The developing world now spends US $13 on debt payment for every US $1 it receives in grants.

The low-income countries pay US $2.30 in debt service for every US $1 it received in grant-in-aid.

It is estimated that 60 least developed and developing countries borrowed $540 billion loans, paid $550 billion in debt service (including principal + interest) over the last three decades, yet there exists $ 523 billion as debt burden.

In short, the poor countries have already paid the loan amount in full but the same amount is still pending on these countries. The developed countries are acting as the unscrupulous moneylenders for the low-income countries. The poor nations and poor people are in extreme poverty; they are in extreme need for debt relief on the outstanding balance to breath freely. However, this suffocation has attracted the world activist organizations to claim for debt relief. The Jubilee Debt Campaign, AFRODAD, CAFOD, OXFAM and Make Poverty History have organized mass rallies in different parts of the world to advocate on behalf of their poor brethren for protecting the basic human rights and human dignity.

The inhabitants of the low-income countries are disgusted of hearing terms like "debt, trade, aid, grants, donations, industrialization, infrastructure credit, visit of World Bank and IMF officials and structural adjustment programs intended for the benefits of the poor people and poor countries".

The advices of funding institutions and developed countries have caused counter- productive results in these countries. The number of starving people has reached one billion and another two billion people are devoid of proper diet and the problem is increasing. The reckless and self-interested lending of rich world has resulted in increase of poverty, debt, disease, migration and terrorism. Let the rich countries chalk out plans and programs for food security, healthcare, primary education, peace, humanity and development for all.

The suggestions are:

(a) 100 per cent debt relief should be awarded on Multilateral Debt and Bilateral Debt as on **December 31, 2015** to low-income countries and by **December 31, 2016** to low-middle-income countries.
(b) The developed countries should increase in current level of aid to HIPCs from $15 billion to $ 46 billion per year for fulfilling MDGs
(c) Military spending of all countries should be reduced by international law.
(d) Developed countries should donate 0.7 per cent of national income for the welfare of poor countries and poor people.
(e) Human rights and human dignity must be upheld in all countries. Discrimination must be ended.
(f) Empowering people regardless of their race, gender, religion, or politics
(g) Funding for global health and eradication of HIV / AIDs, Malaria, TB and other diseases

(h) Elimination of all conditionalities attached to new loans and debt relief
(i) Reduction of agricultural subsidies by developed countries
(j) Support for institutional good governance
(k) Ensuring food security and adequate livelihood to poor and vulnerable people and investing in rural development
(l) All IDA countries (66 countries) should avail debt relief.
(m) Odious debts must be cancelled.
(n) Corruption must be combated in all LDCs through anti-corruption drive and speedy legal action
(o) Encouraging world organizations for peace-keeping and conflict resolution

In short, these international organizations emphasize on 100 per cent debt relief, reduction of poverty in all the LDCs and protection of human rights for ensuring justice to all. In other words, debt relief assumes a pivotal role in strengthening world peace. The developed countries should not exploit the poor but can render advices and assist the poor people and poor countries for mutual advantages.

+++++

Chapter- VII

G 8 COUNTRIES AND DEBT RELIEF

DILEMMA IN GRANTING DEBT RELIEF

Poverty is not natural. It is man-made and it can be overcome and eradicated by the actions of human beings. And overcoming poverty is not a gesture of charity. It is an act of justice. It is the protection of a fundamental human right, the right to dignity and a decent life.

- Nelson Mandela

Our planet needs partnership of donor and debtor countries for securing 'world peace' – a world free of terror, a world free of hunger and a world of humanity. It is possible if the low-income countries emphasize on true democracy, accountability, and transparency in administration. But these countries mis-utilize borrowed funds; engage in factional fighting or war with neighboring countries; and procure war equipments for the purpose of border disputes. These countries encounter ethnic problems, conversion of religion, political-administrative corruption and lawlessness. They face problems like poverty, hunger, starvation, unemployment, illiteracy, and absence of healthcare facilities, human trafficking, and illicit trade of drugs, refugee problems and internally displaced persons. But the rich and developed countries accrue benefits from these low-income countries at the cost of millions of starving people through excessive advices, conditionality, credits, grants and aids. If the developed countries do not trade with poverty and hunger but assist the low-income countries with a humanitarian approach, we can achieve world peace.

If G8 countries extend debt relief, assistance in the fight against AIDS, Malaria, TB, and adopt fairer trade with the poor countries, poverty of poor countries can be minimized. These countries should advise the debtor countries for pro-poor, pro-agricultural and pro-rural policies to benefit 100 per cent of people of the poor countries. As long as deaths by starvation is an usual phenomenon in the low-income countries, it would speak that donor countries are advising wrong policies and the debtor countries are violating the basic human rights of the poor. In this chapter, the role of G8 countries and their action plan have been incorporated as these countries have the capacity to make the world free of hunger. So, their policies on poverty reduction and debt relief have been included.

The G-7 (Group of Seven) Summits, which comprised of France, USA, UK, Germany, Japan, Italy, and Canada, were launched in 1975 with three objectives:

(a) Developing collective management of the world economy to replace American hegemony
(b) Reconciling the domestic and external pressure generated by interdependence; and
(c) Mobilizing political leadership to resolve problems beyond the reach of bureaucracies.

The G-7 (Group of Seven) was converted to G-8 (Group of Eight) in the year 1997 with addition of Russia and officially it became G-8 in 1998. During the three decades, the G-7 / G-8 have assumed more importance as these nations have the capacity to change the world economy. The Summits' communiqués include more of economic resolutions and less of political resolutions. The G-7 / G-8 Summits were held annually on the invitation of host countries since 1975 and since the 1990s, the Summits are held in three phases. These are official level, ministerial level and President / Prime Minister Level. The Summits also invite World organizations like the World Bank, IMF, WTO, and UN for expert views. At the Denver Summit (1997), Mr. Bill Clinton, the President of USA proposed help for the poverty stricken African countries. Similarly, at the Cologne Summit (1999), Mr. Gerhard Schroeder, the Chancellor of Germany proposed debt relief for poor countries. The Cologne Summit also decided to cancel US $ 100 billion of the debts owed by the worlds most Heavily Indebted Poor Countries.[171]

In this chapter, the salient resolutions of Toronto Summit (1988), London Summit (1991), Lyon Summit (1996), Koln Summit (1999), Okinawa Summit (2000), Genoa Summit (2001), L'aquila (Italy) Summit (2009), have been discussed to draw conclusions on the proposals of G7/G8 countries and their commitments towards debt relief and poverty eradication in the least developed and less developed countries. In addition to Summit proposals, Four ministers on a Common Cause, Joint Report on Progress on Cologne Debt Initiative, Canada Announces Debt Relief for Asian Countries, G-8 Proposal for HIPC Debt Cancellation, G-8 Africa Action Plan, Motion for Resolution in the European Parliament, G-8 Agrees Cancellation of World Bank

---

[171] Bayne, N " Decision Making in the G7 / G8 System" Paper for ECPR Workshops, Grenoble, April 2001

and IMF Debt, Contribution of German Government, and G-20 Leaders' Statement: The Pittsburgh Summit have been added to highlight the importance of debt relief for the low and least developed countries.

G-7 – Toronto Summit

June 19 - 21, 1988

The Heads of State or Government of seven major industrial nations and the President of the Commission of the European Communities, have met in Toronto for the fourteenth annual Economic Summit. In the present study, we have included resolutions on 'Developing Countries and debt relief'.[172]

Developing Countries and Debt

1. The performance of developing countries is increasingly important to the world economy. Central to the prospects of the developing countries are a healthy global economic environment and an open trading system, adequate financial flows and, most important, their commitment to appropriate economic reform. The problems of many heavily indebted developing countries are a cause of economic and political concern and can be a threat to political stability in developing countries. Several countries find themselves in that situation in various regions of the world: Latin America, Africa and the Pacific, particularly the Philippines, and that merits our special attention.

---

[172] Resolutions on environment, human frontier science program, International Economic Policy Cooperation on Macroeconomic Policies and Exchange Rates, Structural Reforms, Multilateral Trading System/Uruguay Round, Newly Industrializing Economies and bio-ethics. Moreover, political declarations on securing democracy such as resolutions on East-West, Terrorism and Narcotics and political issues on Middle-East, South Africa, and Cambodia are not included.

Middle Income Countries

2. Numbers of highly indebted middle-income countries continue to have difficulties servicing their external debt and generating the investment necessary for sustainable growth. The market oriented, growth led strategy based on the case-by-case approach remains the only viable approach for overcoming their external debt problems.

3. G-7 is encouraged that many indebted countries have begun the difficult process of macroeconomic adjustment and structural reform necessary for sustained progress, encouraging the return of flight capital and new investment flows. The success of these efforts is essential for improving the economic performance and strengthening the creditworthiness of these countries.

4. Official financing has played a central role in the debt strategy through the Paris Club (U.S. $73 billion of principal and interest have been consolidated since 1983) and the flexible policies of export credit agencies. The international financial institutions will continue to have a pivotal role. We endorse the recent initiatives taken by the International Monetary Fund to strengthen its capacity to support medium-term programs of macroeconomic adjustment and structural reform, and to provide greater protection for adjustment programs from unforeseen external developments. G-7 strongly supports the full implementation of the World Bank's U.S. $75 billion General Capital Increase to strengthen its capacity to promote adjustment in middle-income countries. G-7 also supports greater awareness by international financial institutions of the environmental impact of their development programs.

5. Commercial banks have played an important role in supporting debtor countries' reform efforts through an expanded menu of financing options, which has

facilitated the channeling of commercial bank lending into productive uses. Their continued involvement is indispensable to the debt strategy. In this regard, the World Bank and IMF can play an important catalytic role in mobilizing additional financing from private (and official) sources in support of debtor countries' adjustment programs.

6. G-7 notes that in recent years there has been increasing recourse to innovative financing techniques. The important characteristics of these techniques are that they are voluntary, market oriented, and applied on a case-by-case basis. The "menu approach" has engendered new financial flows and, in some cases, reduced the existing stock of debt. The further broadening of the menu approach and the encouragement of innovative financing techniques to improve the quality of new lending would enhance the flexibility of the present strategy, but particular initiatives would have to be carefully considered.

7. International direct investment plays an important role in spurring economic growth and structural adjustment in developing countries. Thus it contributes to alleviating debt problems. Developing countries should welcome and encourage such investment by creating a favorable investment climate.

Debt of the Poorest

8. An increase in concessional resource flows is necessary to help the poorest developing countries resume sustained growth, especially in cases where it is extremely difficult for them to service their debts. Since Venice, progress in dealing with the debt burden of these countries has been encouraging. Paris Club creditors are rescheduling debt at extended grace and repayment periods. In addition, the recent enhancement of the IMF's Structural

Adjustment Facility, the World Bank and Official Development Assistance (ODA) agencies enhanced program of co-financing. And the fifth replenishment of the African Development Fund will mobilize a total of more than U.S. $18 billion in favor of the poorest and most indebted countries undertaking adjustment efforts over the period 1988/90. Out of this total, U.S. $15 billion will be channeled to Sub-Saharan African countries.

9. G-7 welcomes proposals made by members to ease further the debt service burdens of the poorest countries that are undertaking internationally approved adjustment programs. G-7 has achieved consensus on rescheduling official debt of these countries within a framework of comparability. Rescheduling allows official creditors to choose among concessional interest rates usually on shorter maturities, longer repayment periods at commercial rates, and partial write-offs of debt service obligations during the consolidation period, or a combination of these options.

This approach allows official creditors to choose options consistent with their legal or budgetary constraints. The Paris Club has been urged to work out necessary technicalities to ensure comparability by the end of this year at the very latest. This approach will provide benefits over and above the impressive multilateral agreements to help the poorest countries over the past year. G-7 also welcomes the action taken by a number of creditor governments to write-off or to remove the burden of ODA loans, and also urge countries to maintain a high grant element in their future assistance to the poorest.[173]

---

[173] U.S. Department of State, *Bulletin*, No 2137, (August 1988): 49-52; Canada, Department of External Affairs, *Toronto Economic Summit Economic Declaration* (Ottawa, 1988) [unpublished].

G-7 London Summit

Economic Declaration, July 17, 1991

1. The Heads of State and Government of the seven major industrial democracies and the representatives of the European Community, met in London for our seventeenth annual Summit.

2. The spread of freedom and democracy, which we celebrated at Houston, has gathered pace over the last year. Together the international community has overcome a major threat to world peace in the Gulf. But new challenges and new opportunities confront us. G-7 seeks to build world partnership, based on common values, and to strengthen the international order. Its aim is to underpin democracy, human rights, the rule of law and sound economic management, which together provide the key to prosperity. To achieve this aim, we will promote a truly multilateral system, which is secure and adaptable and in which responsibility is shared widely and equitably. Central to our aim is the need for a stronger, more effective UN system, and for greater attention to the proliferation and transfer of weapons.

3. The Group of Twenty-four (G-24) process, inaugurated by the Arch Summit and chaired by the European Commission, has mobilized $31 billion in bilateral support for these countries, including balance of payments finance to underpin IMF-supported programmes. Such programmes are in place for Poland, Hungary and Czechoslovakia. G-7 welcomes the contributions already made for Bulgaria and Romania. G-7 is intensifying the G-24 co-ordination process and the members reaffirm their shared willingness to play their fair part in the global assistance effort. A single topic on 'developing countries and debt' is as follows.[174]

---

[174] The Ministry of Foreign Affairs of Japan, July 17, 1991. However resolutions on other nine sub-chapters are not

Developing Countries and Debt

4. Developing countries are playing an increasingly constructive role in the international economic system, including the Uruguay Round. Many have introduced radical policy reforms and are adopting the following principles:

(a) Respect for human rights and for the law, which encourages individuals to contribute to development
(b) Democratic pluralism and open systems or administration, accountable to the public;
(c) Sound market-based economic policies to sustain development and bring people out of poverty.

5. G-7 commends these countries and urges others to follow their example. Good governance not only promotes development at home, but also helps to attract external finance and investment from all sources. Its steadfast commitment to helping developing countries, in conjunction with a durable non-inflationary recovery of their economies and the opening of their markets, will be the most effective way for enhancing prosperity in the developing world.

6. Many of these countries, especially the poorest, need our financial and technical assistance to buttress their own development endeavours. Additional aid efforts are required to enhance both the quantity and the quality of our support for priority development issues. These include alleviating poverty, improving health, education and training and enhancing the environmental quality of our aid. G-7 endorses the increasing attention being given to population issues in devising strategies for sustainable progress.

---

included. These are' Building World Partnership, economic policy, international trade, energy, drug etc.

7. Africa deserves special attention. Progress by African governments towards sound economic policies, democracy and accountability is improving their prospects for growth. This is being helped by G-7's continued support, focused on stimulating development of the private sector, encouraging regional integration, providing concessional flows and reducing debt burdens. The Special Programme of Assistance for Africa, co-coordinated by the World Bank and providing support for economic reform in over 20 African countries, is proving its worth. G-7 will provide humanitarian assistance to those parts of Africa facing severe famine and encourage the reform of United Nations structures in order to make this assistance more effective. G-7 will also work to help the countries concerned remove the underlying causes of famine and other emergencies, whether these are natural or provoked by civil strife.

8. In the Asia-Pacific region, many economies, including members of the Association of South-East Asian Nations (ASEAN) and the Asia-Pacific Economic Co-operation (APEC), continue to achieve dynamic growth. G-7 welcomes the efforts by those economies of the region, which are assuming new international responsibilities. Other Asian countries, which are strengthening their reform efforts, continue to need external assistance.

9. In Latin America we are encouraged by the progress being made in carrying out genuine economic reforms and by developments in regional integration. G-7 welcomes the continuing discussions on the Multilateral Investment Fund, under the Enterprise for the Americas Initiative, which, together with other efforts, is helping to create the right climate for direct investment, freer trade and a reversal of capital flight. It is recognized with satisfaction the progress being made under the strengthened debt strategy. Some countries have already benefited from the combination of strong

adjustment with commercial bank debt reduction or equivalent measures. G-7 encourages other countries with heavy debts to banks to negotiate similar packages.

Important observations

10. The agreement by the Paris Club on debt reduction or equivalent measures for Poland and Egypt should be treated as exceptional cases and the Paris Club's continued examination of the special situation of some lower middle-income countries on a case-by-case basis.

11. The poorest, most indebted countries need very special terms. G-7 agrees on the need for additional debt relief measures, on a case-by-case basis, for these countries, going well beyond the relief already granted under Toronto terms. G-7 therefore calls on the Paris Club to continue its discussions on how these measures can best be implemented promptly. It is recognized the need for appropriate new financial flows to developing countries. G-7 believes the appropriate way to avoid unsustainable levels of debt is for developing countries to adopt strengthened policies to attract direct investment and the return of flight capital. The Summit notes the key role of the IMF, whose resources should be strengthened by the early implementation of the quota increase under the Ninth General Review and the associated Third Amendment to the Articles of Agreement.

G-7 Lyon Summit

Economic Communiqué: Making a Success of Globalization for the Benefit of All, June 28, 1996

The Heads of State and Government of seven major industrialized democracies and the President of the European Commission have met in Lyon for our 22nd annual Summit. Their discussions have taken place within the framework of a reflection on benefits and challenges posed by increasing economic globalization. The Summit considered the following:

(a) Strengthening economic and monetary cooperation,
(b) Promoting strong and mutually beneficial growth of trade and investment,
(c) Enhancing our approach to employment problems,
(d) Implementing a new global partnership for development: An ambition for the 21st century,
(e) Enhancing the effectiveness of multilateral institutions for the benefit of development,
(f) Providing the necessary multilateral support for development, and
(g) Toward successful integration of countries in transition into the global economy

However, in the present study, the resolution on 'Multilateral Support for Development' is included

Multilateral Support for Development

1. The replenishment of the concessional resources of the multilateral financial institutions must be completed. G-7 welcomes the fact that all donors have agreed to contribute to IDA-XI and the activation of the Interim Trust Fund. This agreement will enable the Association to lend up to USD 22 billion over three years. This is a major success. It is important that all donors ensure the success of IDA-XI by fully respecting their commitments on time. G-7 also welcomes the replenishment of the resources of the African Development Fund, whose work is of vital importance for this continent, recognizing the reforms already made by the management of the Bank. Timely replenishment of the Asian Development Fund is also important.

2. G-7 is committed to a continuing Enhanced Structural Adjustment Facility (ESAF) as the centerpiece of the International Monetary Fund support for the poorest countries. G-7 welcomes the proposals of the Managing Director of the IMF for greater concession in ESAF lending for a limited number of poor and highly indebted countries, as the IMF's contribution to putting them in a sustainable position. G-7 will examine constructively and positively the options for financing the needed subsidies, using primarily resources held by the IMF, without excluding bilateral contributions. If needed, the IMF should consider optimizing its reserve management in order to facilitate the financing of ESAF. This will enable the IMF to hold out to the poorest countries the prospect of macro-economic stability and structural reforms aimed at growth.

3. G-7 welcomes progress achieved in the alleviation of the debt problems and the active implementation, by the Paris Club, of the Naples terms. However, for some heavily indebted poor countries, G-7 acknowledges the need for additional action, in particular to reduce debts owing to multilateral institutions and other bilateral creditors that are not members of the Paris Club. Following the proposals developed by the Bretton Woods Institutions, G-7 looks forward to a concrete solution being agreed by next autumn at the latest on the following basis:

(a) The solution should provide an exit for unsustainable debt and be based on a case-by-case approach adapted to the specific situation of each country concerned, once it has shown its commitment to pursuing its economic adjustment,

(b) The continuation of ESAF will provide the basis for a reduction in the burden of the debt to the IMF for these countries,

c) G-7 welcomes the proposal by World Bank management to commit $500 million to this initiative and substantial amounts for future years. G-7 will support and work together for an overall World Bank contribution of the order of $2 billion for this initiative. G-7 looks forward to the World Bank together with the Regional Development Banks to develop practical funding mechanisms for treating debt owed to these institutions; and

(d) G-7 is committed to work in conjunction with a maximum possible contribution by the World Bank and the IMF, to achieve financial viability and debt sustainability for all these countries, which undertake the necessary adjustment efforts. G-7 acknowledges Official Development Aid/debt cancellation already given by some creditor countries. G-7 urges the Paris Club creditor countries, where they deem appropriate, on a case-by-case basis, to go beyond the Naples terms for these countries. These efforts would include, on a voluntary basis, debt conversion schemes up to 20 percent instead of currently 10 percent of the stock of debts, and increased debt alleviation.

G8 KÖLN Summit 1999

The Heads of State and Government of eight major democracies and the President of the European Commission, met in Köln for the 25th Economic Summit. On the threshold of the new millennium they discussed growing opportunities as well as forward-looking solutions to the challenges facing nations and the international community. The Summit endorsed 10 recommendations as follows:

(a) Getting the World Economy on Track for Sustained Growth
(b) Building a World Trading System That Works for Everyone
(c) Designing Policies for More Employment
(d) Investing in People

(e) Strengthening Social Safeguards
(f) Deepening the Development Partnership
(g) Launching the Köln Debt Initiative
(h) Redoubling Efforts to Protect the Environment
(i) Promoting Non-proliferation Arms Control and Disarmament
(j) Tackling Global Challenges

However, the preset study has incorporated resolutions on two topics namely 'Deepening the Development Partnership and Launching the Köln Debt Initiative.'[175]

Deepening the Development Partnership

Developing countries are essential partners in a globalize world. G-8 is committed to working with them, especially with the poorest countries, to eradicate poverty, launch effective policies for sustainable development and develop their capacity to integrate better into the global economy, thus benefiting from the opportunities offered by globalization.

G-8 will continue to provide substantial support and assistance to developing and transition economies in support of their own efforts to open and diversify their economies, to democratize and improve governance, and to protect human rights.

G-8 will strive gradually to increase the volume of official development assistance (ODA), and to put special emphasis on countries best positioned to use it effectively.

---

[175] Ministry of Foreign Affairs, Japan However, resolutions on World Economy, World Trading System, More Employment, and Investing in People, Social Safeguards, Development Partnership, Arms Control and global Challenges are not included.

To ease future debt burdens and facilitate sustainable development, G-8 agrees to increase the share of grant-based financing in the ODA it provides to the least developed countries.

Non-governmental organizations also have an important role to play.

While international assistance and debt relief is clearly important, their positive effects depend on sound national efforts towards economic and structural reform and good governance, where the private sector and civil society are able to play productive roles.

G-8 intends to step up work with developing countries and multilateral institutions to improve developing country capacity to exercise their rights and meet their obligations in the global trading system so as to ensure that they derive the full benefits of liberalized trade and thus contribute to global economic growth.

G-8 calls on the UN and the IFIs to help developing countries mobilize sufficient means for social services and basic infrastructure and continue to support and to mainstream democratization, good governance and the rule of law into country development strategies.

G-8 reaffirms support for the OECD mandate to finalize a recommendation on untying aid to the least developed countries. G-8 calls on OECD members to bring this effort to a successful conclusion as soon as possible.

G-8 reaffirms commitment to contribute to the achievement of economic and social development in Africa, Asia and Latin America. G-8 will review the situation in that regard every year, on the basis of reports by the IFIs and the relevant regional development banks, on the alleviation of poverty.

Launching the Köln Debt Initiative

G-8 has decided to give a fresh boost to debt relief to developing countries. In recent years the international creditor community has introduced a number of debt relief measures for the poorest countries. The Heavily Indebted Poor Countries (HIPC) framework has made an important contribution in this respect. Recent experience suggests that further efforts are needed to achieve a more enduring solution to the problem of unsustainable debt burdens. To this end G-8 welcomes the 1999 Köln Debt Initiative, which is designed to provide deeper, broader and faster debt relief through major changes to the HIPC framework. The central objective of this initiative is to provide a greater focus on poverty reduction by releasing resources for investment in health, education and social needs. G-8 also supports good governance and sustainable development.

G-8 is aware that new proposals will require additional substantial financing. While several means of financing are under consideration, credible progress in identifying additional funding possibilities is needed, and G-8 stands ready to help with financing solutions. G-8 recognizes the importance of fair burden sharing among creditors.

G8 Okinawa Summit, 2000

(Kyyushu-Okinawa), 23 July 2000

The Leaders of eight major industrialized democracies and the President of the European Commission, met together here in Okinawa for the 26th Summit in the year, which heralds a new millennium. G-8 reflected upon the challenges faced and progress made since the First Summit in Rambouillet in working toward peace and prosperity throughout the world, and the members discussed the role the G8 should play as it evolves in the 21st century.

During the last quarter of the 20th century, the world economy has achieved unprecedented levels of prosperity, the Cold War has come to an end, and globalization has led to an emerging common sense of community. Driving these developments has been the global propagation of those basic principles and values consistently advocated by the G-8. These are: democracy, the market economy, social progress, sustainable development and respect for human rights. Yet G-8 is keenly aware that even now in many parts of the world poverty and injustice undermines human dignity, and conflict brings human suffering. G-8 will continue to exercise leadership and responsibility in addressing these persistent problems and squarely face new challenges as they arise. G-8 must tackle the root causes of conflict and poverty. However, in the present study, resolutions on development and debt are discussed.[176]

Development

1. The 21st century must be a century of prosperity for all, and G-8 commits to the agreed international development goals, including the overarching objective of reducing the share of the world's population living in extreme poverty to half its 1990 level by 2015. G-8 welcomes the Report on Poverty Reduction by Multilateral Development Banks (MDBs) and the International Monetary Fund (IMF), which G-8 requested in Cologne, and it looks forward to receiving an annual poverty report as it reviews progress each year in reducing poverty across the globe. This report shows that progress is possible

---

[176] Ministry of External Affairs, Japan. However, resolutions on 'World economy, information and communication technology (IT), development, debt, health, education, trade, cultural diversity, crime and drugs, aging, biotechnology / food security, human genome, nuclear safety, conflict prevention, disarmament, non- proliferation ad arms control and terrorism are not included here.

where the right conditions are created for growth and social development. While the percentage of poor in developing countries declined from 29 per cent in 1990 to 24 per cent in 1998, there are still 1.2 billion people living on less than one dollar a day and there are marked differences both within and between regions. In particular, many developing countries, notably in Africa, are growing too slowly. The HIV/AIDS pandemic aggravates the situation.

2. As the report indicates, many countries have made significant progress in overcoming poverty in the past quarter century, and their example is a beacon of hope for others. From their success, it is learned that poverty can best be overcome in resilient, peaceful, and democratic societies with freedom and opportunity for all, growing and open economies and dynamic private sectors, and strong and accountable leaders and institutions.

3. Robust, broad-based and equitable economic growth is needed to fight poverty and rests on expanding people's capabilities and choices. Government must, in co-operation with the private sector and broader civil society, establish economic and social foundations for broad-based, private sector growth. Small and medium sized enterprises, together with the opportunities presented by IT can be powerful tools for development. G-8 will work with developing countries to put in place policies, programmes and institutions that offer people a fair chance to better their lives. G-8 therefore welcomes the constructive discussions of the Tenth Meeting of the United Nations Conference on Trade and Development (UNCTAD X) in Bangkok, and will work in the United Nations and other fora to further reduce poverty, especially in the Least Developed Countries (LDCs).

4. G-8 also welcomes the increasing co-operation between the International Labour Organization (ILO)

and the International Financial Institutions (IFIs) in promoting adequate social protection and core labour standards. G-8 urges the IFIs to incorporate these standards into their policy dialogue with member countries. In addition, G-8 stresses the importance of effective co-operation between the World Trade Organization (WTO) and the ILO on the social dimensions of globalization and trade liberalization.

5. Trade and investment are critical to promoting sustainable economic growth and reducing poverty. G-8 commits to put a higher priority on trade-related capacity-building activities. G-8 is also concerned that certain regions remain marginalized as regards foreign direct investment, and that the 48 LDCs attract less than 1 per cent of total foreign direct investment flows to the developing countries. G-8 urges multilateral development organizations and financial institutions to support developing countries' efforts to create a favourable trade and investment climate, including through the Poverty Reduction Strategy Papers (PRSPs) and the Integrated Framework (IF).

6. G-8 is particularly concerned about the severity of the challenges facing the LDCs, particularly those in Africa, which are held back from sharing in the fruits of globalization by a debilitating and self-reinforcing combination of conflict, poverty and weak governance.

7. G-8 is committed to mobilizing the instruments and resources of the international community to support and reinforce the efforts of these countries to combat and overcome these challenges, with particular priority on promoting equitable distribution of the benefits of growth through sound social policies, including regarding health and education.

G-8 has agreed to:

(a) Push forward the Heavily Indebted Poor Countries (HIPC) debt initiative;
(b) Provide significantly improved access to our markets;
(c) Strengthen the effectiveness of our official development assistance (ODA);
(d) Implement an ambitious plan on infectious diseases, notably HIV/AIDS, malaria and tuberculosis (TB);
(e) Follow up vigorously the conclusions of the recent Dakar Conference on Education by ensuring that additional resources are made available for basic education;
(f) Address the widening digital divide;
(g) Implement measures to prevent conflict, including by addressing the issue of illicit trade in diamonds.

8. ODA is essential in the fight against poverty. G-8 commits to strengthening the effectiveness of ODA in support of countries' own efforts to tackle poverty, including through national strategies for poverty reduction. G-8 will take a long-term approach favoring those countries where governments have demonstrated a commitment to improve the well being of their people through accountable and transparent management of resources devoted to development. G-8 resolves to work with OECD in the least developed countries to increase the effectiveness of ODA. G-8 believes that this agreement should come into effect on 1 January 2002. In the meantime, G-8 urges those countries, which maintain low levels of untying of ODA to improve their performance. G-8 will also seek to demonstrate to the public that well-targeted ODA gets results, and on that basis will strive to give increased priority to such assistance. Well co-coordinated assistance is helpful for developing countries and the member countries will consider how best to improve such co-ordination. G-8 also agrees

to give special attention to three issues - debt, health, and education, as a spur to growth.

Debt

9. Last year in Cologne, G-8 agreed to launch the Enhanced HIPC Initiative to deliver faster, broader and deeper debt relief, releasing funds for investment in national poverty reduction strategies. G-8 welcomes endorsement of this initiative by the international community last autumn.

10. Since then, while further efforts are required, progress has been made in implementing the Enhanced HIPC Initiative. Nine countries (Benin, Bolivia, Burkina Faso, Honduras, Mauritania, Mozambique, Senegal, Tanzania and Uganda) have already reached their Decision Points and are seeing the benefits of the Initiative. Total debt relief under the HIPC Initiative for these countries should amount to more than US $15 billion in nominal terms (US $8.6 billion in Net Present Value).

11. G-8 welcomes the efforts being made by HIPCs to develop comprehensive and country-owned poverty reduction strategies through a participatory process involving civil society. IFIs should, along with other donors, help HIPCs prepare PRSPs and assist their financial resource management by providing technical assistance. G-8 is concerned by the fact that a number of HIPCs are currently affected by military conflicts, which prevent poverty reduction and delay debt relief. We call upon these countries to end their involvement in conflicts and to embark quickly upon the HIPC process. G-8 agrees to strengthen efforts to help them prepare and come forward for debt relief, by asking its Ministers to make early contact with the countries in conflict to encourage them to create the right conditions to participate in the HIPC Initiative. G-8 will work together to ensure that as many countries as possible reach their Decision Points, in

line with the targets set in Cologne. G-8 will give due consideration to the progress of economic reforms and the need to ensure that the benefits of debt relief are targeted to assist the poor and most vulnerable. G-8 will work expeditiously together with HIPCs and the IFIs to realize the expectation that 20 countries will reach the Decision Point within the framework of the Enhanced HIPC Initiative by the end of this year. In this regard, G-8 welcomes the establishment of the Joint Implementation Committee by the World Bank and the IMF. G-8 will promote more responsible lending and borrowing practices to ensure that HIPCs will not again be burdened by unsupportable debt.

12. G-8 notes the progress made in securing the required financing of the IFIs for effective implementation of the Enhanced HIPC Initiative, and welcomes pledges including those to the HIPC Trust Fund. G-8 reaffirms commitment to make available as quickly as possible the resources it has pledged in the spirit of fair burden sharing.

G-8 summit in Genoa, Italy, 2001

The heads of state and government of eight major industrialized democracies and the representatives of the European Union met in Genoa for the first summit of the new millennium. In a spirit of cooperation, they discussed the most pressing issues on the international agenda.

G-8 believes in the fundamental importance of open public debate on the key challenges facing the societies. G-8 will promote innovative solutions based on a broad partnership with civil society and the private sector. G-8 will also seek enhanced cooperation and solidarity with developing countries, based on a mutual responsibility for combating poverty and promoting sustainable development.

G-8 is determined to make globalization work for all citizens and especially the poor. Drawing the poorest countries into the global economy is the surest way to address their fundamental aspirations. But resolutions on "strategic Approach to poverty reduction, debt relief, healthcare and education of poor countries" are cited in this manuscript.

Strategic Approach to Poverty Reduction

1. The situation in many developing countries—especially in Africa—calls for decisive global action. The most effective poverty reduction strategy is to maintain a strong, dynamic, open and growing global economy. G-8 pledges to do that.

2. G-8 will also continue to provide effective development assistance to help developing countries' own efforts to build long-term prosperity. Consistent with the conclusions of the LDC III Conference and the Millennium Declaration, G-8 supports a strategic approach centered on the principles of ownership and partnership. In the common interest of donors and recipients of aid, G-8 will ensure the efficient use of scarce resources.

3. Open, democratic and accountable systems of governance, based on respect for human rights and the rule of law, are preconditions for sustainable development and robust growth. G-8 helps the developing countries to promote:

(a) Accountability and transparency in the public sector
(b) Legal frameworks and corporate governance regimes to fight corruption
(c) Safeguards against the misappropriation of public funds and their diversion into nonproductive uses

(d) Access to legal systems for all citizens, independence of the judiciary, and legal provisions enabling private sector activity
(e) Active involvement of civil society and Non Governmental Organizations (NGOs)
(f) Freedom of economic activities

G-8 will:

(a) Implement fully the OECD Bribery Convention
(b) Support efforts in the U.N. to pursue an effective instrument against corruption
(c) Encourage Multilateral Development Banks (MDBs) to help recipient countries strengthen public expenditure and budget management.

Debt Relief and Beyond

4. Debt relief -particularly the Enhanced Heavily Indebted Poor Countries (HIPC) Initiative - is a valuable contribution to the fight against poverty, but it is only one of the steps needed to stimulate faster growth in poor countries. G-8 is delighted that 23 countries have qualified for an overall amount of debt relief of over $ 53 billion, out of an initial stock of debt of $ 74 billion. G-8 must continue this progress.

5. G-8 looks forward to countries affected by conflict to turn away from violence. When they do, G-8 strengthens efforts to help these countries to receive debt relief. G-8 confirms that HIPC with strong domestic policies and responsible lending by donors is designed to lead to a lasting exit from unsustainable debt.

6. Beyond debt relief, G-8 focuses discussion on three mutually reinforcing elements:

(a) Greater participation by developing countries in the global trading system
(b) Increased private investment

(c) Initiatives to promote health, education and food security

7. Open trade and investment drive global growth and poverty reduction. That is why G-8 has agreed to support the launch of an ambitious new round of global trade negotiations with a balanced agenda.

8. While opening markets through global negotiations provides the greatest economic benefit for developing countries, G-8 fully endorses measures already taken to improve market access for the least developed countries (LDCs), such as Everything But Arms, Generalized Preferences and all other initiatives that address the same objectives. G-8 confirms its pledge made at the UN LDC III Conference to work towards duty-free and quota-free access for all products originating in the least developed countries. G-8 supports efforts made by LDCs to enter the global trading system and to take advantage of opportunities for trade-based growth.

9. Increased market access must be coupled with the capacity to take advantage of it. Developing countries benefit from open markets through trade-related assistance to:

(a) Provide bilateral assistance on technical standards, customs systems, legislation needed for World Trade Organization (WTO) membership, the protection of intellectual property rights, and human resource development
(b) Support the work of the Integrated Framework for Trade-Related Technical Assistance
(c) Encourage the international financial institutions to help remove obstacles to trade and investment, and establish the institutions and policies essential for trade to flourish

(d) Urge countries to mainstream trade expansion by including it in their poverty reduction strategies.

10. Increased private sector investment is essential to generate economic growth, increase productivity and raise living standards. To help developing countries improve the climate for private investment, G-8 urges MDBs and other relevant international bodies to support domestic reform efforts, including the establishment of public-private partnerships and investment-related best practices, as well as codes and standards in the field of corporate governance, accounting standards, enhanced competition and transparent tax regimes. G-8 calls on the World Bank to provide additional support for programs that promote private sector development in the poorest countries. To promote further investments in the knowledge-based economy, G-8 calls on the WTO and the World Intellectual Property Rights Organization, in collaboration with the World Bank, to help the poorest countries comply with international rules on intellectual property rights.

11. Official development assistance (ODA) is essential. G-8 will work with developing countries to meet the International Development Goals, by strengthening and enhancing the effectiveness of our development assistance. G-8 commits to implement the landmark OECD-DAC Recommendation on Untying Aid to LDCs, which should increase aid effectiveness and achieve more balanced effort sharing among donors.

12. As the November 2001 "World Food Summit: Five Years Later" approaches, food security remains elusive. Over 834 million people remain seriously malnourished, including at least 250 million children. So a central objective of poverty reduction strategy remains access to adequate food supplies and rural development. Support to agriculture is a crucial

instrument of ODA. G-8 will endeavour to develop capacity in poor countries, integrating programs into national strategies and increasing training in agricultural science. Every effort should be undertaken to enhance agricultural productivity. Among other things, the introduction of tried and tested new technology, including biotechnology, in a safe manner and adapted to local conditions has significant potential to substantially increase crop yields in developing countries, while using fewer pesticides and less water than conventional methods. G-8 is committed to study, share and facilitate the responsible use of biotechnology in addressing development needs.

13. G-8 will target the most food-insecure regions, particularly sub-Saharan Africa and South Asia, and continue to encourage South-South co-operation. G-8 will support the crucial role international organizations and NGOs play in relief operations. G-8 believes national poverty reduction and sectoral strategies should take due account of the nutritional needs of vulnerable groups, including newborns and their mothers.[177]

G8 Gleneagles Summit 2005
6-8 July 2005

The two themes of the UK G8 Presidency in 2005 were Africa and Climate Change. The main outcomes are summarized below:

Africa

(a) A doubling of aid by 2010 - an extra $50 billion worldwide and $25 billion for Africa
(b) Writing off immediately the debts of 43 of the world's poorest countries, most of which are in Africa (21 countries have received 100 percent

---

[177] www.cnn.com/indepth specials - Resolutions on health, education and TRIPS are not included here.

debt relief so far, with $36 billion worth of debt written off. This could rise to over $50 billion as more countries qualify)

(c) Writing off $18 billion of Nigeria's debt, in the biggest single debt deal ever
(d) A commitment to end all export subsidies and to reduce domestic subsidies, which distort trade
(e) Developing countries will "decide, plan and sequence their economic policies to fit with their own development strategies, for which they should be accountable to their people".
(f) Universal access to HIV treatment by 2010
(g) Funding for treatment and bed nets to fight malaria, saving the lives of over 600,000 children every year
(h) Full funding to totally eradicate polio from the world
(i) All children will have access to good quality, free and compulsory education and to free basic health care by 2015
(j) An extra 25,000 trained peacekeeping troops to help the Africa Union to better respond to security challenges like Darfur.

Climate Change

The G8 leaders agreed that climate change is happening now, that human activity is contributing to it, and that it could affect every part of the world. Global emissions must slow, peak and then decline, moving us towards a low-carbon economy. Unless global emissions of greenhouse gases are reduced and development is made more resilient to climate change, the gains made on African and global development is put at risk. A package of measures was agreed to make energy generation and use more sustainable, and to reduce greenhouse gas emissions. G8 will work with organizations like the World Bank and the African Development Bank to make sure that major investments in infrastructure or other energy intensive sectors are made more energy efficient. The G8 leaders agreed to put procedures in place to help manage the risks from climate change for donor-funded development investments. A major focus is on supporting improvements in monitoring climate change in Africa to increase the availability of climate data. Also on improving Africa's ability to use this data effectively for the planning needs of agriculture, water and healthcare at the local level.[178]

G–8 L'aquila (Italy) Summit - 2009

July 8-10, 2009

G8 Pledges $20 billion to fight hunger and food price volatility in poor countries:

G-8 members pledged $20 billion over three years to finance agriculture projects in poor countries and help fight hunger and food price volatility. The U.S.-sponsored food security plan aims to provide poor farmers in developing countries with seeds, fertilizers and the infrastructure needed to boost food production as a long-term solution to combat hunger and spiking food prices. Until now, most of the money to combat hunger in poor countries, especially in Africa, has been in the form of food donations or emergency aid as a short-term fix when famine strikes. In a fact sheet issued after the close of the G8 summit here, the new administration of U.S. President Barack Obama administration said it would provide at least $3.5 billion of the funds over the three-year period. The total figure was originally set at $15 billion, but Italian Premier Silvio Berlusconi said a further $5 billion was collected thanks to help from all the 30 or so countries at the L'Aquila global summit, which includes key emerging nations like China, Brazil and India. Although aid campaigners welcomed the food security plan, they questioned

---

[178] DFID

whether all of the money would be new and pressed leaders to ensure that promises are kept this time.

Priority actions should include improving access to better seeds and fertilizers, promoting sustainable management of water, forests and natural resources. Last month, a United Nations agency predicted that the number of people going hungry every day will hit 1.02 billion in 2009. The U.S. Department of Agriculture economists have also made dire projections, citing affordability. The food security initiative also aims to prevent the sharp rise in prices seen last year, which sparked riots in some countries. Though many crop prices have since fallen back, the unrest helped make the complex issue of food security a major focus for G8 political leaders, who are concerned about social and political consequences. The world consumed more grain than its farmers could produce for most of this decade, thanks to surging food demand from a growing middle class in emerging nations such as China and India. Even large harvests last fall and the global recession this year haven't returned prices of many crops back to their normal levels. Since June 2008, international prices have come down but average prices are still 25 percent above the levels of 2005 and 2006 in real terms.[179]

In short, the G-8 countries have no agenda for discussion on 'poverty and debt relief' of the low-income countries during St. Petersburg Summit 2006 and the Heiligendamn Summit 2007. They have planned to fight with 'world hunger' in 2009. Food safety can possibly check starvation deaths but cannot fight against poverty and huge debt burden of low-income countries. The poor countries would

---

[179] Luca Di Leo, Dow Jones Newswires, G8 Pledges $20 billion For Food Security To Poor Nations, G–8 L'AQUILA (Italy) July 10, 2009

depend upon the developed countries for a longer period for donations, food-aid, and credit.

II
Suggestions for Debt Relief

More over, joint reports undertaken by Finance Ministers of the industrial countries, government reports, and committee reports are presented to highlight the paths the developed countries had adopted for reduction of poverty and instituting debt relief of the LDCs to foster world peace. Some of the reports are as follows:

(A).Four Development Ministers on a Common Course: Debt Could Be Mitigated

The Development Ministers of United Kingdom, the Netherlands, Germany and Norway (1999) suggested that the problem of debt overhang and difficulties in servicing the debt could be mitigated. They have suggested that the developing countries should undertake special care of the following factors:

Combating corruption: Corruption is stealing from the poor; it is a major obstacle to development, hampering not only economic development, but also undermining democracy and destroying the credibility of government. Both through control systems, public systems reform and punishment of the perpetrators should be addressed.

Strengthening democracy and good governance:

Democracy, competent and strong public authorities are the best guarantees for sustainable development. Lack of democratic participation and weak public sectors are major challenges that need to be met by developing countries and donors alike.

Preventing conflicts: Peace is a fundamental prerequisite for development. This is a responsibility of all actors. Conflicts that have reached a peaceful settlement may arise again unless underlying causes are removed. Development efforts should be used strategically not just to prevent and settle conflicts, but also to consolidate peace when settlement has been reached.

Implementing poverty reducing policies: Developing countries themselves have to create an enabling environment to stimulate private sector investment, ensure an equitable distribution and make public expenditure more efficient and transparent. Moreover, they have concluded that the developed countries or donors should work together and fix up action plan for each country for better utilization of their funds in poor countries. The donors should emphasize on the following steps.

Increased co-ordination: All donors must be prepared to adjust their programs to achieve better co-ordination and thereby more effective assistance. The recipient country should be in the driver seat. The comprehensive Development framework proposed by the World Bank and the United Nations Development Assistance Framework (UNDAF) provide and excellent basic and should be implemented.

Untying of aid: Untying of development assistance will imply increased efficiency, improved quality and more development for every Euro or US $ the poor countries receive. OECD members should strive to unite financial and investment related development assistance and food aid to the Least Developed Countries as soon as possible.

Institutional and financial gap: Closing the institutional and financial gap between humanitarian assistance and long-term development cooperation is vital. Too often neglect of development needs leads to new conflicts and humanitarian catastrophes.

Greater coherence off all policies affecting developing countries: Better aid practices are not enough. Donor countries need to be equally concerned to put in place coherent policies on matters such as trade, investment and environment, which support sustainable development.[180]

(B) Joint Progress Report

On Strengthening the International Financial Architecture and on Implementation of the Cologne Debt Initiative

At the Cologne Summit in June 18 – 20, 1999, the G-7 Heads of State or Government endorsed a report by G-7 Finance Ministers on strengthening the international financial architecture. The implementation of agreed reforms remains key factor to financial stability both at domestic and international level. These are:

(a) The Interim Committee was transformed into a permanent committee of the Board of Governors of the IMF with the new name International Monetary and Financial Committee (IMFC). The joint committee of IMFC and Development committees (DC) will be held on HIPC.

(b) An informal mechanism for dialogue among systemically important countries, within the framework of Bretton Wood institutional system, was launched by the G-7 at the time of their 25 September 1999 meeting in Washington. This group is known as G –20. This committee discusses on; the role and objectives of the G-20, the domestic policy responses to globalization and the role of the

---

[180] Four Development Ministers on a Common Course, Utstein, Norway, 26-27 July 1999

international community in reducing vulnerabilities to financial crises.

(c) The Financial Stability Forum (FSF) will present reports on highly - leveraged financial institutions, capital flows and offshore financial centers. The Forum will work on development of international best practices for deposit insurance schemes, and assess the desirability and feasibility of enhanced public disclosures by financial institutions.

(d) The Code of Good Practices on Transparency and Financial Policies was adopted at the Annual Meeting in September 1999.

(e) The Cologne Debt Initiative adopted core principles of corporate governance, improving coordination of technical assistance for implementation of standards, and monitoring compliance with standards. Moreover transparency and accountability within IMF has been enhanced.

(f) The G 7 Finance Ministers will continue to work together to ensure the full implementation of all the reforms that have been endorsed at the Cologne Summit. They attach particular importance to reducing vulnerabilities to financial crisis of individual countries and of the system as a whole and fostering well-functioning international capital markets by implementing the agreed G-7 framework on private sector involvement in crises.

(g) The Cologne report emphasizes on dissemination of best practices in the area of debt management. It desires to evolve appropriate exchange rate regimes for emerging market economies and on important issues involved in managing the risks posed by large-scale capital flows.

(h) The G-7 Finance Ministers welcome the closer cooperation of IMF and World Bank on financial sector issues in advising emerging countries.

The Cologne Summit emphasized the need to strengthen social infrastructure to give globalization a human face and asked the IFI to support and monitor the development of sound social policies and to develop a set of policies and practices that can be drawn upon in the design of adjustment programs. The World Bank with UN agencies and other institutions are developing a set of good practices of social policies, based on the principles set out in the Copenhagen Declaration announced at the March 1995 World Summit for Social Development.

The IMF has replaced the 'Enhanced Structural Adjustment Facility' (ESAF) by the new "Poverty Reduction and Growth Facility" (PRGF), which aims at making poverty reduction efforts among low-income countries a key and more explicit element of a renewed growth-oriented economic strategy.

At the Cologne Summit, leaders asked for faster, broader and deeper debt reduction for qualifying poorest countries, emphasized the need for a stronger link between debt relief and poverty reduction, and called on the International Financial Institutions (IFIs) and Paris Club to work with countries to ensure that three-quarters of eligible countries received debt relief by the end of 2000.

The Paris Club was asked to increase the debt cancellation rate to 90 per cent or more if needed to achieve debt sustainability. IFIs were encouraged to maximize the use of their own resources in meeting their costs.

The leaders agreed for an expanded HIPC Trust Fund. They called for appropriate burden sharing among donors taking into account all relevant aspects, including the magnitude and quality of ODA already extended and past ODA forgiveness, and high recognizing the contributions of countries with high ODA loans outstanding relative to GDP.

Bilateral contributions to the HIPC Trust Fund of the World Bank were expected to add up to US $ 2 billon. The Summit decided that interim relief should also be provided to eligible countries between the decision and completion points.[181]

(C) Canada announces debt relief for Asian Countries

December 31, 2004

Canada has announced a moratorium on debt payments from countries affected by this week's deadly earthquake and tsunami in Southeast Asia. Foreign Affairs Minister Pierre Pettigrew, who was joined by Defense Minister Bill Graham and International Co-operation Minister Aileen Carroll at a news conference Thursday, said the moratorium would last until the foreseeable future. "In this way we will address not only the immediate crisis, but also provide significant support in helping the rebuilding efforts of these countries," he said. Debtor nations include Indonesia – which owes the most at $588 million – Sri Lanka, Thailand, India, Kenya, Malaysia, Maldives and Myanmar. Pettigrew said he hopes Canada's announcement will encourage the same response from members of the Paris Club, a group of creditor countries which try to find payment solutions for debtor nations. The government will also provide $15 million for specific aid projects in Southeast Asia, as well as $25 million to match donations made by individual Canadians, for a total of $40 million.

If Canadians donate more than $25 million to tsunami relief efforts before the middle of January, the federal

---

[181] Economic Summit in Cologne 1999, Report Number 3085

government will increase its contribution dollar for dollar above the $40-million figure. Graham said the best way Canadians can help is by donating cash to relief organizations, rather than trying to send goods or supplies. Pettigrew said Canadians who have friends and relatives in the area hit by the tsunami should not travel to the region, saying their presence could hamper relief efforts. Graham also announced that a 17-member team of Canadian Defense, foreign affairs and health experts left Ottawa Thursday for Sri Lanka to assess the situation. The 17-member team includes 11 members of the Canadian Forces Disaster Assistance Response Team which will make recommendations on whether DART should be deployed.

Ottawa has come under fire for not deploying the 200-member rapid response unit, which can operate a mobile command center, a medical facility, and water purification equipment capable of producing 100,000 liters of clean drinking water. During the news conference, reporters questioned Pettigrew and Carroll, who returned to Ottawa Thursday, about why they didn't cut short their vacations sooner after learning about the disaster. Both ministers defended their actions, saying they have been in constant contact with their staff during the crisis.[182]

(D). G8 Proposals for HIPC debt cancellation

The G8 Finance Ministers discussed on 'Development and HIPC debt cancellation' in London on 10-11 June 2005. The suggestions are as follows:

Donors agree to complete the process of debt relief for the Heavily Indebted Poor Countries by providing additional development resources, which will provide significant support for countries' efforts to reach the goals of the Millennium Declaration (MDGs), while

---

[182] CBC NEWS, OTTAWA - 31 December 2004

ensuring that the financing capacity of the IFIs is not reduced. This will lead to 100 per cent debt cancellation of outstanding obligations of HIPCs to the IMF, World Bank and African Development Bank. Additional donor contributions will be allocated to all IDA and AfDF recipients based on existing IDA and AfDF performance-based allocation systems. Such action will further assist their efforts to achieve the MDGs and ensure that assistance is based on country performance. G8 Finance Ministers ask the World Bank and IMF to report to them on improvements on transparency on all sides and on the drive against corruption so as to ensure that all resources are used for poverty reduction. G8 believes that good governance; accountability and transparency are crucial to releasing the benefits of the debt cancellation. G8 reaffirms for future bilateral and multilateral assistance to these countries.

Key elements:

1. Additional donor contributions will be allocated to all IDA and AfDF recipients based on existing IDA and AfDF performance-based allocation systems.

2.100 percent IDA, AfDF and IMF debt stock relief for Completion Point HIPCs.

3. For IDA and AfDF debt, 100 per cent stock cancellation will be delivered by relieving post-Completion Point HIPCs that are on track with their programmes of repayment obligations and adjusting their gross assistance flows by the amount forgiven. Donors would provide additional contributions to IDA and AfDF, based on agreed burden shares, to offset dollar for dollar the foregone principal and interest repayments of the debt cancelled. Additional funds will be made available immediately to cover the full costs during the IDA-14 and AfDF-10 period. For the period after this, donors will commit to cover the full costs for the duration of the cancelled loans, by

making contributions additional to regular replenishments of IDA and AfDF.

4. The costs of IMF debt stock relief in full, without undermining the Fund's financing capacity, should be met by the use of existing IMF resources. In situations where other existing and projected debt relief obligations cannot be met from the use of existing IMF resources (e.g. Somalia, Liberia, and Sudan), donors commit to provide the extra resources necessary. G-8 will invite voluntary contributions, including from the oil-producing states, to a new trust fund to support poor countries facing commodity price and other exogenous shocks.

5. G-8 is committed to meeting the full costs to the IMF, World Bank and African Development Bank. G8 will provide on a fair burden share basis resources to cover difficult-to-forecast costs, in excess of existing resources, to the IMF, IDA and AfDF over the next three years. Subject to further analysis by the institutions G8 will provide up to $350-500 million for this purpose. G8 is also committed, on a fair burden share basis, to cover the costs of countries that may enter the HIPC process based on their end-2004 debt burdens. G8 will also seek equivalent contributions from other donors to ensure all costs are covered and G8 will not jeopardize the ability of these institutions to meet their obligations. Utilize appropriate grant financing as agreed to ensure that countries do not immediately re-accumulate unsustainable external debts, and are eased into new borrowing.

6. G8 calls upon all shareholders to support these proposals, which would be put to the Annual Meetings of the IMF, World Bank and African Development Bank by September. The following 18 countries would be eligible immediately: Benin, Bolivia, Burkina Faso, Ethiopia, Ghana, Guyana, Honduras, Madagascar, Mali, Mauritania, Mozambique, Nicaragua, Niger, Rwanda, Senegal, Tanzania, Uganda, and Zambia. As

the remaining unsustainable HIPCs reach Completion Point they will also become eligible. Additional donor contributions would be provided on the basis of IDA-13 and normalized AfDF-10 burden shares.[183]

(E) G8 Africa Action Plan:

UK Progress Report 2005

Africa set out its vision for transformation in the New Partnership for Africa's Development (NEPAD) – a pledge by African Leaders to their people to promote democracy, peace and security, economic development and poverty reduction. At the G8 Summit in Kananaskis (2002), the UK and other G8 countries responded with the Africa Action Plan (AAP) to support the realization of NEPAD's aims. Subsequent G8 Summits at Evian (2003) and Sea Island (2004) built on the original plan, agreeing on more specific ways to support areas such as peace keeping, tackling HIV and AIDS and expanding access to clean water.

The Commission for Africa report was published in March 2005. Building on NEPAD and the G8 Africa Action Plans, this set out the case for a comprehensive response to poverty by Africa and its international partners. The UK has committed to doing its share to meet the challenge. This is a report of UK progress against the Africa Action Plan since the last update in 2003. The report highlights on the following aspects:

(a) Peace and Security
(b) Strengthening Institutions and Governance
(c) Trade, Investment, Economic Growth and Sustainable Development
(d) Debt Relief
(e) Education and Digital Opportunities

---

[183] G8 Finance Ministers' Conclusions on Development, London, 10-11 June 2005

(f) Improving Health and Tackling HIV and AIDS
(g) Increasing Agricultural Productivity
(h) Water Resource Development and Management.

However, aid, debt relief and food security proposals have been included in this chapter.

More and better aid

1. The Africa Action Plan committed G8 members to increasing aid to African countries that demonstrated commitment to NEPAD principles. Africa will not meet the MDGs without radically increased aid flows – the Commission for Africa has reinforced this analysis. UK aid has grown steadily over recent years. In 1997/8, the UK bilateral development programme in Africa spent less than £300 million. By 2002/3, this had risen to £663 million. Just three years on, this has grown to £1.1 billion in 2005/6. It will rise to at least £1.25 billion by 2007/8. The UK is committed to increasing official development assistance to 0.7 percent of gross national income (GNI) by 2013.

2. G8 has also encouraged others to increase their aid. The UK played a major role in the recent commitment by EU Member States to double their combined aid by 2010. But even such growth is not enough. For this reason, the UK has proposed an International Finance Facility (IFF) to provide an additional US $50 billion per year between now and 2015. It would do this by issuing bonds on the international capital markets on the basis of (existing) donor commitments. This would provide a step-change in aid levels and effectiveness. We will continue to press for this.

3. The UK has consistently lobbied internationally for improvements to the quality of aid. The UK has argued that aid should go to the poorest countries, support a country's own priorities, and be sufficiently

predictable for countries to take on longer-term commitments (such as employing more teachers or providing anti-retroviral drugs). The UK has also been leaders in harmonization – for example, ensuring donors work jointly to reduce the transaction costs placed on African countries and donors themselves. Much of this culminated in March 2005, when a high-level meeting of donors and partners agreed the 'Paris Declaration on Aid Effectiveness'. The challenge is now to ensure the 56 Paris commitments are put into practice.

Looking ahead

The UK will improve predictability of aid by expanding the number of development partnerships based on ten-year agreements. The UK currently has ten-year Memorandums of Understanding with Rwanda, Sierra Leone, Ethiopia and Democratic Republic of Congo.

The UK agrees with the Commission for Africa that mechanisms must be put in place to enable mutual accountability between African countries and donors. Donors should be held accountable for keeping their promises to improve the amount and quality of aid. The UK will be seeking rapid agreement on such a mechanism.

Debt Relief

4. There has been remarkable progress on relieving some of the world's poorest countries from debt. The UK has been a leading supporter of the Heavily Indebted Poor Countries (HIPC) programme. Moreover, five African countries have completed the HIPC initiative and received irrevocable debt reduction. In addition to being a key driver of the HIPC initiative, the UK has gone beyond this to offer 100 per cent debt relief to all HIPC countries on both ODA and non-ODA debts. We also hold in trust all payments from HIPC countries yet to benefit from the

initiative – such that the UK no longer benefits from any debt repayments from HIPC countries.

5. Despite this important progress, multilateral debt service continues to crowd out more productive investments in areas such as health or infrastructure. The G8 have therefore agreed to complete the process of debt relief for the Heavily Indebted Poor Countries by providing additional development resources, which will provide significant support for countries' efforts to reach the goals of the Millennium Declaration (MDGs). Moreover, G8 ensure that the financing capacity of the International Financial Institutions is not reduced. For International Development Association (IDA) and African Development Fund (AfDF) debt, 100 per cent stock cancellation will be delivered by relieving post-Completion Point HIPCs that are on track with their programmes of repayment obligations. 32 African HIPCs are potentially eligible. On top of this, several African non-HIPCs are potentially eligible for the UK's multilateral debt relief initiative whereby we will pay our share (10 per cent) of debt service owed to the World Bank and African Development Bank.

6. In line with the Commission for Africa, the UK has supported important moves by the World Bank and IMF to revise the criteria used for measuring debt sustainability. This has involved moving away from a 'one-size-fits-all' analysis of debt sustainability, to one, which considers the country's situation and puts new focus on the needs of these poor countries. Reducing the heavy burden of servicing debt releases substantial funds – which can then be spent on areas such as health and education. For example, debt relief in Uganda over the last 7 years has allowed a doubling of the proportion of discretionary budget spent on poverty-reducing sectors, such as primary education, district health and rural roads. Nearly nine out of ten boys and girls are now going to primary school in Uganda – and the number is rising.

Food Security in Africa

7. Progress towards eradicating hunger is slow in sub-Saharan Africa. The proportion of underweight children is actually rising. The situation is particularly bad in areas affected by conflict. For example, three out of four people living in the Democratic Republic of Congo are undernourished.

8. In 2002, a consultation process led to publication of the 'Eliminating Hunger' strategy paper. This looked at the root causes of food insecurity and how the UK and international community can work to address these and help achieve the Millennium Development Goal on hunger. The UK continues to respond to humanitarian crisis: from 2002 to 2004 we provided over £270 million in bilateral humanitarian assistance to Africa. But the UK is increasingly concerned with addressing the underlying causes of famine, in order to prevent the recurrence of crisis and help households to recover.

9. In Ethiopia, the UK provided over £50 million in humanitarian assistance from 2002 to 2004. In collaboration with the government, EU, and US, the UK are now putting in place a groundbreaking national safety net, moving away from emergency food relief towards predictable cash payments for the vulnerable. The UK aims to provide £70 million over 2 years in support of 5 million of the poorest people. The aim is to go beyond saving lives with emergency relief, and help lift people out of destitution and into a position from which they can support their families in the long-term. In Zambia, £14.5 million will be spent over the next five years on a similar cash transfer programme for the chronically poor.[184]

---

[184] HM Government, G-8 Africa Action Plan: UK Progress Report 2005, DFID, 1 Palace Street, London, UK, Crown Copy right, 2005

(F). Motion for a Resolution in the European Parliament, 5 January 2005

1. The European Parliament welcomes the measures announced at the G8 Summit in Evian on implementing debt relief and achieving long-term debt sustainability and applauds the Commission's efforts to reduce the debt burden in the context of the reinforced HIPC initiative.

2. Underlines the importance of the NEPAD initiative and the pledge by African leaders to the people of Africa to consolidate democracy and sound economic management, and to promote peace, security and people-centered development.

3. Considers that the enhanced HIPC initiative is still inadequate in the current context of economic globalization, even though it acknowledges the failure of earlier programs based purely on macroeconomic strategies. Enhanced HIPC initiative is designed to establish a link between debt alleviation and poverty reduction (a formula based on the Poverty Reduction Strategy Papers) by making the eligibility criteria faster, more flexible and less restrictive.

4. Considers that traditional austerity measures imposed by the International Monetary Fund (IMF) should be reassessed and that particular attention should be paid to ensuring that economic reforms do not produce further poverty.

5. Stresses the need to adapt the current HIPC initiative to meet the requirements of eligible countries, which have not yet reached the decision point, due to extreme political instability.

6. Stresses the importance of a more result-oriented conditionality and considers that the public-debt relief process should be deepened in countries whose governments respect human rights and the principles

of sound governance and give priority to poverty eradication.

7. Calls on resources released by debt reduction to be used for education and health programs, and to promote local development of civil society and local economic activities through instruments such as micro-credit.

8.Stresses that long-term debt sustainability will depend upon the maintenance of sound economic policies, strengthened debt management and the provision of appropriate financing, as well as export performance and particularly export diversification.

9. Calls for strict monitoring and transparency of the operation of the HIPC mechanisms and the additional debt-relief measures in order to guarantee fair, efficient and workable debt relief and stresses, in this regard, that involvement of stockholders and donors in this review process will be essential.

10. Calls on the Commission and Member States to ensure through effective coordination within the G8 group, the World Bank and the IMF so that no country genuinely committed to poverty reduction, good governance and economic reform is denied the chance to achieve the Millennium Development Goals through lack of finance.

The European Parliament adopted a resolution on debt relief for developing countries on the basis of previous resolutions on debt relief such as New Partnership for Africa's Development (NEPAD) initiative adopted in October 2001 in Abuja (Nigeria) and G-8 resolutions adopted in Kananaskis and Evian on 3 June 2003 as per Rule 103(2) of its Rules of Procedure.

The European Parliament resolved:

(a) It is essential to attack the root causes of poverty to break the poverty spiral,
(b) Mobilization of additional debt relief should be seen as part of the total effort to strengthen resources in support of political and human development objectives and targets.
(c) Managing the global debt crisis as initial aid has not provided a lasting solution;
(d) The majority of Heavily Indebted Poor Countries (HIPCs) are located in sub-Saharan Africa;
(e) Africa's debt burden is estimated at about US $ 230 billion,
(f) According to estimates, low-income African countries pay out about $ 39 billion per year to service their debt, while receiving only $ 27 billion in aid;
(g) Africa's future is primarily dependent on the commitment of African nations to govern justly, invest in their own people and promote economic freedom;
(h) Debt forgiveness should be envisaged for the most heavily indebted low-income countries; and
(i) Trade is an important source of growth and poverty reduction[185]

(G). G8 Agrees Cancellation of World Bank and IMF Debt: A Step Forward

Bretton Woods Project, June 13, 2005

G8 finance ministers (excepting Russia) agreed to write off $40 billion to $55 billion of debts owed to the World Bank, IMF and African Development Bank (AfDB) in a meeting in London.

---

[185] European Parliament: Motion for a Resolution, Last updated: 6 January 2005 Legal notice

100 per cent debt stock cancellation will be delivered immediately to the 18 countries, which have completed the Heavily Indebted Poor Countries (HIPC) initiative by the World Bank's concessional lending arm, the International Development Association (IDA), the AfDB and the IMF. 14 countries are in Africa - Benin, Burkina Faso, Ethiopia, Ghana, Madagascar, Mali, Mauritania, Mozambique, Nicaragua, Niger, Rwanda, Senegal, Tanzania, Uganda and Zambia - plus Bolivia, Guyana and Honduras. Nine other countries such as Burundi, Central African Republic, Comoros, Republic of Congo, Coted'Ivoire, Liberia, Somalia, Sudan and Togo will be considered after completion of HIPC Initiative.

The Americans agreed to pay an additional $1.75 billion to the World Bank and AfDB before 2015. The UK earmarked $1 billion for the new initiative. As part of the final compromise, the Germans and Japanese have demanded additional 'performance criteria' to prevent corruption.

UK chancellor Gordon Brown said that additional countries, which were not part of the HIPC process, will come through the process quite soon and would be covered by the communiqué. He also committed to continue pushing other wealthy countries to follow the UK's lead in cancelling its share of multilateral debt for all low-income countries. He insisted that the deal be not just about aid, trade and development, but also about the empowerment of a continent.

Language on aid effectiveness and trade included for the first time in a G8 finance ministers' communiqué, marked a significant shift from previous positions. On aid effectiveness, the ministers committed to (a) enhance efforts to untie aid, (b) deliver aid in a more predictable way and (c) called on the Development Assistance Committee of OECD countries for ambitious and credible targets to measure the progress of donor commitments to improve the way that they deliver aid.

But the global network of southern-based organizations working on the debt issue said that the amount of debt cancelled was a miniscule part of total debt, saying that the debt of African countries alone stood at over $300 billion. They reiterated their demand that any debt cancellation must be unconditional and take into account the illegitimacy of the debt claim held against southern countries.

African governments welcomed the deal. The governor of Tanzania's central bank said that they can expand health and education services with this relief. Uganda's information minister said that they would be able to expand infrastructure and could use the money to better the lives of people.

On trade, the communiqué recognized that not all countries would benefit from reductions in trade barriers. In a marked departure from previous insistence on the universal benefit of unilateral trade liberalization, the communiqué recognized that poor countries face particular problems and need the flexibility to decide, plan and sequence reforms to their trade policies to fit with country-owned development programs. In response, the IFIs are to submit proposals at the annual meetings for additional assistance to countries to develop their capacity to trade and ease adjustment in their economies.

In a meeting with NGOs and faith groups following the announcement, the Bretton Woods Project pressed the chancellor on the gap between the language on trade in the communiqué and the reality of BWI pressure for trade liberalization at the country level. The chancellor encouraged NGOs to enter into a dialogue on how the World Bank and IMF should interpret the language. He said that for its part, the

UK would be talking to the Department of Trade and Industry.[186]

(H). Contribution of the German government

G8 Africa Action Plan - Report to the G8 Summit in Gleneagles, 6–8 July 2005

The G8 Africa Action Plan, which was adopted on 27 June 2002 at the G8 Economic Summit in Kananaskis, Canada, is a political programme elaborated by the world's eight biggest economies in response to the African reform initiative "New Partnership for Africa's Development" (NEPAD), which was founded in 2001. With this Action Plan, the G8 countries have established a new partnership with reform-oriented Africa, thereby affirming their will to deepen this partnership in all areas, in order to tackle the huge challenges involved in overcoming economic marginalisation, poverty and the causes of violent conflict together. Our partnership with Africa now has a new quality – thanks to NEPAD. This is because NEPAD represents a convincing commitment by the countries of Africa to far-reaching political reforms and to global values such as democracy, human rights, rule of law and good governance.

The German government's co-operation with Africa within the framework of the Action Plan, which is based on this new reform partnership, is more than just a commitment for the G8 countries; it is also a conscious political signal. The German government can clearly see that for many people, poverty and conflicts – especially in sub-Saharan Africa – are what characterize Africa's image. However, this does not change in any way the huge importance that the African continent holds for us and for peace, stability and prosperity in the world. Africa in particular is a region where investments in human and economic

[186]Global Policy Forum, 777 UN Plaza, Suite 3D, and New York, NY 10017, USA, web: globalpolicy@globalpolicy.org

welfare are especially rewarding. The German government ensures that Africa handles its crises using its own resources and begins to overcome poverty. The German government wants to do through political support, by creating an international climate, which is conducive to development and through effective development policy. However much support is given, one thing must always be clear: Africa is itself responsible for its own development. And Africa has begun to face up to this task. Despite clear progress in recent years, the challenges remain huge. That is because Africa is still the continent with the most difficult development conditions. Yet there is encouraging political and economic progress.

New political dynamic in Africa

The countries of Africa are taking on responsibility for peace and development. The African Union (AU) and its reform programme NEPAD testify since 2001 to this new quality in Africa. Yet, the continent still lacks institutions and capacities at the national and regional levels in order to be able to really meet these responsibilities. Building up such structures is the big challenge, which the countries of Africa are currently facing. The government cannot expect fast solutions. However, there are encouraging signs that a lasting change is taking place:

Within just four years since its foundation, the African Union has become the key mouthpiece and contact partner for Africa. The AU has made an active start on building new African security architecture and is making good its claim to take responsibility for conflicts within the African continent. The peace missions in Burundi and Sudan show this. Proof that the idea of democracy is being strengthened can also be found in the fact that the Pan-African Parliament has begun its work.

With NEPAD, a group of African countries has launched a reform process aimed at creating prosperity and economic development, upholding human rights, reinforcing the rule of law and strengthening democratically legitimated governments. The central instrument for checking a country's achievements is the African Peer Review (APR), a formalized process of mutual appraisal, which was begun in Ghana, Kenya, Mauritius and Rwanda back in 2004. Up to spring 2005, a total of 23 African countries had made a binding commitment to take part in this review process.

There are positive economic trends in Africa, particularly in political reform states: in 2004, the figure for average growth, which was five percent, was the highest for eight years, whilst inflation was at a record low.

Reform partnerships

Unless national governments make their own efforts and demonstrate the necessary political will, effective co-operation and sustainable development will not be possible. That is why the new political dynamic in Africa is now making a new quality in the partnership with Africa possible. The German government is therefore concentrating its co-operation within the framework of the G8 on the political and economic reforms that many governments are seeking to carry out and on institutional change. As part of this, reform and development processes in individual countries are being supported – for example democratization processes or economic reforms – and regions and regional associations (NEPAD/AU, regional organizations) are being strengthened. For us too, the reform partnership means a new form of co-operation. The donor-recipient relationship is an outdated concept. Instead a partnership is developing that is based on shared goals, mutual responsibility, transparency and accountability on both sides. A prerequisite for this is co-operation on an equal footing, leaving behind all paternalistic or even colonial attitudes.

As encouraging as the reforms, which have been made so far, are – they will need continuity and time. Yet, they in turn are creating the prerequisites for more comprehensive and effective support – and that is vital if the countries south of the Sahara are to have a realistic chance of achieving the United Nations Millennium Goals. More prosperity, schooling for all children, reduced maternal mortality rates, clean drinking water for all and secured property rights – these things represent developments which require more financial resources, but at the same time they are things which cannot simply be bought. They will only become possible if the people and governments of Africa keep up their efforts and if there are better government policies and functioning institutions and organizations. The German government will continue to support these processes, which are the way forward.

Priority Areas by the German government

The present report is the second report by the German government on the implementation of the G8 Africa Action Plan. The first one was elaborated for the G8 Summit in Evian in 2003. The German government is actively involved in all eight areas of this Action Plan: peace and security, good governance, trade and investments, debt relief, health, education, agriculture and water. The German government's contribution is guided by the basic prerequisites for sustainable development as formulated by NEPAD, with the accent clearly on:

(a) Promoting peace and security,
(b) Strengthening good governance,
(c) Promoting the private sector and
(d) Co-operation in the water sector

The G8 Africa Action Plan was conceived as a political response by the G8 to political processes in Africa – and not as a financing initiative. Nevertheless, the implementation of this reform partnership also needs to be financed. The German government is providing a considerable volume of funds for this: the German government's contributions in support of Africa in 2003 to 2005 amounted to some 2.5 billion euros. Germany has been working hard from the start to fulfill the pledges it made in the G8 Africa Action Plan and meet the international commitments it entered into at the Conference on Financing for Development in Monterrey in 2002. This was confirmed at the Council for General Affairs and External Relations on 24 May 2005: 2015 will make 0.7 per cent of GNP made available for development co-operation.

Important progress has also been made with regard to the issue of debt relief. The G8 finance ministers agreed on 10/11 June 2005 to grant those HIPC countries that have already reached completion point in the HIPC Initiative a 100 per cent multilateral cancellation of their debts to the IDA (World Bank), African Development Bank and the International Monetary Fund. The other countries are to be granted this debt stock cancellation once they reach completion point. This would further lighten the debt burden of the countries concerned, which will help them invest more in their own sustainable development. The resources freed up by the debt cancellation can be used in important areas, which serve to reduce poverty.

This second implementation report outlines the German government's involvement, although it – intentionally – does not provide a complete list of all Germany's political and development cooperation with Africa. Instead, it concentrates on the specific contribution that the German government is making towards the implementation of the G8 Africa Action Plan.

Implementation and concrete progress

When it comes to the German government's key political topics and priority areas, concrete progress has been made on the implementation of the G8 Africa Action Plan together with our African partners.

(a) Peace and security:

The German government has been contributing since 2003 to the new African security architecture. Implementing the joint Africa/G8 Peace Plan to enhance African capabilities to undertake peace support operations, which was a product of the Berlin Process, is an important matter for us. This includes as a priority strengthening African institutions, training peace forces and developing regional training centers for peacekeeping forces. For example, 15.5 million Euros has been provided for developing the capacities of the AU and the regional organizations and for the development of an early warning network.

(b) Good governance:

A functioning administration, transparent decision-making processes, and the rule of law and the possibility of democratic participation – these are central prerequisites for sustainable development. The NEPAD countries have committed themselves to these principles. Supporting good governance and thus being actively involved in shaping a partnership for reform is therefore a priority area for the German government. That is why, for example, we are providing a total of 2.4 million euros to support the implementation of the Peer Review and have made a commitment to help the Peer Review countries implement their national reform strategies.

(c) Private sector and promoting investment:

NEPAD and the German government are together in backing reforms to do with the rule of law and economic and financial policy. The aim is a stable and resilient macro-economic and institutional framework for the private sector that reduces uncertainties and risks. This is the only way to achieve dynamic, sustainable economic growth and create the prerequisites for investments by private companies and from the public purse. The German government is therefore supporting the gradual removal of trade barriers, for example and the harmonization of trade and economic policy by African regional organizations in southern and east Africa.

(d) Water:

Clean water is the key to improving the living conditions of many people. Yet water is a resource that is in short supply. More than 300 million people in Africa have no access to clean drinking water. Water is also a source of conflict: there are more than 50 rivers in Africa that are shared by two or more countries – more than in any other continent. In recent years African institutions and programmes have increasingly been giving priority to better water supplies. The German government is therefore also supporting African institutions that serve to jointly regulate the use of water, especially rivers. Germany, with 140 million euros a year, is the biggest bilateral donor in the water sector in Africa.

A dialogue with a future

The new, intensive dialogue between the G8 and the group's African partners since 2001 has provided essential support for African reform efforts. The second implementation report shows what has been accomplished and what kind of challenges are there for future co-operation. The German government task has not yet been completed and will therefore continue to follow a consistent line in pursuit of the G8's reform partnership with Africa.[187]

(I) The Multilateral Debt Relief Initiative:
Implementation Modalities for IDA

The G8 agreed a proposal to cancel 100 percent of outstanding debts of eligible Heavily Indebted Poor Countries and also directed the IMF, IDA and African Development Fund to provide additional resources. This would also ensure that the financial capacity of the IFIs is not reduced, as set out in the statement of 11 June 2006 and reaffirmed by G8 Heads of State at the Gleneagles Summit on July 8, 2005. By June 2006, the G8 had confirmed their commitments to the MDRI and started their internal processes toward securing the resources.

The Multilateral Debt Relief Initiative (MDRI) follows the following implementation modalities as per guidelines of IDA. These are:

(a) The G8 countries have proposed to augment debt relief to completion point HIPCs, leading to 100 percent cancellation of debt owed by them to IDA, the IMF, and the African Development Fund (AfDF).
(b) The objective of the Initiative is to provide additional support to HIPCs to reach the MDGs while ensuring that the financing capacity of the IFIs is preserved.

Key features of the MDRI: The MDRI calls for 100 percent cancellation of IDA, AfDF and IMF debt for countries that reach the HIPC completion point.

---

[187] The Contribution of the German Government to the implementation of the G8 Africa Action Plan, Bundesministerium fur wirtschaftliche Zusammenarbeit und Entwicklung

The MDRI also commits to providing additional resources, to ensure that the financing capacity of the IFIs is preserved.

The MDRI will affect IDA and AfDF "gross assistance flows" through a two-step process.

The MDRI will give beneficiary countries an opportunity to reduce debt payments very substantially and, through continuing or enhanced performance, secure additional resource flows to help countries for attaining their MDG objectives.

Implementation modalities

There are three major variables when determining the eligibility for debt relief under the MDRI. These variables include the cut-off date of eligible debt stock, the credit coverage of the debt to be cancelled, and the group of countries to be covered under the MDRI.

It is proposed to use a cutoff date of end-2003 for debt cancellation.

The donors agreed for July 1, 2006 as the start date for implementation of MDRI for IDA.

For the group of completion point (CP) HIPCs, delivery of debt relief under the MDRI is to start on July 1, 2006.

For HIPCs yet to reach the completion point, delivery of debt relief will start at the beginning of the fiscal year immediately following confirmation of a country's eligibility by the Executive Directors.

Debt relief under the MDRI will cover all remaining debt service obligations on eligible IDA credits, through the end of their maturity.

Credit coverage under the MDRI will be defined as the stock of eligible debt based on debt outstanding and disbursed (DOD) as of the cutoff date.

In addition, there are 4 further potentially eligible IDA countries that may qualify as HIPCs by end-2006 under the HIPC **'sunset clause'**, and which could subsequently also qualify for debt cancellation under the MDRI if and when they reach their HIPC completion points in the future.

For other countries, limited data availability introduces further uncertainty as to whether they would fulfill the HIPC Initiative's indebtedness criteria.

The estimated costs of IDA from debt cancellation, based on debt outstanding and disbursed as of December 31, 2003 for the 38 HIPCs plus the 4 'sunset clause' countries would be equivalent to about USD 37 billion (SDR 24.8 billion).

The MDRI can be interpreted as an extension as well as a deepening of the HIPC Debt Relief Initiative.

For IDA, AfDF and the IMF, the criteria used to confirm eligibility for debt relief under the MDRI would therefore reflect HIPC completion point criteria. These include: (a) Satisfactory macro-economic performance under an IMF poverty reduction and growth facility (PRGF) program or equivalent; (b) Satisfactory progress in implementing a poverty reduction strategy (PRS); and The existence of a public expenditure management (PEM) system that meets minimum standards for governance and transparency in the use of public resources. Countries will need to meet all three criteria in order to be eligible for debt relief.

The Fund assesses satisfactory progress under the PRGF. The Bank and the Fund will also assess satisfactory implementation of the PRS and the adequacy of public expenditure management systems.

These assessments will be prepared in time to provide input into Bank and Fund Board papers that request authorization to provide debt cancellation. Furthermore, for debt relief to be provided by IDA, HIPCs will need to be in compliance with existing reporting requirements on external borrowing under OP14.10.

Cost estimates for IDA depend on the expected time profile when HIPCs would reach their completion points and become eligible for debt cancellation under the MDRI.

Forgone credit reflows of IDA due to debt cancellation under the MDRI are denominated in SDR. (a) SDR-denominated IDA credits. (b) USD-denominated IDA credits.

Following the procedures currently used under the Enhanced HIPC Initiative, IDA's costs under the MDRI will be updated periodically.

Debt relief under the MDRI will have an important impact on IDA's financial statements and its reported total assets.

MDRI debt relief will affect IDA's assistance flows through a two-step process.

IDA will allow increasing total assistance flows – including new IDA commitments and forgone re-flows – over the IDA14 period, including to most of the HIPCs eligible for MDRI debt relief.

A consensus has emerged among IDA's Executive Directors and IDA Deputies that the donor replacement resources would be reallocated to all IDA-only countries, excluding 'gap' countries.

The amount and terms of post-relief borrowing by the recipient countries are also critical to ensure that the benefits of debt relief materialize

Executive Directors and IDA Deputies underlined that measures should be taken to prevent the re-accumulation of unsustainable debt, particularly from non-concessional sources.

Compensation of the Contribution Process

Compensation from donors for IDA's cost of debt relief under the MDRI will be added to IDA's resources following the regular, established procedures for IDA Replenishments.

In line with the procedures followed in IDA replenishments, donors will be asked to pay their subscriptions and contributions through the deposit of Instruments of Commitments.

Building on the example from some countries, in particular the United States and Italy that legislative processes are underway to authorize the full amount of contributions for the MDRI, donors will be asked to deposit one IoC for the full amount of the cost of debt relief. The IoC will cover 3 time periods:

(a) Remaining IDA 14- period (FY07-FY08).
(b) Remainder of the first decade (FY09-FY16)
(c) Subsequent 3 decades (FY2017- FY2044)

The strength of the commitments made over the **entire period of 40 years**–in relation to the estimated total costs to IDA – will be a factor to be considered by the Executive Directors in assessing the extent of the impact of the debt cancellation on IDA's finances.

IDA's forgone reflows are denominated in SDRs. Contributions for each individual donor in national currency will depend on agreed burden shares and on agreed foreign exchange reference rates.

Is the cost of IDA's debt relief provided under the MDRI will fluctuate **over the 40-year period;** the compensation arrangements will include a mechanism to adjust the amounts payable over time.

The G8 countries have proposed that the IDA13 burden-sharing framework will be followed for this debt relief initiative.

Taking account also of the shares of other donor countries, under IDA13 total donor shares add up to 90.61 percent, leaving an un-funded structural financing gap of 9.39 percent.

Debt cancellation will be made subject to effectiveness of the new increase in resources for debt relief costs.

Under IDA13 and IDA14, the effectiveness threshold has been set at 60 percent of total donor contributions, and it is proposed to use the same threshold for the increase in resources for debt relief costs.

The contribution and payment arrangements for donors and non-donors will be similar to those in regular IDA replenishments.

The payment schedule attached to the IoC corresponds to an encashment schedule reflecting the timing of IDA's forgone credit reflows.

Contributions will be denominated in national currencies, in SDRs or, with the approval of IDA, in any convertible currency of another member country.

For the purpose of establishing the equivalence of value among different currencies and the SDR, the average daily exchange rate for the period April 1, 2005, through September 30, 2005 will apply for contributions to compensate IDA for debt relief costs during the IDA14 period.

Donors will receive voting rights for their contributions to this increase in resources for debt relief costs.

The IDA14 commitment authority framework will be amended to reflect the reduced volume of credit reflows available, and the amount of incremental, firm contributions for compensation of debt relief cost from the donors.

The reliance on firm donor contributions, rather than contractual but forgone credit reflows from HIPCs, may lower the amount of reflows available for commitment under the Advance Commitment Scheme of IDA.

As IDA receives unqualified IoCs, they will provide commitment authority under the current replenishment. Qualified IoC will not provide commitment authority. Commitment authority would normally be made available in equal tranches over the replenishment period in which the IoC is received.

Actual higher donor financing is required to ensure the IDA countries to benefit from the MDRI.

In IDA14, regular donor contributions amount to SDR 10,193 million.

With the contribution baseline set with reference to IDA14 regular contributions and assuming an inflation rate of 2.0 percent per annum for the SDR basket of currencies, regular contributions in IDA15 would increase by 6.12 percent over each donor's regular contribution to IDA14 in SDR terms.

Compensatory financing of IDA's forgone credit reflows due to the MDRI will be additional to this contribution baseline.

The agreed contribution baseline would be indicative in nature and intended to demonstrate transparently the higher of debt relief financing.

The following key issues emerge from this Section:

(a) The scope of firm, unqualified financing commitments that each IDA donor will be prepared to provide in its IOC;
(b) How IDA 13 burden shares should be scaled up proportionally to cover the structural financing gap of 9.39 percent.

Decision–making Process for Implementing MDRI in IDA

(a) Implementation of the MDRI will require IDA to provide 100 percent debt relief for eligible countries.
(b) In coming to that determination, IDA's Executive Directors will take into account such factors as the impact on IDA's financial position relative to its current position, on the rights of IDA members and on IDA's institutional framework.
(c) In practical terms, IDA's participation in the MDRI will be presented for formal approval in two interdependent components that would proceed in parallel.
(d) In light of the interdependence of these two components, IDA's Executive Directors will be asked to consider and approve steps (a) and (b) (ii) above at the same time.
(e) The proposed timeline to start implementation of the MDRI was on July 1, 2006. It would be

started by End November 2005 and completed by End May 2006.

(f) Clearly the MDRI will demand significant staff time and resources in terms of changes to information and payment systems necessary for tracking donor contributions as well as changes to credit agreements and accounting systems.

Multilateral Debt Relief Initiative in 2006:

Canada: The allocations to the MDRI are made in the regular budget process for the federal government each year (around February). There is an allocation of CAD $55 million (US $45.4) as Canada's share of the MDRI in 2006.

France: A parliamentary resolution binding the government to finance MDRI over the next 10 years has been approved. Yearly appreciation will take place through budget process.

Germany: There is no binding legal instrument for the entire duration of the initiative. Medium-term financial planning has a much shorter horizon, and is only formally enforceable through the yearly budgetary appropriation.

Italy: The instrument of commitment to pay the first two years of MDRI has already been deposited. The formal commitment holds for the entire time frame of the initiative (40 years for IDA and 45 years for AfDB): to make this binding, the Italian Treasury is working on a multi-annual legislative instrument that will authorize participation in the initiative. In turn, this will allow the yearly appropriation in the budget law.

Japan: Japanese government finances IDA and AfDB through 'Government Financing Bonds' (Shushi-Kokusai). Cancelling portions of IDA / AfDB debt is done on a yearly basis. The procedure itself is different between AfDB / IDA depending on the exact terms of financing of each instrument / institution.

U.K.: The UK submitted its "Instruments of Commitment" for financing the IDA part of MDRI to the Bank in mid-May. This was approved by a debate and vote in the Parliamentary Standing Committee on Delegated Legislation. It sets out the payment schedule for the next 40 years, starting with US $ 49 million on January 15, 2007. The language makes these commitments absolutely firm for 10 years, but payments for years 11 to 40 are subject to revision, and need to be finally approved by another parliamentary process in 2016.

U.S.A.: The US administration submitted its "Instruments of Commitment" to IDA in mid-May and to AfDB in mid-June. It provides a commitment to finance the foregone principal and interest repayments associated with MDRI. Annual payments are subject to annual approval by Congress. The 2006 obligation was met.

The Compensation Schedule for IDA Donors is

(a) Remaining IDA 14 Period (January 15, 2007 - January 15, 2008) = 546 Million SDR
(b) Remainder 1st Decade (Year 2009 - Year 2016) = 4721 Million SDR
(c) From January 15, 2017 to January 15, 2044 = 19,529 Million SDR
(d)Total Relief = 24, 796 Million SDR[188]

---

188 The Multilateral Debt Relief Initiative, Implementation Modalities for IDA, International Development Association, November 18, 2005, 46 pages

(J). G-20 Leaders' Statement: **The Pittsburgh Summit**, September 24 - 25, 2009

The G-20 Pittsburgh summit (2009) has recommended the following actions for the people and countries. The statement includes on: A Framework for Strong, Sustainable, and Balanced Growth, Strengthening the International Financial Regulatory System, Modernizing our Global Institutions to Reflect Today's Global Economy, Reforming the Mandate, Mission and Governance of the IMF, Reforming the Mission, Mandate and Governance of Our Development banks,Energy Security and Climate Change,Strengthening Support for the Most Vulnerable, Putting Quality Jobs at the Heart of the Recovery,and An Open Global Economy. In the present analysis, we have included suggestions on 'Global Economy, Reforming the Mandate, Mission and Governance of the IMF and Development banks' to re-shape the global economy and financial sectors.

1. Global Economy**:** Modernizing the international financial institutions and global development architecture is essential to our efforts to promote global financial stability, foster sustainable development, and lift the lives of the poorest. We warmly welcome Prime Minister Brown's report on his review of the responsiveness and adaptability of the international financial institutions (IFIs) and ask our Finance Ministers to consider its conclusions.

2. Reforming the IMF: Our commitment to increase the funds available to the IMF allowed it to stem the spread of the crisis to emerging markets and developing countries. This commitment and the innovative steps the IMF has taken to create the facilities needed for its resources to be used efficiently and flexibly have reduced global risks. Capital again is flowing to emerging economies.

3. We have delivered on our promise to treble the resources available to the IMF. We are contributing over $500 billion to a renewed and expanded IMF New Arrangements to Borrow (NAB). The IMF has made Special Drawing Rights (SDR) allocations of $283 billion in total, more than $100 billion of which will supplement emerging market and developing countries' existing reserve assets. Resources from the agreed sale of IMF gold, consistent with the IMF's new income model, and funds from internal and other sources will more than double the Fund's medium-term concessional lending capacity.

4. Our collective response to the crisis has highlighted both the benefits of international cooperation and the need for a more legitimate and effective IMF. The Fund must play a critical role in promoting global financial stability and rebalancing growth. We welcome the reform of IMF's lending facilities, including the creation of the innovative Flexible Credit Line. The IMF should continue to strengthen its capacity to help its members cope with financial volatility, reducing the economic disruption from sudden swings in capital flows and the perceived need for excessive reserve accumulation. As recovery takes hold, we will work together to strengthen the Fund's ability to provide even-handed, candid and independent surveillance of the risks facing the global economy and the international financial system. We ask the IMF to support our effort under the Framework for Strong, Sustainable and Balanced Growth through its surveillance of our countries' policy frameworks and their collective implications for financial stability and the level and pattern of global growth.

5. Modernizing the IMF's governance is a core element of our effort to improve the IMF's credibility, legitimacy, and effectiveness. We recognize that the IMF should remain a quota-based organization and that the distribution of quotas should reflect the

relative weights of its members in the world economy, which have changed substantially in view of the strong growth in dynamic emerging market and developing countries. To this end, we are committed to a shift in quota share to dynamic emerging market and developing countries of at least five percent from over-represented to under-represented countries using the current IMF quota formula as the basis to work from. We are also committed to protecting the voting share of the poorest in the IMF. On this basis and as part of the IMF's quota review, to be completed by January 2011, we urge an acceleration of work toward bringing the review to a successful conclusion. As part of that review, we agree that a number of other critical issues will need to be addressed, including: the size of any increase in IMF quotas, which will have a bearing on the ability to facilitate change in quota shares; the size and composition of the Executive Board; ways of enhancing the Board's effectiveness; and the Fund Governors' involvement in the strategic oversight of the IMF. Staff diversity should be enhanced. As part of a comprehensive reform package, we agree that the heads and senior leadership of all international institutions should be appointed through an open, transparent and merit-based process. We must urgently implement the package of IMF quota and voice reforms agreed in April 2008.

Reforming the Development banks

6.The Multilateral Development Banks (MDBs) responded to our April call to accelerate and expand lending to mitigate the impact of the crisis on the world's poorest with streamlined facilities, new tools and facilities, and a rapid increase in their lending. They are on track to deliver the promised $100 billion in additional lending. We welcome and encourage the MDBs to continue making full use of their balance sheets. We also welcome additional measures such as the temporary use of callable capital contributions from a select group of donors as was done at the InterAmerican Development Bank (IaDB). Our Finance Ministers should consider how mechanisms such as temporary callable and contingent capital could be used in the future to increase MDB lending at times of crisis. We reaffirm our commitment to ensure that the Multilateral Development Banks and their concessional lending facilities, especially the International Development Agency (IDA) and the African Development Fund, are appropriately funded.

7. Even as we work to mitigate the impact of the crisis, we must strengthen and reform the global development architecture for responding to the world's long-term challenges.

8. We agree that development and reducing global poverty are central to the development banks' core mission. The World Bank and other multilateral development banks are also critical to our ability to act together to address challenges, such as climate change and food security, which are global in nature and require globally coordinated action. The World Bank, working with the regional development banks and other international organizations, should strengthen:

(a) Its focus on food security through enhancements in agricultural productivity and access to technology, and improving access to food, in close cooperation with relevant specialized agencies;
(b) Its focus on human development and security in the poorest and most challenging environments;
(c) Support for private-sector led growth and infrastructure to enhance opportunities for the poorest, social and economic inclusion, and economic growth; and

(d) Contributions to financing the transition to a green economy through investment in sustainable clean energy generation and use, energy efficiency and climate resilience; this includes responding to countries needs to integrate climate change concerns into their core development strategies, improved domestic policies, and to access new sources of climate finance.

9. To enhance their effectiveness, the World Bank and the regional development banks should strengthen their coordination, when appropriate, with other bilateral and multilateral institutions. They should also strengthen recipient country ownership of strategies and programs and allow adequate policy space.

10. We will help ensure the World Bank and the regional development banks have sufficient resources to fulfill these four challenges and their development mandate, including through a review of their general capital increase needs to be completed by the first half of 2010. Additional resources must be joined to key institutional reforms to ensure effectiveness: greater coordination and a clearer division of labor; an increased commitment to transparency, accountability, and good corporate governance; an increased capacity to innovate and achieve demonstrable results; and greater attention to the needs of the poorest populations.

11. We commit to pursue governance and operational effectiveness reform in conjunction with voting reform to ensure that the World Bank is relevant, effective, and legitimate. We stress the importance of moving towards equitable voting power in the World Bank over time through the adoption of a dynamic formula which primarily reflects countries' evolving economic weight and the World Bank's development mission, and that generates in the next shareholding

review a significant increase of at least 3% of voting power for developing and transition countries, in addition to the 1.46% increase under the first phase of this important adjustment, to the benefit of under-represented countries. While recognizing that over-represented countries will make a contribution, it will be important to protect the voting power of the smallest poor countries. We recommit to reaching agreement by the 2010 Spring Meetings.[189]

Conclusion

The G-8 countries adopt resolutions on debt relief, economic policy, multilateral trading systems, political problems, democracy, terrorism, narcotics and other matters relating to world affairs in their annual summits.

Resolutions on debt relief are as follows:

(a) Increase in concessional resource flow to the poorest countries
(b) The Pars Club of creditors to study case-by-case basis of debtor countries beyond Naples' term
(c) Providing multilateral support for development
(d) Enhanced Structural Adjustment Facility (ESAF) of IMF to support the poorest countries for reduction of debt burden
(e) The IMF / WB to undertake necessary adjustment efforts on debt servicing
(f) Integration of Transition countries into global economy
(g) Building on world trading system that works for every one

Investment in people

[189] Pittsburgh summit, media center, No. 129639

(a) IFIs to support and monitor the development of sound economic policy and infrastructure in developing countries
(b) Deepening the development partnerships
(c) Launching the Koln Debt Initiative
(d) Emphasis on HIPC Initiative, strengthening the effectiveness of official development assistance (ODA), and strategic approach to poverty reduction
(e) LDCs to enter global trading system
(f) Paris Club was asked to increase the debt cancellation rate to 90 per cent or more if needed to achieve debt sustainability
(g) 100 percent IDA, AfDF and IMF debt stock relief for completion point HIPCs.
(h) 100 percent debt cancellation of outstanding obligations of HIPCs of the IMF, World Bank, and African Development Bank
(i) UK promised to offer 100 percent debt relief to all HIPC countries on both ODA and non-ODA debts
(j) Canada announced debt relief for Asian countries
(k) G7 countries (except Russia) finance ministers agreed to write off US$ 40 to US$ 55 billion of debts owed to the World Bank, IMF and AfDB.

G-8 Summits have made promises for debt write-offs of the poor countries many times. They have agreed a $ 50 billion boost in aid. These countries agreed full debt cancellations for the poorest 29 countries. G-8 countries have never expressed that they shall undertake full debt cancellation of south Asian countries, Pacific and Caribbean countries. G8 have not yet declared debt relief for all African countries. G-8 countries have not yet successful to check starvation deaths, child sale, child pornography, child mortality, and problems of child missing in the south Asian countries. G-8 countries have differentiated poor people between African countries and other least or less developed countries. They have forgotten that the highest number of people in absolute poverty is found in India. G8 countries pledge to control Malaria, TB, fight with HIV /AIDs in all developing countries, but the aid amount is insufficient to reach the target. G8 promised a target of $ 829 million for Polio eradication and $ 1.5 billion a year for action against Malaria, but they did not specify how much to contribute for these goals.

G8 countries encourage NGOs and Civil Societies for research, advocacy, awareness, and control of diseases, private entrepreneurship and other charitable activities. By that they encourage corruption, data manipulation and create touts in the LLDCs. They believe in advertisement.

G8 countries fail in trade reform and have ignored small-scale farming, rural agricultural markets, and insurance coverage of the poor in all the LDCs. G8 countries have not yet contributed 0.7 percent of GDP for poverty alleviation of LDCs in spite of their own promises.

The spread of debt relief over 40 years would cover from the grand father to grandchild in the LDCs. Do they really desire a world free of hunger, starvation related deaths and debt relief of the poor countries?

G8 countries emphasize on climatic change and advance grants to the poor countries although these countries are more responsible for climatic change. The greenhouse effects are originated in developed countries to the extent of 80 per cent of carbon dioxide. Rich countries must reduce farm subsidies and open their markets. Trade policy of developed countries induces poverty of LDCs.

Resource-rich poor countries should not be tempted or forced to sell minerals or lease mines, oil tanks or any other primary product through foreign direct investment (FDI) in industries or ports or export business.

Grants of assistance should not include cost of consultancy, sale of capital-intensive products or sale of fighter planes for military purposes. G8 countries encourage the governments of LLDCs to privatize hospitals, schools, and Universities and reduce government employees, where starvation deaths are common occurrence and school dropouts are alarming. Their advices have created havocs in LLDCs.

G8 countries encourage industrialization in poor countries through Foreign Direct Investment or private sector or public-private partnership (PPP) to utilize (exhaust) natural resources of resource-rich LDCs. G8 countries intend to privatize water in poor countries.

Rich people and rich countries own the media and control public awareness. Hence, exposure of poverty related ground reality is neglected. Let the governments of LDCs emphasize on poverty reduction programs to achieve success in the projects for rural employment, rural markets and free healthcare facilities. And, it is possible.

+++++

Chapter VIII

WORLD ORGANIZATIONS AND DEBT RELIEF

Indeed, the test of orderliness in a country is not the number of millionaires it owns, but the absence of starvation among its masses.

Mahatma M.K. Gandhi,
Economic and Moral Progress, December 22, 1921

Multilateral debt is the country's external debt burden owed to international financial institutions (IFIs) such as the International Monetary Fund (IMF) and the World Bank. For the world's most impoverished countries, multilateral debt looms larger than other debts because the IFIs provide low-interest balance-of-payment loans, giving them 'preferred creditor' status. This status means that payments to them must be given the highest priority, over private and bilateral (government to government) debt. These institutions also maintain that their bylaws prohibit them from granting debt relief or writing off debts, as governmental and private creditors often do. Debtor governments have a special incentive to stay current with their multilateral debts, since IFIs determine the creditworthiness of countries: until the IMF gives its stamp of approval, which requires adherence to the economic policies it stipulates, impoverished countries generally cannot get credit or capital from other sources.

Multilateral debt is a problem for the entire globe, but it is particularly acute for the most impoverished countries. The impact of debt is felt in two ways - through the diversion of national resources to servicing and through the effects of structural adjustment programs (SAPs), which are designed to transform economies from production for the local market to a globalize model of production and export of whatever garners the most hard currency.

SAPs have almost invariably caused increased poverty, unemployment, and environmental destruction and have usually led to an increase in the overall size of a country's multilateral debt.[190]

Borrowed funds are mostly mis-utilized. A study of utilization of borrowed funds indicate that out of $100 borrowed, $25 goes back to funding agency, $30 goes to the administrators, $20 goes to the rural people and $ 25 is allocated for urban elites. And the actual utilization is hardly $25 per $100 borrowed.

In some countries the borrowed funds is utilized mostly for political expenses or simply deposited in fake personal accounts inside the country or outside the country such as Swiss Bank.

---

[190] Ambrose, Soren, "Multilateral Debt burden", volume 5, number 4, March 2000
Web: www.fpif.org/briefs/vol15/v5n04debt_body.html

In this chapter, the activities of the UNO, the World Bank, the IMF and Paris Club have been discussed as these organizations can ensure debt relief to the indebted countries for the purpose of world peace.

The United Nations Organization

The Charter of the United Nations was signed on June 26, 1945 in San Francisco, at the conclusion of the United Nations Conference on International Organization, and came into force on 24 October 1945 by 51 countries committed to preserving peace through international cooperation and collective security. Today, nearly every nation in the world belongs to the UN: membership totals 191 countries. When States become Members of the United Nations, they agree to accept the obligations of the UN Charter, an international treaty that sets out basic principles of international relations. The Statute of the International Court of Justice is an integral part of the Charter. The UN has four objectives:

(a) To maintain international peace and security;
(b) To develop friendly relations among nations;
(c) To cooperate in solving international problems and in promoting respect for human rights; and
(d) To be a center for harmonizing the actions of nations

The United Nations is not a world government and it does not make laws. It does, however, provide the means to help resolve international conflicts and formulate policies on matters affecting all of us. At the UN, all the Member States—large and small, rich and poor, with differing political views and social systems—have a voice and a vote in this process. The United Nations has six main organs. Five of them—the General Assembly, the Security Council, the Economic and Social Council, the Trusteeship Council and the Secretariat—are based at UN Headquarters in

New York. The sixth, the International Court of Justice, is located at The Hague in the Netherlands.

The United Nations is central to global efforts to solve problems that challenge humanity. Cooperating in this effort are more than 30 affiliated organizations, known together as the UN system. The UN and its family of organizations work to promote respect for human rights, protect the environment, fight disease and reduce poverty day in and day out. The UN agencies define the standards for safe and efficient air travel, help improve telecommunications and enhance consumer protection. The United Nations leads the international campaigns against drug trafficking and terrorism. Throughout the world, the UN and its agencies assist refugees, set up programmes to clear landmines, help expand food production and lead the fight against AIDS.[191]

In this chapter, the outcome of two important conferences conveyed by the United Nations has been discussed. These conferences were held in May 2001 and September 2005. Albeit, the UNO is the highest organization in the world with six main organs, it has limited role in solving the problems of **terrorism, hunger, starvation and debt** prevailing in most of the countries. This coveted organization has not yet taken steps for permanent 'world peace'.

The UN could not and cannot control arms manufacture and arms trade. Even a number of developed countries and low-income countries are now in possession of nuclear weapons. This suggests that the UN charter needs to be amended and updated to solve the emerging world problems. It should be a democratic organization with legislative power and operate with joint responsibility for the benefit of humanity.

---

[191] UN in Brief

(1) Third United Nations Conference on Least Developed Countries (May 2001)

The LDC Watch Report (2003) has reported that over half of the population in 49 Least Developed Countries (LDCs) lives on less than $1 a day. These countries are caught in a poverty trap and the current form of globalization is making the situation worse. Current international trade and finance relations reinforce the poverty cycle as, while these countries are encouraged to trade themselves out of poverty, they are shut out of Western markets by trade barriers. Their overall share of world exports is just 0.4 per cent and they are burdened by unsustainable debts.

The Third United Nations Conference on Least Developed Countries was held in Brussels in May 2001 and the conference delegates drew up an action plan designated the Brussels Programme of Action (BPoA) to run until the next conference planned for 2010. The programme comprised seven 'commitments' tailored to help LDCs work their way out of poverty:

(a) Fostering a people – centered policy framework;
(b) Building good governance nationally and internationally;
(c) Building human and institutional capacities;
(d) Building productive capacities to make globalization work for LDCs;
(e) Enhancing the role of trade in development;
(f) Reducing vulnerability and protecting the environment; and
(g) Mobilizing financial resources.

The LDC agenda was based on reports from LDC civil society organizations from Asia, Africa, and the Pacific and from international organizations. Each LDC is different, and the way governments' view NGOs will depend on the political, economic, and military situation and whether they feel their country is under threat. Secondly, their reports demonstrate how plans drawn up in an international arena are played out on the ground in the countries themselves. Small difference at a local level can make a big difference internationally. Many NGOs suggest extremely concrete action – build more roads, stabilize the currency, reform the tax system, develop agriculture, while others have a more international impact – bring down trade barriers, and reform development policies.[192]

(2) The Development Agenda

After the 2005 Millennium Summit (A checklist of uncompleted tasks), 14–16 September 2005

It was supposed to be a historic summit meeting, and in terms of the sheer numbers of politicians who attended, it really was. 154 heads of state and government and over 900 ministers came together on 14th-16th of September 2005 at the United Nations in New York, to take stock of progress so far on the implementation of the 2000 Millennium Declaration. They decided on concrete steps towards the realization of the Millennium Development Goals (MDGs) and the reform of the UN.

The Secretary-General of the UN, Kofi Annan remarked, "Let us be frank with each other, and with the peoples of the United Nations. We have not yet achieved the sweeping and fundamental reform that many others and I believe is required. Sharp differences, some of them substantive and legitimate, have played their part in preventing that." Five days later, though, he had regained his duty-optimism and highlighted the progress made in the summit in a piece for the Wall Street Journal, concluding that the glass was "at least half full".

---

[192] LDC Watch Annual Report 2003

Now that the dust the largest summit meeting of all time stirred up has settled it is time to evaluate more precisely where we stand. In the following paper I hope to do so with a particular focus on the world summit's outcomes for development politics. What decisions were made despite all disagreements, and must now be translated into reality? Which issues remained unresolved right up to the summit and must now be negotiated in the coming months? And in which areas do serious disagreements remain between governments despite the pressure to negotiate? The answers to these questions should indicate which topics would define the development agenda in the coming years and where public pressure and critical monitoring by civil society is particularly necessary.

(a) Development Co-operation and the Millennium Development Goals

The Millennium Project report under Jeffrey Sachs, Kofi Annan's report "In Larger Freedom" and the numerous analyses and studies produced by NGOs in the context of the Global Call to Action against Poverty (GCAP) demanded that governments take radical steps to realize the MDGs by 2015. This text is part of the Series of Briefing Papers produced by the Friedrich-Ebert-Stiftung and Global Policy Forum Europe. The text includes hardly any new decisions, but for the most part simply "reaffirmed" old ones and "welcomed" or "took note with interest of" new initiatives which individual groups of countries launched in the run-up to or on the fringe of the summit. One can of course presume that some of these new initiatives would not have come about without the summit there to create pressure to negotiate.

There was some progress made around the summit especially in development and debt relief. However the influence that capital markets and international finance and monetary politics wielded over development was not even up for discussion by the governments in New York. The outcome document also contains only a few meaningless platitudes on world trade policy. Because it shows once again that as far as governments are concerned, the United Nations has long ceased to be the place where disputes on trade politics are resolved – that whole side of things now happens at the WTO.

National MDG Strategies

In order to reach the Millennium Development Goals (MDGs), governments commit themselves to adopt and implement comprehensive National Development Strategies as per the New York summit outcome document. They do not go into any further detail, leaving it unclear whether these development strategies are to be carried out in addition to the Poverty Reduction Strategies already in place in many countries. How they will relate to other development strategies such as the national strategies for sustainable development formulated in the Rio follow-up process, and how parliaments and civil society will be involved in developing the strategies. It is also unclear whether industrialized countries are also committed by this decision to adopt strategies to realize the MDGs. If so, these countries would have to concentrate in particular on MDG 8. The initiative to adopt national development strategies originates from the Millennium Project Report, which demands amongst other things that each developing country should come up with a detailed 3-5-year plan listing concrete political measures necessary for achieving the MDGs by 2015 (MDG-based poverty reduction strategies). These strategies would also include a budget plan showing to what extent national resources could be mobilized and how high the deficit is to be filled by external financing in the form of development aid.

Time table for increasing ODA

In the area of financing for development, governments simply repeated at the summit what individual countries and groups of countries had already announced in the run-up to it. The EU decision on a timetable to increase ODA is particularly worth highlighting.

With the consensus decision of the European Council in June 2005, the 25 member-states' ODA is to rise to a EU average of 0.56 per cent of GDP by 2010 and to 0.7 per cent of GDP by 2015. According to the European Council's calculations, this means a doubling of European ODA from around 33 billion Euros in 2003 to around 67 billion Euros by 2010, with a further increase to 92 billion Euros by 2015. German ODA would have to double from 6.005 billion Euros in 2003 to 12.655 billion Euros in 2010, and almost triple to reach 17.661 billion Euros by 2015. This in practice means an annual increase of at least a billion Euros of German ODA. Other countries have set themselves even more ambitious goals, France aiming for the 0.7 per cent goal in 2012 and Great Britain in 2013.

A central question is, of course, whether or not ODA will be increased with "fresh money". If this is the case, it should be possible to see increases in ODA in national budgets for 2006. It is unfortunately likely, however, that governments aim to reach their goals by other means, for example by counting debt relief as aid. Donor countries agreed in the OECD that under certain conditions, debt relief could be counted as ODA. This bookkeeping trick means ODA figures rise without the South getting a single extra Euro. It is to be expected that additional debt cancellation, especially to Iraq, will significantly dress up ODA statistics.

Creditor countries in the Paris Club pledged a debt cancellation to Iraq in November 2004 of $31 billion in total, to be realized over the next four years. Debt relief for heavily indebted countries is without doubt urgently necessary and sensible for development. But it must not become a replacement for the supply of "fresh money" necessary to fund the MDGs.

Cancelling Multilateral Debt

The newest debt relief initiative from the recent G8 is also greeted in the New York outcome document. The heads of state and government at the G8 suggested at the July summit in Gleneagles that the IDA (daughter-fund of the World Bank), the IMF and the ADB should cancel the multilateral debts of 18 of the most heavily indebted poor countries. These debt cancellations, which were formally confirmed at the annual IMF and World Bank meeting in September 2005, have a nominal value of $40 billion and cover a period of 40 years. The 18 countries will thus effectively save $1billion per year in debt payments. This is still not a 100 per cent cancellation for these countries, as they will continue to pay debts back to other multilateral creditors.

Other heavily indebted countries are not yet granted debt cancellations at all. Action Aid, Christian Aid and the British Jubilee Debt Campaign had calculated in the run-up to the summit that a total of 62 countries need a 100 per cent debt cancellation in order to reach the Millennium Development Goals by 2015. In addition, the IDA and the ADB will be reducing future gross aid payments by the amount of debt cancelled, and the relieved funds are to be distributed to all IDA or ADB countries according to the relevant distribution code. This does of course mean that the 18 countries in question will benefit much less from the debt relief.

In order that the IDA's and the ADB's financing capacities are not limited by the gap that reduced debt payments will leave, donor governments have agreed to make up the balance by contributing extra funds themselves. It remains to be seen and closely monitored whether governments will honour this agreement in the next replenishment rounds.

Neither the G8 nor the New York summits gave rise to an agreement on any steps that might reach further, for example the long-demanded redefinition of debt sustainability or the introduction of an insolvency procedure.

The Paris Declaration on Aid Effectiveness

Besides the quantitative aspects of aid, governments at the UN summit also addressed the quality of aid. In doing so they referred mainly to the Paris Declaration on Aid Effectiveness adopted by 90 industrialized and developing countries in March 2005. The declaration contains concrete obligations to structure and co-ordinate aid more closely around the strategies of recipient countries, to reduce transaction and processing costs, to untie aid and to strengthen the accountability of donor and recipient countries to citizens and parliaments.

In order to measure progress on the realization of these obligations, the Paris Declaration includes a list of 12 targets (including the indicators that go with them), which are to be realized by 2010. To improve the transparency of financial flows and to ensure integration of aid into respective national development strategies, for example, at least 85 per cent of ODA flows to the government sector are to be reported on the national budget of the recipient country by 2010. At least 75 per cent of ODA is to be given in the context of one-year or multi-year plans in order to increase the predictability of aid flows for recipient countries. The proportion of ODA not tied to goods and services from companies in donor countries is to be increased steadily between now and 2010. And within five years' time, donors should be putting 25 per cent of ODA towards programme-based approaches (as opposed to small-scale support for individual projects). So far, only small circles of development experts have really taken note of the Paris Declaration. At first glance it appears technocratic, but it could have tangible effects on development praxis.

(b) Reforming the Economic and Social Area of the United Nations

The debate about UN reform dominated the negotiations in the run-up to the summit and even overshadowed discussions on development aid. Security Council reform was at the Center of attention, and was pursued with great diplomatic pressure by the G4 (Germany, India, Japan and Brazil). Although the reform was already put on hold during the run-up to the summit because of the un-resolvable differences of interest between governments, governments did make some decisions for the economic and social area, which should result in concrete institutional reforms. However, they also left many questions unanswered, which must now be negotiated after the summit. This is the case, for example, for the planned Human Rights Council and the new Peace building Commission.

Economic and Social Council

In the outcome document, governments confirm the role of the ECOSOC as the principal UN body for questions of economic and social development. The Council is to meet annually on a ministerial level. Its task is now primarily monitor follow-up of the outcomes of the major United Nations conferences and summits, including the internationally agreed development goals. It will hold a biennial high-level

Development Cooperation Forum to "review trends in international development cooperation, including strategies, policies and financing, promote greater coherence among the development activities of different development partners and strengthen the links between the normative and operational work of the United Nations". The upgrading of the currently politically insignificant ECOSOC to a sort of 'MDG Council' might be a step forwards. At the same time though, this would restrict its area of competence more closely to development issues. Its competence in the human rights area would be transferred to the new Human Rights Council (see below).

Questions of economy, monetary and trade policy are in any case decided on outside the UN, as the United Nations continues to leave these issues to the IMF, the World Bank and the WTO. Consequently the governments in New York did not take up the demands either for substantial reform of these organizations or for a high-level decision-making body for economic issues to be situated within the UN, as a sort of 'Economic Security Council'. Instead, they limited themselves to a few half-hearted steps towards repositioning the ECOSOC. Whether or not this leads at least to a gradual strengthening of the ECOSOC will depend in particular on whether governments accept its new role, and actually send their respective ministers to the annual meetings in New York or Geneva. If they do not, the postulated renewal of the Council will only have happened on paper. The ECOSOC meeting in July 2006 will deliver the first indication either way.

Peace Building Commission

The summit decided to create a **Peace-building Commission** as an international advisory body to support countries in the transition process from violent conflict to lasting peace. The Commission is to support countries in rebuilding after conflict, mobilize financial resources and formulate recommendations improving the co-ordination between all key parties. Its mandate is thus considerably vague than as formulated in the original suggestions made by Kofi Annan and the High-Level Panel on Threats, Challenges and Change. Governments could reach no agreement on where the Commission should be based within the UN. The G77 would like it to be affiliated to the General Assembly, while some industrialized countries would rather have it under the Security Council and others between the Security Council and the ECOSOC.

The Commission is to decide on all issues by consensus. This in other words effectively gives every member the veto. The membership of the Commission is to vary according to the conflict. Its core will consist of a Standing Organizational Committee in turn made up of Security Council members including the P5, members of ECOSOC, and the largest UN contributors of finances and troops respectively. The outcome document does not say anything about the precise number of members.

Neither do the governments mention the role of civil society in the Commission's work. They do, by contrast, explicitly provide for the involvement of the World Bank, the IMF and other institutional donors.

The Commission is to be supported by a Peace-building Fund fed by voluntary contributions, and by a "small office" within the UN secretariat. The Commission is to start work at the latest by the 31st of December 2005 – one of the few clear deadlines given in the document.

By then these as yet undecided issues of membership, mandate and positioning of the Commission within the UN must be resolved.

Human Rights Council

In principle, governments agreed to establish new UN Human Rights Council. But they were not able to agree on all further details and mandated the President of the General Assembly to co-ordinate negotiations. The mandate, function, size, configuration and working practice of the planned Council, are to be resolved by the end of the 60th session, i.e., by the 11th of September 2006. The outcome document does not even specify whether and when the new Human Rights Council will replace the existing Human Rights Commission. It is also entirely unclear to what extent the future Council will adopt the positive aspects of the Human Rights Commission, such as the close involvement of NGOs, the Special Rapporteurs etc. As the governments currently making decisions on the reforms are the very same governments, who have been responsible for the political deficits and deficiencies of the Human Rights Commission up to now. Therefore, there is a danger that some of these positive elements will be lost in the course of negotiations, leaving the UN's human rights work in fact more weakened than strengthened through these 'reforms'.

Nonetheless, it is a positive signal that the summit decided to double the Office of the UN Human Rights Commission's budget over the next five years. It is, however, unclear whether this will mean extra funds, or whether the UN budget will simply be re-jigged at the cost of other areas.

In short, The Millennium +5 Summit undoubtedly did not give rise to the decisions necessary for improving international development and strengthening the United Nations institutionally. Yet it would be wrong to suggest that nothing at all came out of the summit. In the outcome document and in the various declarations made in the context of the summit, governments did make some concrete pledges to which they can be held account. It would be hasty to evaluate these pledges as successes at this stage, though. For the most part, they are simply political declarations of intent, which governments must implement after the summit (for example the EU ODA timetable). Some of the decisions seem so vaguely formulated that it is not even clear yet whether the final results of negotiations can be evaluated as positive or not. This is the case, for example, with the creation of the Human Rights Council. It will be the task of civil society organizations to scrutinize and evaluate whether and how governments realize the resolutions and commitments recorded in the UN outcome document. The following checklist summarizes some of the decisions particularly relevant to development, which demand critical monitoring in 2006 and beyond.

(a) National MDG Strategies: Will governments adopt National Development Strategies in 2006 to realize the MDGs, and how will civil society and parliaments be involved in formulating these strategies?

(b) ODA Timetable: Do the aid budgets of the 25 EU member-states reflect the incremental increases in ODA necessary to realize the binding EU ODA timetable?

(c) Cancellation of Multilateral Debt: Will the IMF and the ADB fully implement the debt cancellation pledged for 18 of the most heavily indebted poor countries by 2006? Will donor countries provide the promised additional funds to the IDA and the ADB and which countries will benefit? Will further debt cancellations for the 20 other HIPCs and other heavily indebted non-HIPCs follow?

(d) Solidarity contributions on air tickets: Which countries will introduce the air ticket levy? How much income will be generated and for what exact development purposes will it be put to use?

(e) IFF for Immunization: To what extent will the IFFIm mobilize extra funds on capital markets in 2006? How high are the interest and transaction costs of front-loading? For what purposes will the funds be put to use?

(f) Further innovative sources of financing: What progress will be made on realizing other suggestions for innovative sources of financing, as discussed for example by the Lula Group? This question is especially interesting regarding the introduction of a currency transaction tax.

(g) Paris Declaration: Will we soon see the first interim results of the implementation of the 12 targets formulated in the Paris Declaration on Aid Effectiveness?

(h) ECOSOC reform: Will the ECOSOC meet at ministerial level in 2006? How will it go about fulfilling its task of monitoring the implementation of the internationally agreed development goals including the MDGs? How will the ECOSOC's structure and working practice reflect its thematic re-orientation?

(i) Peace-building Commission: How will the Standard Organizational Committee of the Commission be configured? Will northern rich countries dominate as feared? To which main UN organs will the Commission be subordinated? Which countries will it deal with in 2006? How will the Commission support these countries effectively in making a transition to lasting and peaceful development?

(j)Human Rights Council: Will the new Human Rights Council succeed in taking over the positive aspects of the Human Rights Commission's work to date? Will NGOs have the same consultative and participatory rights in the Human Rights Council as in the Human Rights Commission? What will happen to the Sub-commission for the Promotion and Protection of

Human Rights? How will the transition from Human Rights Commission to Human Rights Council be organized?

These are some of the questions, which will define the development agenda and debate on reforms in the economic and social field of the United Nations in the aftermath of the UN summit, in 2006. Only when these questions have been answered will it be possible to evaluate whether the 2005 Millennium Summit will go down in the history of the United Nations as the summit that failed, or rather as an important interim step in the global effort to strengthen multilateral co-operation.[193]

The World Bank

The World Bank was established on July 1, 1944 by a conference of 44 governments in Breton Woods, New Hampshire. Their dream is a world free of poverty. It is one of the world's largest sources of development assistance. Its primary focus is on helping the poorest people and the poorest countries. The World Bank Group consists of the following organizations:

1. International Bank for Reconstruction and Development (IBRD)
2. International Development Association (IDA)
3. International Finance Corporation (IFC)
4. Multilateral Investment Guarantee Agency (MIGA)
5. International Center for Settlement of Investment Disputes (ICSID)

The "World Bank" is the name that has come to be used for the International Bank for Reconstruction

---

[193] UN General Assembly 2005: World Summit Outcome. New York: UN (UN Doc. A/60/L.1, 15 September 2005). Jens Martens, Head of the European Office of Global Policy Forum, in Bonn has quoted.

and Development (IBRD) and the International Development Association (IDA). Together these organizations provide low-interest loans, interest-free credit and grants to developing countries. Some 10,000-development professionals from nearly every country in the world work in the World Bank's Washington DC headquarters or in its 109 country offices. The World Bank is one of the United Nations' specialized agencies, and is made up of 184 member countries. These countries are jointly responsible for how the institution is financed and how money is spent. Along with the rest of the development community, the World Bank centers its efforts on reaching the Millennium Development Goals, agreed to by UN members in 2000 and aimed at sustainable poverty reduction.

The World Bank is like a joint stock company, with its member countries as shareholders. The number of shares a country has is based roughly on the size of its economy. The United States is the largest single shareholder with 16.41 per cent of votes, followed by Japan (7.87 per cent), United Kingdom (4.31 per cent), and France (4.31 per cent). The rest of the shares are divided among the other member countries. A Board of Governors represents the World Bank's government shareholders. Generally, the governors are ministers, such as Minister of Finance or Minister of Development. The governors are the ultimate policy makers in the World Bank. They meet once in a year at the Bank's Annual Meetings. An Executive Director represents every member government of the World Bank Group.

The United State of America nominates the World Bank's president, as this country is the largest shareholder. He holds the office for a period of five-year and chairs meetings of the Board of Director.

Role of the World Bank:

(a) Provides support for poverty reduction through investments in health and education
(b) Promotes economic development and structural reform in developing countries
(c) Assists developing countries through long-term financing of development projects and programs
(d) Provides special assistance to the poorest developing countries through the International Development Association
(e) Stimulates private enterprise development and private investments in developing countries primarily through its affiliates, the Internal Finance Corporation and the Multilateral Investment Guarantee Agency
(f) Secures most of the financial resources by borrowing on International capital markets
(g) Enhances the flow of capital and technology for productive purposes to developing countries by providing investment insurance against non-commercial risks for investments in developing countries.[194]

World Bank (IBRD & IDA)

The World Bank's mission is to reduce poverty - an important commitment to which the Bank should be held and against which its activities should be evaluated. In its first year of operation, 1946, the Bank lent less than $500 million. Today, the World Bank[195] provides between $20 and $30 billion annually for activities ranging from agriculture to trade policy, from health and education to energy and mining.

---

[194] World Bank Group: Working For A World Free of Poverty
[195] Bank Information Center, info @ bicusa.org

The World Bank is among the largest sources of public financing in the world. However its various roles as lender, knowledge broker, and gatekeeper to development finance collectively serve another purpose: to steer investor dollars and aid flows to targeted countries and sectors.

But the poverty focus of these investments is often questionable.

The World Bank as lender

The World Bank lends money to low and middle-income governments for two general uses: investment projects and policy reforms. Investment project lending typically supports public works such as water systems, roads and schools. The World Bank also lends money for economic, institutional or other policy reforms, often known as "structural adjustment" or "development policy" lending. These reforms can influence the amount and composition of public spending in your country and the design of your government's economic and social policies, affecting things like the cost of electricity and water, labor laws and investment regulations.

World Bank lending can take the form of loans or grants, and the poorest countries often receive both. In recent years, the Bank has increased the proportion of its financing provided through grants.

The Bank typically requires certain actions of borrowing countries in advance of loan/grant approval and/or in the course of a project's implementation - known as "conditions" or "conditionality." Conditions can range from requiring a government to privatize its state-owned companies or adopt lower trade tariffs, to mandating new budget and procurement procedures. The Bank's imposition of controversial conditions on borrowing governments has been heavily criticized over the years, as a violation of a country's sovereignty and an undemocratic way to force reforms that can have substantial consequences on people and planet.

The World Bank as knowledge broker

The Bank has cornered the market on development research, publishing numerous books and reports that frame the debate on development issues. In the absence of alternative sources of information, many countries get their information about economic policies and development models from the World Bank. In 2000, the World Bank created its own research and training group – the World Bank Institute (WBI) – to directly influence development discourse. The WBI conducts trainings of government officials, including parliamentarians, and civil society representatives on various dimensions of development policy and planning.

The WB as Gatekeeper to Development Finance

Finally, the World Bank influences the overall amount and composition of development financing available to countries. Both the World Bank's own lending and other donors' decisions are shaped by the Bank's research and analysis – in particular, by Bank studies like the Country Policy and Institutional Assessments (CPIA) and Investment Climate Assessments (ICA), which rate countries largely on the basis of their economic policies and openness to foreign investment. Since many donors take their lead from the Bank, the institutions financing decisions and evaluations of country development strategies affect borrowing country access to capital from a broad spectrum of sources. The Bank's gatekeeper role is much stronger for aid-dependent countries without credit ratings than for countries that have access to international capital markets.

IBRD

The IBRD lends only to sovereign governments or for projects guaranteed by sovereigns. During fiscal 2008, the IBRD committed $13.5 billion for 99 operations, new loans, guarantees, and guarantee facilities for middle-income countries. Development-policy lending represented 29 percent of total IBRD lending, up slightly from 28 percent in fiscal 2007. IBRD borrowers are generally considered to be middle-income countries, roughly defined by the IBRD as countries with a per capita income US $936 to US $11,455. Countries with higher per capita incomes may borrow from the IBRD under special circumstances, as may some countries with lower income levels, but which are deemed creditworthy for IBRD lending. The IBRD offers loans at near-market terms but with more time to repay than if they borrowed from a commercial bank-typically 15 to 20 years with a three-to-five-year grace period before repayment of principal begins. IBRD borrowers typically have some access to private capital markets.

With a US$4.4 billion share of total IBRD commitments in 2008, Latin America and the Caribbean had the highest lending percentage among the regions at 32 percent. Europe and Central Asia followed with US$3.7 billion (28 percent) and East Asia and Pacific with US$2.7 billion (20 percent). The IBRD has lent over US$440 billion since its founding over 60 years ago. While the IBRD had new lending commitments for 99 operations in 2008, 53 percent of total IBRD lending went to the five largest borrowers - Argentina, China, India, Turkey and Colombia - down from 56 percent in fiscal 2007. Major attention was paid to transportation lending. Figures of regional lending by theme and sector are recorded in the World Bank annual Report. IBRD has developed a large range of lending products.

IBRD loans generally take two forms: investment lending for specific projects (roads, dams) or adjustment lending conditioned on structural and policy reforms by the borrower. IBRD adjustment lending has ranged from 35-64 percent of total commitments over the past five years despite Bank policy not to exceed a 25 percent cap.

IBRD is financed primarily by selling bonds to private investors in international capital markets, backed up by the pledges of its member governments. Upon joining the IBRD, member governments must "subscribe" to a portion of the Bank's capital stock, in effect promising to purchase a specified number of shares. Members are required to purchase only a small portion of their subscription ("paid-in capital") while the remaining portion ("callable capital") remains an outstanding pledge (which Bank has never needed to request). In 2008, the IBRD had paid-in capital of US$11.5 billion and callable capital of US$178 billion. With capital backing of nearly US$200 billion from its member governments, the IBRD is able to raise significant funds on international capital markets at preferred "AAA" credit rates and then lend those funds to borrowers at rates slightly below those offered by commercial lenders. In fiscal 2008 the IBRD raised US$19 billion at medium to long-term maturities.

Conservative financial and lending policies and practices instill a high degree of investor confidence in IBRD securities. These policies and practices also instill a high degree of discipline in the IBRD's relations to its borrowers. These policies and practices include:

(a) All loans are made directly to, or guaranteed by, a member country of IBRD.
(b) IBRD is recognized by the major credit rating agencies to enjoy a preferred creditor status

with its borrower-shareholders, in effect, putting the IBRD first in line for debt repayment.

(c) Since its inception in 1945, IBRD has never written off a loan.

(d) The IBRD freezes loan approvals and disbursements if a country fails to pay obligations on time.

(e) Strict limits are set on loan concentration in individual countries.

(f) It is IBRD practice not to reschedule interest or principal payments on its loans (though this does occur from time to time).

(g) The IBRD has made a profit every year of its existence-over US$1.65 billion in 2007.

(h) The IBRD is committed to make further improvements to the services it provides its members. To meet the growing demands of middle-income countries, the IBRD is overhauling financial and risk management products, broadening the provision of free-standing knowledge services and making it easier for clients to deal with the Bank.

International Development Association (IDA)

The International Development Association - the Bank's "concessional," or low-cost lending arm, **provides funding to the poorest member governments** of the World Bank. These governments have been assigned credit ratings so low that they are unable to borrow from commercial lenders or from the main lending arms of the MDBs. IDA is an important source of credit for these countries, with average annual lending commitments of US$10.8 billion over the last 3 years (compared to US$8.3 billion over the previous 3-year period).

Since its inception in 1960, IDA has lent over US$182 billion, with over US$100 billion outstanding for repayment. IDA's largest single borrowers are India,

Pakistan, Nigeria, Vietnam, and Ethiopia. In fiscal 2008, IDA commitments reached $11.2 billion for 199 operations ($7.8 billion in credits and $3.4 billion in grants). In 2008, major attention was paid to public administration lending (including law and justice) who received $2.9.

Seventy-nine countries are currently considered eligible to borrow from IDA. To be eligible, IDA borrowers must (a) lack sovereign creditworthiness, (b) have a per capita income of less than US$1,095 (in fiscal year 2009) and (c) must meet certain "performance" criteria set by the World Bank.

The IDA loans (known as credits) have 20, 35, or 40 year repayment periods with a 10-year grace period on repayment of principal. IDA credits do not carry interest charges per se, but do carry a 0.75 percent "service charge" on disbursed funds (no grace period on this fee). In the past several years IDA has increasingly provided a portion of its funding in the form of grants.

IDA is funded through three main sources:

(a) Re-flows from previous loans
(b) Transfers from IBRD net income
(c) Contributions from IDA donors

Negotiations over the 15th Replenishment of IDA came to a conclusion in December 2007 with records pledges of US$27.3 billion Special Drawing Rights (SDR) (about US$41.7 billion) The funding is divided into $25.2 billion in new pledges made by donors; $16.5 billion from previous pledges for financing the cost of debt relief, IDA's credit re-flows and investment income; and $3.5 billion from internal financing from the World Bank Group. Re-flow payments from past loans to the poorest countries have become an increasingly important source of IDA resources. However, with the implementation of the

Multilateral Debt Relief Initiative (MDRI), some internal resources are no longer available.

IDA donors come together every three years to negotiate the amount of new resources required to replenish IDA's lending program and to discuss lending policies and priorities. The fifteenth replenishment (IDA -15) advances finances for projects over a three-year period 2009 - 2011. During the IDA15 replenishment meetings, donors provided additional contributions for the MDRI replenishment of SDR 4.1 billion (US$6.3 billion), in order to cover IDA's debt relief costs due to the MDRI during the IDA15 disbursement period (FY09-19) as agreed under the MDRI. Donors will meet to review the progress of IDA15 at a Mid-Term Review Meeting to be held in the fall of 2009. The IDA replenishment process provides a degree of influence on setting development priorities by the IDA Deputies.

IDA lending flows to an immense array of programs and projects, from basic health and education provision to economy-wide adjustment operations, from water supply and sanitation to oil, gas, and mining projects.

Over the past decade adjustment lending has comprised anywhere from 16 to 27 percent of IDA annual commitments. Generally the IDA lending supports individual investment projects. In recent years IDA has become, according to the Bank, "the single largest source of donor funds for basic social services to the poorest countries." IDA has increased its investment lending in social sectors from roughly 20 percent of overall commitments in the late 1980s to around 40 percent by the mid-1990s. Over the past several years IDA has targeted 50 percent of its new commitments to countries in Africa.

The Enhanced HIPC Initiative:

September 2006 marked the tenth anniversary of the HIPC Initiative. Started in 1996, the Initiative was enhanced in 1999 as an outcome of a comprehensive review by IDA and the IMF, including public consultations. The Initiative's debt-burden thresholds were adjusted downward, which enabled a broader group of countries to qualify for larger volumes of debt relief. Moreover, a number of creditors, including the main multilateral, started to provide earlier assistance to qualifying countries in the form of interim relief at decision point. Finally, the "floating completion point" was introduced, providing incentives to speed up reforms and increase country ownership.

The international community has focused on strengthening the links between debt relief and poverty-reduction efforts. Debt relief is linked to progress implementing the country's Poverty Reduction Strategy (PRS). Consequently, in addition to the financial benefits debt relief has delivered, it has strengthened countries' reform efforts. Nominal debt service relief under HIPC to the 29 countries that have reached their decision points has been estimated to amount to about US $62 billion. Nominal debt service relief under HIPC to the 20 completion point countries has been estimated to amount to US $44 billion.

The poverty-reducing expenditures of HIPCs have increased since 1999, while debt-service payments have been declining. Debt service paid by the 29 post-decision point HIPCs has declined from about 4 percent of GDP in 1999 to about 2 percent in 2005. During the same period, poverty-reducing expenditures have increased from about 7 percent of GDP in 1999 to over 9 percent in 2005. In absolute terms, poverty-reducing expenditures amounted to nearly US$15 billion in 2005, more than five times debt-service payments. Pro-poor spending is expected to increase further from 2006 onwards with additional assistance under the MDRI. Challenges remain to ensure that debt burdens do not return to unsustainable levels:

(a) Establishing a track record of reform in the remaining countries potentially eligible for HIPC, several of these countries are affected by conflict and several have problems of protracted external arrears.
(b) Strengthening management of debt and public finances.
(c) Ensuring full participation by creditors.

Beyond debt relief, long-term debt sustainability requires efforts by borrowers, lenders, and donors to promote prudent borrowing, suitably concessional finance, sustained economic growth, diversified exports, and greater access to markets in developed countries. Last but not least, "free-riding" concerns could arise if some creditors profit from the borrowing space created by debt relief by increasing their own lending.[196]

Debt Relief at a Glance

(a) The Bank provides debt relief to low-income countries through the Debt Relief Initiative for Heavily Indebted Poor Countries (the HIPC Initiative), created in 1996, and the Multilateral Debt Relief Initiative (MDRI), created in 2006.

(b) Twenty-nine countries are receiving debt service relief under both these initiatives, worth over US$100 billion over time if all creditors participate, with eleven other countries potentially eligible.

(c) For these 29 countries, World Bank debt relief under the HIPC Initiative and the MDRI will total about US$40 billion over time (US$14 billion under HIPC and US$26 billion under the MDRI).

---

[196] The World Bank, Economic Policy and Debt

(d) If all potentially eligible countries qualify, this total could rise to well above US$50 billion. In countries receiving debt relief, reforms have been reinforced, debt service cut by two-thirds, and spending on anti-poverty programs increased from US$4 billion to US$11 billion a year since 1999.
Overview

Following the buildup of foreign debt owed by many low-income countries throughout the 1970s and 1980s, low growth, falling commodity prices, and other economic shocks left many nations with unsustainable debt burdens. By 1992, the 33 most indebted low-income countries faced debts whose present value had more than doubled in ten years to over six times their annual exports. Starting in the late 1980s, the Paris Club and other bilateral creditors rescheduled and forgave many of these debts. But by the mid 1990s, with an increasing share of debt owed to multilateral lenders such as the World Bank, the IMF, and regional development banks, a new debt relief initiative was called for, involving these creditors, to address the concern that poor countries' debts were stifling poverty reduction efforts. In response, in 1996 the International Development Association (IDA, the World Bank's concessional lending arm for poor countries) and the IMF launched the HIPC Initiative. The Initiative is comprehensive - it calls for the voluntary provision of debt relief by all creditors, whether multilateral, bilateral, or commercial - and aims to provide a fresh start to countries struggling to cope with foreign debt that places too great a burden on export earnings or fiscal revenues.

The HIPC Initiative was enhanced in 1999 to provide deeper, more rapid relief to a wider group of countries, and to increase the Initiative's links with poverty reduction. To date, 29 countries are benefiting from HIPC debt relief, 19 having reached the completion point, at which debt relief becomes irrevocable.

Ten more are receiving some debt relief and a further eleven are potentially eligible for HIPC debt relief, pending the agreement of macroeconomic reforms, poverty reduction strategies, or arrears clearance plans. In 2006, following the 2005 Gleneagles Summit of the G8 group of nations, the World Bank joined the IMF and the African Development Bank in implementing the Multilateral Debt Relief Initiative (MDRI), forgiving 100 percent of eligible outstanding debt owed to these three institutions by all countries reaching the completion point of the HIPC Initiative. The MDRI will effectively double the volume of debt relief already expected from the enhanced HIPC Initiative.

The HIPC Initiative in Practice

A country is potentially eligible for the HIPC Initiative if it meets income and indebtedness criteria. Its annual per capita income must be below the threshold for eligibility for concessional borrowing from both the World Bank and the IMF and external public debt must exceed 150 percent of its exports (or in certain cases 250 percent of fiscal revenues). There are 40 such potentially eligible HIPCs. To become eligible, the country must also have had a program with the IMF at some point since the start of the Initiative in 1996. The provision of debt relief then depends on policies being in place to ensure that it effectively contributes to poverty reduction. The fraction of debt that creditors' are asked to forgive (the common reduction factor) is then calculated to bring the country's debt ratio back to a sustainable level (150 percent of exports or in certain cases 250 percent of fiscal revenues).

The first stage of qualification is the decision point, at which the country must have a current track record of satisfactory performance under an IMF program, a Poverty Reduction Strategy (PRS) or an interim PRS in place, and an agreed plan to clear any arrears to foreign creditors. At the decision point, many creditors, such as the World Bank, the IMF, multilateral development banks, and Paris Club bilateral creditors, begin to provide debt relief, although many of these institutions maintain the right to revoke this if policy performance falters.

Debt relief from participating creditors becomes irrevocable at the completion point. At the decision point, the country agrees on a short list of completion point triggers, upon which the country will "graduate" from the HIPC Initiative. These include a continued track record of satisfactory performance on an IMF program and the implementation for at least one year of the PRS. Some triggers may relate to progress in social areas such as health and education, while others may relate to improving governance or fighting corruption to give donors sufficient confidence that debt relief assistance will be well used.

Completion point: Nineteen countries have reached the completion point. These are: Benin, Bolivia, Burkina Faso, Cameroon, Ethiopia, Ghana, Guyana, Honduras, Madagascar, Mali, Mauritania, Mozambique, Nicaragua, Niger, Rwanda, Senegal, Tanzania, Uganda, and Zambia.

Decision point: Ten countries have reached the decision point and these are Burundi, Chad, the Democratic Republic of Congo, the Republic of Congo, The Gambia, Guinea, Guinea-Bissau, Malawi, São Tomé and Príncipe, and Sierra Leone.

Potentially eligible: Eleven countries remain potentially eligible such as Central African Republic, Comoros, Côte d'Ivoire, Eritrea, Haiti, the Kyrgyz Republic, Liberia, Nepal, Somalia, Sudan, and Togo.

Many of these have been beset by civil war, cross-border armed conflict, and governance challenges (including in some cases the buildup of substantial arrears on external debt).

The design of the HIPC Initiative also takes into account changes in economic circumstances brought on by external factors beyond the government's control during the interim period between the decision point and the completion point. When the country reaches the completion point, additional debt relief (topping up*)* may be granted to mitigate the impact of external shocks and ensure that the debt ratio at the completion point is sustainable.

A review of the HIPC Initiative by the World Bank Group's Independent Evaluation Group found that it has enabled higher spending on countries' social programs and poverty reducing investments but also noted the need to manage expectations of what debt relief can realistically achieve. Long-run debt sustainability ultimately relies on countries' broader success in building the institutions to support sustained economic growth.

Cent per cent Debt Cancellations:
The Multilateral Debt Relief Initiative

On March 28, 2006, the Board of IDA approved IDA's participation in the Multilateral Debt Relief Initiative (MDRI), requiring IDA to cancel all debt outstanding and disbursed owed by HIPCs to IDA as of end-2003 as soon as these countries reached the HIPC completion point. The Bank began providing MDRI debt relief on July 1, 2006.

The MDRI provides HIPCs that have reached the completion point irrevocable, up-front cancellation of debt owed to IDA, the African Development Fund, and the IMF. Debt cancellation under the MDRI will be in addition to debt relief already committed under the HIPC Initiative.

The full benefit of the MDRI from all three institutions will be over US$50 billion: about US$37 billion for IDA, US$8.5 billion for the African Development Fund and US$5 billion for the IMF.

The MDRI aims to provide additional resources to help countries reach the MDGs, at the same time preserving the financing capacity of the International Financial Institutions. IDA donors therefore agreed to compensate IDA for all MDRI assistance provided.

MDRI donor contributions to IDA are used to benefit all IDA recipients: they are attributed to countries according to the performance-based allocation mechanism used by IDA. For the 18 countries that had reached completion point as of March 2006, retroactive assessments were conducted to detect any subsequent dip in the main policy areas upon which completion point was originally assessed. All 18 have now received MDRI assistance. For newly qualifying completion-point HIPCs (Cameroon was the first in May 2006), qualification for MDRI is automatic.

Avoiding the Need for another Debt Relief Initiative:

The Debt Sustainability Framework for Low-Income Countries

The debt sustainability framework is a forward-looking approach to guide borrowing and lending decisions to devote resources toward achieving the MDGs without creating the buildup of unsustainable debt. By assessing each country's circumstances, the framework balances the need for funds with current and prospective ability to repay debt. This approach puts responsibilities on both borrowers and creditors. Low-income countries that seek new loans are responsible for strengthening policies and institutions to enhance capacity to manage debt and reduce vulnerability to shocks. Creditors, for their part, review long-term debt projections, which incorporate forward-looking economic analysis and account for possible shocks.[197]

World Bank 2009

In June, the World Bank announced record levels of lending with much of the funding for infrastructure projects, where the Bank's record has been particularly controversial.

Earlier this year, in response to the economic crisis, the Bank promised to substantially increase its lending, particularly to middle income countries. Provisional figures released by the Bank show that it spent a record $58.8 billion in fiscal year 2009 (which ended in June), $20.6 billion more than the previous fiscal year.

The International Bank for Reconstruction and Development (IBRD), the Bank's arm which lends mostly to middle-income countries) was the main source of the Bank's expansion, lending $32.9 billion, up from $13.5 billion the previous year. Almost half IBRD lending went through development policy loans. Concessional lending through another Bank arm, IDA, increased by $2.8 billion to reach $14 billion, of which $2.6 billion was provided as grants.

Most of this cash was raised through the money markets, though the Bank press release claimed that donors have given it an extra $6.8 billion over and above previous commitments to the institution. Despite reports that the Bank's borrowing costs were increasing as governments' pumped money into their banking systems; it is still able to borrow at a far

---

[197] The World Bank, News and Broadcast

cheaper rate than developing countries. While a $6 billion short-term bond issuance in March was expensive, a €3 billion ($4.2 billion) bond offered in May was the cheapest 10 year bond any supranational lender had issued this year.

In Africa, governments are turning to the Bank for emergency support as their public finances deteriorate. In June, the Bank approved $535 million for Ghana: $300 million to support the government's budget and $235 million for transport. Mozambique is seeking $120 million from the Bank and Fund, and Nigeria and Kenya are in exploratory talks with the Bank for around $1 billion.

Big boost to infrastructure

The Bank has recently announced its intention to increase spending in several sectors, including health, education and agriculture, but the biggest boost is reserved for infrastructure.

Education lending is set to double to $4.1 billion per year, agriculture loans increase from $4 billion in 2008 to $6 billion per year for the next two years, and social protection funding rise from $2 billion to $6 billion per year for the next two years. The Bank also intends to increase its facility for the food crisis to $2 billion, up from the $1.2 billion it initially earmarked.

Infrastructure, however, accounted for $20.7 billion, over a third of all Bank-lending in the 2009 fiscal year. The newly established Infrastructure Recovery and Assets Platform (INFRA) promises $45 billion in infrastructure lending over the next three years, an annual increase of around $5 billion per year. Latin America seems set to be a major recipient. In the year to June, Bank lending to Latin America rose to $17.1 billion, an increase of 70 per cent. The Bank expects to maintain this level of lending in the region and to continue to focus on infrastructure projects and social programs.

This big boost to infrastructure has forcefully made the low-income and low-middle-income countries perennially indebted, and people of these countries have been made dependent on others and left their traditional practices and engagement in agriculture. They prefer corruption over hard work.

Outstanding Loan

The World Bank lending was US $ 18,513.2 million in 2003, US $ 20,080.1 million in 2004, US $ 22,307.0 million in 2005, US $23,641.2 million in 2006, US $24,695.8 million in 2007 and US $ 24,702.3 million in Fiscal 2008.

The IBRD Loans outstanding was US $ 99,050 million and the IDA Credit outstanding was US $113,542 million in Fiscal 2008. In other words, the World Bank credit outstanding was to the extent of US $ 212,592 million by Fiscal 2008.

International Monetary Fund (IMF)

The International Monetary Fund as established by the Bretton Woods Agreements is a substitute for the old gold standard, and an alternative to both a system of completely free exchange rates and a system of extreme exchange control. In other words, the Fund is a mixed standard employing within itself some features of the gold standard and the paper standard. It represents an attempt at "an improved system of international currency," in Keynes' words.[198] The IMF is an international organization of 184 member countries. It was established to promote

---

[198] . Kurihara, K. K. (1978), "Monetary Theory and Public Policy", Kalyani Publishers, New Delhi, P. 339

international monetary co-operation, exchange stability, and orderly exchange arrangements; to foster economic growth and high levels of employment; and to provide temporary financial assistance to countries to help ease balance of payments adjustment. The operations of IMF, which involve surveillance, financial assistance, and technical - have developed to meet the changing needs of its member countries in an evolving world economy.

Purpose:

(a) To promote international monetary cooperation through a permanent institution this provides the machinery for consultation and collaboration on international monetary problems.
(b) To facilitate the expansion and balanced growth of international trade, and to contribute thereby to the promotion and maintenance of high levels of employment and real income and to the development of the productive resources of all members as primary objectives of economic policy.
(c) To promote exchange stability, to maintain orderly exchange arrangements among members, and to avoid competitive exchange depreciation.
(d) To assist in the establishment of a multilateral system of payments in respect of current transactions between members and in the elimination of foreign exchange restrictions, which hamper the growth of world trade?
(e) To give confidence to members by making the general resources of the Fund temporarily available to them under adequate safeguards, thus providing them with opportunity to correct mal-adjustments in their balance of payments without resorting to measures

destructive of national or international prosperity.

(f) To shorten the duration and lesson the degree of dis-equilibrium in the international balances of payments of members[199]

Role:

(a) Oversees the international monetary system and promotes international monetary co-operation

(b) Promotes orderly exchange rate relations among member countries

(c) Provides short- to medium- term financial support to members facing balance of payment difficulties

(d) Draws its financial resources primarily from the quota subscriptions of its members

The IMFC Report

The Global Economy and Financial Markets—Outlook, Risks, and Policy Responses:

1. The Committee[200] welcomes the ongoing global economic expansion, although it notes that growth divergences between countries remain wide. Global growth is expected to continue, although downside risks to the outlook have increased, especially high and volatile oil prices, recently exacerbated by the effects of Hurricane Katrina, the widening of global imbalances, increasing protectionist sentiment, and the possibility of tighter financial market conditions. While core inflation generally is contained and inflation expectations remain well anchored, higher oil

[199] Articles of Agreement – Article 1: Purposes, International Monetary Fund, Washington, DC

[200] The International Monetary and Financial Committee held its twelfth meeting in Washington, D.C. on September 24, 2005 under the Chairmanship of Mr. Gordon Brown, Chancellor of the Exchequer of the United Kingdom. Washington, DC

prices remain a risk to price stability. The Committee notes that these areas should be a particular focus of IMF surveillance and policy advice in the coming months.

2. The Committee emphasizes that oil producers, oil consumers, and oil companies will all have their part to play in working together to promote greater stability in the oil market. First, the Committee welcomes the action by members of the International Energy Agency and oil-producing countries to continue to increase supplies to the market. Second, the Committee calls for further investment both now and in the long term throughout the supply chain, particularly in refining capacity including of heavy oil, and for efforts to create a favorable investment climate. Third, the Committee also stresses the importance of policies to promote energy conservation, efficiency, and sustainability, including through new technologies, alternative sources of energy, and reducing subsidies on oil products. Fourth, the Committee encourages closer dialogue between oil producers and consumers, and further efforts to improve oil market data and transparency to improve market efficiency. Fifth, the IMF should stand ready to provide assistance to help members, especially poor countries, deal with oil price shocks.

3. The Committee welcomes recent progress in implementing the agreed policies to address global imbalances and foster growth, but urges further action to promote orderly adjustment in view of the heightened risks to the outlook. This includes: fiscal consolidation to increase national savings in the United States; greater exchange rate flexibility in emerging Asia; further structural reforms to boost potential growth in the euro area; and further structural reforms, including fiscal consolidation, in Japan, where the economy is regaining momentum. Measures to promote a more investor-friendly environment, including in a number of emerging

market economies, would also contribute to reducing imbalances. Oil-exporting countries will also need to play their part, including through efficient absorption of higher oil revenues in countries with strong macroeconomic policies.

4. Steps to strengthen medium-term fiscal positions remain crucial for supporting global growth and stability. Fiscal deficits in many industrial countries need to be lowered further, and reforms to address pressures from aging populations and ensure the sustainability of pension and health care systems need to be accelerated. Improvements in the fiscal positions and debt structures of many emerging market countries are welcome, but in countries with high public debt levels continued fiscal consolidation efforts are needed. The Committee also calls for more ambitious efforts to address rigidities in labor and product markets in many countries. Regulatory and supervisory authorities should remain alert to risks stemming from ample global liquidity and associated risk taking and leverage.

5. The Committee emphasizes that a successful outcome to the Doha Round by the end of 2006 remains of critical importance for global growth and poverty reduction. Serious challenges remain in reaching agreement at the WTO ministerial meeting in Hong Kong SAR in December. As finance ministers and central bank governors of WTO member countries, we have a vital interest in successful multilateral trade liberalization. Mr. Pascal Lamy, the Director-General of the WTO, and the Committee called for all countries to ensure progress on ambitious trade liberalization with the urgency that the timetable now demands. Key areas for action are: increasing market access, especially for developing countries; significantly reducing trade distorting domestic support; eliminating all forms of export subsidies in agriculture; and making significant progress on services, including financial services, and

on issues of intellectual property. The Committee welcomes the joint IMF-World Bank staff report on proposals to enable low-income countries to benefit fully from trade liberalization, and urges the Executive Board to consider these proposals expeditiously.

6. The Committee welcomes the enhanced growth performance and prospects of many of the world's poorest countries, reflecting improvements in their underlying policies. With ten years remaining to meet the Millennium Development Goals (MDGs), those countries should move rapidly to strengthen policies needed for sustainable growth and poverty reduction. These countries should include sound macroeconomic frameworks and build the sound, accountable, and transparent institutions that are essential for fostering growth and supporting vibrant private sector growth. Also, the international community must follow through expeditiously on its renewed commitments to provide additional resources, including at the Gleneagles Summit and the Millennium Review Summit. An ambitious outcome to the Doha Round is also essential for poverty reduction.

IMF Objectives and Medium Term Strategy

7. The Committee welcomes and supports the broad priorities set forth in the Managing Director's Report on the Fund's Medium-Term Strategy to improve the IMF's effectiveness in support of its members. In the coming years the IMF will continue to work to help members meet the economic challenges of globalization within its mandate in the macroeconomic and financial areas. The Committee looks forward to specific proposals and timelines on the main tasks identified in the medium-term strategy in the Executive Board's work program, within the context of the IMF's medium-term budget framework and the staff compensation review.

8. The broad priorities set out in the Managing Director's report are to:

(a) Make surveillance more effective;
(b) Adapt to new challenges and needs in different member countries;
(c) Help build institutions and capacity;
(d) Prioritize and reorganize the IMF's work within a prudent medium-term budget; and
(e) Address the issues of fair quotas and voice.

The Committee agrees that the IMF needs to deepen its analysis of globalization and continue to develop its strategy for responding to the long-term challenges it poses.

IMF Supports Low-Income Countries

9. The Committee reiterates that the IMF has a critical role in supporting low-income countries through policy advice, capacity building, and financial assistance. The PRGF remains the main instrument for IMF financial support for low-income country members. The Committee agrees that the IMF's concessional lending should be financed at an appropriate level as assessed by the IMF. The Committee calls for incorporation of the lessons from the recent review of the design of PRGF-supported programs in the future work of the IMF in low-income countries.

10. The Committee welcomes the progress made on new instruments that will strengthen IMF support for low-income countries. The Policy Support Instrument (PSI) will be available to members that do not need, or want, IMF financial assistance, but voluntarily request IMF endorsement and continued assessment of their policies as meeting the standard of upper credit trances conditionality. The country-owned policy frameworks designed by the authorities would

consolidate medium-term macroeconomic and financial stability, and deepen reforms in support of poverty reduction and economic growth. A new window in the PRGF Trust will also be available to complement existing instruments by providing timely concessional support to low-income members without a regular PRGF arrangement and who are facing exogenous shocks, and we look forward to contributions from countries.

11. The Committee supports the proposal to provide 100 percent cancellation of debts owed by Heavily Indebted Poor Countries (HIPCs) to the IMF, the International Development Association and the African Development Fund. This will provide significant additional resources for countries' efforts to reach the MDGs and reinforce longer-term debt sustainability. The Committee welcomes the approach subsequently discussed in the IMF to ensure that the IMF's resources will be used consistently with the principle of uniformity of treatment. It stresses the importance of ensuring that the IMF's capacity to provide financing to low-income countries is maintained, and therefore welcomes G-8 countries' commitments to provide additional resources. It also emphasizes that countries benefiting from irrevocable debt relief should have demonstrated sound policies and high standards of governance. Following this agreement now reached on all the elements, the Managing Director has informed the Committee that he will now call the Executive Board together to complete its approval of the arrangements to deliver debt relief by the end of 2005. The implications of debt cancellation for the new debt sustainability framework should be addressed in the review scheduled for spring 2006. There should be a regular report on progress at future meetings of the Committee.

12. The Committee underscores the importance of full creditor participation, including by non-Paris Club

creditors and private creditors, in contributing their share to implementing the enhanced HIPC initiative. It takes note of the work on identifying low-income countries with unsustainable debts as of end-2004, with a view to finalization by early 2006 of the list of countries potentially eligible for HIPC assistance.

13. The year 2005 is the International Year of Micro-credit. The Committee notes the IMF's role in improving data availability on micro-credit and in addressing micro-credit issues in the Financial Sector Assessment Program.

Other Issues

14. The Committee welcomes the rapid progress on the inclusion of collective action clauses in international sovereign bonds, and the efforts by emerging market issuers and private sector creditors to broaden the consensus on the "Principles for Stable Capital Flows and Fair Debt Restructuring in Emerging Markets." The Committee looks forward to further work on the orderly resolution of financial crises, including the implementation of the IMF's lending into arrears policy.

15. The Committee calls for continued actions by all countries to develop strong programs on anti-money laundering and combating the financing of terrorism (AML/CFT). The Committee supports the IMF's efforts to implement its intensified AML/CFT work program, and notes the critical importance of supporting countries' efforts with well-targeted and coordinated technical assistance.[201]

16. The Committee recommends members' acceptance of the Fourth Amendment of the Articles of Agreement. The Committee reiterates that the IMF's effectiveness and credibility as a cooperative

---

[201] International Monetary and Financial Committee

institution must be safeguarded and further enhanced. Adequate voice and participation by all members should be assured, and the distribution of quotas should reflect developments in the world economy. The Thirteenth General Review of Quotas presents an opportunity to address the issue, and we look forward to progress on this issue and a report back at our next meeting.

IMF grants US $ 3.3 billion (£1.9billon) debt relief to world's poorest countries

The International Monetary Fund has granted immediate debt relief to 19 of the world's poorest countries, amounting to a total of $3.3billion (£1.9billion), though Mauritania in North Africa will not benefit from the decision. Rodrigo de Rato, managing director of the IMF, said after the meeting of the IMF's executive board late on Wednesday that this was "a historic moment, which would allow those countries to increase spending in priority areas to reduce poverty and make progress towards the millennium development goals". The IMF said the countries, most of which are in Africa, will receive debt cancellation in early 2006.

The day before the meeting campaigners had expressed fears that six of the eligible countries promised a debt write-off could face new delays because of perceived backsliding on their economic and fiscal policies. Mauritania was denied immediate relief because of a "substantial deterioration" in budget formulation, execution, reporting and public expenditure tracking. An IMF spokesperson said after the board's meeting that Mauritania should be able to get the write-off in the coming months. Gordon Brown, who has campaigned for debt relief for years, welcomed the decision. He said: "It will ensure that urgently needed resources are made available now in the world's poorest countries to tackle poverty and provide essential health and education." He urged similar moves from the World Bank and the African Development Bank, to whom the bulk of the US $40 billion poor countries' debt is owned. The write-off was promised in June at the Gleneagles summit by the G8 countries, which represent the world's richest nations.[202]

IMF and Debt Relief

Debt Relief under the Heavily Indebted Poor Countries (HIPC) Initiative

The Joint IMF-World Bank's comprehensive approach to debt reduction is designed to ensure that no poor country faces a debt burden it cannot manage. To date, debt reduction packages under the HIPC Initiative have been approved for 36 countries, 30 of them in Africa, providing US$72 billion in debt-service relief over time. Four additional countries are potentially eligible for HIPC Initiative assistance.

Debt relief key to poverty reduction

The HIPC Initiative was launched in 1996 by the IMF and World Bank, with the aim of ensuring that no poor country faces a debt burden it cannot manage. Since then, the international financial community, including multilateral organizations and governments have worked together to reduce to sustainable levels the external debt burdens of the most heavily indebted poor countries.

In 1999, a comprehensive review of the Initiative allowed the Fund to provide faster, deeper, and broader debt relief and strengthened the links between debt relief, poverty reduction, and social policies.

In 2005, to help accelerate progress toward the United Nations Millennium Development Goals

[202] Maren Peters, The Guardian, Friday December 23, 2005

(MDGs), the HIPC Initiative was supplemented by the Multilateral Debt Relief Initiative (MDRI). The MDRI allows for 100 percent relief on eligible debts by three multilateral institutions—the IMF, the World Bank, and the African Development Fund (AfDF)—for countries completing the HIPC Initiative process. In 2007, the Inter-American Development Bank (IaDB) also decided to provide additional ("beyond HIPC") debt relief to the five HIPCs in the Western Hemisphere.

Two step process: Countries must meet certain criteria, commit to poverty reduction through policy changes and demonstrate a good track-record over time. The Fund and Bank provide interim debt relief in the initial stage, and when a country meets its commitments, full debt-relief is provided.

First step: decision point. To be considered for HIPC Initiative assistance, a country must fulfill the following four conditions:

(a) Be eligible to borrow from the World Bank's International Development Agency, which provides interest-free loans and grants to the world's poorest countries, and from the IMF's Extended Credit Facility, which provides loans to low-income countries at subsidized rates.
(b) Face an unsustainable debt burden that cannot be addressed through traditional debt relief mechanisms.
(c) Have established a track record of reform and sound policies through IMF- and World Bank supported programs.
(d) Have developed a Poverty Reduction Strategy Paper (PRSP) through a broad-based participatory process in the country

Once a country has met or made sufficient progress in meeting these four criteria, the Executive Boards of the IMF and World Bank formally decide on its eligibility for debt relief, and the international community commits to reducing debt to a level that is considered sustainable. This first stage under the HIPC Initiative is referred to as the decision point. Once a country reaches its decision point, it may immediately begin receiving interim relief on its debt service falling due.

Second step: completion point. In order to receive full and irrevocable reduction in debt available under the HIPC Initiative, a country must:

(a) Establish a further track record of good performance under programs supported by loans from the IMF and the World Bank.
(b) Implement satisfactorily key reforms agreed at the decision point
(c) Adopt and implement its PRSP for at least one year.

Once a country has met these criteria, it can reach its completion point, which allows it to receive the full debt relief committed at decision point.

Countries receiving debt relief: Of the forty countries eligible or potentially eligible for HIPC Initiative assistance, 32 are receiving full debt relief from the IMF and other creditors after reaching their completion points. Four countries have reached their decision points and some of them are receiving interim debt relief. Four countries, which have been identified as potentially eligible for HIPC Initiative assistance have not yet reached their decision points.

Factsheet: The IMF at a Glance

September 15, 2011

The International Monetary Fund (IMF) works to foster international monetary cooperation, secure financial stability, facilitate international trade, promote high employment and sustainable economic growth, and reduce poverty around the world. Created in 1945, the IMF is governed by and accountable to the 187 countries that make up its near-global membership.

Why the IMF was created and how it works

The IMF, also known as the "Fund," was conceived at a United Nations conference convened in Bretton Woods, New Hampshire, United States, in July 1944. The 44 governments represented at that conference sought to build a framework for economic cooperation that would avoid a repetition of the vicious circle of competitive devaluations that had contributed to the Great Depression of the 1930s.

The IMF's responsibilities: The IMF's primary purpose is to ensure the stability of the international monetary system—the system of exchange rates and international payments that enables countries (and their citizens) to transact with one other. This system is essential for promoting sustainable economic growth, increasing living standards, and reducing poverty. Following the recent global crisis, the Fund has been clarifying and updating its mandate to cover the full range of macroeconomic and financial sector issues that bear on global stability

Facts on the IMF

(a) Membership: **187 countries**
(b) Headquarters: Washington, D.C.

(c) Executive Board: 24 Directors representing countries or groups of countries
(d) Staff: Approximately 2,470 from 141 countries
(e) Total quotas: US$383 billion (as of 8/18/11)
(f) Additional pledged or committed resources: US$600 billion
(g) Loans committed (as of 8/18/11): US$282 billion, of which US$213 billion have not been drawn
(h) Biggest borrowers (amount agreed as of 8/18/11): Greece, Portugal, Ireland
(i) Biggest precautionary loans (amount agreed as of 8/18/11): Mexico, Poland, Colombia
(j) Surveillance consultations: Consultations concluded for 120 countries in FY2010 and for 88 countries in FY2011 as of 02/11/11
(k) Technical assistance: Field delivery in FY2010—192.5 person years
(l) Transparency: In 2009, over 90 percent of Article IV and program-related staff reports and policy papers were published

Original aims: Article I of the Articles of Agreement sets out the IMF's main goals:

(a) Promoting international monetary cooperation;
(b) Facilitating the expansion and balanced growth of international trade;
(c) Promoting exchange stability;
(d) Assisting in the establishment of a multilateral system of payments; and
(e) Making resources available (with adequate safeguards) to members experiencing balance of payments difficulties

Surveillance: To maintain stability and prevent crises in the international monetary system, the IMF reviews country policies, as well as national, regional, and global economic and financial developments through a formal system known as surveillance. Under the surveillance framework, the IMF provides advice to its 187 member countries, encouraging policies that foster economic stability, reduce vulnerability to economic and financial crises, and raise living standards. It provides regular assessment of global prospects in its World Economic Outlook, financial markets in its Global Financial Stability Report, and public finance developments in its Fiscal Monitor, and publishes a series of regional economic outlooks. The Fund's Executive Board has been considering a range of options to enhance multilateral, financial, and bilateral surveillance, including better integrating the three; improve our understanding of spillovers and the assessment of emerging and potential risks; and strengthen the traction of IMF policy advice.

Financial assistance: IMF financing provides member countries the breathing room they need to correct balance of payments problems. A policy program supported by IMF financing is designed by the national authorities in close cooperation with the IMF, and continued financial support is conditioned on effective implementation of this program. In an early response to the recent global economic crisis, the IMF strengthened its lending capacity and approved a major overhaul of the mechanisms for providing financial support in April 2009, with further reforms adopted in August 2010.

In the most recent reforms, IMF lending instruments were improved further to provide flexible crisis prevention tool to a broad range of members with sound fundamentals, policies, and institutional policy frameworks. In low-income countries, the IMF doubled loan access limits and is boosting its lending to the world's poorer countries, with interest rates set at zero through end-2011.

SDRs: The IMF issues an international reserve asset known as Special Drawing Rights (SDRs) that can supplement the official reserves of member countries.

Two allocations in August and September 2009 increased the outstanding stock of SDRs almost ten-fold to total about SDR 204 billion (US$328 billion). Members can also voluntarily exchange SDRs for currencies among themselves. In a recent paper, IMF staff explores options to enhance the role of the SDR to promote international monetary stability.

Technical assistance: The IMF provides technical assistance and training to help member countries strengthen their capacity to design and implement effective policies. Technical assistance is offered in several areas, including tax policy and administration, expenditure management, monetary and exchange rate policies, banking and financial system supervision and regulation, legislative frameworks, and statistics.

Resources: The IMF's resources are provided by its member countries, primarily through payment of quotas, which broadly reflect each country's economic size. At the April 2009, G-20 Summit, world leaders pledged to support a tripling of the IMF's lending resources from about US$250 billion to US$750 billion. To deliver on this pledge, the current and new participants in the New Arrangement to Borrow (NAB) agreed to expand the NAB to about US$590 billion, which was approved by the Executive Board of the IMF on April 12, 2010 and became effective on March 11, 2011 following completion of the ratification process by NAB participants. When concluding the 14th General Review of Quotas in December 2010, Governors agreed to double the IMF's quota resources to approximately US$767 billion and a major realignment of quota shares among members. When the quota increase becomes effective, there will be a corresponding rollback in NAB resources.

Historically, the annual expenses of running the Fund have been met mainly by interest receipts on outstanding loans, but the membership recently agreed to adopt a new income model based on a range of revenue sources better suited to the diverse activities of the Fund.

Governance and organization: The IMF is accountable to the governments of its member countries. At the top of its organizational structure is the Board of Governors, which consists of one Governor and one Alternate Governor from each member country. The Board of Governors meets once each year at the IMF-World Bank Annual Meetings.. Twenty-four of the Governors sit on the International Monetary and Financial Committee (IMFC) and normally meet twice each year.

The day-to-day work of the IMF is overseen by its 24-member Executive Board, which represents the entire membership; this work is guided by the IMFC and supported by the IMF staff. In a package of reforms approved by the Governors in December 2010, the Articles of Agreement will be amended so as to facilitate a move to a more representative, all-elected Executive Board. The Managing Director is the head of the IMF staff and Chairman of the Executive Board, and is assisted by four Deputy Managing Directors.[203]

Debt relief frees up resources for social spending

Debt relief is one part of a much larger effort, which also includes aid flows, to address the development needs of low-income countries and make sure that debt sustainability is maintained over time. For debt reduction to have a tangible impact on poverty, the additional money needs to be spent on programs that benefit the poor.

---

[203] International Monetary Fund, 2011

Boosting social spending: Before the HIPC Initiative, eligible countries were, on average, spending slightly more on debt service than on health and education combined. Now, they have increased markedly their expenditures on health, education, and other social services. On average, such spending is about five times the amount of debt-service payments.

Reducing debt service: For the 36 countries receiving debt relief, debt service paid, on average, has declined by about two percentage points of GDP between 2001 and 2009. Their debt burden is expected to be reduced by about 80 percent after the full delivery of debt relief (including under the MDRI).

Improving public debt management: Debt relief has markedly improved the debt position of post-completion point countries, bringing their debt indicators down below those of other HIPCs or non-HIPCs. However, many remain vulnerable to shocks, particularly those affecting exports as seen during the current global economic crisis. To reduce their debt vulnerabilities decisively, countries need to pursue cautious borrowing policies and strengthen their public debt management.

IMF debt relief complemented by other sources

About 45 percent of the funding comes from the IMF and other multilateral institutions, and the remaining amount comes from bilateral creditors.

The total cost of providing assistance to the 40 countries that have been found eligible or potentially eligible for debt relief under the enhanced HIPC Initiative is estimated to be about $75 billion in end-2009 net present value terms.

The IMF's share of the cost is financed primarily by the investment income on the proceeds from off-market gold sales in 1999 that were deposited to the

IMF's PRG-HIPC Trust. Additional contributions to this trust have been provided by member countries.

Resources available in the trust are currently insufficient to finance the cost of debt relief to all countries that meet the initial conditions for debt relief and reach the decision point. The original financing plan did not include the cost of debt relief to Sudan and Somalia, as well as to other countries that entered the Initiative after 2006. Should these countries progress to the decision point, there would be an urgent need to mobilize resources.

Challenges remain

Many of the 8 countries that have not yet completed the requirements for full debt relief face common challenges, including preserving peace and stability, and improving governance and the delivery of basic services. Addressing these challenges will require continued efforts from these countries to strengthen policies and institutions, and support from the international community.

Another challenge is to ensure that eligible countries get full debt relief from all their creditors. Although the largest creditors (the World Bank, the African Development Bank, the IMF, the Inter-American Development Bank, and all Paris Club creditors) provide debt relief in line with their commitments under the HIPC Initiative, and even beyond, others are lagging behind. Smaller multilateral institutions, non-Paris Club official bilateral creditors, and commercial creditors, which together account for about 25 percent of total HIPC Initiative costs, have only delivered a small share of their expected relief so far.

Non-Paris Club bilateral creditors as a whole have delivered close to 40 percent of their share of HIPC

Initiative debt relief, but about half of these creditors have not delivered any relief at all.

The delivery of debt relief by commercial creditors has increased markedly in recent years through a few large operations. A number of commercial creditors have initiated litigations against highly indebted countries, raising significant legal challenges to burden sharing among all creditors, including the multilateral institutions.

Given the voluntary nature of creditor participation in the HIPC Initiative, the IMF and the World Bank will continue to use moral suasion to encourage creditors to participate in the Initiative and to deliver fully their share of HIPC Initiative debt relief.

The IMF and World Bank will also continue to improve their ability to monitor the delivery of HIPC Initiative debt relief. The IMF will continue to address issues related to participation in the HIPC Initiative during its regular consultations and other missions to creditor countries. List of Countries That Have Qualified for, are Eligible or Potentially Eligible and May Wish to Receive HIPC Initiative Assistance (As of December 17, 2010)

Post-Completion-Point Countries (32):

Afghanistan, Ghana, Nicaragua, Benin, Guinea Bissau, Niger, Bolivia, Guyana, Rwanda, Burkina Faso, Haiti São Tomé and Príncipe, Burundi, Honduras, Senegal , Cameroon Liberia Sierra Leone, Central African Republic Madagascar Tanzania, Republic of Congo, Malawi Togo , Democratic Republic of Congo, Mali, Uganda, Ethiopia, Mauritania, Zambia, The Gambia , Mozambique,

Interim Countries (Between Decision and Completion Point) (4): Chad, Côte d'Ivoire, Comoros, and Guinea

Pre-Decision-Point Countries (4): Eritrea, Kyrgyz Republic, Somalia, Sudan[204]

Paris Club

The Paris Club is an informal group of official creditors whose role is to find co-coordinated and sustainable solutions to the payment difficulties experienced by debtor nations. Paris Club creditors agree to re-scheduling debts due to them. Rescheduling is a means of providing a country with debt relief through a postponement and, in the case of concessional rescheduling, a reduction in debt service obligations. The first meeting with a debtor country was in 1956 when Argentina agreed to meet its public creditors in Paris. Since then, the Paris Club or adhoc groups of Paris Club creditors have reached 405 agreements (breakdown by year) concerning 84 countries. Since 1983, the total amount of debt covered in these agreements has been $509 billion (breakdown by year). In spite of such activity, the Paris Club has remained strictly informal. It is the voluntary gathering of creditor countries willing to treat in a co-coordinated way the debt due to them by the developing countries. It can be described as a "non institution". The Paris Club does not have legal status to follow rules and principles agreed by creditor countries. It helps a co-coordinated agreement only.

The Paris Club makes decisions on a case-by-case basis in order to permanently adjust itself to the individuality of each debtor country.

(a) Consensus: no decision can be taken within the Paris Club if it is not the result of a consensus among the participating creditor countries.
(b) Conditionality: debt treatments are applied only for countries that need a rescheduling

---

[204] Fact Sheet, International Monetary Fund, September 6, 2011

and that implement reforms to resolve their payment difficulties. In practice conditionality is provided by the existence of an appropriate programme supported by the IMF, which demonstrates the need for debt relief.

(c) Solidarity: Creditors agree to implement the terms agreed in the context of the Paris Club.

The Paris Club preserves the comparability of treatment between different creditors, as the debtor country cannot grant to another creditor a treatment less favourable for the debtor than the consensus reached in the Paris Club.

Rules and conventions of Paris Club agreements

The practical implementation of these principles has led to a number of rules and conventions, which assist the conclusion of negotiations. Among the different types of debt, Paris Club agreements generally only apply:

1. to the debts of the public sector: As the agreement is signed with governments of the debtor countries, which are unable to meet their external obligations. Debts owed by private entities and guaranteed by the public sector are considered to be part of the public sector.

2. to medium and long-term debts: Short-term debt (debt with a maturity of one year or less) is excluded from the treatments, as their restructuring can create a significant disruption of the capacity of the debtor country to participate in international trade.

3. To credits granted before the 'cut of date': When a debtor country first meets with Paris Club creditors, the "cut off date" is defined and is not changed in subsequent Paris Club treatments and credits granted after this cut off date are not subject to future rescheduling. Thus, the cut off date helps restore

access to credit for debtor countries facing payment difficulties.

From the creditor side, the debts treated are credits and loans granted, or commercial credits guaranteed by the Governments or appropriate institutions of Paris Club creditors. Claims of other creditors are divided in two parts: (i) multilateral claims are not rescheduled (ii) other claims are treated (by the debtor country) in a manner comparable to the Paris Club agreement. Debt that was already treated in the context of a previous Paris Club agreement is normally not treated again, except for those countries where the financing gap is large or where all pre-cutoff-date debt was already rescheduled. When previously rescheduled debt is treated again, the earlier debt treatments are conducted before the later ones.

Flow treatments

A standard Paris Club agreement provides a way of tiding a debtor country through temporary balance of payments difficulties. This is described as flow relief and works in the following way:

(a) The period of time to which the agreement refers is usually the period when the IMF programme shows a financing gap that can only be covered by debt rescheduling. This period is called the "consolidation period"

(b) Payments falling due to Paris Club creditors in this period and covered by the Paris Club agreement are then "consolidated" and the payment of these debts is then made on a new schedule ("rescheduling"). The typical terms of a rescheduling are described in section 3 below

The standard consolidation period is one year. However, creditor countries have accepted to reschedule the debt falling over two or three years, corresponding with a multiyear arrangement with the IMF that shows a financing gap (arrangement under an Extended Arrangement, arrangement under the Poverty Reduction and Growth Facility).

Stock treatments

Some Paris Club treatments apply not only to the payments falling due in a particular period of time, but also to the entire stock of debt from which those payments fall due. The intention of any agreement, which deals with the stock of debt in this way, is to provide a country with a final treatment by the Paris Club called an exit rescheduling. These agreements are implemented in two sets of circumstances:

(i) In the context of the HIPC initiative, Paris Club creditors provide their share of the effort defined in the context of the initiative through a Cologne terms stock treatment at completion point

(ii) In other cases, stock treatments may be implemented, on a case-by-case basis, for countries having established a satisfactory track record with both the Paris Club and the IMF and for which there is sufficient confidence in their ability to respect the debt agreement.

(iii) Stock treatments generate interests on the consolidation that are larger than the ones resulting from flow treatments. As a consequence, stock treatments provide long-term debt relief, but debt service relief is smaller in the short-term than for a flow treatment.

Payment terms resulting from Paris Club agreements

Throughout its existence, the Paris Club has aimed to produce agreements, which lead to levels of payments, which are sustainable for the debtor. Over time practice and theory have developed and two trends have emerged in the terms of Paris Club agreements:

(a) Longer repayment periods have been considered. In early Paris Club agreements, repayment terms did not exceed ten years including a grace period (in which only payments of interest on the consolidation are due). For poorer countries, these terms have been constantly extended that the maximum repayment period is now 23 years (including 6 years of grace) for commercial loans with up to 40 years for official development aid loans (including 16 years of grace).

(b). Debt cancellation has been increasingly used. In December 1994, the Paris Club agreed to implement a new concessional treatment on the debt of the poorest and most indebted countries, called 'Naples terms' ", raising the level of cancellation up to 67%. In November 1996, the cancellation effort of the creditors was raised up to 80% (Lyon terms) for the countries eligible to the initiative for Heavily Indebted Poor Countries (HIPC).

In November 1999, following the approval by the international financial community of the enhanced HIPC initiative, Paris Club creditors accepted to raise the level of cancellation up to 90% Cologne terms) or more when necessary to reach debt sustainability.

Debt Swap Provision

Paris Club agreements may contain a provision, which makes it possible for creditors to voluntarily undertake debt swaps. These operations may be debt for nature, debt for aid, debt for equity swaps or other local currency debt swaps. These swaps often involve the sale of the debt by the creditor government to an investor who in turn sells the debt to the debtor government in return for shares in a local company or for local currency to be used in projects in the country. In order to preserve comparability of treatment and solidarity among creditors, the amounts of debt swaps that can be conducted are capped at a certain percentage of the stock of the claims of each individual creditor. The terms under which these operations can take place are contained in the standard terms of treatment. To ensure full transparency between creditors, debtors and creditors submit a report to the Paris Club Secretariat informing about transactions undertaken.[205]

Functioning: The creditor countries meet for negotiation sessions, to discuss among themselves of the external debt of debtor countries or methodological issues on the debt of developing countries. These meetings are held in Paris. The Chairman is a senior official of the French Treasury. Deputies to the Chairman in the French Treasury serve as co-president and vice-president.

The permanent Paris Club members (19) are: Austria, Australia, Belgium, Canada, Denmark, Finland, France, Germany, Ireland, Italy, Japan, Netherlands, Norway, Russian Federation, Spain, Sweden, Switzerland, United Kingdom, and United States of America.

The creditors (13) invited on a case-by-case basis are: Abu Dhabi, South Africa, Argentina, Brazil, Korea, Israel, Kuwait, Mexico, Morocco, New Zealand, Portugal, Trinidad and Tobago, and Turkey.

Paris Club had business transactions with 84 countries by December 2006.

---

[205] Paris Club, web: www.clubdeparis.org

(B)The World Bank and the IMF
Two Important Committee Reports

In order to study the working of the World Bank and the International Monetary Fund, two important committees were appointed to study in detail the activities of these institutions and suggestions for improvement. Moreover, the views of two economists have been added on the 'Meltzer Report' to study the impact of the Fund and Bank on the fate of poor people living in Low-income and low-middle-income countries. These are as follows:

(1) US House Banking and International Relations Committees Report

The struggle for debt cancellation and economic justice for the benefit of the low-income countries was reflected in the US House Banking and International Relations Committees on October 14, 1999 for the 'Leach Bill' (HR 1095), which emphasized on the three suggestions. These are:

(a)De-link debt relief from structural adjustment. This amendment would bar the conditioning of debt relief on any SAP designed or monitored by the IMF,

(b)Put necessary restrictions on the use of proceeds from International Monetary Fund gold transactions. This amendment would condition the required Congressional approval for gold transactions on the IMF cancelling all debts owed it by the HIPC countries and abiding by more comprehensive requirements for transparency and accountability; and

(c)Cancel debts owed by the most impoverished countries to the IMF as a pre-condition of future IMF funding. This amendment would withhold further US appropriations to the IMF until the institution has used its own resources to cancel those debts.[206]

The Senators have urged that only by reducing the power of the IMF can debt cancellation have a lasting impact, and only by wiping out the un-payable mountains of debt can the people of much of Africa, Latin America, the Caribbean, and Asia have a hope of better futures. But the Meltzer Commission has gone into details of financial structure of the World Bank and International Monetary Fund and rendered valuable suggestions.

(2) The Meltzer Commission

The Meltzer Commission—established by the U.S. Congress as part and parcel of the legislation adding $18 billion to the U.S.'s capital contribution to the IMF—issued its *Report*. The press registered that the Commission had called for thoroughgoing reforms of the World Bank and IMF. But it quickly dropped from sight: the *Report* was more than 100 pages long. Much of it was written in economics language, that peculiar language that only academic economists speak with fluency.

J. Bradford De Long says, "This is too bad, but not because the *Report* gave a clear description of the current flaws in the IMF and World Bank and laid out a straightforward roadmap for their reform—far from it, for the *Report* is a confused document, riddled with internal contradictions. But the *Report*'s internal contradictions mirror the dilemmas of global financial, monetary, and development funding management. Understand the contradictions within the **Meltzer Commission Report**, and you have a keen grasp of

---

[206] Keep the pressure on: cancel the debts! Diminish the IMF's power! , 50 years is enough: US Network for global economic justice 202 / IMF-Bank, Capitol Switchboard, October 21, 1999

the inevitable tradeoffs and un-resolvable dilemmas placed on global managers by our highly idiosyncratic and vastly imperfect global economic structure.

What are these contradictions?
Consider the Report:

First, the Commission approves of the overall principle of lending to solvent but illiquid governments—governments that will repay their loans in the long run but cannot borrow private-sector money in the short run, yet condemns the IMF’ s 1995 loans to Mexico, the most recent clear example of this practice.

Second, the Commission assigns the IMF the role of lender of last resort in international financial crises, but fails to give it the resources needed to fulfill such a role (in fact, the Commission strongly recommends against any increases in the IMF’s resources).

Third, the Commission urges that the IMF and World Bank forgive their loans to heavily indebted poor countries, but also proposes that neither ever again lend on a scale that could ever make debt relief important.

Fourth, the Commission urges that the international financial institutions should not be tools of US policy and playthings of US government, yet also urges that these institutions be decisively reformed according to their recommendations—the recommendations of a US-only Commission.

It is possible to confidently speculate on the reasons for these contradictions. Consider a Commission with a chairman—Allan Meltzer—sufficiently hostile to our international financial institutions to have called in 1998 at a Brookings Institution conference for the abolition of the IMF. But to repeat the 1998 vintage of Meltzer would not get a majority of Commission members to sign on. So make concessions to Commission members interested in key issues in order to approach consensus, even if in the process intellectual coherence is lost. And the resulting contradictions trace the fault lines in the Commission's internal debates.

The first contradiction shows the split between those who believe that international financial markets work well in the absence of public intervention, and those who believe that public authorities have the role that Walter Bagehot prescribed more than a century ago—to guard against a collapse of liquidity by lending freely to organizations that would be solvent if there were no crisis and will be solvent if the crisis is successfully resolved. For the first group, the fact that private-sector lenders were unwilling to roll over Mexico's debts in early 1995 means that no one should have loaned to Mexico in early 1995--even though the U.S. Treasury and IMF that did lend to Mexico earned very healthy profits on their loans, even though the loans did not lead the Mexican government to adopt unsustainable inflationary policies, even though after the fact the private-sector lenders cannot give coherent reasons for their panicked flight from Mexico. For the second group the Mexican crisis was handled properly—or, rather, would have been handled properly had loans to Mexico been larger, made for longer periods of time with less conditionality, and had the U.S. Treasury not felt under so much pressure from then-Senator D'Amato to prematurely demand repayment and so slow Mexico's recovery.

For the first group, the fact of the Mexican rescue package must have created "moral hazard"—induced over-speculation and over-lending—and thus set the stage for the East Asian financial crisis (never mind that "moral hazard" can be generated only when someone pays out and never gets paid back, and that the IMF gets paid back). For the second group, the absence of pre-1997 forecasts of an East Asian financial crisis is convincing proof that an expectation of bailouts could not have induced the East Asian crisis—for if there is no expectation of a crisis, what would happen if there were a crisis has no effect on anyone's investment decisions.

The second contradiction shows a split between those who understand that a lender of last resort's actions *must* be decisive and must end all doubt about whether a lent-to organization will in turn meet all of its obligations—and hence know that when a lender of last resort intervenes it must have the potential to do so on a nearly-unlimited scale—and those who want to keep public institutions lean out of the fear that large-scale government failure will lead to mammoth wastes of resources. The Meltzer Commission's report tries to bridge this gap by calling for the IMF to be a "quasi" lender of last resort, and tries to avoid facing the possibility that such a "quasi" organization may lack sufficient resources to restore confidence in a crisis yet still waste enormous amount of money.

The third contradiction finds the Commission stuck between its realization that demanding repayment from heavily-indebted poor countries where loans have been corruptly stolen and bureaucratically wasted imposes an extraordinary degree of inhumane misery on such countries' citizens, and its fear that forgiving loans—allowing policy makers to gain access to IMF and World Bank loan money and never repay it—does induce "moral hazard" and lead to bad borrowing policies. The solution is to close down the possibility that truly poor countries will ever be able to borrow on a large scale from the IMF and the World Bank again. But this solution in turn ignores the fact that the poorest countries are the scarcest countries, and hence the ones where the social benefits from financing that are well used to promote investment are the highest.

The fourth contradiction is one of governance. Members of the Meltzer Commission are uneasy that the technocratic economic mission of the IMF was distorted in the 1990s by the wish on the part of the Executive Branch of the U.S. government to make a few high-stakes bets on Russian reformers, and on the U.S. Executive Branch and Federal Reserve's willingness to use the IMF to undertake a Mexican peso-support program that the Congress was unwilling to explicitly approve. They wish for an IMF that is less politicized—and they want to use one final act of politicization in order to attain their goal, just as in the past Presidents have confidently undertaken the war to end all wars or colonels have launched the coup that will be the last coup.

I don't have clear and convincing arguments to demonstrate the proof of my own views of which side of these fault lines is the right one—or rather of where the proper points are that do the best job of balancing vital concerns. (I do, however, recommend Barry Eichengreen's -Toward New International Financial Architecture: A Practical Post-Asia Agenda- for the most clear and convincing arguments that there are.) I do think that the final positions of the Meltzer Commission that paper over these fault lines are clearly faulty. Yet I also wish more people would read the Commission's Report and think about the issues. There is now no international financial crisis: it is sunny, and hence there seems to be no urgency about fixing the roof. But the worst possible time to try to fix a roof is in the rainstorm".[207]

Meltzer Report on Bretton Woods Twins Builds Case for Abolition but Hesitates.

---

[207] J. Bradford De Long, " The Meltzer Report", May 2000, delong@econ.berkeley.edu/ http://www.j-bradford-delong.net/

During the heated debate on whether or not to raise the US quota in the IMF in 1998, the US Congress voted for the quota increase but attached several conditions, including the creation of an independent body to look at the missions and performance of the World Bank and the International Monetary Fund. The report of the International Financial Institution Advisory Commission, better known as the "Meltzer Report" after its chairman Alan Meltzer, serves as a striking confirmation from the mainstream of what progressive critics of the Bretton Woods Institutions have been saying for the last 25 years. Walden Bello opines that among the most important claims in the corpus of critical literature is that the report supports the following:

(a) Instead of promoting economic growth, the International Monetary Fund institutionalizes economic stagnation,
(b) The World Bank is irrelevant rather than central to the goal of eliminating global poverty;
(c) Both institutions are to a great extent driven by the interests of key political and economic institutions in the G-7 countries-particularly, in the case of the IMF, the US government and US financial interests; and
(d) The dynamics of both institutions derive not so much from the external demands of poverty alleviation or promoting growth but to the internal imperative of bureaucratic expansionism or empire building.

There is little in the report that was not earlier documented in such works as Cheryl Payer's The Debt Trap, Bruce Rich's Mortgaging the Future, Susan George's Faith and Credit, and the Food First trilogy Aid as Obstacle, Development Debacle: The World Bank in the Philippines, and Dark Victory: The US, Structural Adjustment, and Global Poverty. But then the importance of the document lies not only in its critique but in the fact that a significant part of the establishment has embraced much of the progressive analysis, and, even more significantly, has made fairly radical proposals for the future of the Bretton Woods twins. Criticisms of the IMF have found a very receptive global audience recently owing to the devastating performance of the Fund during the Asian financial crisis. To the credit of its authors, the Meltzer Report was not taken in by the World Bank's propaganda that, in contrast to the IMF, it has turned a new leaf. The report shows that the much vaunted Poverty Reduction Strategy or Comprehensive Development Framework articulated by ideological entrepreneur James Wolfensohn is largely a public relations effort to save the Bank and that, although it is billed as a new development paradigm, it is largely devoid of substance.

The IMF: No Redeeming Value

While diplomatic in its language when discussing the IMF, the report finds little of redeeming value in the institution. It shows that the Fund's foray into macroeconomic reform via structural adjustment institutionalized economic stagnation, poverty, and inequality in Africa and Latin America in the 1980's and 1990's-precisely what we had documented in detail in our 1994 book Dark Victory: the US, Structural Adjustment, and Global Poverty. It confirms that the Fund's duty of ensuring a stable global financial order was derailed by its prescription of indiscriminate capital account liberalization for developing countries, its habit of assembling financial rescue packages that simply encouraged moral hazard or irresponsible lending and speculative investment, and its prescribing tight fiscal and monetary policies that merely worsened the situation in the crisis countries instead of reversing it. The report is on the right track when it recommends the closure of the structural and extended structural adjustment programs, now renamed the "Poverty and Growth Facility."

And it is correct in recommending downsizing the IMF in both size and its scope of responsibilities, though as we shall argue below, it would do better to recommend an outright abolition of the Fund.

The report is, however, wrong in its recommendation that the IMF should serve as a "quasi-lender of last resort" to countries suffering a liquidity crisis. The IMF, by the Commission's own account, has handled this function badly in the past. Moreover, the Commission's recommending of strict conditions under which the IMF may extend credit contradicts its own criticism of "the use of IMF resources and conditionality to control the economies of developing nations."

Particularly objectionable is the Commission's proposal that the Fund provide liquidity assistance only to those countries that "permit freedom of entry and operation for foreign financial institutions" on the ground that these entities would, among other things, "stabilize and develop the local financial system."

This recommendation is problematic for two reasons. First, foreign financial institutions such as hedge funds, which have taken full advantage of "free entry and operation," have helped precipitate one financial crisis after another. Second, forcing countries to adopt western-style free market norms governing ownership of foreign financial subsidiaries and their local operations violates the first core principle it proposes for IMF reform-that is, "sovereignty-the desire to ensure that democratic processes and sovereign authority are respected in both borrowing and lending countries."

This contradiction between the logic of the analysis and the prescription reminds us that the Commission is, after all, a US government-appointed body, many of whose members come from the banking sector, conservative think tanks, and establishment universities who are very wary about placing significant restrictions on the free flow of finance capital globally, even when the evidence they are staring at underline the destructiveness of unchecked capital mobility.

The World Bank: Hype versus Substance

When it comes to the World Bank, the report is equally devastating. The rhetoric about focusing on poverty alleviation, it says, is contradicted by the reality that 70 per cent of the Bank's non-aid lending is concentrated in 11 countries, while the Bank's 145 other member countries are left to divide the remaining 30 per cent. Moreover, 80 per cent of World Bank resources have gone, not to poor countries with poor credit ratings and investment ratings, but to countries that could have raised the money in international private capital markets owing to their having investment grade or high yield ratings.

In terms of achieving a positive development impact, the Bank's own evaluation of its projects shows an outstanding 55-60 per cent failure rate.

The failure rate is particularly high in the poorest countries, where it ranges from 65 per cent to 70 per cent. And these are the very countries that are supposed to be the main targets of the Bank's anti-poverty approach. The picture that is drawn of the World Bank is that of a massive institution that is driven to lend more by institutional imperatives than actual need in the recipient countries, that is burdened by high failure rates both in its project lending and its program (adjustment) lending, that has poor monitoring capabilities of the sustainability of its projects, that competes with rather than supplements the regional development banks (Asian Development Bank, Inter-American Development Bank, and African Development Bank).

The stark reality is that of a dinosaur that is slowly sinking in a bog of its own making but which flags a new approach of "Poverty Reduction" or "Comprehensive Development" to mask a fundamental crisis of identity and direction.

Reform or Abolition

The Meltzer Report's basic conclusion is that the IMF and the Bank are monolithic institutions that have outlived their usefulness. Now, institutions should be saved and reformed if their functioning, while defective, nevertheless broadly achieves their basic objectives. They should be abolished if they have become fundamentally dysfunctional in achieving their basic objectives.

The IMF, in the Report's view, has become part of the problem rather than part of the solution in global development and financial governance. The World Bank likewise has become irrelevant rather than central to the alleviation of poverty.

Despite adjustments here and there, the two institutions are imprisoned within paradigms and structures that cannot handle the multiple problems confronting the world economy during this phase of globalization. To borrow the language of Thomas Kuhn's classic Structure of Scientific Revolutions, both institutions are like paradigms in crisis, and the solution when a paradigm is in fundamental crisis is not to try to reform it with endless minute adjustments that merely prolong its inevitable demise, but to cut cleanly from it in favour of a simpler, more relevant, and more useful paradigm-in a manner similar to the way the founders of early modern science simply junked the old, hopelessly complex Ptolemaic paradigm for explaining the cosmos (the sun and other celestial bodies moving around the earth) in favour of the simpler Copernican paradigm (the earth moving around the sun).

In other words, rather trying to find a function for the Fund and assigning to it the role of being a lender of last resort, we would do better to scrap it totally and create a new institution that does not have the baggage of institutional failure and an obsolete institutional mindset and is thus better positioned to manage financial crises in this era. Rather than expect the highly paid World Bank technocrats who live in the affluent suburbs of Northern Virginia to do the impossible-designing anti-poverty programs for folks from another planet.

Therefore, it would be more effective to abolish an institution that has made a big business out of "ending poverty".

And completely devolve the work to local, national and regional institutions better equipped to attack the causes of poverty. This task should not fall to the regional development banks so long as they are imprisoned by World Bank-type structures.[208]

Recommendations of the Meltzer Report:

In short, the Meltzer Report has recommended the following:IMF and the World Bank, regional development banks should write off in entirely all claims against the heavily indebted poor countries that implement an effective economic and social

---

[208] Walden Bello, "Meltzer Report on Bretton Woods Twins Builds Case for Abolition but Hesitates", www.focusweb.org/publications/2000 /

development strategy in conjunction with World Bank. IMF should restrict its lending to the provision of short-term lending. Extending long-term lending should end. The frequency and severity of recent crises raise doubts about the system of crisis management now in place and the incentive of private actions that it encourages and sustains. The World Bank, in evaluating its own performance has a 73 per cent failure rate in Africa. Only one in four programs achieved satisfactory results.

The Commission wants the IMF/World Bank and development banks to become more accountable with clear focus. The IMF should serve as a quasi lender of last resort to emerging economies. Lending should be limited to the provision of liquidity to solvent member governments. Liquidity loans should have short maturation, be made at a penalty rate (above borrower's recent market rate), is secured by a clear priority claim on the borrower's assets. Except in unusual circumstances, where the crisis poses a threat to the global economy, loans would be made only to countries in crisis that have met pre-conditions that establish financial soundness. To function more effectively, the development banks must be transformed from capital-intensive lenders to sources of technical advice, providers of regional and global public goods, and facilitators of an increased flow of private sector resources to the emerging countries. The common goals should be to reduce poverty.

Proposed pre-conditions to liquidity

(a) The World Bank group should sanction loans on:

(b) Performance based grants

(c) Institutional reform loans–screw being tightened

The commission further recommends: The World Bank would be renamed as 'the World Development Agency'. The IMF must be structured as a smaller institution with three responsibilities, would increase global stability, improve the functioning of market and help the countries to improve domestic and fiscal policies.[209]The report by Alan Meltzer is one of the best reports to save the low-income countries from debt overdue, debt overhang and debt management.

Conclusion

1. The United Nations, the World Bank, the International Monetary Fund, and the Paris club have the capacity, ability and resources to make the world free of hunger, free of poverty and can contribute immensely for a peaceful living of billions of people around the world, if these organizations accept moral responsibility to uplift the poor countries and poor people, who are hungry, indebted, and face debt over-hang.

2. The World Bank, the IMF, Paris Club, IFI, and international banks should adopt 100 per cent debt relief to 54 low-income countries as on **December 31, 2015,** and other 58 low-middle-income countries as on **December 31, 2016**. Debt relief is the most desired destination of all the indebted countries.

3. The donor countries and the multilateral, bilateral, international organizations can try to restore human rights of poor people living in hamlets, forests or deserts or anywhere.

4. Common people in all the indebted countries, excepting the political leaders, **disapprove the World Bank and the IMF** because they feel that these organizations have made them hungry, poorer, unemployed and restless. The World Bank and the IMF have intentionally encouraged pro-rich, pro-industry and pro-urban policies in all the indebted

[209] The Meltzer Report, International Financial Institution Advisory Commission

low-income countries through structural adjustment programs. They opine that these coveted World organizations are working to make the low-income countries poorer and bonded. Their assistance and advices through newspapers or seminars resemble the activities of the unscrupulous village moneylenders of remote areas, who finance, guide, console, and ultimately harass the poor; forcefully take the possession of land including homestead land and dwelling thatched houses to their possession. The ultimate result is that the poor people become nomads and beggars.

5. The United Nations should discuss the matter in Security Council as the World Bank and the International Monetary Fund are working against one billion of hungry people and two billions of undernourished people the world, who become sympathizers of anti-government movements of Terrorists, Maoists and Naxalites organizations. The World Bank and IMF are directly and indirectly involved for loss of peace and security of the world. The United Nations General Assembly should also probe and discuss the matter, as the situation is worsening each day and likely to aggravate in near future.

6. Transactions by multilateral organizations, Foreign Banks, Paris Club, International Finance Institutions with low-income countries support political, administrative, and defense corruption. This corruption induces the debtor countries to wage wars among themselves and become involved in governmental terror, state involvement in terror or state sponsorship of terrorism. In other wards, the states also fund terrorists groups to remain in power. The defense arms and arsenals become available to these terrorists easily and quickly. Terrorists are aspiring to own nuclear power to fight against the governments in their own country and abroad.

7. A rich country should finance another country for genuine purposes at an interest rate accepted by both the parties. A rich country must know that the loaned countries do not spend the amount for the purpose it is sanctioned; rather it becomes a source of high corruption of the politicians and bureaucrats in the low-income countries. This amount becomes black money of few individuals, political expenses of party-in-power, disparity of income among people, growth of cities, and creation of lawlessness in society and diversion of funds for non-productive projects. This fund is ultimately shared by Terrorists, Naxalites and Maoists, who purchase modern arms and ammunitions and cause terror. As a result, war is caused between the government and the guerrillas in the countryside.

8. But a group of developed countries financing a group of developing or least-developed countries jointly or through a group-organization is more political and dangerous than an economic and humanitarian endeavour. Economists working in the World Bank, the IMF and other organizations are generating development reports, which act as suicidal reports for millions and billions of poor people of the world. Most of the suicides occur in poor families because of hunger, poverty and debt. **Hunger causes more deaths than wars.**

9. The United Nations should not be a poster organization; it should act as the WORLD GOVERNMENT of the 21st Century. The United Nations should be stronger legally, politically and economically. The UN should have four organs instead of six organs. The organs are: The United Nations Peace Council, The United Nations War Council, The United Nations Law Council and The United Nations Secretariat. All the four organizations should be strengthened with statutory powers for ensuring permanent world peace.

Chapter- IX

WORLD PEACE IS POSSIBLE

Even at the MDG halfway point, around 75 million children of primary school age were not in school; 190,000 children under five died every week from preventable disease; 10,000 women died every week from treatable complications of pregnancy; more than 2 million people died from AIDS annually, close to 2 million from tuberculosis, and about 1 million from malaria; around 1 billion people suffered from hunger; about 2 billion people were undernourished; and about half of the developing world lacked access to basic sanitation — grim numbers that would be far lower if the world were on track on the Millennium Development Goals.

--- **Global Monitoring Report 2009**

Globally, the 20th century was marked by: (a) two devastating world wars; (b) the Great Depression of the 1930s; (c) the end of vast colonial empires; (d) rapid advances in science and technology, from the first airplane flight at Kitty Hawk, North Carolina (US) to the landing on the moon; (e) the Cold War between the Western alliance and the Warsaw Pact nations; (f) a sharp rise in living standards in North America, Europe, and Japan; (g) increased concerns about the environment, including loss of forests, shortages of energy and water, the decline in biological diversity, and air pollution; (h) the onset of the AIDS epidemic; and (I) the ultimate emergence of the US as the only world superpower.

The planet's population continues to explode: from 1 billion in 1820, to 2 billion in 1930, 3 billion in 1960, 4 billion in 1974, 5 billion in 1988, and 6 billion in 2000. The world population was 6,525,170,264 in July 2006. For the 21st century, the continued exponential growth in science and technology raises both hopes (e.g., advances in medicine) and fears (e.g., development of even more lethal weapons of war).[210]

But the world encounters a number of critical problems, which needs immediate solutions.

These are:

- (a) Rapid depletion of nonrenewable mineral resources,
- (b) Repletion of forest areas and wetlands,
- (c) Extinction of animal and plant species,
- (d) Deterioration in air and water quality (especially in Eastern Europe, the former USSR, and China),
- (e) Growth of terrorists attacks,
- (f) Change of climate and decrease of rainfall,
- (g) International disputes,
- (h) Problems of refugees and internally displaced persons,
- (i) Trafficking in persons,
- (j) Increase use of illicit drugs,
- (k) Increase of major infectious diseases and new fatal diseases,
- (l) Increase of HIV / AIDS deaths,

[210] CIA – The World Fact book -World

(m) Increase of intra-country and inter-country rich – poor gap,
(n) Religion based conflicts and wars,
(o) Increase of defense expenditure
(p) Unfavourable agricultural prices and terms of trade; and
(q) Shortage of foodstuffs and drinking water

The number of people living in extreme poverty has increased by almost 100 million while total world income has increased by an average of 2.5 per cent annually since the 1980s. At least 54 countries are poorer now than two decades ago. A recent FAO publication (2006) has reported that the world is having 854 million of people who are chronically undernourished. They are residing mostly in the developing countries such as India (212 million), sub-Saharan Africa (206 million), Asia / Pacific (excepting India and China) 162 million, China (150 million), Latin America / Caribbean (52 million), Near East and North Africa (38 million), Transition countries (25 million) and Industrialized countries (9 million). More than 13 million children have died because of diarrhea related diseases and, every year, over half a million women die during pregnancy or childbirth. The deterioration of poverty conditions is accompanied by an increase in global inequality. The richest 1 per cent of the world's population now receives, as much income as the poorest 57 percent, and the income of the richest 25 million of Americans can be compared with that of almost two billion of the world's poorest people.

South Asia remains one of the world's poorest regions and because it is heavily populated, it is home to the largest number of poor people. More than one-third of South Asians lack access to sanitation, one-third are in poverty, one-quarter are hungry, one-fifth of children are out of school, and one out of ten children die before they reach age five. Two of five poor people live in South Asia, and one in four in East Asia and the Pacific. Forty per cent of world's undernourished people live in South Asia and 24 percent in East Asia and the Pacific.[211]

In African, it can be explained that they lack access to basic education, health care facilities, food and clean water. More than 300 million people in sub-Saharan Africa – nearly half the region's population – live on less than $1 per day. The World Bank expects this number to rise to 404 million by 2015. 28 million people in Sub-Saharan Africa are living with HIV / AIDs, comprising between 60–70 percent of world's total. Almost 40 million people are threatened by starvation in Africa.[212]The poor and hungry are the products of historical processes of marginalisation, mal-development, expropriation and exploitation. The attempt of world organizations, donor countries, the World Bank and the International Monetary Fund to reduce poverty through financial assistance could not achieve the desired results. Starvation deaths could not be completely checked till date.

IMF Crimes against Humanity

Greg Palast (2000) has explained that by November 1, 2000, Ecuador government raised the price of cooking gas by 80 per cent through a secret document by the International Monetary Fund strategy for Ecuador. As a result, it eliminated 26,000 jobs and halved real wages for the remaining workers by 50 per cent in four steps in months specified by the IMF. It began to transfer ownership of its biggest water system to foreign operators by July and granted one Arco subsidiary the right to build and own an oil pipeline over the Andes.

---

[211] The Millennium Development Goals and the Eradication of Extreme Poverty and Hunger – discussion paper- Asia-Pacific Civil Society Forum, Bangkok, Thailand, October 6-8, 2003

[212] UNAID: world Food Program estimates

The IMF's 167 loan conditions look less like an assistance plan and more like a blueprint for a financial coup d'état. In 1983, the IMF forced Ecuador government to take over the soured private debts owed by Ecuador's elite to foreign banks. For this bailout of local financiers and US, Ecuador borrowed US $1.5 billion. To pay this loan, the IMF dictated price hikes for electricity and other necessities. And when that didn't drain off enough cash, yet another assistance plan required the state to eliminate 120,000 jobs.

The IMF and the World Bank have advised Tanzania to charge for hospital visits and school fees. This advice resulted cut in hospital visits by 53 per cent in Dares Salaam and 80 per cent to 66 per cent in school enrolment. The involvement of the IMF and the World Bank in Tanzania since 1985 has resulted in Tanzania's GDP falling from $309 to $210 per capita, literacy rate is falling and abject poverty has jumped to 51 per cent of the population in 2000. These two world organizations instead of debt relief, they received structural assistance plans listing an average of 114 conditionalities in return for capital. The dreaded structural assistance plans of the Fund and the Bank have been renamed as Poverty Reduction Strategy Papers.[213]

The Disinvestments Campaign:

The campaign explains, "Why Boycott the World Bank?" In its opinion, the World Bank, one of the most powerful agents of neo-liberalism and economic globalization, enforces policies that sacrifice human and labour rights and the environment to the dictates of multinational corporations and powerful governments. The World Bank, along with the

[213] Greg Palast (2000), "IMF crimes against humanity", ***Observer*** (London), October 8, 2000

International Monetary Fund (IMF), encourages the privatization of government services, requires the weakening of labour laws, and undermines small business and farmers. Through its devastating structural adjustment lending, the Bank also encourages poor countries to increase fees for health and education by requiring the cutting of spending on vital government services. With the help the World Bank and the IMF, corporate giants have become richer while most of the world's poor people are becoming poorer.

Despite increasing criticism and appeals from numerous civic organizations and governments in the North and South, the World Bank continues to increase its rate of structural adjustment and harmful lending.

(a) The World Bank refuses to cancel 100 per cent of the debts of poor countries.
(b) The World Bank refuses to implement recommendations from the World Commission on Dams.
(c) Despite the World Bank's verbal support of workers' rights to organize its pro-corporate privatization policies undermine workers' rights.
(d) The World Bank refuses to cease promoting drastic cuts in social spending, leaving governments no alternative but to impose 'user fees' on basic services such as primary health care and education.
(e) The World Bank refuses to adopt measures of transparency and remains unaccountable and undemocratic.
(f) The World Bank ignores concerns of local people and civil society by imposing a 'one style fits all' model economics on debtor nations.[214]

[214] The Dis-investment Campaign

Debt Cancellation Should Be Implemented

As the World Bank and International Monetary Fund prepared to hold their spring meetings in Washington, D.C., in April 2005, debt cancellation activists were poised to claim a long-awaited victory. Earlier this year, for the first time, the Group of Seven wealthy nations agreed in principle to require the World Bank and IMF to cancel up to 100 percent of the debts of a number of impoverished countries. This breakthrough was the result of years of pressure from activists in Africa and throughout the Global South.

Sony Kappor et al (2005) have reported that debt owed by IMF, World Bank is growing faster and the multilateral funding institutions are now the major creditors of low-income countries. Cancelling multilateral debt has three advantages. These are:

(d) **Policy conditionality:** The World Bank and the IMF impose restrictions on debtor countries while lending money. These policy conditions are called conditionalities, which covers government's policies in a wide range of areas, from economic and fiscal policies to governance, human rights and the social sector. This conditionality promotes privatization, trade and capital account liberalization, reduced spending in the social sectors and cannot reduce poverty in poor countries.

2. **Equal burden sharing**: Most multilateral debt cancellations are generally financed by additional bilateral contributions. This effectively turns grants into loans - as the money contributed by donor countries is then recycled as additional loans by the institutions. Multilateral debt cancellation using the multilateral own resource is one way to redress this imbalance.

3. **Moral hazard**: The International financial Institutions are treated as preferred creditors. The debtor countries must have to repay the multilateral debt for fear of being cut off by all funding sources including private and official bilateral repayment obligations. The Paris Club does not consider for debt reduction unless it is signed up to an IMF sponsored adjustment program. Irresponsible lending decisions by the IFIs cause moral hazards to the low-income countries. Because new loans provided to a country is often paid-off for old loans and do not serve any real development purpose. The practice of defensive lending also causes moral hazard.

4. **The moneylender cum trader adopts this practice in Indian villages; even cooperative banks in India adopt this paper-adjustment practice without any benefit to the customers. How the same procedures are being followed by the multinational organizations?**[215]

Booker and Njehu (2005) have strongly advocated that for African countries, in particular, the burden of illegitimate and un-payable debt has taken a devastating human toll over the past 25 years. The $300 billion that African countries owe to foreign creditors such as the World Bank and IMF represents a crippling burden that has severely undermined economic and social progress.

Sub-Saharan Africa alone pays $13 billion to wealthy creditors including the IMF and World Bank each year. The UN estimates the same amount to combat HIV/AIDS in that region too.

Meanwhile, dozens of African nations still spend more of their budget on debt service than on health care in the midst of the HIV/AIDS pandemic. It has long been clear that previous efforts at debt relief,

---

[215] Sony Kapoor et al (2005), www.eurodad.org

particularly the Heavily Indebted Poor Countries (HIPC) Initiative, have failed to resolve the debt crisis in the most impoverished countries. After years of activist pressure on the immorality of this outflow of resources, there is finally an acknowledgment on the part of creditors that this dynamic is unsustainable.

But the deal is not yet done. The G-7, World Bank and IMF are still discussing various options for dealing with the debt crisis, and it is not yet clear that the 100 percent cancellation that is so urgently needed will actually be realized. This is indeed a critical moment. The world's wealthiest countries must now agree on a plan that will go far beyond the HIPC framework to include 100 percent cancellation for all impoverished and deeply indebted countries, without imposing harmful conditions. The Bush administration has proposed to its G7 allies that the debts owed by about 40 of the most impoverished countries to the World Bank and IMF be completely written off. The list of countries is too short, but the U.S. proposal, uncharacteristically, is the most progressive on the table. The other G7 countries must resist the distraction of a U.K. plan that would accomplish far less, but which has gotten far more media attention.

Anything less than 100 percent debt cancellation will fail to resolve the debt crisis.

Moreover, most of the debts claimed by the wealthy creditor nations and institutions are illegitimate to begin with. The vast majority of impoverished country debts are the result of irresponsible lending to dictators who stole the loans or used the money to oppress the very people who are now footing the bill. Shortly after invading Iraq in 2003, the United States began actively pursuing the cancellation of Iraq's debt as a means to support the country's "transition to democracy." Earlier this year, after the tsunami wrought such devastation in the Indian Ocean, creditors offered to freeze bilateral debt repayments for some of the impoverished countries worst affected, to enable them to prioritize their own domestic needs. It is past time those African countries and other impoverished and deeply indebted countries receive the same consideration.

Independent studies show that 100 percent debt cancellation can be financed from the resources of the World Bank and IMF themselves, without negatively affecting their credit rating or their ability to continue their operations.

This can be achieved primarily by closing down its Poverty Reduction and Growth Facility and through an easily designed market-neutral sale of the IMF's vast gold reserves, a point on which the U.S. must resist mining companies' unfounded concerns about gold market fluctuations. In addition, the World Bank can direct part of its ample annual surplus to a measure that should be its top development priority. The British government, which will host the annual G8 summit in July, has declared that addressing Africa's poverty is a top priority, and has indicated it hopes a deal on debt, may be reached at this summer's meeting. But time is of the essence. The World Bank and IMF meetings this month represent yet another opportunity for rich-country creditors to do the right thing on debt. Financing options for debt cancellation will be explored and discussed, and decisions should be made. Every further delay means African countries must continue starving their children to pay their debts.[216]

Learning form History

Debt relief for the least developed and low developed countries have assumed the greatest challenge to the

[216] Salih Booker and Njoki Njoroge Njehu, "Debt Cancellation Should Be Considered", Seattle Post - Intelligencer, April, 15, 2005

developed countries and world organizations in the first decade of the 21st century. The creditors are not legally bound to allow debt relief; but they are bound to allow debt relief on ethical, moral and humanitarian grounds to the debtor countries to ameliorate their poverty, hunger, and inhumane conditions of living. The rich and poor should go together for a healthy living and for security and peace. The rich controls the empire but the poor build the country and protect all. The rich cannot live without the assistance of the poor. The rich lives a healthy life because he feels he is fortunate as compared to the poor. Let us study why Egyptians devoted hundreds of years to enrich humanity and welfare.

Egyptians had given many thoughts to the nature of universe and to the social and ethical problems of humanity. The achievements of Greece (sixth century B.C.) were rather the development of philosophy in a more inclusive manner. They attempted to find answers to every conceivable question about the nature of universe, the problem of truth, the meaning and purpose of life.

Thales, the founder of Milesian School, perceiving that all things contained moisture, taught that the primary substance is water. Anaximenes declared that the original material of the universe is air. Air when rarefied becomes fire, when condensed it turns successively to wind, vapor, water, earth and stone. Pythagoreans interpreted philosophy largely in terms of religion. Democritus developed the atomic theory in fifth century B.C. In the same century an intellectual revolution in Greece and it accompanied the high point of democracy in Athens. Protagoras, a leading Sophist, declared, "Man is the measure of all things". By this he meant that goodness, truth, justice and beauty are relative to the needs and interest of man. The Sophists condemned slavery and the racial exclusiveness of the Greeks. They were champions of liberty, the rights of common man, and the practical and progressive point of view. They perceived the folly of war and ridiculed chauvinism of many Athenian citizens. Perhaps most important, they broadened philosophy to include not only physics and metaphysics, but also ethics and politics. As the Roman Cicero expressed it, they" they brought down from heaven to the dwellings of man".

Moreover, scholars like Socrates (birth 469 BC), Plato (birth 429 BC), and Aristotle (birth 384 BC) were born in Greece. They expressed, "if there is no final truth, and if goodness and justice are merely relative to the whims of individual, then neither religion, morality, the state, or society itself can long be maintained." The result of this conviction was the growth of a new philosophic movement grounded upon the theory that truth is real and that absolute standards do exist. These three great persons are the most famous individuals in the history of thought. Socrates was condemned to the death in 399 B.C. on a charge of "Corrupting the youths and introducing new Gods".

Plato's philosophy of ideas, ethical and religious philosophy crowned him as a political philosopher.

Aristotle's religious doctrine and ethical philosophy included politics on the structure and functions of government. He dealt primarily with the broader aspects of political theory. He advocated measures to prevent the concentration of wealth. He defended the institution of private property, but he opposed the heaping up riches beyond what is necessary for intelligent living.

He recommended that government provide the poor with money to buy small farms or to 'make a beginning in trade or husbandry' and thus

promote their property and self-respect. He was the founder of the Science of Biology.

Pythagoras developed theory of mathematics. Anaximander developed Biology. Empedocles developed Medicines. Homer developed Greek epics, the Iliad and the Odyssey.[217]

All the great persons were basically philosophers but they developed new ideas for human welfare. They will be remembered for their selfless contributions to the world. They are the torchbearers. Cannot we solve the problem of hunger in this twenty-first century? We can do it. To solve this greatest challenge, the international communities need not be worried for solving the Millennium Development Goals by 2015. The world will be a peaceful place to live in if they simply implement 100 per cent debt relief for all low-income countries as on 31st December 2014 and the low-middle income counties by December 31, 2015.

Debit money is generally assumed as the surplus money. The donor countries, world organizations, international funding institutions and even the international banks can try managing the loss of their organizations, if they desire to solve the greatest problem facing the humanity. These countries / institutions can sacrifice for the cause of world peace – a new generation of civilization of 21st century. Of course, the new loans from the New Year of 2015 should be entertained with interest. Debt relief of 100 per cent to low-income countries would fulfill the target of MDGs without any assistance of international communities and donors.

---

[217] Burns, EM et al, " World Civilizations – Their History and Their Culture" Western Civilization – 7th Edition, Indian Edition, New Delhi, pp188-200

Absence of foreign funding on industrialization, grants to governments, NGOs and civil societies will check corruption in all developing countries.

This practice may be followed for a couple of years to check massive corruption in all developing countries. Donations should not encourage corruption at any cost. There should not be politics in giving food aid to the hungry and awarding a cash prize to the poor for relieving his mental strain.

In all LDCs, there exist conflicts between the paths of development and the path of peace. Development neglects social and political factors and is often derailed by conflicts. Agricultural economy can slowly accept the development through setting up agricultural related industries.

But imposing industrialization of the economy overnight will jeopardize the growth of both agriculture and industry. The state of Orissa in India adopted industrialization overnight after the general election of 2004 and the state has turned into a conflict-ridden state within a year. The result will be disillusionment and disappointment.

The African countries are facing conflicts because of borrowed capital and borrowed policies. The ultimate aim is peace in mind and peace everywhere.

Imposing new rules and police administration for growth of industrialization in poor pockets of the world will rekindle internal disturbances, arms trade and will enter into civil war. Politicians generally activate conflicts through inefficiency of bureaucracies, massive corruption, and false propaganda and the general public losses peace of mind and fights with the government with stones, sticks or crackers.

The world organizations like United Nations Conference on Trade and Development (UNCTAD), and World Trade Organization (WTO) cannot enrich the heavily indebted poor countries because the rich countries offer high subsidy to their farmers. The farmers of poor countries cannot compete with the farmers of rich countries in quality, prices and varieties of grains or fruits or finished products. These organizations can further enrich USA and Japan as against Ethiopia or Bangladesh. Similarly, the Paris Club, Official Development Assistance (ODA), Foreign Direct Investment (FDI), Multilateral Investment Guarantee Agency (MIGA), partial debt relief and debt restructuring cannot allow the poor to live in peace. The developed countries know the art of increasing their wealth-building capacity.

The donors did transcend humanitarian assistance during natural calamities in Indonesia, India, Bangladesh, Mozambique, and Ethiopia and in Darfur of Sudan. But the government officials were engaged in massive misappropriation of foreign-assisted funds in poor countries during relief operations and the commodity-relief was black marketed openly in the receiving countries.

Opinion of Mr. Gordon Brown

Gordon Brown says, "We will be judged on how we deliver the resources to prove that making poverty history was not a passing fashion. Having taken the first steps to make poverty history, we must ensure 2005 is remembered as the start of something – not the end. We must learn from our achievements and failures, not least the depressing lack of final agreements on trade. So when finance ministers meet in Moscow next month, I will propose a post-Gleneagles agenda, founded on delivering the G8 commitments, for the empowerment of developing countries. It should, as a matter of urgency, include:

(a) A new US $4 billion to US $5 billion on-call facility for disaster relief and reconstruction
(b) Full debt relief for not 38 but all the world's poorest countries
(c) A new environmental fund for developing countries
(d) A delivery plan produced by developing countries themselves for achieving the millennium development goals
(e) A push by world leaders to restart and complete the trade talks

At the heart of this empowerment agenda we should offer a global new deal: rich countries honoring commitments on finance, debt, trade and the environment; poor countries, freed from the shackles of debt, under-funding and protectionism, enabled to grow, invest and trade, and defeat hunger, illiteracy, disease and underdevelopment. A century ago people talked of "What we could do to Africa". Last century, it was "What can we do for Africa?" Now, in 2006, we must ask what the developing world, empowered, can do for itself. If Make Poverty History shifted from the old calls for charity to the new demand for justice, 2006 must see campaigners and governments moving the agenda beyond addressing the consequences of poverty to attacking its root causes. The delivery of aid is not the final goal, but just the first stage in the process of empowerment. That is why all developing countries must now produce their own poverty-reduction and development plans – not just for economic empowerment through transparent monetary, fiscal and corporate policies to tackle corruption, but also for social empowerment through universal free schooling and healthcare.

As we start of 2006, preventable diseases such as malaria and tuberculosis still kill 7 million children a year, and in South Africa half of all 15-year-olds are expected to die from Aids. By front loading aid and investing an extra $4 billion in vaccination now, the path-breaking international finance facility for immunization could save 5 million lives by 2015, and a life-saving vaccine could soon be available for malaria to save 1 million lives each year. So next month, I will ask the G8 to put the most innovative financial mechanisms at the service of the most innovative medical research. We should create the first mechanism whereby rich countries underwrite the research, development and bulk production of affordable vaccines and treatments. And by reducing the price of drugs and building healthcare systems, we should meet our promise of universal access to HIV/Aids treatments by 2010.

If past generations said, "If only we had the knowledge, the technology, the medicine and the science to act", today we have no such excuse. As we start 2006, there are 110 million children who, far from being empowered, do not go to school. So our new resolution for every country must be universal free education - the best and most empowering investment we could ever make. And 2006 must also start by agreeing not just better, swifter and more coordinated responses to emergencies and disasters but - learning another lesson from 2005 - major reforms of the way international institutions tackle poverty. For while last year showed that round the world there is not compassion fatigue but a mountain of goodwill, 2005 also exposed deadly disarray in the world's response to humanitarian crises.

Rich countries should finance with compassion and charitable activism to the UN disaster-relief and reconstruction fund. From their $1.2 trillion windfall, oil-producing countries should help finance our proposed IMF shocks facility. The IMF's surveillance work - monitoring how countries implement the codes and standards vital to economic stability and growth - must be stepped up and conducted independent of politics. To coordinate the war on poverty there should be a regular summit of the

World Bank, the IMF and all UN agencies. And recognizing that the recent doubling of oil prices has hurt poor countries most, we propose the World Bank consider a new US $20 billion loan and grant fund for investment in alternative energy sources and energy efficiency.

An empowerment agenda for economic self-sufficiency requires world trade agreements that finally address the scandal of rich countries' agricultural protectionism. But they must do more than open the door to trade: poor countries must have the strength to walk through. So part of any deal must include funding infrastructure and education to enable poor countries to compete effectively. But empowerment of the poor will be a false hope until the decades-old debt crisis is fully resolved. In December, 100 per cent multilateral debt relief was finally achieved for the first 19 highly indebted poor countries - and, despite prior worries, with no extra conditionality.[218]

In Britain's view, all 67 of the poorest countries should secure debt relief. By paying our share of their debt service, we will unilaterally lead debt cancellation for up to another 30 countries, and I will urge others to follow. These are more than crumbs of comfort. They are a signal that globalization could mean not just global flows of capital, but social justice on a global scale too. In 2006 we will be judged not just on willing the millennium development goals but on delivering the resources to achieve them. All involved will have to prove that making poverty history is not just a passing fashion but also a commitment for our generation".

---

[218] Gordon Brown, The Guardian, Wednesday January 11, 2006, Gordon Brown was the Chancellor of the Exchequer and now the Prime Minister, UK

Both the WB and IMF Reject 100 Percent Debt Relief

The World Bank and the International Monetary Fund assail for rejecting debt relief. Their arguments are as follows:

(a)With total public external debt for low-income countries standing at some $460 billion, the world's poorest debtors are increasingly dependent on funding from bilateral and multilateral lending agencies on concessional terms.

(b)Total cancellation of their debt could imperil these funds. It would also undermine the confidence of existing and potential investors whose funds are vital for the long-term development of the low-income countries.

(c)The HIPC initiative is making a crucial difference in the lives of the poor because for the first time, debt relief is delivered within a framework that is transparent and comprehensive. In addition, the relief is delivered only to those countries, which have demonstrated the commitment and capacity to use the resources effectively. These principles reflect the fact that debt relief comes at a cost.

(d)Eliminating their debt in one stroke would make it difficult for the poorest countries to receive development assistance in the future because donor agencies would have to write off loans, forcing them to raise interest rates on other lending programmes.

That could put some lenders at risk and threaten IMF programmes for the poor, such as its Poverty Reduction and Growth Facility (PRGF), formerly the Enhanced Structural Adjustment Facility, which is funded by outside contributions and borrowing. For the Fund, total debt cancellation in the absence of full funding by bilateral donors would do serious damage by fundamentally changing its role as an anchor for the international financial system based on the revolving character of its resources. Debt cancellation would not only eliminate PRGF lending, but also impair the Fund's financial integrity.

Why these organizations do not want 100 percent debt relief?

(e)The industrial countries have adopted a new technique to control all the low-income countries through excessive debt. Even the policy adopted by the Sunset Law has sincerely tried to control all the 'third world countries' for at least 50 – 60 years or for three generations.

(f)**These countries have successfully utilized their surplus funds in the debtor countries with the knowledge that these countries can never be able to repay back the amount.**

(g)The British started trade and commerce initially in all these countries but after that they ruled these countries during 16th to 20th century. Now these rich countries are undertaking money-lending business through the World Bank and IMF in the guise of helping the poor. But their advices and activities have resulted in one billion of hungry mouths.

(h)**The politicians- administrators – contractors are now ruling the states, amassing huge private wealth, depositing foreign borrowed funds in Swiss Banks in private names and are selling land, mines, minerals, forests and allowing business in education through private educational institutions including Universities. They have started an age of corruption, torture, terror and loss of peace everywhere.**

(i)**Interest payments for borrowed funds have exceeded expenditure on education and health care combined in all the low-income countries.**

Where We Stand Now

It is a fact that all international advocacy organizations such as Jubilee 2000, AFRODAD, LDYS, CAFOD, OXFAM, the Churches and Religious organizations, Women's organizations and 'Make Poverty History' are undertaking massive protests for 100 percent debt relief. Moreover, a large number of professional and renowned economists (chapter II) have suggested for 100 percent debt relief. They have proved that multilateral and bilateral debts to the low and least developed, low-income and middle-income countries have increased more burdens as compared to the benefits in those countries. The debt for infrastructure development has caused massive political corruption and administrative corruption.

Easy flow of funds to the low developing countries has caused massive defense expenditure and huge corruption. This debt of the IMF and the World Bank has resulted in price rise of essential commodities, increase of poverty, hunger, starvation, massive unemployment, environmental degradation, and rise of Terrorists, Naxalites and Maoists in all indebted countries.

Even the policy for collection of User's Fee in government hospitals, public-private partnership for infrastructure development, concretization of village roads, and maximization of irrigated areas through of River Valley Projects have simply forced the countries into debt trap.

The World Bank and IMF have made all the low-income economies (54) and most of the lower-middle-income countries (58) as bonded countries.

Even in the Twenty-first century there occur starvation deaths, child sale, pornography, human trafficking, farmers' suicides, and international trade in illicit narcotics. And 1.3 billion people are hungry.

Problems Can Be Solved

Problems can be solved and can be attempted successfully through debt relief, regards for other religions, peace movements, reduction of defense budget, solving boundary problems and humanitarian approach towards poverty reduction for strengthening world peace. The world is having 54 low-income countries (or less economically developed countries or developing countries with per capita GNI less than $875 in 2007), which speak that these countries are poor and indebted. There are other 58 Lower-Middle-Income countries, which are also indebted. So to start with, planning should aim at a hunger-free, debt-free, and a peaceful world through debt relief of these 54 low-income countries.

The total external debt of the very poorest countries 54 countries (the low income countries, which have an annual average income of less than $875 per person) was US $412 billion at the end of 2005. During 2005, these countries paid nearly $43 billion to the rich world in debt service (payments of interest and principal). In other words, these poorest 54 countries paid $118 million a day. Moreover, all the poorest and indebted 152 countries owed an external debt of $2.8 trillion at the end of 2005, and over the course of that year they paid $511 billion servicing these debts. These are the latest figures available – there has been some debt cancellation in 2006, but there will also have been new debts taken on. The overall figures are unlikely to have changed hugely.[219]

---

[219] Jubilee Debt Campaign, The Grayston Centre, London

However, we have made a modest attempt for world peace through debt relief.

Peace was prevalent on Earth since living organisms were created through evolution. The religious priests call it as God's creation. In the pre-Vedic era, human beings and animals were living together. Even today poor people remain in the same thatched house along with domestic animals. The rich persons also treat pet dogs and cats as permanent guests of the family. It is love and affection that creates relationship between animals, people, and among different classes, castes, groups, and religions. When love and affection don't cost anything; why we will not give respect to people of other religion, caste, colour, gender or country and treat them as our friends?

Our mind and heart can be enlarged to accommodate the entire world as our native place, where we are born and where we will perish one day. Each one of us should feel pity with those people, who encounter hunger, pain, sufferings or mental stress. The rich, therefore, should extend his helping hands to the poor for relieving his poverty. It is said, "Service to the poor is service to God".

The world is classified into different countries for political reasons; religions for different faiths; North and South blocks for economic factors; and different zones on the basis of natural resources. The world is also classified on the basis of agro-climatic considerations and on the basis of colour and physique of inhabitants. But we can consider the entire world as our home and the poor people as our brethren.

History speaks the rich becomes richer by oppressing the poor. And in this twenty-first century, the present world can change the history, if the donor countries and world organizations do assist the poor for relieving their misery. It is possible if the donors really desire to assist the poor countries and are prepared to sacrifice some amount for social welfare of billions of poor people around the world. The donor countries and world organizations should take decisions on 'debt relief' on priority consideration rather than undertaking new projects for poverty reduction worldwide. Let all the citizens on this planet including the poor of the third-world countries feel that there prevails peace everywhere and they possess the right to live on.

The IMF desperately needs a non-European

An international organization with a capital and lending capacity of hundreds of billions of dollars will have a vacancy at its top almost immediately as a result of the personal indiscretion of its managing director that has been an acute embarrassment to himself and the International Monetary Fund.[220]

Everyone may agree that the IMF requires a comprehensive overhaul under visionary leadership. But the race to lead the IMF is not open to the swifter, higher, stronger — in the words of the Olympic motto — but confined to a narrow clique of European central bankers and politicians. This is because, by convention, the IMF's chief executive is appointed by the Fund's 24-member executive board, and to date, the chief executive has always been chosen from a West European country. The latest and tenth managing director, Dominique Strauss-Kahn, from France was to retire in any case in October. In 2009, after a full decade of working groups, position papers and learned reports, it was agreed that the IMF should adopt "an open, merit-based and transparent process" of selection for the top management, but this formula, apparently, has not

---

[220] Krishnan Srinibasan (2011), " View from Below", The Telegraph, June 1, 2011, Wednesday

yet been applied to the selection of its chief executive.

The Bretton Woods institutions, the IMF, the World Bank and the World Trade Organization, are part of the United Nations family. The governing structure of the IMF and the World Bank is heavily weighted in favour of the industrialized countries, although their clientele, in numerical terms, is from the developing world. At the end of 2010, India and Brazil were given additional quotas to join China and Russia among the top ten IMF shareholders, but strong economies like India and China, even with the added powers, together still possess less than 10 per cent of the voting strength. This anachronistic dispensation requires revision in keeping with the changed world order. To restrict the leadership of the World Bank to the United States of America, and that of the IMF to Europe — the two regions responsible for the global meltdown and financial panic in the first decade of this century — is patently absurd.

When this writer asked an economics professor, one closely identified with the now discredited and dis-empowered Communist Party of India (Marxist) regime in West Bengal, whether the IMF should mark a departure by appointing a non-European at its head, he loftily enquired why it should matter who takes over the leadership of that international financial organization. The riposte to the academic's pomposity is that the leadership issue does matter, and it is something the developing world has been struggling to extract from the grip of the developed countries in recognition of the shift in the balance of power from the industrialized economies to the new emerging powers illustrated by the BRICS — Brazil, Russia, India, China and South Africa.

Gordon Brown, until last year the Labour Party prime minister of the United Kingdom, has said that had he known better, he would have more strictly regulated the banking industry. This sent his former finance minister, Alistair Darling, into a sharp reaction. Darling alleged that he had repeatedly urged the then prime minister to do just that, and had been rebuffed. While the Labour Party shows disunity even in its retrospective reflections on the parlous state of the British economy, the Conservative Prime Minister, David Cameron, is mulling over whether to support Brown's undeclared but obvious plan to be the next managing director of the IMF. Cameron has declared that this international financial organization needs someone who understands the dangers of excessive debt and excessive deficit, implying that the present British government is more aware of the problems and their remedies than its predecessor. This is interpreted as a thumbs-down for Gordon Brown.

If the credentials of the new managing director are such that will make him or her wary of debts and deficits, as suggested by Cameron, such views will be of relevance to the world. But that is hardly the full prospectus of what the IMF badly needs at this time, which is nothing less than root and branch reform. The organization was shown to be ineffective during the Asian financial crisis of 1997, and its advice was resented and discounted by the affected countries in making their recoveries, especially in matters of capital controls that placed restrictions on free movement of currencies across trans-national borders. The IMF also failed to anticipate or deal with the global financial meltdown of 2008, which was caused by, and afflicted most gravely, its leading shareholders, namely the western developed economies, all of which are still languishing in various phases of the financial doldrums. In fact, the IMF's favoured policies of free capital flows have pushed several countries into crises, such as Spain, Portugal, Greece, Ireland and Iceland. Its prescriptions are rigid and its one-cap-fits-all solutions are belatedly considered to be ill conceived, to say the least.

The IMF has lately been progressively overshadowed by the G20, a body that sets out policies for the world economy but without any executive ability. The G20 agreed to expand the IMF's ability to lend to countries hit by recession, but the Fund has managed to advance only about 15 per cent of the monies at its disposal, and its conditions remain stringent, emphasizing the restoration of fiscal balance through restrictions of wage and employment opportunities, essentially through cuts in social spending. At the same time, volatile capital movements have continued unhindered, and they threaten to create instability in the finances of vulnerable nations. Poor and middle-income countries complain bitterly that their economies are being knocked off the course as a flood of hot money assails their markets as a result of policies adopted in the West.

Whether the IMF has finally learnt to slip out of its monetarist straitjacket is very debatable. It is still wedded to controls being used sparingly, in specific conditions and only temporarily. It prefers to concentrate on capital inflows, investments, reserve requirements and lock-in periods rather than outflows, which have always had a more pernicious effect. Countries that have large capital inflows are unlikely to be the developing countries, where such a phenomenon would, in fact, be welcomed as providing Bottom of the Pyramid support. In other words, these are nations that would have no need for advice from the IMF in the first place. Chile, Brazil, Thailand and Malaysia had instituted controls on capital inflows well before the IMF changed its traditional tune. In countries with BoP problems, the IMF still persists in advocating open capital accounts and further liberalization to secure investor confidence, and there is no evidence of any introspection despite IMF nostrums having made the maladies worse for several patients in the past.

What does the IMF think about the high food and fuel prices, commodities futures markets, or financing facilities without conditionality's? Would the forthcoming leadership change in the IMF be able to make any difference? It is facile for the economist in Calcutta to scoff and be cynical, but at one of the most turbulent times since World War II, the appointment of the next IMF head acquires considerable significance. The new leader should give due recognition to the essential role of State spending in maintaining incomes and employment. Historian Hugh Trevor-Roper once wrote, "it is European techniques, European examples, European ideas which have shaken the non-European world out of its past, and the history of the world for the past five centuries, insofar as it has significance, has been European history."

Such opinions have no contemporary relevance. The membership of the Fund has increased from the initial 29 to 187. While the Euro-zone has lurched into an existential crisis, a so-called advanced European economy is as likely to apply to the IMF for a bail-out as one in Saharan Africa, and the biggest borrowers in value terms are now Greece, Portugal and Ireland. A massive change has taken place in moving the centre of gravity of the global economy away from the industrialized West, and solutions and practical examples offered by the new emerging economies will be more apposite for the IMF's role than the failed policies of the past.

An IMF managing director from outside Europe will be better placed to re-position the organization. Such an appointment will also reflect a welcome and overdue awareness that history has moved on from a handful of nations in the West to a much larger group in the South. It is an irony that one of the few world leaders who had consistently pressed for the reform of the IMF and a new global financial architecture is none other than Gordon Brown. Even if he is ruled out by his successor, it is far from clear if any non-European candidate is ruled in.

Measurement of Peace

The economic growth of a country is measured by Gross National Product (GNP), Gross Domestic Product (GDP), and by per capita income. But we feel that this calculation could neither solve poverty of people nor award peace to a region, country or the whole world. We want to devise a new measurement theory, which can ensure comparatively a more practical solution of solving human sufferings, and could bring or at least try to award permanent peace to a region, country or the world. We feel that each Government should measure its efficiency by measuring the Gross Domestic Peace of a Country (GDPC). The Government can try to award peace to the citizens by studying the following factors and evaluate its performances. People of the country should also cooperate with the government in peace measurement and peace movement.

The **Suresh–Pritam Model** for peace measurement is as follows. These factors are:

G D P C = f (S, D, H, W, C, E, O, F, P, X)

(a) Food Secured families (S)
(b) Debts sustainable families (D)
(c) Families those can bear medical, educational, social and Household bills (H)
(d) Area free from Rebellion, War and Terrorists (W)
(e) People's perception of Corruption-free politics and administration ©
(f) Forest coverage for clean Environment (E)
(g) Employment Opportunity (O)
(h) Families without Court cases (F)
(i) Share of State Income in Budget Expenditure Proposal (P)
(j) Other Factors Contributing to Peace (X)

Gross Domestic Peace of a Country (GDPC) can also be calculated with a single factor or with a multiple of factors in percentages. But more number of factors would bring better results. The data could be drawn from official records of the government or from published reports of researchers. We can also collect latest data by observing statistical procedures. The end result of a region, state, country or the entire globe can be classified as Highly Peaceful with >80 percent output, 60-80 percent as Peaceful, 40-60 percent as Moderately Peaceful, 30-40 Percent as Doubtful Peace Area and <30 percent as No-peace Zone. (Ref: world Peace Vol. one)

Conclusion

Debt relief is a global problem. It covers both the developed countries and low-income countries. Moreover, the low-middle-income countries would be benefited if the multilateral creditors, bilateral creditors, commercial creditors, the Paris Club, Non-Paris Club creditor governments, international organizations and developed countries would be convinced to free the poor people from debt burden.

Legally the indebted countries are bound to pay the amount, but they have misled the poor countries to borrow more for unproductive and un-payable infrastructure development. Similarly, the governments of low-income countries are urging the donors for astronomical figures of credit because these rulers, ministers are appropriating huge amounts for personal gain out of this grant. As a result the number of hungry people has crossed more than a billion and an additional two billion of poor people. The World Bank and International Monetary Fund have projected that the structural adjustment policy would yield benefits to poor people and low-income countries. The truth is: the unused wealth of developed countries and petrol-money of military rulers or emperors was safely invested in low-income countries through the WB and the IMF.

The International Forums, researchers and writers claim that the donors have already received their invested capital from the low-income countries. But the interest portion in cumulative form has not been paid and these organizations therefore, request to the donors for debt relief on behalf of the debtor countries. The developed countries are not making any loss by awarding debt relief, but the debtor countries would gain much as they would be free from debt bondage and would spend more on food security, elementary education and healthcare.

Similarly many problems crop up each day but people do not get answers to their problems. Can the problems of the poor be solved? Would the donors implement Debt Relief to the low-income countries? The suggestions include 'Reorganization of United Nations' and 'Debt Relief would strengthen World Peace'. The United Nations should try to solve the problem of DEBT RELIEF because it involves 54 low-income countries and 58 low-middle-income countries. The suggestions for 'Reorganization of United Nations' arise because global problems are increasing at a faster rate in the twenty-first century. The present form of United Nations, possibly, cannot solve all the problems. Hence, suggestions are mentioned to make the United Nations as an effective and active organization to function as the WORLD GOVERNMENT.

The world is passing through problems. The worst problem is starvation-death as it causes humanitarian crises in all the least and less developed countries. So, our suggestion is **'100 per cent debt relief'** to all LDCs and low-middle-income countries can change the turbid world into a peaceful world. If the developed countries again ask us, "What is your second choice?" We would again say, "100 percent debt relief". If the media interviews us, "What is your third suggestion? We will simply say '100 percent debt relief'.

The developed countries, multilateral, bilateral, and commercial and international funding institutions should accept 100 per cent debt relief for the least and less developed 54 countries as on December 31, 2015 and should consider debt relief for 58 other low-middle-income countries by December 31, 2016.

Debt relief can secure 'world peace' for all people living in this planet.

The developed countries may stop donating funds for achieving the MDGs, but they should consider the possibility of debt relief at the earliest for the low-income and low-middle-income countries.

Debt Relief can convert a world of injustice, hunger, illiteracy, terrorism, Maoism, Naxalism and rebellion into a state of WORLD PEACE. Debt relief is not a political slogan; it is a necessity for achieving World Peace. [221]

Debt relief can be solved through humanitarian approach that can benefit about half of the human population. Debt Relief would benefit 54 low-income countries and 58 low-middle-income countries.

Imagine a World, where there is no war, no debt, and no starvation! These LDCs would try to achieve the MDGs by themselves provided they are free from debt burden. Jennifer Henry of the Canadian Jubilee said: The debt crisis is a death crisis. We are calling for an end to the war against the poor.

---

[221] Seminar on "Debt, Structural Adjustment and Jubilee", Inter-Church Coalition on Africa, Updated No.6, July 2000

The U N should not be a poster organization; it should act as the WORLD GOVERNMENT in the 21st Century and beyond.

The United Nations should be stronger legally, politically and economically. The UN should have four organs instead of six organs. The organs are: The United Nations Peace Council, the United Nations War Council, the United Nations Law Council and the United Nations Secretariat. All the four organizations should be strengthened with statutory powers for ensuring permanent world peace. The task of the UN is to achieve a world free of war, annexations, anxiety and fear. It should activate the peace process in all sectors.

The United Nations Peace Council should monitor peace activities through out the world and award United Nations Peace Prizes to 100 individuals (not institutions) each year on 24th October for their activities, contributions and sacrifices towards strengthening 'World Peace'.

We feel that 'poverty of people' should neither be criticized nor used as a cause of laughter as it nudges a smoldering fire into the bellies of hungry people. Moreover, poverty should not be traded for economic gain and used as a source of political mileage.

The developed countries and multilateral organizations should consider, discuss, decide and take actions on the problems of 'DEBT and STARVATION' of poor countries for a peaceful solution.

Their noble and sympathetic consideration with humanitarian approach could make 100 percent 'debt relief' possible for a long drive towards peace, happiness and calmness in all the indebted countries. And WORLD PEACE is possible.

ANNEXURE

Low-income Economies (54)

Afghanistan, Bangladesh, Benin, Bhutan, Burkina Faso, Burundi, Cambodia, Central African Republic, Chad, Comoros, Congo, Democratic Republic, Cote d'Ivoire, Eritrea, Ethiopia, The Gambia, Ghana, Guinea, Guinea-Bissau, Haiti, India, Kenya, Democratic Republic of Korea, Kyrgyz republic, Lao PDR, Liberia, Madagascar, Malawi, Mali, Mauritania, Mongolia, Mozambique, Myanmar, Nepal, Niger, Nigeria, Pakistan, Papua New Guinea, Rwanda, Sao Tome and Principe, Senegal, Sierra Leone, Solomon Islands, Somalia, Sudan, Tajikistan, Tanzania, Timor-Leste, Togo, Uganda, Uzbekistan, Vietnam, Yemen, republic, Zambia, Zimbabwe

Lower-middle-income Economies (58)

Albania, Algeria, Angola, Armenia, Azerbaijan, Belarus, Bolivia, Bosnia and Herzegovina, Brazil, Bulgaria, Cameroon, Cape Verde, China, Colombia, Republic of Congo, Cuba, Djibouti, Dominican Republic, Ecuador, Arab Republic of Egypt, El Salvador, Fiji, Georgia, Guatemala, Guyana, Honduras, Indonesia, Islamic Republic of Iran, Iraq, Jamaica, Jordan, Kazakhstan, Kiribati, Lesotho, FYR Macedonia, Maldives, Marshall Islands, Micronesia Federal States, Moldova, Morocco, Sri Lanka, Suriname, Swaziland, Syrian Arab Republic, Thailand, Tonga, Tunisia, Turkmenistan, Ukraine, Vanuatu, West Bank and Gaza

Source: World Bank Report 2007

AUTHOR INDEX

Abbott George C. : 67
Abrego, Lisandro : 86
Acharya, Shankarsan : 59
Adler, Oliver : 52
Aizenman, Joshua : 43, 55
Alan Gelb : 92
Alfred M. : 60
Arslanalo S. : 90
Arora, Vivek B. : 66
A. Milne : 89
Ambrose, Soren : 378
Ann Pettifor : 263
Andrabi, Tahir : 68
Andrea Ripa : 68
Armendariz de Aghion, Beatriz: 70
Armendariz de Hinestrosa : 70
Arora, Vivek B. : 66
Arslanalo S. : 161
Arthur, Patrick : 83
A. Javier Hamann : 84
Asiedu, Elizabeth : 84,303
Bailey, Norman A : 37
Belessakos, Elias : 75
Benn Eifert : 92
Buerthelemy, J C : 91
Berthelemy, Jean Claude : 58
Bird, Graham : 89
Boot, Arnold W.A : 71

Boote, Anthony R : 73
Bowe, Michael : 28, 72
Brazelon, Coleman : 54
Bulir, Ales : 84
Bulow, Jeremy : 160
Burnside C. : 161
Burns, E M : 468
Calvo, Guillermo A. : 48, 54
Cheru, Fantu : 81
Christou, Costas : 75
Cline, William R. : 38, 71
Claessens, Stijn : 53
Cockburn, John : 70
Cohen, Daniel : 42, 53,64,82,88
Cohen, Richard : 37
Corden, W. Max : 39, 40, 43
Cordella Tito : 88
Cornwall, A : 167
Cutler, David M. : 75,162
Dagdeviren, H : 85
David Dollar : 160
Denise Froning : 23
Dean, James W : 28,72
Dellas, Harris : 75
Dent Martin : 76
Di Meana : 86
Dijkstra, G. : 27, 53
Diwan, Ishac : 50, 59
Dooley, Michael P. : 42, 47, 51
Doris C. Ross : 86
Dombusch, Rudiger : 50
Elbadawi, Ibrahim A. : 79
Egli Dominik : 69
Fischer, Stanley : 39
Fishlow, Albert : 39
Froot, Kenneth A. : 46
Eaton, Jonathan : 27
Easterly, William : 80
Edwards, S. : 87
Fernandez, Raquel : 27
Fernandez, Jorge : 69

Frenkel, Jacob A. : 51
Franke, Gunter : 57
Gail Lerner : 285
George Ayittey : 24
Ghani,Ejaz :74
Ghatak,Subrata :64
Gensollen, Anne : 83
Giradin Eric : 58
Gilman Martin : 167
Gordon Brown : 470,473
Greene, Joshua : 48, 63
Greenhill, R : 218,264
Gracia Aldaz, Jesus : 76
Greg Palast : 460
Griffith Jones, Stephany : 57
Hajivassiliou, Vassilis : 49
Hayri, Aydin : 73, 82
Helleiner G.K :62
Henry, Peter B. : 90
Hermes, CLM : 28
Hermes, N : 27
Horwitz, Jill R. : 75
Huizingsa, Harry : 40
Hussain , Aasim. M : 63
Hussain, Ishrat : 50
Jacques : 58
James wolfsaon : 447
J. Bradford De Long : 441,445
J. Weeks : 85,162
Jayanti Ghosh : 213
Jeffrey Sachs : 262
Jorgensen, Erika : 45
Jose Antynio Ocampo : 33
Kanatas, George : 71
Kamel, Nawal : 43
Kaminsky, Graciela L. : 54, 60
Kenneth R. : 161
Klein, Martin : 53
Koren,Stephan : 61
Krugman, Paul R. : 44
Krugman, P. : 160

Krishnan Sriniasan : 479
Kunibert Raffer : 262
Kurihara, K K : 413
Lackwood, Sharon : 67
Lagae, W. : 56
Lagos,Richado A : 62
Landskroner, Yoram : 42
Levine,paul : 63
Luca Di Leo : 331
Makin, John H : 50
Mahatma M K Gandhi : 377
Marchesi, Silva : 80
Marcesi, S : 91
Maren P. : 425
Michael Wang : 89
Miana di : 68
Mkapa : 157
Michelson, Jan Giehm : 59
Mitchael, Wang : 89,168
Missale, A. : 91
Mistry, Percy S : 68
Morisset : 58
Morrissey, Oliver : 85
Mrak, Mojmir : 52
Mullineux, Andrew W : 65
Mulima Kufekisa Akapelwa : 254
Myers, Stewart : 160
M.K Gandhi : 19
Nasution, Anwar : 80
Nelson Mandela : 301
Niels Hermes : 86
Nioki Nioroge Niehu : 465
Paroush,Jacob :42
Pastor, Manuel, Jr. : 61
Pereira, Alfredo M : 60
Peter, Bill : 76
Peter Blair Henry : 161
Rauscher, Michael : 49
Raussor, Gorden C. : 54
Rubbens Ricupero : 29
Sachs, Jeffrey : 40

Sachs, Jeffrey D. : 45, 46
Salih Booker : 465
Schwartz, Herman : 47
Sharma, Ruchir : 25
Sony Kapoor : 463
Soto Marcelo : 88
Sri Chinmoy : 36
Stephens, Malcolm : 74
Stewart Frances : 89, 168
Stiglitz, Joseph E. : 25
Stymne, Joakim : 49
Summers, L : 159
Swarna Kumar Anand : 151
Thomas, Jonathan P. : 80
Thugge, Kamau : 73
Tideman Nicolous : 67
Yilmaz Akyuz : 262
Van Wijnbergen, Sweder : 55
Walden Bello : 451
Wayne Mitchell : 167
Weeks, J : 85
Wickham, Peter : 51
William Harris : 154
Williamson, John : 41
Zang, Hyoungsoo : 74
Zlowe, David : 50

+++++

SUBJECT INDEX

Ability to pay - 66
AFRODAD – 237,256,257
African Development Fund – 344
Almaty Program of Action- 244
Anti-corruption Act-156
Atlas methodology classification -100
Bangkok Recommendations - 242
Blanchard's Overlapping Generation – 52
Brady Deal-53, 55
Bretton Woods Project-334
Brussels Program of Action - 381
Build, Operate and Transfer (BOT) - 251
CAFOD – 256,272
Cancelling Multilateral Debt-386
Causes of Debt Crises – 27
Cent percent debt cancellation-409,486
Churches & Religious Organization - 276
Civil Society Organization-235,236
Common Country Assessment - 173
Commonwealth – 234
Commonwealth Debt Sustainability Forum-245
Combating corruption – 292,332
Completion Point Countris-208,408
Country Economic Memorandum – 123
Crisis in Africa – 283
Cycle of Indebtedness-23

Debt Buy Back – 59
Debt Forgiveness as Imperialism – 211
Debt Relief –29, 61,108,127,161,213,289,343
Debts over hang – 42
Debt Relief with Strings - 267
Debt Swap Provision – 438
Debt and Starvation-18
Default Forestalling-41
Development Agenda – 382
Decision Point Countries-209,408
Dis- investment Campaign – 460
Dilemma in Granting Debt-relief-301
Economy – Mozambique –120
Economy - Uganda – 133
Economy – India – 143
ECOSOC – 388
Enhanced HIPC Initiative – 403
Enhanced Structural Adjustment Facility -336
Eradication of Poverty - 222
Ethiopian People's Revolutionary
External Debt of India – 145,146
Food Security in Africa -345
Foreign Policy Focus-34
Free Decision Point Countries-209
Free the Entire World From Want-263
Full Debt Relief-156
G-8 Africa Action Plan-341
Gap between rich and poor Widening-273
Gleneagles Summit – 328
Global Call to Action against Poverty-383
Global Monitoring Report 2009-456
Grady deal-55
Good Governance – 291,356
Genoa Summit – 323
Gross National Happiness – 228
Gross Domestic Product – 131
Harvard Humanitarian Initiative – 118
HIPC- 21,30,84,90
HIPC, Initiative – 161
HIPC Initiative Progressive Report-208
Human Rights Council – 390

Humanitarian Crises – 116
IBRD-411
IDA-108,401
International Monetary Fund-413
IMF Crimes against Humanity – 459
International Comparison Program (ICP) - 101
International Financial Institutions – 336
International debt Facility-44
Jubilee Research-68
Jubilee Debt Campaign – 258,264
Justice Not Charity - 273
Koln Summit – 314
Laffer curve -44, 62, 79
L'Aquila Summit – 330
Launching the Koln Debt Initiative - 317
Least Developed Countries – 64
Learning from History - 466
Liberal Democrat Youth and Students – 270
London Club – 66, 94
London Summit – 308
Lyon Summit - 311
Make Poverty History –285,294
Meltzer Commission –441
Measurement of Peace - 483
Millennium Development Goals -35,157,387
Multilateral Debt Initiative-366
Multilateral Debt Cancellation-252
National Long-term Planning Strategy – 177
Necessity of Debt Relief-159
ODA-78
OECD-77
Opinion of Golden Brown-470
Okinawa Summit – 317
OXFAM-278
Oxfam America – 118
Paris Club – 21, 66, 94,434
Peace Keeping and conflict Resolution-296
Peace Building Commission - 389
Pittsburgh Summit-368
Poverty-114
Poverty in Ethiopia - 114

PRSP-109,167
--, Reduction Growth Facility (PRGF) – 191,192,336
Problems can be solved -152
Purchasing power parity – 101
Rapid Public Health Assesement-118
Research Center for Civic and Human rights-118
Recommendations of Meltzer Report-451
SADC Trade Protocol – 124
SAARC – 227
Sunset Clause –165,211,360
Suresh – Pritam Philosophy-252
Suresh-Pritam Model-484
Starvation-6
Structural Adjustment Program-378
Think Tanks – 155
The World Bank-206,394,439
Third UN Conference on LDC-381
Third World External Debt -69
Trafficking in Persons - 148
Toronto Summit – 291
Toronto terms for debt Resibling-63
Trade in Services-287
UN Country Team Support-182
UN Anti-corruption Organization-155
UN Development Assistance Framework – 173
UNCTAD – 29
UNDAF-173
United Nations Peace Prize – 455,488
World Government – 455,487

THE END

AUTHOURS

Professor Suresh Chandra Mallick (b 1944) was a faculty member of the OUAT, Bhubaneswar (India) during 1968 - 2004. He is a researcher, writer, thinker and social worker. He is an Agricultural Economist with specialization in Agriculture, Poverty, Marketing, Policy and World Peace to motivate people's involvement in peace process. He held the post of Vice President, Indian Society of Agricultural Marketing during 2003-05. At present, he is the Chairperson of the Institute of Development Studies & Policy Research, Bhubaneswar.

Pritam Mallick (1975-2006) was extremely noble, friendly and knowledgeable and possessed extraordinary memory. He received B.A. (Honors) from Utkal University, M.A. from Central University, Hyderabad and M. Phil. Degree from JNU and completed Ph. D. courses in JNU. He was a specialist in Monetary Economics and Econometrics. He remembered the Oxford Dictionary and Roget's Thesaurus to master English literature. He acquired deep knowledge in Astrology, Palmistry, Mathematics and Statistics. He contributed enormously for WORLD PEACE manuscripts as co-author. But his heavenly demise occurred on August 4, 2006.

Published – Published - Published

WORLD PEACE

BY
PROFESSOR SURESH C. MALLICK
AND
PRITAM MALLICK

Volume: 1 : Poverty and Peace
Volume: 2 : Corruption and Peace
Volume: 3 : War and peace
Volume: 4 : Debt and Peace
Volume: 5 : Farmer and Peace
Volume: 6 : Food Security and Peace
Volume: 7 : Humanity- A Religion
Volume: 8 : Environment and Peace
Volume: 9 : Politics and Peace
Volume: 10 : Woman and Peace
Volume: 11 : Governance and Peace
Volume: 12 : Mind and Peace
Volume: 13 : Terrorism and Peace
Volume: 14 : Democracy and Peace
Volume: 15 : Country and Peace
Volume: 16 : Water and Peace
Volume: 17 : Economics and Peace
Volume: 18 : People and Peace
Volume: 19 : Media and Peace
Volume: 20 : Land and Peace
Volume: 21 : Justice and Peace
Volume: 22 : Health and Peace
Volume: 23 : Culture and Peace
Volume: 24 : Faith and Peace
Volume: 25 : Life and Peace

A MOVEMENT FOR A PEACEFUL WORLD